FREEDOM AND REASON

Morris Raphael Cohen

FREEDOM AND REASON STUDIES IN

PHILOSOPHY AND JEWISH CULTURE

IN MEMORY OF *Morris Raphael Cohen*

EDITED BY
SALO W. BARON, ERNEST NAGEL, AND KOPPEL S. PINSON

1951 · THE FREE PRESS · GLENCOE · ILLINOIS

EDITORIAL BOARD

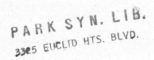

Contents

PART THREE—ESSAYS IN JEWISH CULTURE

Preface

$\mathcal{M}$ORRIS R. COHEN was fond of characterizing himself as being primarily a logician, and he was even wont to declare that logic was the only subject he ever taught. As he conceived the subject, however, logic was not identical with a specialized branch of formal analysis. It was for him co-extensive with the exercise of critical reason and with a passionate concern for intellectual rectitude and clarity. He thus took all knowledge for his province, and he possessed an intimate familiarity with the materials of widely separated disciplines. He was a thoroughgoing naturalist in his conception of the world and of man's place in it; but although he believed that the physical sciences provide the most reliable knowledge that men have yet been able to achieve in any domain, he retained a deep attachment to the humane wisdom that is so often the fruit of the less exact disciplines. The range of his special interests included not only philosophy in its more technical and professional phases but also the philosophy and the history of the sciences, the philosophy of law and of history, political and social theory, the history of ideas, and the development of Jewish thought.

The present collection of essays dealing with problems in many departments of human concern, is an attempt to do homage to the memory of a many-sided thinker. A number of the contributors to this volume were one-time students of Morris R. Cohen, and experienced his influence directly; the others felt the impact of his thought and personality in less formal ways. But to all the contributors he was a stimulating guide, an invaluable critic, and an example. Circumstances have prevented the inclusion of essays in this volume to represent all areas of Cohen's interests; but it is hoped nevertheless that the present collection constitutes a fair sample of the range of studies he cultivated.

The initial stimulus for preparing a memorial volume came from the Conference on Jewish Relations; and without the continued interest and support of the Conference the practical difficulties in publishing a scholarly volume of this sort might not have been surmounted. The Editors wish to acknowledge with particular gratitude the generous financial assistance of the following Directors of the Conference on Jewish Relations: George Backer, Salo W. Baron, Felix S. Cohen, Maurice Finkelstein, Bernard H. Goldstein, Louis Gottschalk, William Gresser, Joseph J. Klein, Arthur S. Meyer, Harry Rosenfield, Etta L. Rosensohn, David Rosenstein, Alan M. Stroock, and Israel S. Wechsler. Without their (and some of their friends') help, this volume would undoubtedly not have seen the light of day. We also wish to express our thanks to Mr. Ralph Colin for his help in the arrangements for the publication of this volume.

The Editors have also been fortunate in having available for their guidance the advice of the distinguished group of men who consented to serve on the Editorial Board for this volume. Final responsibility for the inclusion of the essays contained in it rests with the three editors; but they wish nonetheless to acknowledge their great debt to the members of the Editorial Board for their unfailingly helpful suggestions and good judgment.

It had been originally planned to include in the present volume the addresses delivered at the Memorial Meeting for Morris R. Cohen held at the New School on February 2, 1947, as well as a complete bibliography of Cohen's writings. Neither seems now necessary, for a number of the memorial addresses have since been published elsewhere, and a complete bibliography is included in Cohen's *A Dreamer's Journey*.

THE EDITORS.

PART ONE

Morris R. Cohen

The Life and Mind of Morris R. Cohen*

✍ BY MILTON R. KONVITZ
Cornell University

*B*ORN in Minsk, Russia, on July 25, 1880, Morris Raphael Cohen received the traditional education of an orthodox Jewish boy in eastern Europe. When he was twelve his parents brought him to the United States. Eight years later he received his bachelor's degree from the College of the City of New York through which he had worked his way by doing various jobs, including that of poolroom attendant. In 1899 Cohen met Thomas Davidson, founder of the Fabian Society, the Fellowship of the New Life and the Aristotelian Society. Under Davidson's inspiration and guidance Cohen began to teach at the Educational Alliance on New York's East Side. Seven years afterward he was awarded the degree of Doctor of Philosophy by Harvard University, where he had studied under William James and Josiah Royce.

I.

In 1902 Morris Cohen began to teach mathematics at City College, an assignment in which he continued for almost ten years. He was not happy teaching mathematics, although his interest in the subject was very keen. It was a study of mathematical philosophy, especially Bertrand Russell's *Principles of Mathematics,* he said, which liberated him "from the feeling of helpless philosophic bewilderment" and enabled him "to undertake an independent journey."

Cohen's first love was philosophy. He felt it had been awakened in him in his early years by his grandfather, a poor tailor in the

---

* A complete bibliography of the published works of Morris R. Cohen is to be found in his *A Dreamer's Journey* (1949) p. 291-303.

Russian town of Nesviesh. "Though he never learned to write and had only a moderate reading knowledge of Hebrew," Morris Cohen wrote, "he had become the master of an extraordinary amount of knowledge and wisdom. Walks and talks with him first stimulated my imagination about the world at large and its history. From him, also, I acquired a certain ineradicable admiration for the ascetic virtues and a scorn for the life of wealth, ease, creature comforts and all that goes under the old name of worldliness."

To Morris Cohen to philosophize seemed "as natural and desirable in itself as to sing, to dance, to paint, or mould, or to commune with those we love." The opportunity to teach his favorite subject came to him in 1912 when he was appointed assistant professor of philosophy at City College. This meant to him "the end of a long valley of humiliation. I had labored for six years with the Leah of mathematics yearning for the Rachel of philosophy."

For twenty-six years Cohen taught philosophy to thousands of students at City College. During various periods of his lifetime, both before and after retiring from City College, he also taught and lectured at other institutions, among them The New School for Social Research, Johns Hopkins, Columbia University, Yale, the University of Chicago, St. John's Law School and Leland Stanford University. It was not until seven years before he retired from his position at City College in 1938 that *Reason and Nature*, his major work, was published; yet for a quarter of a century his name had been known throughout the length and breadth of the country wherever men were devoted to a pursuit of wisdom. This was, indeed, a remarkable achievement, matched in recent times only by the reputation of Felix Frankfurter; for the renown of each was due chiefly to the opinion and devotion of thousands of students.

Cohen made no effort to acquire disciples. He conceived it his duty as a teacher to be the critic rather than the prophet or the system-builder. This position exposed him to the charge of being "merely critical, negative, or destructive." "I have always been ready," he said, "to plead guilty to that charge." He considered it an important service "in the cause of liberal civilization to develop a spirit of genuine regard for the weight of evidence, to inculcate the habit of admitting ignorance when we do not know and to nourish the critical spirit of inquiry which is inseparable from the love of truth that makes men free." He once said to a student who reproached him for his destructive criticism: "You have heard the story of how Hercules cleaned the Augean stables. He took all the dirt and manure out and left them clean. You ask me: 'What did he leave in their stead?' I answer: 'Isn't it enough to have cleaned the stables?' "

Morris Cohen challenged accepted dogmas, fashionable opinions, uncritical acceptance of beliefs and views, no matter by what authority they were supported. He compelled his students—future physicians, lawyers and teachers—to think critically about the problems they would face as specialists and as citizens. He wanted to make of his students responsible thinkers, not disciples. Some of his students became eminent philosophers in their own right. They include Ernest Nagel and Herbert W. Schneider of Columbia University, Sidney Hook of New York University, and Paul Weiss of Yale University.

Morris Raphael Cohen's family life was rich in sentiment and love. His devotion to his parents, to his wife and to his children never flagged. In addition he enjoyed the close friendship of men like Justices Holmes, Brandeis, Cardozo, and Frankfurter; Albert Einstein, Arthur S. Meyer, A. A. Himwich, Harold J. Laski, John Dewey, Irwin Edman, Alvin Johnson, Huntington Cairns, and countless others. His gift for friendship was an essential part of him.

Despite his physical frailties, Morris Cohen pushed himself hard, worked constantly on his lectures, articles and books. In 1923 he edited a collection of Charles S. Peirce's philosophical essays under the title *Chance, Love and Logic.* Before he retired from teaching in 1938 he had published, besides numerous articles and reviews, *Reason and Nature* (1931), *Law and the Social Order* (1933) and, with Ernest Nagel, *An Introduction to Logic and Scientific Method* (1934).

Cohen had plans for eleven other books—a volume on metaphysics, a treatise on law, a book on logic, a statement of his philosophy of liberalism, an autobiography, a volume on the will to illusion, an introduction to philosophy, a volume on Jewish problems, a philosophy of history, a history of science, and a study of the development of American thought. However, he felt that he would not be strong enough to accomplish this program if he continued to teach, so in January 1938 he retired from active teaching at City College—the institution with which he had been intimately associated since 1895.

By the time of Cohen's death on January 28, 1947, at the age of sixty-six, he had seen nine more books published or in process of publication: *A Preface to Logic,* dedicated to the City College and its students "who gave zest to my life," appeared in 1944; *The Faith of a Liberal* was published in 1946; *The Meaning of Human History,* the Carus Lectures delivered in 1944 at the City College, and *A Source Book on Greek Science,* prepared with the collaboration of I. E. Drabkin, came out in 1948. The correspondence between Mr. Justice Holmes and Cohen was also published in 1948 in the pages of the *Journal of the History of Ideas.* His autobiography, *A Dreamer's Journey,* and *Studies in Philosophy and Science* appeared in 1949 and *Reflections of a Wondering Jew* and *Reason and Law* in 1950. Remaining to be published is his *Currents of American Thought.*

His retirement from City College left Cohen with more time to devote to his studies and writing; but he did not give up teaching entirely. Besides teaching at the University of Chicago from 1938 to 1941 he also gave a number of graduate seminars at Harvard, Yale and Columbia universities.

II.

Morris Raphael Cohen considered himself philosophically "a stray dog unchained to any metaphysical kennel." It seemed to him "better to brave the muddy realities of the unprotected out-of-doors, the uncertain food, the attacks from the watch dogs of comfortable homes, and above all the chilling rains and winds of factual experience. . . . I have never become completely at home in even the greatest of academic philosophies." Bertrand Russell came closer to being his philosophical god than any other thinker. Cohen said that he was faithful to Russell's fundamental teaching even when Russell strayed from the way. He liked to think of himself as a logician, calling his intellectual autobiography in *Contemporary American Philosophy* (1930) "The Faith of a Logician." His emphasis on criticism, skepticism and logical analysis led many persons to view Cohen as a philosophical nihilist, a great nay-sayer, an iconoclast, a destroyer of other men's faiths and philosophies, as one who could effectively wreck but not build. This view of Cohen is, however, only partially true. Cohen had the capacity to build and this capacity he manifested in his more substantial productions, such as *Reason and Nature, Law and the Social Order* and *The Meaning of Human History*.

A look into *Reason and Nature: an Essay on the Meaning of Scientific Method* shows that the book covers a wide range of subjects, disclosing the catholicity and erudition of the author: mathematics, biology, jurisprudence, ethics, the social and physical sciences. From the first page to the last Cohen demonstrates his unqualified devotion to impartial reason: "Our reason may be a pitiful candle-light in the dark and boundless seas of being," he says, "but we have nothing better, and woe to those who wilfully try to put it out."

Cohen's search for fundamental principles of thought and categories of reality led him to attack empiricism or nominalism of the type which admits the existence of only particulars. Logical or mathematical relations are real; their reality justifies the hypothetical and deductive procedures of science. Scientific inquiry discovers abstract relations which characterize the world of phenomena. The reality of mathematical relations makes possible a "biting into the world." Relativism, nihilism or skepticism fails to disclose the nature of mind or reality. It does not follow from this, however, that *a priori* rationalism must, therefore, be accepted. An understanding of the logical and hypothetical character of mathematics destroys the ground of any assertion that space must be Euclidean.

On the one hand, said Cohen, one sees that the laws or postulates of mathematics or logic are the invariant forms or relations of all possible objects; they are the laws of all possible being but are themselves neither physical nor mental. On the other hand, one sees that from purely formal considerations no material facts are deducible. Science involves logic; on the one hand we see that it is rational, that phenomena conform to laws of logic; on the other hand we see that phenomena involve an element of contingency.

The discussion thus far of the laws of logic and the nature of science shows Cohen's adherence to what he called the principle of polarity, which occupied a central place in his thought. There is a polarity of terms and relations; neither is reducible to the other; terms and relations involve one another. Opposites "such as immediacy and mediation, unity and plurality, the fixed and the flux, substance and function, ideal and real, actual and possible," all involve each other when applied to any significant entity.

This principle of polarity seems to be the central fact of Cohen's metaphysics of science. Polarity is a supplement to the principle of causality; for a natural event must have a cause, but the cause is opposed by some factor which prevents it from producing a greater effect than it actually does; thus protoplasm lives by continually dying. The principle of polarity applies to social as well as to physical and biological events. In all determination there are opposing categories: unity and plurality, identity and difference, activity and passivity.

Thus Cohen's denial of both empiricism and absolutism may be viewed as an instance of the effectiveness of the principle of polarity. He believed that rational structure is a fundamental phase of the world; but he also believed that there is an element of contingency. There is both intelligibility and contingency in the world.

Cohen did not always, in the presentation of his argument, keep himself scrupulously neutral between two poles, between the fixed elements in reality and the flux, between the variant and the invariant characters of the world, between unity and plurality, between the ideal and the real or between idealism and naturalism, between reason and nature. His sharpest barbs were directed at those who are romantically attached to immediacy rather than mediation, who are attached to "life" or "experience." There is no intelligible life without the polestar of invariance or identity; the weight and emphasis of his argument seemed to be on the side of intelligibility as opposed to contingency, on the side of idealism as opposed to naturalism, on the side of reason as opposed to nature, status or fixity as opposed to change.

It is to be doubted, however, if this disparity in the weights of opposite sides of the scale was more than polemical. When Cohen framed his arguments, empiricism was in the ascendant and idealism was on the defensive. Cohen always distrusted ideas that were fashionable, for they threatened to become the new dogmas, displacing the old. There was more danger that men would adopt the new philosophies as absolutes than that they would go back to the discredited faiths. It was, therefore, necessary to fight harder against the new gods, still young and fresh, than against the gods already in the twilight.

III.

Cohen's influence on judges and teachers of law can hardly be exaggerated. The weight of his legal philosophy was felt in high courts, including the United States Supreme Court.

As a young boy Cohen came to look upon the law as chiefly a pattern of life, rather than a set of rules to be memorized and obeyed. The God of the Jews was primarily a law-giver, and Moses was a law teacher. Cohen was exposed to legal studies as soon as he began to study the Old Testament and the Talmud. The law became and remained for him a lifelong interest.

Law and the Social Order: Essays in Legal Philosophy consists of twenty-five essays published in the twenty years preceding 1933. The book discloses an extensive and penetrating knowledge of legal philosophy that was equalled in the United States only by Roscoe Pound and probably was unequalled by any British or continental thinker. The book treats of the legal philosophies of de Tourtoulon, Geny, Duguit, Charmont, Demogue, Ihering, Stammler, Kohler, del Vecchio, Pound, Laski, Gray, Jerome Frank, Holmes, Krabbe and others. The book has notable discussions of property and contract and an attack on what he called the "phonograph theory of the judicial function." Even before Franklin D. Roosevelt's attempt to reorganize the Supreme Court, Cohen had pointed out that the judges of our higher courts generally are elderly gentlemen who in their younger days were successful representatives of the interests of bankers, manufacturers and merchants.

But Cohen's sharp criticism of the jurisprudence of concepts did not mean that he joined the camp of the legal realists. Here, too, the principle of polarity came into play: one must give weight to the abstract legal principle and to the concrete case. Cohen was as opposed to legal anarchy or naked "experience" in legal phenomena as he was to the legal philosophy that saw only the empty abstract rule or doctrine. There must be both discretion and rule; there is a need for both realism and idealism.

In this instance, too, his argument in later years seemed to favor order and reason, rationalism, the unchanging, as against the contingent and the changing. But this emphasis was only, I believe, polemical; for in legal philosophy, too, nominalism of a radical nature appeared to be in fashion and the old conceptualism was losing favor. Cohen distrusted the new movement; he wanted to expose its more extreme manifestations as shallow fads. In his legal philosophy, as in his philosophy of nature, Cohen was no champion of causes, no partisan advocate. He attacked all false prophets, and especially those who made the most noise in his day or appeared to attract more devotees than did competing prophets.

Cohen attacked those who distrusted the Supreme Court less than Congress. When one considers, he said, the long roll of judicial decisions "such as the Dred Scott case, the Lochner case, the Adair case, the child labor cases, the Coppage case, the minimum wage cases up to 1937, the voiding of Congressional legislation to protect the Negroes against lynching and the deprivation of civil rights, or the public against being gouged by ticket scalpers, fraudulent bakers, and conscienceless employment agencies, the sadism of the courts will far outweigh that of Congress even though esthetically the procedure of the courts is more refined."

Long before it became respectable to mention such things, Cohen argued against the hypocrisy of the legal orthodoxy centered in the axiom that judges declare but do not make law. His interest in the judicial function was first stimulated in the early years of the century by the course of decisions in labor cases. The "arbitrary (and often unenlightened) character" of these decisions revealed to him the inadequacy of the dogma that judges are legal phonographs. Judges are influenced by economic and social theories and prejudices; and no study of the law should ignore or fail to evaluate economic and social interests and forces. The judicial process has a human aspect. These and similar statements are commonplace today, but early in the century it took vision and courage to make them. When they became commonplace, Cohen began to point to the opposite pole, which was being neglected; namely, that idealism, tradition and fixity of rule have a necessary and justifiable place in the judicial process.

In the early years of his interest in jurisprudence and the philosophy of law, Cohen received intellectual stimulation from American scholars and thinkers like Roscoe Pound, John Dewey, and Felix Adler. However, Cohen found his chief inspiration in the writings of continental thinkers. That he studied these writings well and beneficially can be easily seen from a reading of *Law and the Social Order.*

Professional legal scholars soon became aware of Cohen. When the Association of American Law Schools appointed an editorial committee to translate, edit and publish the Modern Legal Philosophy Series, Cohen was made a member of the committee, although he was neither a lawyer nor a teacher of law. In 1913 Cohen organized the Conference on Legal and Social Philosophy, the chairmanship of which was taken by John Dewey. The Conference held four meetings, each of which attracted outstanding scholars. The meetings stimulated discussion and thought, and underscored the need for radical and fresh thinking in legal and social philosophy. The Conference on Legal and Social Philosophy and the *New Republic* magazine, founded in 1914, were forums from which Cohen's influence effectively emanated. Holmes and Cardozo, Brandeis and Frankfurter, Learned Hand, Roscoe Pound, and Harold Laski, American courts, philosophers and men of public affairs felt and responded to that influence.

IV.

In *The Meaning of Human History* we see Cohen wrestle "in the field of history, as elsewhere, with such permanent problems as those involved in the reconciliation of the empirical and the rational, the mental and the physical, change and persistence, unity and diversity, value and existence, chance and determination." Since history "unfortunately has not arranged itself to suit the convenience of historians," the facts of human history, like the facts of nature and of mind, challenge philosophical enquiry. Professor Cohen was not one to run away from a problem. He noted a "human disinclination and inability" to learn from history as itself constituting one of the outstanding facts of history; but he himself, as the Carus Lectures eminently demonstrate, was free from this vice. He brought to bear on the methodological, scientific and philosophical problems that the field of history presents the same great qualities of mind and spirit that he employed when coping with the problems of scientific method, with the problems of legal philosophy, with the problems of logic, and with the problems of politics. One ends *The Meaning of Human History* with a refreshed awareness of the fact that its author was the most encyclopedic philosopher our century has thus far known, a twentieth-century Aristotle.

The past, Professor Cohen said, "has left such a mark on the present that in some way it may be said to be always with us." Thus:

If a pebble obstructs the growth of a tree and causes a certain division in it, the tree will always bear the mark. So the experiences of our youth, the language we have learnt, the manners in which we have been trained, become part of our nature. And so the past laws of a country, its old institutions, and the general traditions which constitute its *ethos* and character are active forces in the present, and in that sense history is a necessary guide for the understanding of the present. The past literally continues into the present. Past conditions, such as old ideas and habits, buildings, fields, and laws, continue to operate. Inertia is the first law of history, as it is of physics. Every event is an integral part of a larger segment of history, and the task of tracing causal connections is the task of discovering those elements that persist through, and despite, the arbitrary cuts by which we mark off the event we are at the moment seeking to explain.

Since the past is with us now, the discovery of the persistent elements in human history is a matter of no small importance. The discovery can be made through investigations that are controlled "by the strictest rules of evidence," by testing every general proposition through observation and experiment. Historic investigation, to the extent that it involves scientific investigation and verification, "may be properly called scientific." But the investigation also involves imagination, for the historian needs "an imaginative capacity for seeing threads of connection between historic facts and significant issues." The ideal to which the greatest historians have aspired is that of "an imaginative reconstruction of the past which is scientific in its determinations and artistic in its formulation."

There are, of course, subjective factors that "color" all histories. The historian sees things from his chosen perspective, and his selected theory of causation will determine for him the events that are related. "But this is true also within natural science. The presence of assumptions or hypotheses does not vitiate but rather strengthens an argument, provided we recognize these elements for what they are." Social movements can be explained only in terms of constants or identities, and these "connections or identities the historian must find. He does not create them." If the meaning of an event is found in its relations to other events with which it is connected, "the meaning of history is not created by the historian but discovered by him." What the historian makes is "not the past but findings about it."

These findings, however, should not be in terms only of constants. Nature and history show events that are "accidental or fortuitous coincidences." There is relative necessity and also contingency in history, for these terms are always relative to a selected system that is finite or limited in perspective. It is the same with human events as with physical happenings; their necessity is conditional, for "no event is necessary absolutely or by itself, but only insofar as it is connected with other events and is thus part of a system." Since we may be living in a really pluralistic world, we have accidents when two relatively independent streams of causality meet and their meeting is not deducible from either alone or from the two together. The historian should not try to expunge from the history he is writing "the notion of accident as the coincidence of independent streams of events."

Since the world may be really pluralistic, no single factor or account (political, religious, economic, psychologic, etc.) can give us a complete explanation of the historic process. A purely political, religious or economic account is only a partial story; it can never give us the fundamental interpretation. "General history must work with a number of factors rather than with only one." The monistic approach makes its appeal by reason of its simplicity and apparently definitive character, "but easy simplicity is an evasion rather than a solution of difficulties."

Professor Cohen arrived at these conclusions only after a painstaking examination of the leading monistic philosophies of history, which he discussed in chapters devoted to the geographic, biologic, institutional, and "great men" approaches in the writing of history. These chapters are among the most impressive and valuable in the book.

Toward the end of the book Professor Cohen permitted himself to state some conclusions suggested by his lifelong study of history. While he apparently failed to find sufficient time for their elaboration and for testing their verification, he considered them sufficiently significant to state them.

"To my mind," he said, "the idea of polarity and oscillation between opposite poles has a good deal more to contribute to historiography than the notions of perpetual progress or perpetual degeneration." The dominant forces in human nature which seemed to him relevant for an understanding of history are "the expansive forces, which involve adventure, and the centralizing or organizing forces, which protect us against those elements that would destroy us. Fear and freedom are thus two poles of human life. Without freedom to expand or grow life would become impossible, but without fear, which leads us consciously or unconsciously to guard against danger, life would soon be destroyed." Human history is full of human failures, brutalities and stupidities; human tragedies fill the pages of history. But despair and cynicism need not follow from this. Knowledge of the truth "is in the end the only truly liberating and thus ethically sustaining force." The expansive and centralizing forces in life—the principle of polarity—are the basis of hope which sustains human life. Brute power has defeated many good causes, but history shows "that good causes are more often defeated by negligence in the pursuit of the right than by positive forces of evil; and while it is true that brute power can for a limited time crush the human spirit, history also shows that the spirit of truth has a superior vitality and thus truth, even though for a time crushed to earth, rises again."

One may ask the question whether Professor Cohen could, if challenged, have proved the proposition that history shows that the spirit of truth has a superior vitality. Perhaps this is the sort of proposition that can neither be proved nor disproved. Indeed, Professor Cohen himself has said that "history cannot prove any moral rules"; yet, if history shows the superior vitality of truth, why can it not also show the superior vitality of goodness, which itself may be defined as a species of truth? Professor Cohen speaks of the "fundamental truth" of the saying of Jesus: "What is a man profited, if he shall gain the whole world, and lose his own soul?" Is this a "fundamental truth" of physical nature or of the moral nature of man?

If pressed, I suspect that Professor Cohen would have admitted that he believed in the superior vitality of truth in human history as an article of faith. Faith *can* move mountains. A man's view of what is happening is itself a cause of what happens. "You cannot," said Professor Cohen, "rule human purposes and knowledge out of human life and history. The belief that we are victorious influences our conduct." Had he not believed in the superior vitality of truth, Cohen could not have been the great teacher that he was for over forty years.

"To widen our horizon," said Professor Cohen, "to make us see other points of view than those to which we are accustomed, is the greatest service that can be rendered by the historian." When history is studied with an ethical interest, he said, it will widen our experiences and horizons, "like intelligent visits to foreign countries or conversing with great and unique personalities. Our problems may not thereby be solved, but they are illumined." Has he not in these statements concerning the role and utility of historians in fact stated his own function and significance as a philosopher? One finishes the lectures with a consciousness that one has enjoyed the inestimable privilege of a conversation with a great and unique personality, that one has visited remote "places of nestling green for poets made."

V.

"Like science, liberalism insists on a critical examination of the content of all our beliefs, principles, or initial hypotheses," Cohen said, "and on subjecting them to a continuous process of verification so that they will be progressively better founded in experience and reason." It was socialism, he said, that offered the specific occasion for his entering upon a study of technical philosophy, for socialism seemed to him to offer "the only scientific analysis of the economic evils and political corruption of our age as well as of the main course of human history." The 1896 campaign of Bryan stirred in Cohen a deep interest in politics. Cohen was then teaching workingmen's classes as part of his work for Daniel de Leon's Socialist Labor Party. In 1897 he campaigned for Henry George who ran in the New York mayoralty election.

This was also the period during which Cohen belonged to a Marxist study group; and, as a matter of fact, he never ceased to be grateful for the illumination he found in a study of *Das Kapital*. "It not only helped me to recognize the poverty of most non-economic interpretations of history," he said, "but also prepared me to see that the recurrent breakdowns of capitalist economy are not unforeseeable accidents but a consequence of the private ownership of the machinery of production. . . . It helped me to see that the old optimistic but essentially anarchistic notion that the good of all will best be promoted by 'rugged individualism,' by each pursuing his own selfish economic gain, is a cruel superstition which men possessed of both reason and a decent amount of human sympathy cannot long maintain in the face of the hideous miseries that flourish in the shadow of men's mighty productive powers."

On the other hand, he was repelled by the exaggerated materialism that pervaded Marx's thinking. This materialism was evident at many points in Marxism; it was especially evident, said Cohen, "in the Marxist boast, which I could not swallow, that Marx never spoke of justice."

All his life Cohen maintained an active interest in social problems and social reform. Social injustices aroused his hatred and put him in a fighting mood. He never forgave Roosevelt's imposition of the embargo against the Spanish Republic. Always taking his stand for freedom of thought and inquiry, freedom of discussion and criticism, he opposed Communism and the Russian dictatorship. He did not believe that the "proletarian" dictatorship was necessary as a "temporary" expedient. "The plea that the denial of freedom is a temporary necessity is advanced by all militarists. It ignores the fact that, when suppression becomes a habit, it is not readily abandoned. . . . When the Communists tell me that I must choose between their dictatorship and Fascism, I feel that I am offered the choice between being shot and being hanged.

It would be suicide for liberal civilization to accept this as exhausting the field of human possibility."

In his social philosophy, too, Cohen used the principle of polarity. There must be the principle of order and the principle of freedom; opposing groups must co-operate, for each group must be wise enough "to see the necessity of compromising with those with whom we have to live together and whom we cannot or do not wish to exterminate"; not all property should become communal, nor does an individual have a right to use his property in antisocial ways.

Principles of social aims and policy should not be posited as fixed dogmas; they should be viewed as "provisional hypotheses, to be tried with as much intelligence and persistence as we can summon, but never without watching their consequences to see whether these hypotheses are really confirmed."

A fundamental tenet of his liberalism is that an individual may never assume that he has the whole truth in his possession. Moral humility, tolerance, a belief in the scientific method, freedom of speech and inquiry—a faith in these qualities of mind and action was at the heart of his liberalism.

He did not believe in the inevitability of progress; with Justice Holmes he said that effort is one of the ways through which the inevitable comes to pass. His philosophy of liberalism required only the possibility of progress. But this mere possibility is all a man needs to provide the moral strength for his will, to engage in the fight for social reform. No social cause, however, will bring about universal salvation. The achievement of universal suffrage, popular education or some other end greatly desired brings in its train new disappointments. But despair is not a permanent state of the emotions; new waves of hope arise, and so human history swings between the pole of growth and the pole of decay, between the pole of hope and the pole of despair.

Cohen's liberalism stands between these poles: it is not a set of dogmas or doctrines, but a process, a temper of mind. It means an open eye for alternatives; a questioning of all "self-evident" propositions; a faith in enlightenment, "yet colored with a deep humility before the vision of a world so much larger than our human hopes and thoughts"; a readiness for new risks in new

situations, "in which there is no guarantee that the new will always
be the good or the true, in which progress is a precarious achievement rather than an inevitability"; a liberation of "the energies of
human nature by the free and fearless use of reason."

In this social philosophy, as in his philosophy of nature, his
philosophy of history, and his philosophy of law, Cohen saw the
operations of the principle of polarity: there is the opening up of
new situations with new challenges, but this activity should be
the result of disciplined intelligence rather than of arbitrary forces;
for social life "involves a balance between the expansive or cen-
trifugal forces which make for diversity and adventure, and the
constraining or centripetal forces which make for organization and
safety. . . . The life of civilization, like the life of each organism,
oscillates between opposite extremes."

VI.

Cohen said that piety as defined by Santayana—"reverence for
the sources of one's being"—is but a necessary corollary of the
Socratic maxim "know thyself." If a Jew is to know himself, he
must know the history of the Jewish people—in Biblical, Talmudic
and recent times. Cohen's interest in Jewish history began when he
was still a young boy subject to the influence of his grandfather
and remained a lively one all his life. His essay "Philosophies of
Jewish History," in the first number of *Jewish Social Studies* (reprinted in *Reflections of a Wondering Jew*), is one of the significant fruits of his devotion to this subject.

His mother tongue was Yiddish and for this language he always
maintained a special love. "No other language," he once admitted,
"ever entirely replaced it in the expression of intimate affection."
He owed a great deal of his education, he said, to the Yiddish
press: "It taught me to look at world news from a cosmopolitan
instead of a local or provincial point of view, and it taught me to
interpret politics realistically, instead of being misled by empty
phrases."

The first language Cohen learned to read was Hebrew. Up to
about the time of his *bar mitzva* his life conformed to the tenets
of orthodox Judiasm; thereafter he gave up a belief in a personal
God, and at the age of nineteen discontinued the orthodox ob-

servances. Later he rejected monotheism—and all other forms of theism—on philosophical grounds, for he was not able to reconcile the reality of evil with the idea of a benevolent and omnipotent deity. Nor was he able to understand, he said, any theism that was not anthropomorphic, and "making a God in man's image has always seemed to me to be the height of arrogance."

Nor did he accept Zionism. "I should like to see Palestine, and all its inhabitants, grow in wealth," he said. "I have the deepest admiration for the brave and wise efforts through which Jewish pioneers have rescued the soil of Israel from centuries of neglect and abuse. I should like to see the racial or religious discriminations with which the British exclude Jewish immigrants and restrict Jewish land ownership broken, just as I should like to see similar discriminations in our own land broken. I should, above all, like to see the Hebrew University become a beacon of light throughout the world."

A politically-Zionist Palestine, Cohen felt, would not have free non-Jewish immigration. It would be a state founded on a peculiar soil; there would be no separation of church and state, no free mixing of races or peoples. "Tribalism," he said, "is a creed that leads to grief and massacre, whether it bears the label of Zionism, Aryanism, Anglo-Saxon America, or Pan-Islam." The fine achievements of the *halutzim* did not, he said, presuppose the establishment of a Jewish state, "and I trust that they may be advanced and extended in years to come within the framework of a non-sectarian state that allows equal rights to all—Jews, Christians, Mohammedans and atheists alike."

In any case, he believed Zionism distracted the minds of American Jews from the solution of domestic problems. "To my way of thinking," he said, "the realities before us here and now, where our practical efforts are likely to be most effective, are actual human beings, boys and girls who are our children, who live here, who must adapt themselves to the conditions of American life, and who want to make their lives fuller and richer. A few of them will go to Palestine and cease to be Americans. A few will stay here and cease to be Jews. But the great majority, for generations to come, will be American Jews and, out of self-respect, will want to make the greatest contributions to American life which their heritage, their training and their individual efforts make possible. For them, as for those of us whose hopes as parents and as teachers are bound up with theirs, the problem remains: what can we, with our age-old heritage, contribute to the fullness of American life?"

Cohen rejected Judaism as a theology; he rejected political Zionism; he also rejected assimilationism. "Jewish young men will continue to fall in love with Jewish young women. The highest rate of intermarriage ever known in the heyday of German liberalism was fourteen per cent. Even if centuries of assimilation in an atmosphere of tolerance were unbroken by waves of anti-Semitism it would probably be eighty generations before the Jews would disappear as distinguishable people upon the American scene."

When Cohen began to teach at City College in 1902, and for thirty-six years thereafter, his students were predominantly Jewish boys. He shared their struggles against the discrimination that so many of them faced as they sought to establish themselves in careers. As a citizen he felt he could not be silent "in the face of the great campaign to repudiate the declaration that all men are created equal which culminated in the racist immigration laws of 1922 and 1924." In the early 1920's, alongside his wife, Mary Ryshpan Cohen, he became active in the vocational training work of the ORT. Later, in 1939, he became president of the Jewish Occupational Council. These affiliations should not suggest that Cohen believed that Jews should seek careers and employment in which their "visibility" in public life would be relatively small and thus points of irritation leading to antisemitism would be reduced in number. Why should Americans object to Norwegian immigrants, who possess a maritime tradition, supplying more than their proportionate numbers to American shipping? "If the traditional Jewish love of learning is of value to a liberal civilization, is it not better for the Jews to maintain it, and perhaps transmit it to other portions of the population, rather than retreat from it as a source of danger?"

When Cohen heard of the pogroms in tsarist Russia and later of the massacres by the Nazis, it was natural for him to recognize that, but for the good luck and fortitude of his parents, he and those dearest to him might have been among the victims. He always sought for ways to identify himself with fellow Jews and not to let differences in religious belief or politics stand in the way of practical co-operation. Believing in division of labor, he felt that he could best make his contribution by concentrating on scientific pursuits. In the fight against injustice and cruelty, facts and an understanding of facts are necessary, useful weapons.

Cohen, therefore, in 1933, organized the Conference on Jewish Relations, to which he dedicated a large measure of his energy during the last fourteen years of his life. Not long afterward Cohen took a leading role in the establishment of *Jewish Social Studies*, a quarterly that has won a distinguished place among learned socio-logical and Jewish journals. The Conference has pursued and the journal has published detailed scholarly studies of Jewish social, political and economic problems. Motivated by the same spirit of truth-seeking, Cohen became one of the founders and the first chairman of the Research Institute on Peace and Postwar Prob-lems of the American Jewish Committee.

VII.

Although Cohen gave up a belief in a personal God, he did not give up the Jewish "ideal of holiness that enables us to distinguish between the good and evil in men and thus saves us from the idolatrous worship of a humanity that is full of imperfections." He might have called this "ideal of holiness" by the name of God, but he did not want to cause confusion or be misunderstood. He never returned to any supernatural beliefs, but if by religion is under-stood what he called "the realm of ideal expression," Cohen was a religious man.

Atheists, he said, are as a rule singularly blind "to the limita-tions of our knowledge and to the infinite possibilities beyond us. And those who called themselves materialists appeared to me to be shutting themselves off from philosophy, wisdom and the life of the spirit, which are certainly not material things. Those of my circle who rejected religion *in toto* seemed to me to be casting away the ideals that had sustained our people through so many genera-tions before we had fashioned guide posts to our own lives that could stand up against the sort of buffetings that the old guide posts had withstood. In this some of us lost sight of the larger view that Thomas Davidson had taught, that we have no right to break

away from the past until we have appropriated all its experience
and wisdom and that reverence for the past may go hand in hand
with loyalty to the future, 'to the Kingdom which doth not yet
appear.' "

In Spinoza Cohen saw a kindred spirit and in Spinoza's writings
he found most clearly developed "the rational and tolerant attitude to the values of religion" for which he had been searching.
If "religion consists in humility (as a sense of the mystic potency
in our fellow human beings), and spirituality (as a sense of the
limitations of all that is merely material, actual or even attainable), then no one was more deeply religious than Spinoza." In
these passages Cohen was describing not only Spinoza's religion,
but also—and especially—his own.

In his later years Cohen came to view with more sympathy the
role of ritual "as a primary fact in human religious experience. For
each of us the symbolism of our childhood offers paths to peace
and understanding that can never be wholly replaced by other
symbolisms. For me the ancient ceremonies that celebrate the coming and going of life, the wedding ceremony, the birth and the
funeral service, give an expression to the continuity of the spiritual
tradition that is more eloquent than any phrases of my own creation. The ritual may be diluted by English and by modernisms, but
the Hebrew God is still a potent symbol of the continuous life of
which we individuals are waves. So it is, too, with the celebration
of the eternal struggle for freedom, in the family service of the
Passover.

"Like vivid illustrations in the book of my life are the prayers
of my parents, the services at their graves, the memory of an old
man chanting funeral songs at the *Yahrzeit* of my dear friend Dr.
Himwich, the unveiling of the monument to the beloved comrade
of my life's journeys, and the celebration of the continuity of
generations in the Passover services in the home of my parents and
in the homes of my children. And though I have never gone back
to theologic supernaturalism, I have come to appreciate more than
I once did the symbolism in which is celebrated the human need
of trusting to the larger vision, according to which calamities come
and go but the continuity of life and faith in its better possibilities
survive."

When Cohen taught in the Thomas Davidson school, he gave courses in the Book of Job and the Hebrew Prophets. When he was a graduate student at Harvard, his work under George Foote Moore formed a major part of his studies. In later years, said Cohen, a considerable part of his reading was in the field of Old Testament literature and criticism, especially in days of depression when he had little energy for writing or professional studies.

The "larger vision" of Professor Cohen, especially after his retirement from the professorship at City College, encompassed many fields of interest. His eye saw through a "dome of many-coloured glass." He was a whole man; he sought the truth and was willing to open many doors in his search. Logical analysis was one door; scientific method was another door; history and tradition also were doors; active devotion to humanitarian causes was still another door; defense of freedom was another door; a religion of humility, charity or love, and spirituality was also a door. He did not always see all doors at one and the same time. But what man does?

He always sought, however, the larger vision and more often than is given to others he had the fortune to see his "father's mansion" in its totality. Yet can one honestly say that any mortal sees this totality? No, Cohen would say, no. For there is a "Kingdom which doth not yet appear"; there are "those human values that the process of time can never adequately realize or destroy." As his teacher William James said in *A Pluralistic Universe*: "the word 'and' trails along after every sentence. Something always escapes. 'Ever not quite' has to be said of the best attempts made anywhere in the universe at attaining all-inclusiveness."

Morris Raphael Cohen did not always agree with William James, but Cohen himself could have written these sentences. He had a sense of the infinite powers beyond any man's scope. His favorite form of expression was the question; his life was a quest. He worshiped no god, yet, like young Samuel, he lived a dedicated life. In the company of Morris Raphael Cohen, Mr. Justice Holmes once said, he felt the presence of a holy man.

Morris R. Cohen as a Teacher of Lawyers and Jurists

ᵉᵹ BY NATHAN R. MARGOLD

*L*IKE thousands of other students who caught from Morris R. Cohen some appreciation of the fundamentals of scientific method and acquired under his guidance habits of thinking and a mental outlook peculiarly helpful in the solution of legal problems, I owe him a great personal debt. An opportunity to acknowledge it publicly is highly gratifying. Beyond this there is also the underlying urge to which that distinguished American, John Dewey, referred when he said, at a dinner in honor of Professor Cohen arranged by his students in the fall of 1927:

> I am sure that consciously or unconsciously all of us, who have come here to do him honor this evening, have done it not merely from personal affection and from loyalty to a friend, but because we feel that in writing ourselves down as his friend, we are in some measure also identifying ourselves with the friends of truth, the friends of freedom, the friends of that freedom which is both the parent and the progeny of truth, the friends of that truth which alone makes humanity free.[1]

To trace the influence of Morris R. Cohen's philosophy upon the practice of the law one must first know what that philosophy is. But try as I may, I can recall no "Cohen philosophy" whose postulates I learned as a student. Indeed, the recollection that stands out the clearest is that no teacher of mine was ever so careful *not* to impose his viewpoint upon his students, nor even to explain what that viewpoint was. Moreover, Professor Cohen was fond of saying that philosophy is for fifty years from now; and the half century point beyond the period of his teaching days in the field of philosophy is still some years away. At most, therefore, my con-

[1] *Morris Raphael Cohen* (published by "the youth who sat at his feet") (1928) p. 20.

tribution so far as it relates to the influence of Morris R. Cohen as
a teacher must be limited to a very narrow—almost autobiographical
—view of how those teachings influenced some of us who found
there our first introduction to the meaning of the law.

What Professor Cohen meant to us who sat in his classroom has
been put so aptly by my fellow student and attorney, Max Gross-
man, that I cannot do better than to quote his words:

> It has been my privilege to be a student of Professor Cohen. Method
> or content in teaching is frequently only a vehicle to the personality of
> the teacher communicating itself to the students. It is particularly true
> in Professor Cohen's case. His classroom may be likened to a laboratory
> where ideas are tested for rational validity. There are no airy vaporings.
> There is no false stimulus of inspirational talk, that by its quick disap-
> pearance leaves a void begetting only disillusionment. It is true that
> more frequently the tests dissolved myths—and woe is me—frequently a
> *Weltanschauung* built meticulously in adolescence crumbled. In the be-
> ginning, I was conscious of an acidic wit that not only dissolved but bit
> too sharply, that destroyed and did not energize recreation. But soon
> there came the realization of the profound earnestness of this seeker for
> genuine ideas. One forgave the surgeon's sharp knife for the healing
> process thereafter. One understood the curative x-ray that pierced to the
> wound. A keen logic sought the foundation of ethics and law, of science
> and philosophy, but it was not a sterile logic. It became fruitful through
> the penetration of the one mysticism that logic readily accepts as its
> love—a faith in its power to reveal truth. Logic is then productive of
> harmonies that are as aesthetically satisfying as is sweet music.
>
> Professor Cohen in his address explained his task as an attempt "to
> relieve the student of needless traditional baggage" and while he leaves
> him in the desert, he has at least taken him "out of the Egypt of Bond-
> age." Let not the statement create an impression of an atmosphere of
> desert and whirling sand. I felt when I came into the class-room that I
> came to a crystal clear spring where the waters were cold and refreshing.
> The "climate of opinion" and the "temperature of ideas" were not suit-
> able for passionate prejudices and half-baked theories. A long cool
> draught at the fountain head cleared the mind of cobwebs and musty
> ideas.[2]

Other students of Professor Cohen who have made distinguished names for themselves in his own chosen field of philosophy
have testified in similar vein. Professor Sidney Hook wrote:

> In my time Professor Cohen was the strongest intellectual force in
> the college. His full strength was felt primarily by the students and

[2] *Op. cit.*, p. xv-xvii.

through them reflected upon the faculty. One instructor was wont to remark that he could always pick out Cohen's students. They were distinguished by an intensity about ideas, by a catholicity of interests and by a keenness and persistency in logical analysis which often outran the limits of social discretion. This absorption in method was really the "mark of Cohen" which they bore in their manner if not on their brow. Sometimes they were not popular with other members of the faculty— they stressed the importance of giving reasons, raised doubts, challenged time-worn dogmas, interrupted the full-flowing periods of rotund rhetoric and were deaf to all arguments from authority. . . .

And yet so profound was his intellectual humility that I can truthfully assert that I have heard him say "I do not know" more often than any other person I have known. Like Socrates he taught that the realization of one's ignorance was the beginning of one's wisdom.[3]

And, in the same key, Professor Ernest Nagel has said:

It is indeed upon integrity in one's beliefs that Professor Cohen still insists as the one cardinal virtue of the philosophic life. No student of his who was worth his salt failed to acquire it in some measure. We learned from him what grasp of subject-matter, what comprehensiveness of range, may contribute to the stature of a man. But we learned, above all, love of honesty and clarity in one's convictions, and humility in the presence of truth, to be the basis of the life of reason. His class-room methods were the expression of his passionate rationality. Ours was the joy in watching the play and penetration of a first-rate mind; and ours too was the pain which his ruthless logic, stooping for no personalities and recognizing no compulsion but that of the subject-matter, inflicted upon our vanities. He taught us, so that some of us will never forget it, that suspended judgments are achievements of intense reflection, not of indolence, and that doctrinal loyalties are not incompatible with catholicity in one's sympathies and understandings. . . .

To be docile to the lessons of experience, but withal to seek blessedness in the shadow of the ideal, has been the substance of his teachings.[4]

Those of us who studied under Professor Cohen were of many minds and many backgrounds. He made all of us see more clearly the implications of our opinions and the inadequacies of the particular set of prejudices which each of us brought with him to the college. As we went our separate ways there was, it is true, no "Cohen philosophy" which any of us could use to solve the problems that faced us in professional life. We were of all parties of politics, of all schools in economics, of all faiths in religion. But

[3] *Op. cit.*, p. 90-93.
[4] *Op. cit.*, p. 96-97.

his teachings impressed one recognizable pattern on us and on our contribution to the life of the law. He trained us to be alert to the superstitions, the prejudices, the frailties in the law and to be steadfast in championing their elimination or correction. This all of us would be impelled to do however much we might disagree among ourselves as to what, if anything, should be substituted for the elements of the legal order that were justly the subject of attack.[5] The list of his students who later entered the legal profession is long. It contains many who have become recognized leaders of the bar, distinguished judges, writers and teachers of law. I think I can truthfully say, on their behalf, that the impact of the early training we received in Cohen's classes is a constant and dominant force in our daily professional lives. In one way or another as opportunity affords, we strive and now and then succeed in justifying his liberal faith. That faith, as I understand it, consisted of an abiding confidence in the power of reason to give arms to that love of humanity which, without arms, is so pitiful a figure in the world of today.

The ranks of Cohen students who join in that endeavor are not limited to the few thousand who had the privilege of sitting in the classrooms that he graced. Justice Holmes once wrote: "I have read his writings with admiration and great profit. I have enjoyed his conversation with equal profit, affection and reverence. I am proud that he calls me friend. I envy the youth who sit at his feet."

And in the same spirit Justice Cardozo wrote:

If insight into the essence of the judicial process, if profound appreciation of the fundamental principles and concepts and methods of the law can make a man a lawyer, then Professor Cohen is a lawyer and a great one, though seeing how many lawyers are entered upon the official roll, I think he will do well to content himself with the title of philosopher. He is teaching a great lesson, which is sinking more and more into our minds. I went over some of his papers last summer while I was doing some work upon pseudo-philosophic lectures. I was amazed at the range of his erudition alike in law and in philosophy, at the keenness of his perceptions, at the freshness and vigor of his thought, and at the compelling and arresting charm and incisiveness of his literary style.

[5] This, too, is in accord with Professor Cohen's own view of his function as a teacher. "It was enough," he said, "that Hercules should have cleaned the Augean stables, without replacing that which he swept out."

Sooner or later he will articulate his thoughts into a volume, and then his power will be felt in every law school in the land. . . .

Last spring, in the course of an opinion on the subject of causation, I ventured to include a citation of Lord Haldane's book *The Reign of Relativity*. Well, I got a letter from a distinguished friend, in which he said that he was greatly shocked that I should have cited such a book in the course of an opinion. He would stand for philosophy, he said, in the philosophical reviews, and for humor in a comic paper, but he did not wish to see humor in an elegy nor philosophy in a legal judgment. Let metaphysics be kept for those to whom physic of that sort is palatable.

Here you have the notion, which reappears again and again and has done so much harm to the law and its development, the notion that law is to be kept in a water-tight compartment and that within that compartment, and no other, is to be found the material by which its growth must be renewed. I can think of no one who has battled against that view more steadily and gallantly than this pseudo-lawyer who has enriched our conception of jurisprudence by the fertilizing waters of a profound and pure philosophy. We shall never get away in education from the study of fundamentals. We shall never get away from it or the need of it in the study of the law. We shall never separate the law from the study of philosophy unless we are ready to condemn it to barrenness and decay. In maintaining the relation between the two spheres of human thought scholars like Professor Cohen are keeping open the road to the steady progress of society along the paths of peace and order.

These comments are typical of other expressions that I have heard from judges of an older generation who studied under Morris R. Cohen, in their chambers if not in his classrooms. But I venture to think that the generations of future judges will owe an even greater debt to America's first legal philosopher.

In days that men of my generation can remember, it was popular for lawyers to assert that judges do not make the law; they merely find it as it already exists in law books and other source material of recognized authority. This notion went unchallenged and exercised a dominant influence over the practical life of the law. Morris R. Cohen was one of the first publicly to challenge it as a myth which, when put to the proof, could find no credible witness to veracity. That it is a myth is now generally recognized. The breakdown of its effect on the law, not yet complete but far enough advanced to be unmistakable, represents a major change in the climate of professional legal opinion within my generation. In this change the voice of Morris R. Cohen was the voice of a prophet who first points out that which becomes obvious to all once it has been declared.

The slogan that judges find the law and do not make it was based on the notion that the law is a self-sufficient body of logically inter-connected propositions to be found in the law books from which a judge, with honesty and moderate intelligence, might deduce or evolve the necessary and only answer to any question arising in the day-to-day life of our modern civilization. From this assumption it followed that a lawyer or judge could become great by mastering the law books, without looking at the world outside, and that the function of a law school was to acquaint students with the contents of the law books and with the methods of reasoning which they embodied. The inadequacy of this assumption was recognized in higher legal circles; but there was a sort of gentlemen's agreement that the general public should not be let in on the secret. Back in the days of Coolidge normalcy, Professor Cohen wrote:

When Theodore Roosevelt, in the days before the World War destroyed his progressivism, pointed out the inadequacies in the legal philosophy with which our courts were choking much-needed social legislation, he was attacked by almost all the leaders of the bar. The argument to which they all resorted, namely, that courts merely declare what the law is and have nothing to do with shaping its policy, was known to legal scholars since Austin as a childish fiction. It is surely a most childish fiction to pretend that our judges have had nothing to do with making our constitutional law what it is today. The leaders of the bar themselves do not make any such silly pretension when they praise John Marshall as the one who effectively moulded our federal constitutional law in the first third of the nineteenth century. What led distinguished lawyers to adopt such an absurd position, in which their hysterical vehemence could not hide the extreme senility of their learning?[6]

To show, as Professor Cohen showed with inexorable logic, that courts make law, and that they find the premises for the law they make not only within, but also outside of, the law books, is to show the need for rigorous scientific canons in incorporating economic, political, and other social data into the legal process. This is the only alternative to blind operation from a base of unexamined

[6] "Legalism and Clericalism," in *The New Republic*, vol. xli (1924) p. 15, reprinted in *Law and the Social Order* (1933) p. 158-59.

prejudices. But, as Professor Cohen was perhaps the first to point out, our courts were not organized to make use of scientific methods and scientific evidence. Again I quote words of Professor Cohen which bring to focus the most serious practical consequences that followed from the prevailing myth of the insulated self-sufficiency of the legal order:

> The American people have been accused, not unfairly, of lacking a due respect for law. In part, our judges are responsible for this fault through their failure to correct their personal opinions by objective tests and factual information. This failure is not primarily a personal one, since all of us find such an effort difficult. The fault is, in the main, with our judicial system which is intellectually the weakest part of our government. It has the least opportunity to get adequate information on the issues which it has to decide. Which of us who wants to inform himself on one of the principal current issues will be satisfied with listening for a few hours to a couple of lawyers and reading their briefs? Much is said about the calm atmosphere of the courts in contrast with the passionate attitudes which exist in the legislative and executive branches of the government. The truth of this is very dubious. Certainly our courts are less in contact with the actual facts of our complicated economic and social life, have no power to initiate investigations, and, by pretending to pass only on the law and not on the facts, leave the door open to most uncritical opinions.[7]

It was back in 1913 that Morris R. Cohen shocked the lawyers and law teachers of America with his epoch-making paper on "The Process of Judicial Legislation." What he said then supplied the text to which the most valuable work of progressive jurists since that time has been commentary. No excerpt can do justice to the productive insights of that essay, but a paragraph points to the intimate dependence of law upon the social sciences, a dependence which was once surreptitious and is now open, public, and on the way to becoming as scientific as human affairs ever can become:

> Law deals with human affairs and it is impossible to legislate or make any judgment with regard to law without involving all sorts of assumptions or theories. The issue, therefore, is not between a fixed law on the one hand and social theories on the other, but between social theories unconsciously assumed and social theories carefully examined and scientifically studied. What provision does our legal system make for the triumph of the more scientific theories? We let arbitrators, who

[7] Introduction to Goldberg and Levenson, *Lawless Judges* (1935) p. x.

are more or less specialists in the matter, sit for months to determine a single case. Yet we expect judges, with long calendars of all sorts of cases, without power to initiate inquiry and without power to call in experts to advise them, to settle all these matters saisfactorily. In ancient times it was comparatively easy for the court to take judicial notice of the established religion, the established Aristotelian philosophy, and various established customs of the realm. But how can judges today pretend to take judicial notice of all the findings of modern science that bear on the issues before them?[8]

The non-legal works that now fill the footnotes of Supreme Court opinions, the increasing reliance upon scientific data in the trial and argument of cases of public interest, and the expanding curricula of our more progressive law schools, all bear witness to the breakdown of the old myth of the self-sufficiency of the law. The technique of the "Brandeis brief," with its accent on social facts, the tendency of the last twenty years to expand the ad-ministrative and investigative side of the judicial process, and the increasing recognition of the role of social outlook in the judicial process, are all indications of the vitality of the philosophy with which Professor Cohen began to break down the walls that sepa-rated law from the social sciences. The trumpets still echo and the walls go crumbling down.

One does not have to wear a gray beard to remember days when it was accepted as a matter of course that major economic and political questions would be decided by leaders of the bar in-vested with judicial authority. The success or failure of a strike was likely to be determined by the character of the injunction that a court might be persuaded to issue, with or without notice to the union enjoined. Whether a given limitation of hours or improve-ment of working conditions or any other measure of public health and safety should be enforced or not was a question that we looked to the courts to decide. The answers to such questions were

[8] This paper was read on April 26, 1913, at the first meeting of the Confer-ence on Legal and Social Philosophy, which Morris R. Cohen organized. It was subsequently published in the *American Law Review*, vol. xlviii (1914) p. 161. Portions of the paper were elaborated in an address before The New York State Bar Association on January 23, 1915, and published under the title "Legal Theories and Social Science," in *International Journal of Ethics*, vol. xxv (1915) p. 469. The two papers are consolidated in *Law and the Social Order* (1933) p. 112, from which the quotation above is taken (at p. 142).

supposed to be extracted by the courts from the terms of state and federal constitutions, without the aid of any social philosophy. It thus became an impertinence to inquire into the social outlook or background of a candidate for judicial office. In such an atmosphere the phrase "government by judiciary" had solid content.

Today a very different view prevails with respect to the judicial function in our society. That judges are human beings, with social outlooks and value judgments not entirely derived from the law books, is no longer the shocking thought that it was when Morris R. Cohen addressed the New York Bar Association in January, 1915, on "Legal Theories and Social Science." Even the title then shocked staid leaders of the bar who were accustomed to contrast the certainty of law with the theoretic or speculative character of social studies. But since 1915 the writings of judges like Holmes, Brandeis, Cardozo, and Frankfurter have made clear, not only to law school students but even to seasoned lawyers, the role of extra-legal factors in the judicial process. It is expected today that a candidate for judicial office will be subjected to examination that covers every aspect of his social attitudes. Until a generation ago Supreme Court posts were generally filled by men who had made their names in private practice as the attorneys of important and powerful clients and had thus attained positions of leadership at the bar. Today that bench is manned entirely by men who have come to it from teaching or from public service.

"Government by judiciary," in its heyday, rested primarily on the foundation myth of a self-sufficient, all-encompassing, mechanical legal system. What Morris R. Cohen baptized the "phonograph theory of justice" was an ever-ready answer to critics of legal decisions. If court decisions in labor cases and other fields of social conflict really came off records made by the founding fathers, it was a waste of breath to direct criticism to the "disc jockeys" on the bench who merely turned on the records on appropriate occasions.

Morris R. Cohen made the phonograph theory of justice intellectually untenable. As judges came to recognize the scope of their creative and responsible role in the legal process, there grew up a more sober attitude of judicial deference to the authority of legislators. At the same time legislators became more aware of the social policy issues involved in constitutional law. There thus arose the practice of including in statutes statements of fact and policy designed to support the constitutionality of the statute. For more than a decade now the Supreme Court has accepted the authority of Congress as embodied in such statements. During that period it has refrained from substituting its own judgment for the judgment of Congress on disputed issues of social fact and policy.

This has been the rule of the present Supreme Court where Congressional legislation was of a progressive stamp. I suspect that the rule will carry over to situations where the legislation in question is not at all progressive. Liberals who do not see the woods for the trees are likely to rail at such decisions. I think they will be wrong. In the long run it is right that Congress, with its superior facilities for fact-gathering and its greater responsiveness to public opinion, should make the decisions in controverted fields of social policy, and face the criticism that wrong decisions will provoke.

This does not mean that our judges will cease to play an important role in our political and economic life. So long as the words of statutes need to be interpreted and fitted to cases that legislatures never foresaw, the role of the judiciary will continue to be important and to reflect the awareness of philosophical and social issues that judges bring to their work on the bench. This will be true even if the tendency of the present Supreme Court to defer to any clearly expressed judgment of Congress on large questions of social fact becomes a permanent part of our law and a characteristic of all our courts.

One of the chief supports of "government by judiciary" a generation ago was the old-fashioned shibboleth of "a government of laws and not of men," which an unkind critic has paraphrased "a government of lawyers and not of men." The assumption that gave force to this distinction was originally the assumption that laws are not human affairs, subject to human tinkering, but god-given and above the battle of human interests. As this assumption was deflated, as the human character of judicial and legislative justice came to be appreciated, the major prejudice against administrative law began to evaporate. A dozen years ago Morris R. Cohen noted, in his incisive "Critical Sketch of Legal Philosophy in

America,"[9] the narrow restraints that had been put upon the development of administrative law:

> Traditional American legal thought not only directed its energy primarily to private and commercial transactions, but it took a certain pride in minimizing administrative law. This, of course, followed from the dogma of the supremacy of the civil courts and the subordination of all public law to the forum where dominate lawyers representing private clients.

The twelve years since 1935 have witnessed a tremendous development of administrative law in national affairs. Essentially this growth has accompanied the heightening recognition that specialized knowledge, which cannot readily be gathered by a court from private litigants and their attorneys, is essential to the intelligent carrying out of social responsibilities of the modern state. The system of administrative law that has developed since early New Deal days was based in part upon a recognition of limitations in the judicial process. These limitations called for the creation of supplementary machinery outside of the regular court system. But this structure could not have flourished if the courts had maintained an unsympathetic attitude toward the substitution of administrative for judicial discretion in many fields of modern life.[10] That the courts accepted this growth of administrative law with sympathy and deference to the democratically expressed will of the people is a token of the change that has begun to come over our prevailing legal philosophy.

Now we face an era of legal development when the outlook that Morris R. Cohen advanced will no longer seem shocking or novel or revolutionary. I do not think that what he had to say will

[9] *Law: A Century of Progress: 1835-1935*, vol. ii, p. 266, 315.

[10] On this matter I can speak out of personal knowledge. As chief legal adviser to the Secretary of the Interior from 1933 to 1942, I had the responsibility of defending in the courts his administrative decisions on a wide variety of highly controversial issues relating to oil, coal, helium, public lands, Indians, Puerto Rico, the Philippines, and the construction and use of the greatest works of public improvement in the United States. In more than thirty instances the litigation reached the Supreme Court itself. Yet in all those nine years, not a single departmental decision was overthrown by the courts. This would not have been possible without genuine appreciation on the part of the courts of the value of the administrative process, without their having attached great weight to the resources of information and expert knowledge available to a great government department.

therefore become less important. That might be the case if he had been only the impatient critic of prevailing irrationalities that some of us saw in his classroom. But he was more than that. He strove mightily, especially in the later years of his life, to understand the basic institutions of the law, property, contract, liability, criminal law, and the Constitution, and to see how an awareness of social issues might affect our understanding of recurring problems in those fields. He was not content to set forth a philosophical out-look—to go down in history as the first American philosopher to interest himself in the law, as Holmes was the first American law-yer to interest himself in philosophy. He followed, with an intel-lectual passion that burned to the very end, the implications of that philosophical outlook through the day-to-day life of our legal system.

We have not really begun to catch up with that phase of his thought. Most of it is still scattered in uncollected legal papers or the cherished private possession of students and friends who have caught from his lips words of insight that nobody has yet coor-dinated. And so I think that Morris R. Cohen was right, as usual, when he said that it takes fifty years to translate philosophy into action. It will be 1963 before his first essay on jurisprudence[11] is fifty years old. Only then, will it be possible to appraise fairly his impact on the life of the law.

[11] "Jurisprudence as a Philosophical Discipline," in *Journal of Philosophy*, vol. x, p. 225 ff.

The Principle of Polarity
in Cohen's Philosophy

◆§ BY DANIEL J. BRONSTEIN

City College of New York

SOMEONE once said that Morris Cohen had an inordinate fear that others might agree with him. He thrived on criticism, which he needed as a stimulus to the development of his own thought. "Without the critical spirit," he wrote, "philosophy degenerates into sheer dogmatism." What more fitting way, then, is there to honor him than by analyzing and criticizing his ideas? I shall, in this paper, consider what is probably his fundamental philosophical conception, an idea both original and fruitful, which has ramifications in all the many areas of human knowledge which he made his province. Whether he was writing on ethics, law, politics, religion, metaphysics, history, or science—sooner or later this theme was bound to appear. It is concerned with the reconciliation of the rational and the empirical, the actual and the ideal, the mental and the physical, the one and the many, change and constancy, etc.

One common pitfall in philosophy, Cohen held, is to regard opposite categories like these as incompatible and hence irreconcilable. This leads philosophers to oversimplify situations and to analyze them in terms of only one of such contrary categories, instead of using both. Another fallacy is what he called "the too facile reconciliation of incompatible alternatives." (RN 399.)[1] While the first error consists in magnifying the opposition of conflicting tendencies, the second results from underestimating the difficulties of resolving certain conflicts.

It was Morris Cohen's oft-repeated contention that we could

[1] I shall use the following abbreviations: RN for *Reason and Nature*, PL for *A Preface to Logic*, FL for *The Faith of a Liberal*, MHH for *The Meaning of Human History*, and DJ for *A Dreamer's Journey*.

avoid both Scylla and Charybdis if we heeded the principle of polarity. What is the principle of polarity? Although Cohen often employs it and attributes many of his finest insights and criticisms to its use, it is seldom formulated; and even when it is, this is done in a sketchy manner with the key concepts conveyed by terms that are either vague or ambiguous. The reader is given the impression that the principle somehow defies exact formulation, and that it is sufficient if he catches its flavor and realizes its importance. The several statements that are given of the principle do not, offhand, seem to be equivalent. Let us examine these formulations (and explanations) in an effort to give them more precision, and to determine whether "the principle of polarity" is one or many.

I. FORMULATIONS OF
THE PRINCIPLE OF POLARITY

Formulation 1.

One of the most explicit expressions of the principle of polarity was given in *Reason and Nature*. There, (p. 165) Cohen says:

> ... opposites such as immediacy and mediation, unity and plurality, the fixed and the flux, substance and function, ideal and real, actual and possible, etc., like the north (positive) and the south (negative) poles of a magnet, all involve each other when applied to any significant entity.

To understand what this means we need to know how the term "opposites" is defined. But no definition of this basic term is given. Also, the word "involves" is particularly troublesome; and the restriction to entities that are significant seems important, but what distinguishes a "significant" entity from others, we are not told. The statement pretty clearly does *not* say that *all* opposites "involve each other when applied etc." because there is a qualifying phrase "such as immediacy and mediation, etc." Well, then, presumably, what it does say is that all opposites of a certain kind "involve each other." Of what kind? It seems from the statement that the kind of opposition referred to is the kind exemplified by the relation between the north and south poles of a magnet. Let us call such opposites, *polar* opposites. Then we have: "All polar opposites involve each other etc." But the illustration of the magnet has been chosen precisely because the opposite poles of a magnet do "involve" each other; that is to say, polar opposites "involve" each other by definition. This produces a tautology: "All opposites (which, like the poles of a magnet, involve each other) involve each other etc." However, this is only a part of the statement of the principle of polarity. There is another, non-tautological, part which, when detached, reads:

> . . . immediacy and mediation, unity and plurality, the fixed and the flux, substance and function, ideal and real, actual and possible, etc. are polar opposites.

This is the significant part of the "principle of polarity." But it is hardly a "principle"; it is a program. It remains to be shown that these categories do "involve each other," whatever that means. It is also necessary to specify with some precision what the qualifications are for admission into the class of polar opposites.

While this first formulation of the principle of polarity appears to be concerned only with those high abstractions of metaphysics which are mentioned, and others like them, there are other descriptions of the principle where the term "opposites" is construed in a more general sense.

Formulation 2.

In *A Preface to Logic* (p. 74), Cohen writes:

> . . . physical entities or complexes of relations admit and often demand contrary determinations within them. Of any given individual it may be true to say that he is generous and not generous at the same time. The truth of both of these statements becomes clear and determinate if we draw a distinction and say he is generous to his family and in public charities, but ungenerous to his employees and economic competitors.

But since "generous to his family" and "ungenerous to his employees" are perfectly compatible and not at all "contrary determinations," the original "contradiction" is shown to be only apparent. It arose because our language was vague. Hence it seems strange to insist that "physical entities admit and often demand contrary determinations within them," though this is, of course, true if by "determinations" we mean to include terms that are so vague that they are indeterminate.

Cohen continues:

. . . to make logic applicable to empirical issues, we must employ the principle of polarity. By this I mean that the empirical facts are generally resultants of opposing and yet inseparable tendencies like the north and south poles. . . . Physical science employs this principle to eliminate the vagueness and indetermination of popular discussion in which opposite concepts, like good and bad, hot and cold, large and small, remote and near, can be applied to the same thing. Such vagueness is eliminated by substituting concepts of numbers and measures, which enable us to pass from relatively indeterminate issues as to whether our object is large or small, hot or cold, to the more definite issue, how many yards, how many degrees of temperature, etc. Similar progress might be made in philosophy if we recognized the indeterminateness of certain issues as to whether certain things exist or not, by asking, exist how or in what sense.[2]

If the principle of polarity means that "the empirical facts are *generally*[3] the resultants of opposing but inseparable tendencies," where "generally" connotes "usually, but not necessarily always," the principle would not enjoin us to employ opposite categories in *all* situations, but would warn us that in *some* cases (where our language is vague and hence indeterminate) contrary categories are both applicable. Thus, *Formulation 2* would make the principle of polarity in the author's words, "a maxim of intellectual search," reminding us that greater clarity and philosophic understanding can be achieved by eliminating the vagueness of ordinary language, and by recognizing the valid insights of opposing points of view.

Formulation 3.

But the temptation to generalize was hard to resist. In the same context we are told:

Philosophically, it [the principle of polarity] may be generalized as the principle, not of the identity, but of the necessary copresence and mutual dependence of opposite determinations." (PL 75.)

Here the principle assumes the form of a metaphysical generalization. As in *Formulation 1*, we have the mutual involvement, but we also have something additional, *viz.* necessary copresence. And since the reference to certain specific categories (as in *Formulation*

2 PL, p. 75.
3 My italics.

1) is omitted, the principle becomes most general in scope. Although Cohen explicitly differentiates his principle from Hegel's identity of opposites, he would not deny, but in fact admitted (RN 167-68) that the principle of polarity has a distinctly Hegelian cast. This became quite apparent when, on another occasion,[4] Cohen said:

> . . . contradiction is essential to the meaning and fruitful application of the concepts of the understanding . . . there is a growing appreciation of the necessary polarity of ideas, that fruitful thought *must* use opposite categories in *every* situation to get adequate insight. (FL 383, my italics.)

There are, in these quotations, two strains of thought, incompatible, but both appealing. Instead of deciding between them, the author offers us both. Together they constitute what I shall call

The Antinomy of Polarity

One view *(Formulation 2)* says: Whenever you find a contradiction in describing a concrete situation, this is because your language is vague. Look for a distinction to resolve the contradiction; there must be one. The other view counters *(Formulation 3):* In every situation there are opposing tendencies in equilibrium. To get a true picture of the world you must use polar categories; it is a mistake to think that every contradiction can be resolved.

How can we explain Cohen's adherence to both of these positions at the same time? Perhaps a few illustrations will help. Some say that Americans are losing their freedom because they can no longer join a political party of their own choosing without the fear of reprisal, while their opponents reply that we are not losing our freedom but making it more secure by protecting ourselves from those who care nothing about freedom and wish only to undermine and then destroy it. To resolve this "contradiction" may not be easy, but there are few who will be inclined to maintain that it cannot be done. We see that the term "freedom" is used with different meanings in the two arguments and we try to explain what this difference is. When we succeed in doing so, we have resolved the "contradiction." The facts are complex enough, and it requires empirical knowledge as well as linguistic ingenuity to describe

---

[4] The Presidential Address to the American Philosophical Association, 1929.

them accurately, but it can be done. It is not simply that we *can* get adequate insight without retaining the original "contradiction," but rather that we do not attain adequate insight until we see how to make the "contradiction" vanish.

Now let us consider another case. It is well known, we are told, that the Democratic Party is full of "contradictions." Truman pledges his party to establish civil rights, and Rankin and his supporters sabotage that pledge. Doesn't the Democratic Party exhibit a "real" contradiction? Can we be true to the facts without noting their contradictory character? Or can we resolve this contradiction by using more accurate language? Here the "contradiction" appears to be in the situation itself because there is a real conflict of forces or interests. There is a collision in reality, and not only a linguistic confusion. Two vehicles traveling in opposite directions on a narrow road may collide. The physicist can determine the mechanical forces involved and explain the situation correctly without employing a contradiction. (In fact, if he did employ a contradiction, we would say his explanation was unsatisfactory.) And we can do the same with the Democratic Party. But there is also a linguistic confusion, in that both Mr. Truman and Mr. Rankin insist on labeling themselves by the same name, Democrat. But this "contradiction" is not a perplexing one, and we have no great difficulty in finding the proper distinction to dispel it.

Our example shows that people may hold opposing views, even contradict each other, and still remain within the same party. But when we say that some Democrats contradict other Democrats, and that therefore "a contradiction exists within the Democratic Party," we do not mean that these two contradictory positions are both true, or that both can prevail at the same time. Whenever the party must act as a unit, one or the other side must yield. We can, if we wish, say that we have here a "contradiction in reality," but if we do, we will be extending the meaning of the term "contradiction" from logical incompatibility to political incompatibility—and if we then forget that we have enlarged its meaning, we are quite likely to get a genuine contradiction, *i.e.*, to contradict ourselves.

Now the *antinomy of polarity*, it seems to me, arises because Cohen does not always make a clear enough distinction between genuine contradictions and apparent ones. At times he maintains that contradictions occur because we use language that is vague and indeterminate; and that we can resolve them by making the proper distinctions. At other times, he holds that the indeterminateness of our conception reflects an indetermination in "reality." (PL 13, 76.) In these cases, as when we try to describe a complex unit like the Democratic Party, or the United States, or the universe, and find after a while that we have a "contradiction," he feels that the contradiction may be unresolvable; in fact, that it may be the only correct analysis of the situation as it is. He writes:

> Of incompletely determined existence, as in the case of the total universe, contradictory propositions do not annihilate each other (since they refer to a complex of existences); and yet they cannot always (because of the indefiniteness of the subject) be reconciled with each other. This gives rise to the antinomies of metaphysics. (RN 167.)

How can two contradictory propositions not "annihilate each other?" I assume Cohen is referring to a case like:

A. The Democratic Party supports the civil rights program.

B. The Democratic Party does not support that program. His argument would be that if we make a distinction, and interpret A as referring to Truman and his followers, and B as referring to the Dixiecrats, then both propositions are true, *i.e.*, they do not annihilate each other. But if we make this distinction, the propositions are not contradictories, since they refer to different groups. There is an *apparent* contradiction because the term "Democratic Party" seems to have an identical referent in both propositions, but in order to show that they "do not annihilate each other," we must assign two different referents to the term "Democratic Party." This apparent contradiction, in other words, is the result of a lack of analysis. Now, in the above quotation from *Reason and Nature* it is interesting to note the *indefiniteness* is attributed not to our language, but to the *subject*. This might be called a case of misplaced indefiniteness. It is because he transfers the indefiniteness from the realm of discourse, where it belongs, to what we are talking about (the subject), that Cohen is able to maintain that there are contradictions in "the real world."

Philosophers, like Hegel and Bradley, who say that the contradictions are *in rebus,* are content to accept them—even to welcome them. For they are regarded not as signs of inadequate understanding or defective analysis, but simply as blemishes in "the world of appearance." This is tantamount to declaring the contradictions unresolvable, which is to block the road of inquiry. For it assumes that where we can find no adequate solution, none exists. In this connection, Whitehead's comment on Bradley's analysis of space and time is relevant: "He shouldn't have said: 'space contradicts itself and time contradicts *itself*'; he should have said: '*I* contradict *my*self.'"

II. ORIGIN OF THE PRINCIPLE OF POLARITY

Since the abstract formulations of the principle of polarity present us with a number of difficulties of interpretation, and even a fundamental inconsistency, it would seem wise, if we wish to understand what the principle meant to its author, to consider how he came to formulate it, and how he applied it in his own critical studies.

The courses in logic and economics that Cohen took at college had at least one good result. They led him to the writings of John Stuart Mill. But the latter's view that the world consists of a number of independent things, facts, or states of mind, did not satisfy him. Meanwhile his interest in socialism, and readings in Marx and Engels made it only natural, if oversanguine, for him to seek enlightenment in Hegel and the neo-Hegelians. Although Cohen found Hegel's emphasis on the organic unity of things a needed antidote for Mill's atomism, Hegel's Absolute proved to be too large a dose to swallow for one who had respect for logic and the method of the sciences. This left Cohen in an intellectual dilemma which plagued him for several years; and it was not until he read Russell's *Principles of Mathematics* that he found a way out. Just how did Russell help him solve his problem? Here is Cohen's account from his autobiography:

Russell's demonstration that pure mathematics or logic cannot be identified with either psychologic or physical events, but constitutes a part of the real world of thought, seemed to me to offer a well-grounded and fruitful starting point for philosophy. Here was a standpoint that explained the fruitfulness of mathematical method in building up scientific knowledge.

This renewed faith in logic showed me how to avoid both Mill's extreme individualism, which denies real connections, and the absolutism of Hegel and Marx, in which there is no room for real individuality. In mathematics there are no pre-eminent numbers. One is as real as two or three, but not more so. Circles are not more real than squares, equality is not more real than inequality, variables are not more real than constants. Accepting the ultimate validity of logic and mathematics thus made it possible for me to see that unity and plurality, similarity and difference, dependence and independence, form and matter, change and permanence, are equally real. It also showed me that no one of these conceptions can exist or have meaning without the other, just as the opposite blades of a scissors or the north and south poles of a magnet cannot function except in pairs, united in opposition. When any one of these conceptions, unity or plurality, independence or dependence, is blown up to include the entire universe and so swallow up its opposite, it ceases to have any meaning. This standpoint freed me from subservience to false absolutisms in law, in politics, and in metaphysics, as well as in religion. The idea that the nature of things depends upon the equilibrium of opposing forces, and that therefore the way to get at the nature of things is to reason from opposing considerations, came to be a permanent part of my philosophical outlook, reinforced by suggestions that came to me from Professor Felix Adler, from Professor Josiah Royce, and from Marshall's *Principles of Economics*. The idea that opposite viewpoints could each embody elements of truth was strengthened by Wilmon Sheldon, whom I had met at Glenmore in 1899 and under whom I studied at Columbia in 1903-4. I was much impressed by the insight of Sheldon's observation that philosophers were generally right in what they affirmed of their own vision and generally wrong in what they denied of the vision of others. (DJ 170.)

I have included this long quotation because it is such a lucid and succinct description of the origin and function of the principle of polarity. Selecting the valuable insights of opposing philosophers while rejecting their claims to exclusiveness was one of Cohen's great talents, and gives his criticisms their incisive and at the same time constructive character.

The reference in the above selection to opposite categories such as unity and plurality, etc., as "equally real" raises a question. (1) The author can be understood as saying, in effect, what he *did* say on other occasions, *viz.* that "reality" is an honorific term and that "the honorific use of non-discriminating terms [such as unity, plurality, similarity, difference, etc.] can only serve to darken counsel." Hence the contention of the absolutists that one of each pair of such terms represents "the real," while the other represents "appearance," is meaningless. (2) A second interpretation would take Cohen seriously when he says that Russell, who was a Platonist in 1903, taught him that logical relations are "a part of the real world," and when he claims that polar categories are "equally real." But if logical relations are part of the "real world," then contradiction, which is a logical relation, is "part of the real world." But Cohen once said that "strictly speaking, contradictions are always dialectical, *i.e.*, they hold only in a logical universe." (RN 166.) Indeed, if contradictions were "part of the real world," one could not mention anything which would *not* be "part of the real world." If we adopt this second interpretation, we can only conclude that in attributing *reality* to circles and squares, equality and inequality, dependence and independence, etc., Cohen has lapsed into the habit of the absolutists he criticizes, by allowing the term "reality" to become non-discriminating and yet to pose as if it had a descriptive meaning. Of these two interpretations I prefer the first, but I think it is nearer the truth to say that Cohen wavered between the two views and never faced the issue squarely.

III. CHANGE AND PERSISTENCE

Because change is a more arresting phenomenon than persistence, we are apt to overlook the fact that in an institution or culture much remains the same even in the midst of radical changes. In pointing this out, Cohen criticizes those who say, with Heraclitus, that everything is in a state of flux. "As abstract categories," he says, "change and persistence, discontinuity and continuity, are mutually exclusive, but every concrete real existence involves both. Whenever anyone does or suffers anything he remains the same individual. The change has occurred in him." (MHH 63.) This gives us a clue to the meaning of the expression "opposite categories *involve* each other." When he says that "change *involves* persistence" he appears to mean that whenever something changes, it can change only in some respects, and will remain the same in other respects. Now, whether or not this is true will depend on how liberal we wish to be in interpreting the term "respects." When a man grows older he may retain the same recollections, and he does retain the same ancestors. But the water which changes into hydrogen and oxygen as a result of electrolysis does lose its identity. Still, there is something which persists even through such a change, *e.g.*, a certain mass. When Lewis Carroll turns a baby into a pig, size remains invariant. But as Charles Peirce pointed out, *any* two things can be shown to have *something* in common, even when no process of change connects one with the other. To illuminate the notion of change, therefore, Cohen would have to distinguish the type of invariance which holds between A and B when they are phases of one process, from the type which holds even when A and B are completely independent. When the notion of persistence, or invariance, is left undefined, the proposition that "change involves persistence" is an ambiguity; it appears to be a law without exceptions only because on one interpretation it is a tautology. To remove the ambiguity, Cohen would have to classify types of change, and within each type indicate a set of properties which constitute the range of invariance. But then he would have to be prepared to countenance exceptions to his principle.

Cohen considers the case of annihilation and holds that it is no exception to his generalization. He says: "this [annihilation] is a fact of change to a world which includes more than the thing annihilated, just as a table taken out of a room means a change in a room." (MHH 63.) Here there has been a perceptible shift in the meaning of the proposition that "change involves persistence." When invariance cannot be found in the changing thing, it can always be found in the universe. This view contains more than a hint of the Hegelian notion that all change occurs within the Absolute, which is itself unchanging. If every change is imbedded in an environment which includes more than the changing thing, it is not surprising that we can find invariant aspects of this environment even where the process of change results in something so different as to be unrecognizable. While acknowledging the Hegelian tinge of his principle of polarity, Cohen hoped that he could free it of the obscurity and irrationality which he found in Hegel. I am not convinced that he was entirely successful.

We have found, in the writings so far examined, two different meanings of the expression "change involves persistence," *viz.*:

(1) Whenever something changes in some respects, *it* will remain constant in other respects.

(2) All changes are fragments of a larger whole in which there are invariant properties.

A third meaning is sometimes given to this idea, as in the following quotation:

> The world of experience certainly does not show us anything constant except in reference to that which is changing, nor any change except by reference to something constant. We may generalize change as much as we like, saying that even the most general laws of nature that we now know, such as the laws of mechanics, are slowly changing; but this change can be established and have meaning only by means of or in reference to some logical constant. The belief that the world consists of all change and no constancy is no better than the belief that all vessels have insides but no outsides. (RN 412.)

This raises a question which should be asked about any generalization like the principle of polarity. Is the principle a proposition of logic, or a scientific hypothesis? Is it true *a priori,* because of the definitions of its terms, or is it acceptable because it is so well confirmed by experience? Cohen's discussions are ambivalent on this question. Often he presents empirical evidence to support his generalization; but when he is *in extremis* he argues that a contradiction would result if his proposition were denied. If the belief in universal change were no better than a contradiction (like "all vessels have insides but no outsides"), then his own proposition would be analytic, and it would be pointless to look to experience to substantiate it. If, on the other hand, the proposition that "change involves persistence" is not analytic, then it is relevant and necessary to show how it is supported by experience. But then it cannot be claimed that a contradiction would be the result of denying the proposition.

Cohen's reply would be something like this: The principle of polarity belongs neither to logic nor to science, but rather to metaphysics. It is not true simply because of judicious definition, nor because of experimental findings. Polarity is an objective and pervasive feature of the world. In any field of scientific exploration there will be found instances or applications of polarity, but the principle itself is general. Newton's laws of motion are also general; but they deal only with physical reality and require experimental verification. "Metaphysics, however, is not interested in the discovery or formulation of specific laws of nature, or the prediction of specific facts. It is primarily concerned with what Plato and Kant called ideas—i.e. with formulations of those ultimate totalities (or absolutes, if you please) which a changing world can show." (FL 381.) The principle of polarity is one of these absolutes. Our own experience, as well as the factual results of the special sciences at any given time are bound to be fragmentary. The recognition of this fact "does not remove but rather necessitates the metaphysical idea or ideal of a system or world of time and space to which all of our actual experience and knowledge more or less approximates." (FL 382.)

This reply does not meet the foregoing criticisms but assumes that they are not relevant, an assumption which would be justified if the principle of polarity had been consistently interpreted as in *Formulation 2.* It would then have been treated not as a metaphysical truth but as a "maxim of intellectual search," directing us to strive for greater definiteness of expression, and indicating certain ways of avoiding premature one-sided generalizations. But when the principle of polarity is formulated after the fashion of an empirical law, yet is regarded as some kind of absolute which neither needs nor is capable of confirmation by experience, then, in my opinion, the foregoing criticisms *are* relevant, and Cohen's reply fails to meet them. To classify a statement as a metaphysical principle or absolute, does not make its vagueness or ambiguity more tolerable, nor does it confer an immunity from the need of empirical justification.

IV.   LANGUAGE AND REALITY

In calling the principle of polarity metaphysical, Cohen indicates his belief that opposition is a *characteristic* of nature, and not just a way of describing it. "Language," he held, "ceases to be significant if it cannot indicate something beyond language." When he speaks of the "necessary copresence" of opposite determinations like the hot and the cold, the one and the many, the actual and the ideal, self-sacrifice and self-realization, he means not merely that these categories are necessary for intelligible discourse, but that this "necessity corresponds to an objective reality." (MHH 67.) From this point of view, what shall we say of other philosophies which find the world composed not of dyads, but of a single reality (Hegel), or of triads? Charles Peirce held that there are three irreducible categories which are "real constituents of the universe." Are these opposing views necessarily wrong because Cohen has shown that "every concrete real existence" exhibits a *pair* of opposites? Philosophers like Hegel and Peirce often set forth "proofs" of the exclusive truth of their own position. But even when they do not say so explicitly, one gathers the impression that each believes his own doctrine to be the truth about reality, and opposing views to be erroneous. Some of Cohen's discussions of polarity, as when he insists that polar opposites are objective, and necessary in every situation, give his readers the right to infer that he holds similar beliefs about his own doctrine. He argues: either we acknowledge that our categories represent an objective reality or we must admit that they are "a kind of mental trickery that does violence to the universe . . . or, at least, is irrelevant to that universe." (MHH 67.) But this is just the kind of intellectual dilemma the principle of polarity should help us avoid. We can reject both alternatives, and remembering the maxim that "opposite viewpoints can each embody elements of truth," we can regard the categories of each philosopher as possible coordinate systems rather than as necessary constituents of reality.[5] Although language often has a representative function, we need not accept the extreme, and untenable, position that all our linguistic constructions "correspond to an objective reality." One of the examples Cohen uses to support his *realism* is that "the infinite number of different coordinates from which a given line may be located does not prevent it from having an objective and constant length and curve." (MHH 67.) But the mathematician does not assert that one out of all these coordinate systems "corresponds to an objective reality," while the others are "unreal"; though he may find one

[5] This is what Cohen does on one occasion, when, making a concession to the relativistic approach, he writes: "Theoretically, the legal system may be viewed completely from either pole. You may even insist that there is little difference, if any, between a positivism like Gray's which allows for moral judgments upon the law, and an idealism that admits the inherent limitation of any ideal of justice that can be applied to human affairs. There is a sense in which the same system of legal rights and duties might be expressed in positivistic or in idealistic language." (RN 426.)

system more convenient or psychologically simpler. In mathematics, a line has a given length—call it objective if you wish—only because we stipulate that it shall have a certain length, either directly or by other postulates. And it has been shown that "objective" distances in physical space become determinate only after we have made certain *decisions* concerning the measuring instruments we are to use and the action of universal forces on those instruments.

If the principle of polarity in one of its versions is a first cousin of Hegelianism, in another it resembles Aristotles's theory of the golden mean. It is also a close ally of William James' conception of pragmatism as a method of settling metaphysical disputes. No wonder it proved so fertile. But its very richness of meaning, which has only been suggested here, is also its great weakness. Many, including the present writer, who recognize its value as a principle of criticism and its fruitfulness in achieving a synthesis of apparently opposing points of view, have grave doubts concerning the principle of polarity as an ontological law or absolute. Even if its author wished to espouse it in both forms, he could have saved his readers much bewilderment if he had differentiated the various versions of the principle. To clarify the principle of polarity is, I believe, a necessary preliminary in gaining for it the recognition from philosophers that it deserves—and this paper is meant to be a step toward achieving that end.

The Philosophical Method of Morris R. Cohen

✎§ BY ARTHUR FRANCIS SMULLYAN

University of Washington

*M*ORRIS COHEN philosophized not only about the abstract themes of logic but also about the concrete themes of history. His views on these concrete themes were not deductions from metaphysical assumptions. They reflected his concern for empirical fact as well as his concern for philosophical synthesis. Nevertheless, there was a distinctive approach he had to any question on which he wrote or lectured and this distinctiveness of approach, although not his particular conclusions, was largely determined, I think, by his use of two principles. One of these I shall take the liberty of calling the principle of relationality. The other he himself called the principle of polarity. The purpose of the following discussion is to clarify the interrelated meanings of these principles.

Cohen was wont to distinguish himself from those philosophers who regard things as independent units which are endowed with permanent private possessions on the one hand and which enter into adventitious relations on the other. He writes:

To me, the "nature" of a thing seems not to be so private or fixed. It may consist entirely of bonds, stocks, franchises, and other ways in which public credit or the right to certain transactions is represented, And, after all, what are private possessions but publicly protected rights to collect rent, exclude trespassers, etc.? At any rate, relations or transactions may be regarded as wider or more primary than qualities or possessions. The latter may be defined as internal relations, *i.e.*, relations *within* a system that constitutes the "thing." The nature of a thing contains an essence, *i.e.*, a group of characteristics which, in any given system or context, remain invariant, so that if these are changed the thing drops out of our system. Thus, if a banker no longer issues credit or receives deposits he ceases to be a banker. But the same thing may present different essences in different contexts. As a thing shifts from one context to another, it acquires new relations and drops old ones, and in all transformations there is a change or readjustment of the line between the internal relations which constitute the essence and the external relations which are outside the inner circle.

. . . This view, of course, does not deny the existence of terms, literally termini of relations, but it denies that terms have any nature apart from relations. The world of existence is thus a network of relations whose intersections are called terms. These termini may be complex or simple, but the simplicity is always relative to the system in which they enter. . . . The prevailing metaphysic . . . regards things as more fundamental than their relations, but it finds it difficult to tell us what the things are apart from their relations. The metaphysic here suggested starting with the relational structure of things avoids the ontologic ills that beset things in themselves.[1]

Cohen's doctrine is that the qualities of things are respective or relational. Qualities hold of things in respect to a background of systematic relatedness. Accordingly, the principle of contradiction was interpreted by him to mean that the same character cannot both characterize and fail to characterize the same object in the same relation.[2] Cohen argued therefore that there is no inconsistency involved in saying the same object is blue in one context and red in another,[3] or in saying that the same term is mental in one context and non-mental in another,[4] or in saying that the same line subtends an angle of 45° in one perspective and 23° in another,[5] or that points are simple in respect to one system and complex in respect to another,[6] or that permanence in one respect precludes contingency,[7] or, in general, that polar categories preclude one another.[8] Thus, we find him writing:

Is there any contradiction in "describing the same object as 'really' possessing simultaneously all the incongruous qualities which at any

[1] Cohen, Morris R., "Qualities, Relations, and Things," in *Journal of Philosophy*, vol. xi, p. 621-22.

[2] Cohen, "Concepts and Twilight Zones," in *Journal of Philosophy*, vol. xxiv, p. 678.

[3] Cohen, "Qualities, Relations, and Things," *loc. cit.*, p. 620.

[4] Cohen, "The Distinction Between the Mental and the Physical," in *Journal of Philosophy*, vol. xiv, p. 266.

[5] Cohen, "Qualities, Relations, and Things," *loc. cit.*, p. 619.

[6] *Ibid.*, p. 622.

[7] Cohen, *Reason and Nature*, p. 225-26.

[8] *Ibid.*, p. 165.

given moment appear in the perception of different percipients?" I see no difficulty whatsoever in the same object possessing all sorts of contradictory qualities, provided no two contradictory qualities appear in one point of view or relation. Professor Lovejoy admits, for instance, that the same line may simultaneously subtend an angle of 23° from one point of view and 45° from another. Why may not an object be square from one point of view and oblong from another? Why is there no contradiction in the first if there is one in the second? I am told that this question is "a rather curious disregard of the familiar distinction between the relations and the qualities of a thing." Now I am quite willing to confess that I do not pay the usual homage to this familiar distinction, and I hope on some other occasion to pay my respects to its deceptive and treacherous nature. . . .

The difficulty which Professor Lovejoy and others find in conceiving one object possessing contradictory qualities, seems to me to be due to a ghost of the thing-in-itself. "Every real thing," we are told, "has, besides its relations, a 'nature' or character or set of qualities of its own." Now, whatever may be said for the existence of *Dinge-an-sich,* it seems certain that science does not deal with them, and that none of its objects possesses qualities in isolation but only in given systems. If things could not have contradictory qualities, neither could they have contradictory relations or attributes, and all predication would be impossible. I regard Plato as having cleared this up in his controversy with the Megarians.[9]

The principle of relationality is the proposition that a characteristic is *either* a relation *or* is analyzable in terms of relations *or* is at least predicable only in relation to a system. If this principle is true, nothing has a non-relational quality *simpliciter*. In one relation an object may be said to have a certain quality. In a different relation, the object may be said to lack that quality. And apart from all relations, the object is a vicious abstraction from its nature, a point without position or quality, a subject of no possible predication. The principle of relationality does not mean that the possession of qualities is merely associated or empirically correlated with certain features of the environment. The principle affirms that the very meaning of quality-possession involves reference to some relation or perspective, so that the predication of a non-relational quality is incomplete or elliptical unless at the same time a system is specified in respect to which the quality is predicated.

   [9] Cohen, "The Supposed Contradiction in the Diversity of Secondary Qualities—A Reply," in *Journal of Philosophy,* vol. x, p. 511-12. Cohen's reference is to Lovejoy, "Secondary Qualities and Subjectivity," in *Journal of Philosophy,* vol. x, p. 216.

Thus, gold is not yellow except when it is in a certain light. That qualification is necessary to make our expression true and without it we have an incomplete symbol which is sometimes true and sometimes false according to the way we complete it. *When not thus completed it is neither true nor false and therefore not a proposition at all.*[10]

In the interest of clarity it is advisable to distinguish between respective and relational qualities. The distinction is implicit in Cohen's discussion although not formulated in these terms.

Suppose that "a has the property F" is a statement to be analyzed. The principle of relationality, we have seen, directs us *either* (1) to look for a relation, R, such that "a has the property F" will be logically equivalent to a relational proposition in which R is denoted and in which no mention is made of F, *or else* (2) in case F is not eliminable in favor of relations, to regard "a has the property F" as elliptical and requiring for its completion a specification of context. If F is not of the first kind, is irreducible to relations and is of the second kind, let us call it a respective quality. The principle of relationality informs us that properties are of the first or second kinds and that there are no properties of a third kind. We may explain the sense of the principle of relationality more succinctly by saying that the principle of relationality is the proposition that non-relational qualities are respective.

Cohen was not at all sure that there *are* respective qualities but he did defend the view that if a quality were not reducible to relations it would have to be respective.[11] I do not think that Cohen regarded the principle of relationality as self-evident or that he supposed that he had demonstrated the principle. But he probably regarded it as a metaphysical hypothesis for the direction of philosophical inquiry and analysis. And he undoubtedly believed that all the historical arguments which purported to subvert the principle were fallacious or employed dubious premises.

It is important to consider the principle of relationality at greater length both because of the light it throws on Cohen's philosophy and because of its intrinsic interest. Obviously, philosophy is concerned with the analysis of concepts and propositions. But the work of analysis is not a tearing up of an idea into small pieces. The idea to be analyzed is not completely given at the

10 Cohen, *Preface to Logic* (New York 1944) p. 31 [Italics mine].
11 Cohen, "Qualities, Relations, and Things," *loc. cit.*, p. 624.

outset of the analysis. Nevertheless philosophical analysis requires some anticipation of its goal to regulate its proceedings just as empirical inquiry requires hypotheses to regulate its experimental and observational procedures. Without metaphysical hypotheses, the philosophical analysis of a concept would never lead to a unique result. The principle of relationality may thus be interpreted as intending to be a statement of a necessary condition with which a piece of philosophical analysis must comply if it is to be a correct analysis. It is thus a regulative hypothesis.

It is not difficult to provide clear-cut examples of what is meant by a relational quality or quality of the first kind. *Even* is a relational quality because any statement of the form "n is even" is logically equivalent to a statement of the form "n is divisible by ." Again, the property of being one foot long is relational because to say that a given object is one foot long is equivalent to saying that it is congruent with a standard unit of measure. It is clear that relational qualities involve contextual reference.

Consider also a statement of the form "x is tall." It is perhaps the case that some persons have thought that there is a quality of absolute tallness. But it is sufficiently obvious that propositions of the kind in question are here elliptically expressed, so that to clarify the sense we would have to say, "x is at least as tall as some standard object, y." Now, this statement does not refer to a quality of tallness but to the relation *being at least as tall as*. Hence, the adjective "tall" is an elliptical expression of a relational property. The presence of ellipsis is not a sufficient condition for an adjective to denote a respective quality.

Where, then, if anywhere, do we find instances of respective qualities? Consider now a statement which asserts of a *physical* object that it is red. In this case, I think, some of us *know* that we are referring to an intuitable quality which is intuitably different from anything that we are here calling a relational quality. By inspection of that quality, we can see, I think, that it is not reducible to relations. Now, an adherent to the principle of relationality would not necessarily agree but he would in any case respond, "If it is the case that red is non-relational, then it is respective. And if it is respective, then the judgment that a given object is red is incomplete. For it may be red in one relation and not red in another and no complete proposition is expressed pending the specification of the relations in question."

If secondary qualities are objective, psycho-physical dualism has traditionally argued, the same object has at the same time different colors. But it is impossible for the same object to have different colors at the same time. Therefore, secondary qualities are not objective. To this argument Cohen replied that the so-called secondary qualities characterize objects not *simpliciter* but in certain relations and it is not *prima facie necessary*, though it may be true, that these relations involve a reference to consciousness. What the dualistic argument proves at best, according to Cohen, is that sensible qualities are not predicable *simpliciter*. And this is what the principle of relationality would have led one to anticipate.

We are assuming, for the sake of the discussion, that in the perceptual situation a respective quality is discerned and predicated of an object in reference to a context. We now must ask whether "predication" is a univocal term. Is it the same meaning of "predication" which is in question when we predicate properties of the second kind and when we predicate properties of the first kind? What is the relation which obtains between a piece of gold and the hue yellow, which we express by saying that the gold is yellow in light of a certain frequency and under certain psycho-physical conditions? We mean, do we not, that under a certain scheme of optical and spatial relations involving a sensitive, organic subject and an object, the subject obtains yellow sensa. The quality, yellow, is predicable, in one sense of "predicable" of the object. But, in another sense of "predicable," it is predicable of sensa. We shall say that yellow is predicable *simpliciter* of sensa and predicable *conditionally* of material things. Cohen was exclusively interested in the conditional mode of predication so far as his discussion of sense qualities was concerned. But this is not to say that he would have endorsed any *analysis* of this mode of predication, such as the above, which introduces explicitly the assumption of sensa. In point of fact Cohen presented no analysis whatsoever of the concept of conditional inherence of sense qualities in physical objects. Nevertheless, Cohen's doctrine is not comprehensible save in terms of some doctrine of contrasting kinds of predication.

When I predicate a character *simply* there is no ellipsis involved in the statement of predication. However, when I predicate a character conditionally, there is a tacit reference to a context *which is not entailed by the predicated character*. When I predicate yellow of a piece of gold I cannot determine the optical conditions involved in the inherence of yellow merely by scrutinizing the hue in itself. But when I say that a man is a professional money lender, the contextual reference to the world of commerce is involved in the very meaning of being a professional money lender. In the case of such simple predication no qualification is needed to secure significance. In the case of conditional predication the significance of the statement is conditional upon the specification of an extraneous context.

Obviously it would lead to a vicious infinite regress to affirm that all predication is conditional. And to say that no predication is conditional is to deny the patent empirical fact that precision and coherence are achievements of thought rather than its initial state. The growth of precision and coherence in cognition has consisted largely in the progressive definition of the conditions to which our quality characterizations of reality are relative.

We conclude that the more modest thesis is true, namely that some predications are conditional and that some are simple. But this does not clear up the muddle as to what it means to say that a physical object has a sense quality in relation to a context. I have suggested that it means that the quality inheres simply in a sensum which is in turn an appearance of an object to a subject. It is doubtful that Professor Cohen would have welcomed this suggestion and it is possible that more fruitful lines of advance may be developed but Cohen's published work contains no hint of such a development.

We have explained that if a quality is respective, then (and only then) is it predicable conditionally and not simply of a physical object. The respectivity of a quality is itself, therefore, a relational quality. A quality is respective in relation to the physical objects of which it is conditionally predicable. But the respectivity of a quality need not preclude its simple inherence in sensa, if there are any sensa.

To sum up the discussion so far. The principle of relationality is understandable if it be restricted to qualities which are predicable, in any sense of "predicable," of physical objects. It then affirms that the only qualities simply predicable of such objects are relational qualities, analysis of which discloses contextual reference, and that if there are other qualities they are respective and are predicable conditionally of physical objects. If it were implied by the principle of relationality that qualities respective in one context are in no context simply predicable of anything at all, the principle would, I think, clearly be false. For this flash of sensible color which I now see is blue absolutely or simply. But we are now interpreting the principle of relationality to mean only that non-relational qualities are predicable conditionally of physical *objects* and as saying nothing at all concerning the relations of qualities to sensa. As so qualified the principle is intended to have heuristic value.

The reader of the controversy between Professor Cohen and Professor Lovejoy, to which we have been alluding, may notice that Lovejoy was attempting to persuade Cohen that sense qualities do not inhere simply in physical objects, whereas Cohen was attempting to persuade Lovejoy that sense qualities do inhere conditionally in physical objects. The issue between them was therefore never joined. However, this philosophical debate is one of the few sources available to the student of this phase of Cohen's philosophy.

Although the principle of relationality was not explicitly formulated in Cohen's later writings and much of the terminology with which I have explained this principle is not Cohen's, nevertheless it seems to me to explain many diverse aspects of his philosophy.

We have seen that the intention of the principle of relationality is to show how, and in what sense, it is possible for diverse and opposed qualities to inhere in the same thing. But the principle of relationality does not itself assert that opposed qualities do inhere in the same thing. It affirms that an object *may* have a quality in one system of relations and lack it in another. But if there were just one system of relations in which a given thing were embedded, the possibility affirmed by the principle of relationality would be trivial and, in fact, never realized. If an object had a character in reference to the system S, and S was the only system in reference to which the object had a qualitative character, then the object would, in reference to no system, lack the character in question. The principle of polarity, however, affirms that there always is another system, say S′, in reference to which the object lacks the quality which it has in respect to S. Obviously, we are speaking here of respective qualities and not of characteristics which are simply predicable of objects.

The principle of polarity is a form of pluralism. It maintains the irreducible plurality of systems in which one and the same thing is embedded. The non-relational characters of an object possess their respective backgrounds of systematic relatedness. For every such character which belongs to an object in respect to one background, there is an opposed character belonging to the object in respect to a different background. In saying that one character is opposed to another, I mean that the characters cannot characterize the same object in respect to the same background of systematic relatedness or in respect to the same perspective.

If the datum of inquiry is the presence of conflicting predications, the principle of relationality is relevant, directing attention to the systematic relatedness by virtue of which the conflict may be eliminated without resulting narrowness. If, on the other hand, the datum of inquiry is an object characterized in terms of a conventional and stable environment, the principle of polarity is pertinent, directing attention to other backgrounds in reference to which the same object reveals novel characters opposed to those initially given. The two principles are intended to be inseparable in their application to, and direction of, inquiry. The principle of polarity assures us that in any reality there are opposite determinations to be found. The principle of relationality explains that such opposition involves no breach of logic and enjoins us to specify the relevant contexts by reference to which coherent predication is achievable.

Cohen was wont to acknowledge an Hegelian influence upon his thinking. But the difference between the Hegelian dialectic and the principle of polarity must be emphasized. According to Cohen, there are genuinely diverse systems and there is, in the universe, genuine irrelevance. Although the clarification of the meaning of any assertion involves delineating a network of relations, this network need not embrace the absolute totality of being or else predication obviously would in principle be impossible.

Cohen's Philosophical Interpretations of the History of Science

✎§ BY PHILIP P. WIENER

City College of New York

$\mathcal{M}$ORRIS R. COHEN might well have added to the cemetery of human hopes his unwritten philosophical history of science in which he would have brought together his compendious historical knowledge and philosophical understanding of the role of science in shaping our civilization. He was too much of a humanist and metaphysician to confine his interests and limited energy to the sundry details of any one subject, so that he fell back in his own way on the classical manner of philosophizing on the cultural significance and broad presuppositions of scientific method. Yet I recall his telling me in 1935 that he had made extensive notes on the development of the sciences at the University of Padua, where scientists like Vesalius and Galileo had spent their most fruitful years, and of the significance of the proximity of commercial Venice, famous for its arsenal and its defiance of Papal authority. I regret now that I did not see these notes though he offered to give them to me in connection with a paper I was writing on the background of Galileo's methodology. About five years later, Cohen proposed to give to the *Journal of the History of Ideas,* which he helped to found, an article on the subject of this essay, and the readers of this volume will certainly share my regret that he did not do so[1] because of his failing health and the pressure of his other activities in the Conference on Jewish Rela-

---

[1] *Cf.* Cohen, M. R., *The Meaning of Human History,* p. 206, for his brief account of Padua. See also Randall, J. H., Jr., "The Development of Scientific Method in the School of Padua," in *Journal of the History of Ideas,* vol. i (1940) 177-206; Wiener, P. P., "The Tradition Behind Galileo's Methodology," in *Osiris* vol. i (1936) 733-46.

tions. Whatever critical remarks I make here of some features of Cohen's thinking, to which I and many others are so deeply indebted, are made in the very spirit he inculcated in his students.

Metaphysics was wedded to humanism in Cohen's interpretations of the philosophic significance of the history of science. To his humane and philosophical mind there was more to the history of science than its chronological, biographical, and philological details, though he had great respect for the scientific and historical erudition of Mach, Duhem, and Meyerson. If he was critical of the methodological and cultural implications drawn from the history of science by the nominalistic positivism of Mach, the Catholic positivism of Duhem and the identity-epistemology of Myerson, it was primarily because he was himself deeply concerned with the philosophic and cultural significance of the history of science.

Charles S. Peirce exercised the greatest influence on Cohen, and he edited the first collection of Peirce's papers on scientific method under the intriguing title *Chance, Love and Logic.* In his correspondence with Justice Holmes, who was a member of Peirce's Metaphysical Club where the name and doctrine of pragmatism saw the light, Cohen called himself "a logical pragmatist."[2] Cohen was the first to bring Chauncey Wright, a precursor of pragmatism, to the attention of historians of American thought.[3] Wright and Peirce were both close students of Kant's philosophy. Concerning Kant's *Critique of Pure Reason,* Peirce thought that "perhaps the most valuable proposition that the *Critique* contains" is the anti-metaphysical view that "no general description of existence is possible." Peirce described his own philosophy as "the attempt of a physicist to make such conjecture as to the constitution of the universe as the methods of science may present, with the aid of all that has been done by previous philosophers. . . . The demonstrations of the metaphysicians are all moonshine. The best that can be done is to supply a hypothesis, not devoid of all likelihood,

[2] Letter of Cohen to Holmes, Aug. 7, 1920, in "The Holmes-Cohen Correspondence," ed. by Felix S. Cohen, in *Journal of the History of Ideas,* vol. ix (1948) 20.

[3] Cohen, "Later Philosophy," in *Cambridge History of American Literature* (New York 1921) p. 226-65. *Cf.* Wiener, P. P., *Evolution and the Founders of Pragmatism* (Cambridge 1949) ch. iii, "Chauncey Wright, Defender of Darwin and Precursor of Pragmatism."

in the general line of growth of scientific ideas, and capable of being verified or refuted by future observers."[4] However, there is the same conflicting mixture of quasi-positivistic and metaphysical strains in both Peirce's and Cohen's philosophies of science and of its history. Cohen's penetrating discussions of the insurgence against reason in those who appeal to infallible authority, traditionalism, and anti-intellectual intuition, follow Peirce's lessons drawn from the history of science.[5] Both saw clearly that the internal development of scientific method could not be dictated to by extraneous interests without undermining the intellectual integrity and the freedom of inquiry without which no liberal civilization can long flourish. That historical insight rests on a distinction between the internal and external history of science which I wish to define as clearly as I can, for it furnishes us with a key to the philosophical and cultural implications of the history of science.

By the internal history of science I mean the history of the problems and methods which have led to verified discoveries of the properties of specific subject matters and their laws, *e.g.*, Ohm's discovery of the laws of electrical resistance as a result of experimentally investigating Seebeck's thermocouple. By the external history of science I mean the history of the extra-scientific intellectual and social changes which have *both* affected and been affected by the internal progress of science. Anthropologists have long distinguished between (1) the mores and occupations, customs and institutions which over a given period of time generate a cumulative pattern distinctive of a culture or people, and (2) the effects of contact with invading or invaded peoples which pro-

---

[4] Peirce, C. S., *Collected Papers*, ed. by C. Hartshorne and P. Weiss (Cambridge 1931) vol. i, paragraphs 35 and 7.

[5] *Chance, Love, and Logic* (New York 1923), ed. by M. R. Cohen, includes Peirce's "Illustrations of the Logic of Science," beginning with "The Fixation of Belief," *Popular Science Monthly* vol. xii (1877) 1-15, which Peirce claimed was the first printed statement of his pragmatic theory of belief. It had been read, together with "How to Make Our Ideas Clear," (printed the next year in the same magazine and in Jan. 1879 in a French version, in *Revue philosophique*) about six years earlier to the members of Peirce's Metaphysical Club at Cambridge, Mass., though the term "pragmatism" does not occur in any of these articles, and did not gain philosophical currency until William James in 1897 credited Peirce with the origination of the name and doctrine (*Cf.* Wiener, *op. cit.*, ch. ii).

duce borrowed or imposed cultural forms. Since science is both a habit of thinking and an institution that has evolved distinctive traits among those who have pursued it as a vocation or avocation, it is not surprising that its history also has internal and external aspects.

The specific problems with which any science deals and the experimental techniques, habits of thinking and vocabulary that grow among the investigators, competent by virtue of their training to test proposed solutions, constitute the internal cumulative core of the history of that science. Pertaining to the external history of science are sociological and cultural conditions for the pursuit and utilization of science rather than for the truth of its results. The validity of Euclid's geometry or Archimedes' physics does not depend on any geographical, ethnic or political features of Greek culture, though it is perfectly legitimate to inquire into the physical and social ecology of new ideas in the external history of any science.

In order to clarify the distinction between the internal and external phases of the history of science, between the scientific and extra-scientific causes of scientific discovery, let us consider the following remark by George Sarton about the history of the metric system: "Mere scientific reasons do not suffice to explain the creation of the metric system by the French revolutionaries. This creation was also in part a reaction against the 'foot of the king' of the *ancien régime*."[6]

Now scientists, including the aristocrat Lavoisier, guillotined by the French revolutionaries, would agree that the metric system is superior scientifically to the "foot of the king." The British system of units is defended by engineers today not for the sake of the old regime but for the economic reason that takes into account the cost of changing tools and machinery gauged on the older system, without denying the mathematical advantages of the metric

[6] Sarton, G., *The Life of Science, Essays in the History of Civilization* (New York 1948) p. 35. On p. 52, Sarton hints at a distinction between "internal" and "external" comparisons "between the evolution of scientific phenomena and that of other intellectual or economic phenomena." But he does not discuss the failures of the attempts of K. Lamprecht, Comte, and Marx to establish "historical laws" that would hold for both the internal and external history of science.

system. In the technology and economy of science the external and internal phases of science merge, but political and economic needs should not be confused with the logical requirements of scientific research. In the theory of measurement, dimensional analysis is an internal feature independent of all economic and political conditions. The statistical theory of errors cannot logically be subordinated to any political ideology of dialectical necessity.

It is true of the external history of astronomy that commercial interests in navigation explain "in part"[7] why many astronomical discoveries were made. The part internal to astronomic science that would *not* thus be explained would be the greater scientific truth and predictive value that some theories have over others with respect to the starry heavens above all commercial interests. This commonplace fact that the subject matter of natural sciences remains historically independent of social and political changes for the most part—technology, civil and military, does alter the physiognomy of a small portion of the earth—would not be worth mentioning were it not for the tendency of those "sociologists of knowledge" who merely dabble with the history of science, to let their external interpretations be carried away by the storm and stress of contemporary political excitement. Historians of science must be faithful to the internal standards of scientific research even while they are moved deeply to take account of the extra-scientific contexts and social conditions which favor or frustrate the progress of science. As Sarton very well puts it, it is the cumulative character of the internal development of the sciences that makes their history central for the external history and progress of civilization.[8] Buckle went so far as to deny any moral or social progress other than scientific or intellectual, but he wrote at a time when the teaching of the sciences and their cultural force were just begin-

[7] *Ibid.*, p. 37

[8] *Ibid.*, p. 40. (*Cf.* Buckle, T. H., *History of Civilization in England,* 3 vols. (1857, 1861, n. d.). Buckle's comment on the political control of science is still pertinent: "If in the long course and compass of history there is one thing more clear than any other, it is, that whenever a government undertakes to protect intellectual pursuits, it will almost always protect them in the wrong place, and reward the wrong men." (World Classics edition, vol. ii, p. 163). Cohen was fully in accord with Buckle's emphasis on the fact that "no one is a competent judge of scientific excellence unless he is himself scientific" (*ib.*, p. 164).

ning to break through the crust of older traditions and established authority.

It was not much more than seventy-five years ago that the Darwinian controversy revealed the external pressure of natural theology on any science that offered a secular view of man. The cumulative labors of scientists guided by an internal scientific discipline, not subject to ecclesiastical or political authority, present an increasingly formidable obstacle to those who attempt to purge science by means of external racial, religious or political criteria. The only kind of purging that has ever aided science is the logical and experimental de-anthropomorphizing of subject matter and the application of disinterested rules of procedure. Modern physical chemistry does not aim at the alchemists' "philosopher's stone" or any other metaphysical short cut, in order to achieve the transmutation of the elements, a result primarily due to the experimental pursuit of a verifiable theory of atomic structure and radiation. If Cohen was sceptical of the theories of sociologists like Comte and Spencer, it was because he thought that they were heedless of the rigorous requirements of scientific logic and of the disinterested patience that marks the historically cumulative labors of the experimental creators of scientific progress.

Much of Cohen's impatience with positivism in recent years was due unfortunately to his identifying it with Auguste Comte's interpretation of the history of science. Comte's law of three stages —the theological or animistic, the metaphysical or scholastic, and the positive or scientific—and semi-Hegelian hierarchy of the sciences, beginning with abstract mathematics and culminating in concrete sociology, ran counter to Cohen's high regard for Greek science, Roman law, medieval logic, and anti-authoritarian liberalism. Comte's external historical scheme failed to account for and even made impossible certain internal developments of science, such as those about to appear in astro-chemistry (due to Bunsen's and Kirchhoff's use of the spectroscope) and in evolutionary geology and biology (due to Lyell and Darwin). The lessons of Comte's failure are important both for the internal logic of science and its external history. Cohen saw that the logical error of Comte was to restrict scientific inquiry to directly verifiable phenomena and thus to ignore the power of the hypothetico-deductive method and of the long-run frequency theory of probability to enlarge the scope of physical, biological and sociological research. On the political side, Comte's attempted dictatorship of scientific and other social institutions by a priesthood of sociologists indicates the cultural dangers of his interpretation of the historical development of science.

The Marxist interpretation of the history of science based on the Hegelian laws of dialectics and eighteenth-century materialism also failed to recognize the essential probability of empirical laws and the dangers of subjecting scientific inquiry to political overseers. Cohen admitted with Marx that economic conditions affect the external history of science, but he would not accept dialectical or historical materialism as a true explanation of the inner logic and development of scientific discoveries. He knew that no scientific discoveries have been made or promoted by the use of dialectical laws. Borrowed from Hegel, who despised experimental science, these "laws," despite their alleged ontological and historical certitude, do not increase the rigor or fruitfulness of the method practiced by "bourgeois" scientists. The prefaces written by Soviet scientists in high eulogy of dialectical materialism and of their great leader Stalin have as little logical relevance to the inner history of scientific discoveries as the dedicatory prefaces written by Renaissance scientists to their ecclesiastical or princely patrons.

An important feature of the Marxist interpretation of the history of science is, as Veblen saw, the role assigned to technology. But here again confusion results from the failure to distinguish the external application of scientific theories to social or industrial needs, which have stimulated research, from the internal development of scientific techniques and concepts adapted to specific problems and objective properties not limited by those needs. When Kepler said that Napier's logarithms tripled the life of astronomers he was illustrating the internal sense of the role played by what Peirce and Mach called "the economy" of scientific research[9] in the history of science. This internal sense of the "eco-

[9] Peirce has priority over Mach in introducing the term "economy of research" into the history of scientific logic; *Cf.* Peirce, "Theory of the Economy of Research," in *Annual Reports of the U. S. Coast and Geodetic Survey* (1876) appendix 14; Mach, "The Economical Nature of Physical Inquiry," in his *Popular Scientific Lectures* (1895).

nomic" factor in the history of science must logically be discriminated from consideration of the expense and subsidization of research which brings the history of science into close but external relations to the economic and political structure of the society which supports the training and researches of scientists. Scientists, as Cohen often pointed out, have thrived on all sorts of patronage and under all forms of government, despotic and democratic. Cohen might have said, in keeping with his own liberal faith, that a democratic regime is more favorable to scientific progress because there is a greater probability of getting more and freer scientists from a population enjoying democratic equality of opportunities to choose a scientific career, *ouverte aux talents,* than from one which limits the field by extraneous qualifications of race, religion, or nationality.

Nazi historians of science did not contribute to the internal history of science by contrasting the "Jewish formalism" of Einstein's theory of relativity with "Aryan intuitionism." Nationalistic bias affected Duhem when he spoke of French clarity and German pedantic rigor in science, though he did not explain how French clarity came into being from originally Germanic tribes. Protestant as well as Catholic theologians opposed the Copernican astronomy and Darwin's theory of natural selection. The history of the warfare between science and theology belongs to the external history of science along with certain metaphysical interpretations of the history of science that fail to do justice to its internal development.

By "metaphysical" I mean, perhaps unfairly to some metaphysicians, the ascribing of an internal necessity to the history of science which limits its scope in an *a priori* fashion. Comte's and Marx's views, influenced by Hegel, had such a metaphysical character, as do those interpretations of the history of science which attempt to derive scientific progress from some single factor like climate, soil, race, religion, or nationality.

The Kantian historian of science, Rev. William Whewell, was opposed to the Hegelian subordination of science to dialectics, but he also opposed the Darwinian doctrine of the transformation of species and any other scientific theory opposed to his own natural theology. His high *priori* ground was that the history of science— to which he made one of the most notable contributions of the nineteenth century—cannot interfere with the higher supernatural truths of the moral and spiritual world. It is not surprising then that the learned Reverend's historical erudition did not affect his conservative social and educational philosophy. He opposed the liberal Thirlwall on the admission of Dissenters to Cambridge University by upholding the system of a privileged class of clerical Fellows. Priestley would not have been admitted to Whewell's university because of his Unitarian faith and utilitarian ethics of "the greatest good for the greatest number," against which Whewell directed his official moral philosophy. Here is a typical case of the danger to science on its internal side from external authority when, cognizant of the history of science, it interprets that history with *a priori* restrictions on the limits of each science; for Whewell thought that "one of the advantages of the study of the history of science . . . is, that it warns us of the hopeless and presumptous character of such attempts to understand the government of the world by the aid of science. . . . It confines each science within its own limits, and condemns it as empty and helpless, when it pronounces upon those subjects which are extraneous to it."[10]

Nothing is more patent in the history of the sciences than the historical extension of mathematical and physical concepts beyond their original form, and the continual crossing of boundaries resulting in hybrid sciences like biochemistry, statistical mechanics (classical and quantum), etc. Pasteur's germ theory of disease was the result of his studies of molecular dissymmetry and of fermentation. Statistical concepts apply to physical as well as social phenomena, as the "social physics" of Quetelet, astronomer and meteorologist, amply showed. Yet, the idea of "Providential design" persisted in the extra-scientific philosophy of statisticians like Herschel.[11]

Failing to do justice to the inductive and statistical form which physical laws were beginning to assume after Gibbs's and Boltzmann's analyses, Henry Adams, influenced to some extent by

[10] Whewell, William, *History of the Inductive Sciences, from the Earliest to the Present Time*, 2 vols., 3d ed. (New York 1897) vol. ii, p. 572.

[11] Herschel, John, "Quetelet's Letters on the Application of Probabilities to the Moral and Political Sciences," in *Edinburgh Review*, vol. xlii (1850) 1-57; this is a review of O. G. Downes's translation of Quetelet's *Letters on the Application of Probabilities to the Moral and Political Sciences* (London 1849).

Marxian dialectics, produced an abortive synthesis of the physical and cultural sciences:

Any science assumes a necessary sequence of cause and effect, a force resulting in motion which cannot be other than what it is. Any science of history must be absolute, like other sciences, and must fix with mathematical certainty the path which human society has got to follow. That path can hardly lead toward the interests of all great social organizations. We cannot conceive that it should help at the same time the church and the state, property and communism, capital and poverty, science and religion, trade and art.[12]

This line of reasoning, which Adams honestly thought made the doom of capitalism and democracy a rigorous logical consequence of the second law of thermodynamics, is based on a confusion of the internal logic of science (interpreted by Adams in the light of a dogmatic and outmoded theory of causal necessity) and its external relations to the factors of social progress or decay. William James, with his large fund of common sense and pluralistic conception of scientific laws, saw through the speciousness of Henry Adams's reasoning and joshed him for his metaphysical pessimism.[13] Adams had graduated from Harvard in 1858 and had been impressed among all his teachers only by Louis Agassiz,[14] the great anti-Darwinian naturalist who regarded the forms and laws of nature as the eternal thoughts of the Creator. The extra-scientific ground for Agassiz' belief in the immutability and necessity of these forms is revealed in his statement that "a physical fact is as sacred as a moral principle,"[15] though his positivistic teacher Alexander von Humboldt had early in Agassiz' career warned him against using the "symbolical language" of the transcendental *Naturphilosophie*.[16] That language with its rigid hierarchy of forms originated in ancient Pythagorean and neo-Platonic categories tan-

[12] Adams, Henry, "The Tendency of History," a communication to the American Historical Association from its President, December, 1894, in *The Degradation of the Democratic Dogma,* ed. by Brooks Adams (New York 1920) p. 129.

[13] In a characteristic post-card of James to Adams, one of the last things James wrote in 1910 shortly before his death; *cf.* Cater, Harold D., *Henry Adams and his Friends: a collection of his Unpublished Letters* (Boston 1947).

[14] *Education of Henry Adams* (New York 1918) p. 60.

[15] *Louis Agassiz, His Life and Correspondence,* ed. by E. C. Agassiz (Boston and New York 1885) p. 781.

[16] *Ibid.,* p. 228. Letter of A. von Humboldt to L. Agassiz, July 4, 1833.

gential to the more pliable development of scientific method. It did not advance the inductive and experimental procedures of the empirical sciences.

In other words the internal history of science is a dynamic one, faithful only to the complexities of a temporal world. Adaptation to such a world requires a flexible intelligence. Yet the account of scientific reason and its *"cheminement"* given by the philosophical historian of science Emile Meyerson fallaciously takes the classical mechanical conception of reversible phenomena as the form of all causal explanation (identity in time).[17] This is fallacious on two grounds: first, we cannot, as Cohen properly indicated, derive the necessary form of all scientific laws simply by inductive generalization from even a large segment of the past history of science; secondly, Meyerson has not *proven* his thesis that irreversible phenomena (thermodynamic and biological) are irrational, for he has simply and in *a priori* fashion *defined* the rational aim of science as the establishment of identities or equations. As with many *a priori* theories, Meyerson's fallacy consists in selecting one aspect of the internal history of science, its structural form, and making it the essence of science. The history of the shifting standards of logical rigor and of models of demonstrations should make us wary of any theory that regards the *a priori* as anything more than what has already been established within an accepted system; as soon as that system breaks down with fresh evidence or with more fruitful assumptions, its former *a priori* features disappear. Kepler's ellipses in his laws of planetary motion did away with the traditional *a priori* principle that the circle was the most perfect form of motion. The *a priori*, Cohen often indicated, is relative to a system.

Cohen used to quote with approval, Poincaré's dictum that though science is built with facts as a house is with bricks, a collection of facts is no more a science than a pile of bricks a house. Poincaré was, however, more nominalistic than Cohen, and regarded *a priori* principles as hypotheses which simplify the relations among experimental data and help in yielding the greatest possible number of predictions. He distinguished three kinds of

[17] Meyerson, Emile, *Identity and Reality,* translated by K. Lowenberg (New York 1930); *Du Cheminement de la Pensée* (Paris 1931).

hypotheses internal to physical theories: (1) the assumptions common to all theories, *e.g.*, that the effect is a continuous function of the cause. Such broad hypotheses are "perfectly natural and scarcely avoidable. . . . They are the last that ought to be abandoned;" (2) neutral assumptions, *e.g.*, that matter is continuous or formed of discrete particles. "They may be useful, either as devices for computation, or to aid our understanding by concrete images, to fix our ideas;" (3) empirical generalizations which experiment confirms or fails to confirm, *e.g.*, the law of gravitation. "They will be fruitful if not too numerous."[18] Notice that in all these three forms of hypothesis there is no necessary relation assumed to be restrictive of the objective order of phenomena. All that is required is "the approximate homogeneity of the matter studied by the physicist." We shall see that, at times, Cohen took a more stringent view, postulating an invariant order of nature to be reflected in scientific laws. At other times, he seems to agree with Poincaré that the *a priori* is relative to a cumulative body of knowledge.

Cohen agreed also with Duhem that, historically, scientific verification always proceeds from a whole group of accepted hypotheses rather than from the confrontation of an isolated hypothesis with disjointed facts; *e.g.*, isotopes are "facts" inseparable from recent atomic and electrical theories. These theories are subject to revision and are admittedly contingent. But Cohen eschewed the nominalistic positivism of Mach, Poincaré, and Duhem by insisting on an equally pervasive element of necessity in all causal laws corresponding to an invariant order in nature. In this Cohen was influenced by the neo-Platonic metaphysical theory of the inner light of reason reflecting the eternal order of nature, a theory advocated *extra-scientifically* by Galileo, Kepler, Descartes, Spinoza, and the Cambridge Platonists. Cohen's attempt to read this theory into the internal history of science is marred by a serious ambiguity in his accounts of the element of necessity.

On the one hand, necessity is, for Cohen, a purely logical relation such as we have in the deductive reasoning of mathematical, logical, and *a priori* metaphysical systems. Cohen attacked Mill's

[18] Poincaré, H., *Science and Hypothesis*, translated by G. B. Halsted (New York 1905).

notion that two plus two might not equal four in some remote parts
of the universe, because Mill had failed to note that such mathematical statements are purely logical or analytical consequences
of definitions, axioms and rules of inference, independent of spatio-
temporal conditions including the psychological process of counting physical things. On the other hand, Cohen repeatedly insists
that necessity is an essential element in causal relations, including
psychological beliefs:

> A causal relation asserts more than mere past coincidence. It affirms
> that there is some reason or ground why, whenever the antecedent
> occurs, the consequent must follow. The assertion of a causal relation
> may be false in fact or not supported by adequate evidence, but the
> element of necessity, the exclusion of a contrary possibility, is an essen-
> tial part of its meaning.[19] . . . It is really impossible to get along in our
> daily life or in scientific investigation without the idea of necessity.[20]
> If then, the historian is not to fall into the fallacy of regarding every
> antecedent event as the cause of every consequent, he must rely on true
> laws or necessary relations in human nature and social life.[21]

I leave to the logicians the problem of deciding whether the
three meanings of necessity—the logical, the physical and the psychological—are reconcilable in Cohen's writings. It is clear that he
often advocated a neo-Platonic interpretation of logical and mathematical necessity as designating ontological and causally efficacious relations.[22] But it is also clear that he qualified his metaphysical rationalism with such empiricist assertions as:

> Obviously an abstract property cannot operate in time. . . . Since
> history deals with occurrences in time, the element of temporal sequence
> must enter into causality and distinguish it from the relation between
> whole and part, form and content, or any other abstract, purely logical
> or mathematical condition. The laws with which history is concerned
> are descriptions of the connections between events, not prescriptions.[23]
> History begins with general impressions. We think of "the average
> man of common sense," or "the kind of men and women one meets in

[19] Cohen, *The Meaning of Human History*, p. 102.
[20] *Ibid.*, p. 109
[21] *Ibid.*, p. 89.
[22] "The rules of logic and pure mathematics may be viewed not only as
principles of inference applicable to all systems but also as descriptive of certain abstract invariant relations which constitute an objective order characteristic of any subject-matter." *Reason and Nature* (New York 1931) p. 143.
[23] *The Meaning of Human History*, p. 98.

Paris," or "the good-natured Italian people." Statistical analysis may help us to refine these vague concepts. The more precise information at which we arrive as a result of such analysis is by no means a "falsification" of the data from which we start. The process is rather one of refining truth out of a mixture that includes much error and more confusion. Whether or not we ever attain the absolute truth it is important that we understand the direction which the process of rational inquiry takes.[24]

Any trends of direction then, in either the internal or external history of scientific research, should be capable of study by means of the method of empirical correlation. Even the question, to what extent extra-scientific metaphysical ideas have influenced the direction, method or results of science, should be capable of empirical, historical investigation whenever documentary or socio-psychological data are available. Cohen was, inconsistently or not with his neo-Platonism, one of the few philosophers after Peirce to defend the statistical conception of scientific laws. And he often indicated that Quetelet and Buckle fell short of a thoroughgoing statistical empiricism by clinging to the older metaphysical interpretation of "the reign of iron laws of causality."[25] In a subject as complex as the history of science, my view, in accord with the empirical strain in Cohen, is that we can scarcely fall back on any such metaphysical interpretation and discover anything but our own metaphysical predilections.

[24] *Ibid.,* p. 70.

[25] *Ibid.,* p. 94. Cohen fails to note in his historical account of "The Statistical View of Nature" (*Preface to Logic,* New York, 1944, Ch. VII) as "first clearly enunciated by Maxwell (though partly anticipated by Clausius) in connection with the law of entropy" (*ibid.,* p. 139), that Maxwell regarded the statistical method as inferior to the "dynamic" method of explanation which determined the properties of every individual. *Cf.* p. 130 where Cohen makes this point about J. J. Thomson, the successor of Maxwell. John Fiske noted that Clifford attacked Maxwell's belief that "the laws of mechanics are absolutely the same throughout eternity." *The Unseen World* (Boston 1876), p. 18. Maxwell's distinction between the dynamic and statistical method appears in *The Life of James Clerk Maxwell, with selections from his correspondence and occasional writings,* ed. by Lewis Campbell and William Garnett (London 1884) p. 362. Jerome Frank in his *Fate and Freedom* (New York 1945) and in a letter to me quotes some passages from *Selected Papers of James Clerk Maxwell* (ed. by Niven, 1890) vol. ii, p. 253, 365 that would seem to indicate that Maxwell occasionally had doubts about the strictly determined behavior of individual particles. In that case I should say Maxwell had uneasy premonitions about the future developments of his own contributions to statistical mechanics which might lead to the abandonment of his "dynamic method" of explanation.

Cohen's main objection to the use of the method of statistical, empirical correlation was that it could not avoid the fallacy of accidental concomitance. But the history of experimental sciences provides the method of checking such a fallacy; namely, the method of subjecting any hypothesis suggested by a statistical correlation to experimentally controlled or further empirical observations. This was the method Cohen himself used when he criticized Huntington's theory that attributes so much weight to climate, by the obvious statistical consideration that the number of great Greek scientists has not fluctuated with climatic variations, but with the cultural conditions under which schools of mathematics, medicine and philosophy were able to thrive in ancient Greece.[26]

Furthermore, Cohen has more than suggested that "accidents, like necessity, are relative to our system" · of knowledge.[27] This "relative determinism" implies a contextualistic approach to scientific developments. Applied to the internal history of science, such a contextualism would imply that logical necessity is relative to the rules of a deductive system, that causal determinations result from the application of logically elaborated hypotheses to variable empirical situations, and that psychological necessity or the "human need to understand"[28] lies at the center of most metaphysical systems. A *priori* principles, Cohen sometimes admitted (sacrificing consistency to his deep-grained candor) "form a system of human confessions: I can't help believing . . . or, I can't conceive any knowledge that does not assume . . . etc."[29] Here Cohen practically paraphrased the pragmatic empiricism of his sceptical friend Justice Holmes.

Guided by his empirical knowledge of the internal history of science, Cohen discriminated three types of scientific laws: (1) General facts, *e.g.*, gold is yellow; whenever you have a substance

[26] *Ibid.*, p. 151-52.
[27] *Ibid.*, p. 90. "Every problem or question involves certain assumptions and nothing inconsistent with these assumptions will be an answer. This is all the certainty that science needs for the process of investigation—enough certainty to give direction to the growth of knowledge without foreclosing all issues and making such growth unnecessary." (*Reason and Nature,* p. 144.)
[28] *Reason and Nature,* p. 145. These quotations illustrate the empirical side of Cohen's philosophy of science.
[29] *Ibid.*

having the atomic weight of gold, its color is predictable. (2) Empirical sequences and statistical correlations, *e.g.*, much sugar in a diet will be followed by decayed teeth. Cohen revealed his rationalistic bias by regarding these two types as mere preliminaries to a third type: "the statement of a universal abstract relation which can be connected systematically with other laws in the same field."[30] Such systematic laws hold not only for the physical sciences, but they are also the essential object of research in social causation: "the causal relation or the interaction between [events] is predominantly a matter of logical analysis of groups of phenomena."[31] Now the history of science would be incomplete if it contained only the discovery of systematic generalizations, important as they are as leading principles of further research. But for the patient and laborious accumulation of detailed and accurate laws of the first two types, the great scientific generalizations of Galileo, Kepler, Newton, Mendeleyev, Gibbs, Darwin, and Einstein would not have been possible. Even the alchemists whose discoveries were limited to the first two types have contributed to the history of chemistry, and the craftsmen who do not formulate laws have made experimental techniques and apparatus available to scientists engaged in "pure research." The medical and social sciences make sufficient progress, relative to their complex problems of diagnosis and planning, when they can by statistical methods achieve verifiable laws of the first two types. And, for Cohen, the history of medicine illuminates philosophical questions of method (empirical vs. dogmatic schools of medicine), the mind-body problem, and Aristotle's moral principle of the mean (based on dietary laws).

We know that Cohen tried to achieve a metaphysical synthesis of the empirical contingency and particularly of the first two types of law with the logical necessity and universality of his third type by invoking a dialectical principle of polarity, akin to what Nicholas of Cusa and Hegel had elaborated in their theories of the "coincidence of opposites" and *Aufhebung* of contradiction, respectively. I think there is an empirical generalization about the history of thought that underlies Cohen's principle of polarity, namely, the

[30] *Reason and Nature*, p. 357 ff.
[31] *Ibid.*, p. 361

continual oscillation and interaction of experience and reason, particularity and universality, complexity and simplicity, that is characteristic of "the flights and perchings" (to use a phrase of William James, teacher of Cohen) of thought in both its internal and external aspects. Philosophic interpretations of the history of science have attempted to fixate the dynamic and cumulative growth of the sciences by selecting some aspect of scientific thought and treating all other aspects as derivative. Yet all the evidence of the history of science points to the futility of prescribing one type of law for all the diverse fields of scientific research.

PART TWO

Essays in Philosophy and the Social Sciences

Recent Philosophic Importations*

~§ BY JOSEPH L. BLAU

Columbia University

*T*HE importation of philosophic ideas into America is as old
as European settlement in America. From the very beginnings of
cultural life on this continent, our philosophic roots have been
deeply implanted in European soil. In the seventeenth century,
the Ramist philosophy provided the logical foundation for the
expository sermons of Puritan divines; the covenant theory of Ames
was the acknowledged basis for congregational independence in
church government and a rehearsal for later theories of the social
contract and later and more serious theories of national independence. In the eighteenth century, it was John Locke and his English
and Scottish followers in whose terms Americans began the development of an empiricist tradition, while from classical and French
sources, as well as from the political writings of Locke, our enlightened ancestors drew the inspiration that led them to the model of
a government founded on natural law and natural right. In the
early part of the nineteenth century the Scottish philosophy of
"common-sense" realism carried all before it in the colleges, but
away from academic halls German romantic transcendentalism, as
mediated by Coleridge, became the progressive philosophy in the
"golden day" of Emerson, Thoreau, Parker, and Alcott. Later in the
century a stricter discipline in German thought developed both
inside and outside the colleges: inside, in the form of a critical
psychology, as in Noah Porter of Yale, a systematic philosophy of
reason, as in Laurens Perseus Hickok of Union College, or a
dynamic idealism, as in George Sylvester Morris of Johns Hopkins
and the University of Michigan; outside in the study and transla-

* This essay is a revision of a lecture given at the University of Minnesota
in June 1948, as the second of a series sponsored by the American Studies
Program, under the general title "Foreign Influences in American Life."

tion of Hegel's works by a group of devotees in St. Louis under the leadership of William Torrey Harris. Thus for more than two centuries of American life it is possible to say without exaggeration that philosophy in America was transplanted European philosophy, that philosophy in America had no distinctively American characteristics.

This situation changed in the 1870's when an American philosophy began to emerge. One can only guess at some of the factors which led to the change: the retrospective empiricism of the British, involving a correspondence theory of truth, was inverted by Charles Sanders Peirce and his friend William James into a prospective empiricism holding a pragmatic theory of truth; the theory of universals held by the late medieval realists, the followers of Duns Scotus, was revived by Peirce, by Francis Ellingwood Abbot and a little later, by George H. Mead, but in this revival the doctrine was altered—the universal represented not an independently existing entity, but a habit of generalizing; the theories of induction which the Scottish philosophers had elaborated, and to which John Stuart Mill had given full and clear statement, were combined with certain aspects of traditional deductive logical theory into what was called "scientific method" and was glorified by Peirce, Abbot, Mead and John Dewey into the method *par excellence* of all inquiry—in the hands of men such as these logic was considered a technique for the discovery of novelty rather than a mere exploration of the implications of old dogmas. But all of these factors, even all of them taken together, do not serve to characterize the work of two generations in shifting from the profession of European philosophy in America to the construction of an American philosophy. For the factors I have mentioned have been characteristics of a developing naturalism, and recent American idealism has been no less American than American naturalism.

Perhaps we can approximate more closely the factors which led to the emergence of an American philosophy if we recognize that in philosophic speculation men are trying to break through to the meaning of man's experience of himself, of the world in which he lives, and of those elements which seem to transcend both his social and his natural environments. When Americans were content to parrot philosophies which had been formulated in terms of

European experience, they could make no real contribution to philosophy. It was only when experience which was distinctively American, the experience of the American people and of their philosophers, came to be used to extend, to modify, to reconstruct, what others were learning to understand in terms of their experience that American philosophy was born.

Such distinctively American experiences which contributed to American philosophy were the sense of co-operatively created community and of the values of diversity to this community; the sense of man's creative powers, his ability to do something about the improvement of both his natural and his social environment; and the sense that construction, looking towards the future, is more important than maintenance, looking towards the past. Around these, binding them together into a pattern of the American spirit, is the much satirized, and unjustly satirized, sense of gregariousness, the belief that what men do together has more meaning than what they do alone, because to the value of the doing must be added the value of the togetherness.

The nature of the experiences I have detailed is such that, inevitably, it was American political theory which first departed from its European background, and, next, American social science. It was inevitable, too, that when American philosophy emerged, it came, first, in the form of a social philosophy, and only later developed the other disciplines within philosophy. The American spirit as I have described it yielded philosophic fruits in a distinctively American philosophy. I shall state its chief characteristics briefly.

First, a concern for theories of community has developed out of our experience of creating communities. Perhaps the most highly elaborated forms of this theory are to be found in the thought of Josiah Royce, an absolute idealist, and G. H. Mead, a naturalist. Royce, for example, made effective communication central to his theory of community, and therefore stressed the need for a "third," a mediator, an interpreter, to preclude the possibility that rival and conflicting views might call a halt to all development.

Second, our experience of the values of diversity has led us to develop a pluralistic habit of mind. We associate this pluralistic temper chiefly with William James and John Dewey and their opposition to the "block universe" of monistic thought, but it is a far more general and pervasive habit of mind than these two names would indicate.

"Americans are convinced that they are living in a complex universe containing in disordered profusion quite a mess of miscellaneous stuff. Its various parts, to be sure, are not wholly disconnected; each sets up a train of reverberations in the rest. But they can be isolated, and examined, and dealt with by themselves. There is no discoverable neat logical pattern, with a fitting pigeonhole for everything. There are differences, irrelevancies, oppositions. Things are 'relative,' but not in the sense of a vague relativism. They are always 'relative to' some ascertainable context or situation, to some specific problem, and the American is resolved to consider each in terms of its own peculiar setting. Technically, this attitude appears in our philosophies as an 'objective relativism' or 'contextualism.' German thinkers also have been anxious to recognize oppositions and contradictions in experience. But they have usually transformed the brute fact of antagonism into a 'principle of contradiction,' and erected that 'dialectic' structure into the pattern of the cosmos. American thinkers, strive as they may, have never been able to take such a wholesale 'dialectic' seriously." (J. H. Randall, Jr., "The Spirit of American Philosophy," in F. E. Johnson, ed., *Wellsprings of the American Spirit*, New York, 1948, p. 125-26.)

Third, the sense of man's ability to do something about his environment has led American philosophy into the paths of an experimental humanism. This is usually non-supernaturalistic rather than anti-supernaturalistic; it is, in a word, unconcerned about God as a principle of philosophic explanation because it is based upon a faith that man has in himself the powers necessary to explain change, or to understand its natural origin. The humanism to which this gives rise is, partly because of the pluralistic relativism which has been mentioned, experimental in its method and temper. Nothing is more foreign to the American spirit than an abstract and theoretical rationalism which explores, deductively and in isolation from the pulsating currents of experience, the consequences of a single "insight." The American contextualist has to use an experimental procedure in order to find out just when and where his insight—or "hypothesis," as he is likely to call it—is applicable.

Then, too, experimentalism is the attitude of looking from the present into the future, of seeing the weaknesses—yes, and the constructive possibilities—in the present, and having the faith in man and man's knowledge necessary to stimulate the determination to build a future better than the present. The spirit of traditionalism, the feeling that we represent a decadent, degraded, and debased generation which has fallen far below the achievements of our fathers, has never been able to take firm hold on the American mind. Thus it is that the melioristic temper of pragmatism has found warm response even among those who have ardently opposed any pragmatic movement in philosophy. The distrust of mere verbalization inherent in the pragmatic temper is good Americanism: if the consequences of two statements are identical, the statements, however differently expressed, have the same meaning—this is good American doctrine; indeed, so is its opposite, as witness the frontiersman's "When you say that, smile!"—a recognition of the fact that the same verbal form may have different consequences in different contexts. But, more, this experimental temper is melioristic, neither optimistic nor pessimistic. It does not say with the optimist "This is the best of all possible worlds," nor with the pessimist "This is the worst of all worlds." Either of these attitudes can lead only to acceptance of things as they are. The spirit of melioristic, experimental, humanistic American thought says, rather, "This is a pretty bad world, but, if you take hold there and I take hold here, and we both do our best, maybe we can improve it a little."

Fourth, our living in groups, gregariously, tends to make our thinking take on group perspectives. Even our ancient belief in equality tends to a group expression. We do not think of this man's being equal to that man, but of conditions of life for this group being made equal to conditions of life for that: rural and urban groups, labor and management, native-born and immigrant, and so on. Our tendency is to be hospitable to diversities, provided that the diverse groups show their own willingness to work co-operatively. This means that some compromises, some "deals," whether "square" or "new," must forever be in process of being worked out. Intelligence is practical, instrumental; it is the technique for making adjustment of the conflicting claims of rival groups and rival institutions.

These are some important directions in which American philosophy moved during the two generations just past. Uncompleted, ever open to novelty of theme or novelty of statement, this was the promising infant industry of American philosophy. It was a lusty infant, perhaps somewhat noisy, as infants tend to be, but it was a bold and curious infant, pushing into every corner of every room, getting itself into all manner of trouble, but beginning to learn a lot and to walk by itself in a world it accepted merely as a base of activities for a series of contemplated improvements.

Meantime we are given to understand that the tide has turned. Scarcely have we reached the beginnings of philosophic independence but already colonial dependence rears its head anew. What makes the situation worse is that the newer European philosophies to which we are urged to give ear are philosophies "born of the agonies of European culture," philosophies of retreat, defeat, and despair. They are philosophies which live by the assumption that man is unable to do anything about the alien world in which he lives. It is unfortunate that they have this pervasive aspect of hopelessness, for each of these philosophies records a type of concern from which American thinkers might well profit. It remains to be seen whether these valuable concerns can be divorced by Americans from their foundations in European tragic experience.

Let us note first the philosophy of retreat, Logical Positivism, which we have imported from Vienna. Philosophy in America can derive much benefit from careful consideration of the constructive aspect of logical positivism. The concern of the logical positivist is with the relationship between the structure and the content of our knowledge. His immediately beneficial effect is to turn our minds away from the shallowness of much recent empiricism by calling attention to the fact that our natural knowledge is known by a rational structure. Again the logical positivist holds up before our minds the ideal of a "unity of science," a theoretically conceivable systematization of all experience without residue. Such a goal is certainly worth striving for. Why then do I speak of logical positivism as a philosophy of retreat?

Because logical positivism, like Kant's earlier critique, accents the gulf between the structure of our knowledge and the structure of things. Our logical and mathematical systems, like Kant's system of categories, are made at our own pleasure, in terms of our own minds. We have no reason for making the assumption that our logical systems are descriptive of any reality. Only in the purely theoretical end of days, when there will be an integration of all experience into the unity of science, can we possibly have *authentic* knowledge. In the meantime, if we do ascribe any descriptive value to our logical system, we are led to "metaphysics," that is, to nonsensical or meaningless statements. The logical form is a non-descriptive element which lies at the root of every supposedly scientific description of fact. Since, therefore, our scientific descriptions are thus vitiated, we can come to no speculative understanding of our world. Let us then, says the logical positivist, devote ourselves to the study of logical form *per se* and to cognate fields of linguistic analysis. Thus for logical positivism the servant of philosophic speculation becomes its master, and the instrumentalities of thinking become the object of all thought. In this way is it that logical positivism *retreats* from thinking speculatively about the universe to thinking about thinking.

As the representative of various philosophies of defeat now being offered to the American mind, let us consider neo-Thomism, a Parisian exportation to our shores. It, too, has an engaging quality, reminiscent of the logical positivist's dream of a unity of science; neo-Thomism, too, asserts the possibility of complete knowledge, of a system which can provide all answers. Surely American thought could gain much from a greater concern for system. Further, neo-Thomism, as a part of the great realistic tradition in epistemology, completely avoids the subjective dangers of much recent thought by a forthright insistence that the objects of knowledge are not changed by our getting to know them; that is, neo-Thomism insists that we know the objects of our knowledge as they are. In spite of these valuable qualities, neo-Thomism is here called a philosophy of defeat because this process of things becoming known cannot be an empirical process. Real cognition is limited by the neo-Thomist to the intellect, or reason, which has an insight into real substances and their essential characters. Thus empirical science is largely dismissed from serious philosophic consideration, and rational science, which remains, is religiously conceived as the servant of a higher truth given by revelation. An Aristotelian metaphysics and epistemology is maintained by the neo-Thomist as a dogmatic philosophy to accompany a revived traditionalism, a view that final truth has been stated once and for all time; that learning consists in the remembering of old doctrines rather than the exploration of new paths. Where the logical positivist places the unity of science in an unattainable future, the neo-Thomist places it in the mind and revelation of God. Neo-Thomism, then, is a philosophy of defeat, of the inevitable defeat of human efforts. Because man has not yet built a perfect world, he is charged with being unable to build a better world; he must place his reliance upon God. Neo-Thomism is a philosophy of the *defeat* of humanism in a revived supernaturalism.

Retreat may be strategic; defeat may be temporary; a greater danger than either is despair, for when men despair they are irretrievably lost. Yet despair is what we are offered by both religious and secular Existentialism. Even in these movements there is a salutary factor: the concern with a philosophy of personality, a concern which has been lacking in much American thought. Yet this concern is expressed in a context which makes it extremely unpalatable. Religious existentialism is represented by "neo-orthodoxy" in theology, the new emphasis on the sense of sin, the nameless dread, the *Angst* of Kierkegaard and his followers. There is for Reinhold Niebuhr, the chief preacher of religious existentialism in America, an essential paradox in our human nature, which involves us necessarily in sin—sin which persists even in the life of the redeemed. The root of this paradox lies in the fact that man is both finite and transcendent—that in his very knowledge of his own finiteness he gives evidence of his self-transcendence. Man is insecure; he is involved in natural contingency. Yet he seeks to overcome his insecurity by a will to power which overreaches his creaturely limitations. Man assumes that his transcendent mind can gradually overcome its finite limitations and become identical with the universal mind. This is the sin of pride. On the other hand, man is transcendent, he is free; yet he sinks himself in some aspect of "the world's vitalities." This is the sin of sensuality. Free yet bound, bound though free, man cannot avoid sinning either in pride

or in sensuality. In his being inextricably immured in the paradoxical destiny of being free and bound, man's spiritual state is one of
anxiety not to sin, and this very anxiety is itself the precondition
of sin. Here is, if ever there was such, a basis for the tragic sense
of life, from which salvation can come only by throwing ourselves upon the infinite but arbitrary grace of God. This is the
element of hope—if not in man, why, then, in God—in religious
existentialism.

There is no such hope in secular existentialism, the existentialism of recent literary faddism. Here the basic experience is that of
the absurdity of existence. The failure of our existence is complete.
We are bound to the world, but the world does not fulfil the
requirements of our minds. It is not that it has this meaning or that;
it is that it has *no* meaning at all. The world is not absurd, nor is
man absurd. But in the confrontation of man and the world—that
is, in existence—absurdity inevitably resides. Faced with this fundamental absurdity, terminable only by death, man's only choice,
man's one freedom, lies in his selection of the role he will enact
in the playing out of the farce. Borrowing from the French resistance movement for his illustrations, Sartre describes three possible
courses as those of the "stinker," the "coward," and the "existentialist." The "stinker" lets the world run riot over his reason; the
"coward' sways from side to side, now asserting his reason, now
letting the world dominate; the "existentialist" leads the resistance
to the world, now playing the part of the hero, as at another time
he might play the part of lover, conqueror, or artist, but he does
so in full consciousness of the complete futility and gratuitousness
of the parts he plays. He does not forget that after a time our globe
will be dead and the civilizations on which we pride ourselves will
have disappeared. All glory, he knows full well, is ephemeral, but
he knows, too, that there is less of delusion in the glory which is
enjoyed in the present than there is in that which is deferred to the
future. Human existence is thus inevitably characterized by a lack,
a void, a frustration, an incompleteness. Our liberty, which is a
function of this incompleteness, is a function of non-being. It is born
in anguish and carries us only towards that unpredictable realization of our essence which will not be complete till the hour of our
death. Surely this completes the full tale of *despair*.

These philosophies of retreat, defeat, and despair are the recent philosophic importations which are offered us as alternatives to the American philosophy of progress, achievement, and hope. Although they are offered as alternative philosophies, we need not accept them as alternatives. We may accept them, instead, as contributory. Each of them has, as I have said, a valuable concern which has been too little emphasized in American thought. We must carefully consider how to salvage these elements while eliminating the aura of futilitarianism which hangs over these philosophies. Our thought has strength enough and flexibility enough to be able to save whatever has constructive possibilities without discarding the vitality of our recent indigenous thinking.

In the earlier years of our republic, Alexander Hamilton tried to protect our infant industries by the erection of a high tariff wall. Had our philosophic independence been of earlier growth, it, too, might have needed and asked such protection. But it is no longer necessary to protect American philosophy by attempting the exclusion of such philosophies as these. Nor would it be desirable to do so, for it would be altogether opposed to our tradition of hospitality to ideas of all sorts and to our cultural pluralism. Although, however, we should continue to import, we must be careful not to surrender. However attractive for the moment it may seem to beat a retreat from philosophic speculation into logical manipulation, or to cast our intellectual problems into the mind of God, or to wallow soulfully or swinishly in the depths of despair, we must avoid the total acceptance of these patterns. We should maintain the strong sense, fed by our two great generations of creative philosophers, that philosophy is, can continue to be, and by right ought to continue to be, of supreme relevance to life lived creatively, constructively, and hopefully.

Business and Intellect in the Eighteenth Century

⊷ε BY SOLOMON F. BLOOM

Brooklyn College

*F*OR A thousand years, aristocrats and those greater aristocrats, the monarchs, presided over the civilization of Europe. Their pre-eminence was still imposing when the sun of the old regime began to descend in the sky. That regime had long been undermined by the business man and, in the eighteenth century, it was challenged by the man of thought and letters. The merchant had discovered fabulous sources of treasures, but their full exploitation ran counter to the rule and custom of monarchy and aristocracy. The insistence of kings and aristocrats to share in the profit naturally irked him. The new culture of the enlightenment pleased the literate community with the vision of a fairer order of things. The cultivated man with a strong interest in public affairs asserted a right to inde-pendent reflection and expression, and to leadership in society. And so, working from different premises, and toward different destina-tions, the man of letters and the man of affairs converged momen-tarily upon the ruin of their common masters in the American and the French revolutions.

The origin, the ambition and the reputation of the business man are all ambiguous. Who has done more to remake the practical world and who is less admired? His works are appreciated but he is not praised. The novelists have satirized him. The poets have shunned him. Other leaders of workaday existence—knights and pirates, kings, priests, and even landlords—have stirred the imag-ination more although they have advanced comfort less. The tra-ditional clerical and aristocratic antagonism to the business man has indeed passed the bounds of fairness. Even the classic account of the law and custom of business and the greatest defence of its right to freedom, *The Wealth of Nations*, gives a derogatory evaluation of the business man as citizen and statesman: "No two characters seem more inconsistent than those of trader and sovereign." "The government of an exclusive company of merchants is, perhaps, the worst of all governments for any country whatever." Most nations have been chary of entrusting their fate to business men, preferring even generals and lawyers.

The reason seems to be, as Adam Smith pointed out, that the operations and habits of commerce shorten the vision and lengthen the self-regard of the practitioner. They breed invidious rivalry, a narrow sense of clique, and an easy adjustment to circumstances and institutions that offer opportunities of immediate enrichment. A combination of private interest and public accommodation attended the very birth of business in the feudal world. Not a little of the original capital used by medieval traders came from the accumulations and surpluses of ecclesiastical or secular holdings. The agent hired by the bishop and abbot—themselves not cold to accumulation—frequently abstracted enough to set up in business for himself. But he did not fail to pay a due obeisance to religion, or at least to the Church and to the aristocracy. For a consideration, noblemen protected towns and fairs against the depredations of others, and from their own. Those of them who borrowed to go on Crusades—one might say to invest in them—brought back precious plunder from the Byzantine empire and so increased the working capital of western Europe. A group of Crusaders assisted the oligarchs of the commercial empire of Venice to conquer Constantinople, the capital of the Eastern empire. When favored pirates returned from the treacherous sea they were sometimes ennobled by their sovereigns, and always relieved of a goodly share of their spoils. In time, kings and aristocrats were tempted also to become silent partners in commercial enterprise. The princes acquired the habit of borrowing heavily, because prices were ever rising while their landed wealth remained relatively stationary, thus benefiting the banking community; and they spent lavishly, enriching importers and manufacturers of luxuries, and incidentally keeping craftsmen in employment. Bernard de Mandeville observed that

> Luxury
> Employ'd a Million of the Poor,
> And odious Pride a Million more.

The business man thus thrived by contact with clergy and aristocracy. His association with the absolute monarchies was particularly close. The story is familiar: The Hapsburg dynasts of Germany, Spain and America had favored the enterprise of great bankers, miners, and traders, and simultaneously taxed and borrowed from them heavily; as the Tudor monarchy of England had waxed in power, merchants with connections at court, and courtiers with a hand in business, had waxed in wealth; the Bourbon kings of France habitually encouraged commerce and even improved, by direct regulation, the processes of manufacture; and farther east such rulers as Peter the Great spurred foreign trade, and imported forges and skilled craftsmen and manufacturers. By the mid-eighteenth century, commercial development had become, in the more advanced monarchies, a settled policy of state. The ready money of trade and finance could be taxed more fruitfully and quickly than the fixed resources of the landed classes, and such taxation generated less political resistance. The policy naturally assumed the shape of the prevailing system of prerogative: royal charters for a few privileged companies, monopolies for trade and manufacture, import prohibitions or high tariffs to protect native monopolies, reservation of colonial trade for special groups, occasional capitals for investment from the surpluses of the royal treasury—the shape, in short, of mercantilism. The balance of trade was considerably reflected, and it was regarded as being wholly represented, by the movements and transfers of specie, the universal token of value; and the amount of specie in a country was regarded as the measure of national success or failure. Thus, to the privileges and monopolies of the aristocracy were joined the less numerous and profitable, but none the less similar, privileges and monopolies of selected and fortunate groups of merchants.

Capitalism was assimilated to the old regime and the consequences were spiritual and moral as well as economic. The aristocratic society lumped together quite indiscriminately all persons and classes who lived beyond the pale of hereditary rank—rich and poor, townsmen or villagers, professionals or peasants. They composed what used to be called "democracy"; and if this confusion eventually had the political advantage of making it possible to defend the claims of the business men as democratic, it had the immediate social disadvantage of seeming to degrade the rich and ambitious to the level of the mass. The business classes were particularly self-conscious, for in fact they had often been recruited from the "lower orders"; in earlier centuries, many a business man had actually worn the badge of serfdom. They felt a strong need to cut themselves off from their less lucky and successful fellows. A hierarchical scheme seemed therefore desirable, and the aristocratic society was decidedly and sharply hierarchical. There was an elaborate and finely graded scale of privileges, exemptions and honors. High aristocrats, on whom the royal sun shone, were distinguished from provincial nobles, the *noblesse de l'épée* from the *noblesse de la robe*, bishops and abbots from mere monks and parish priests.

The middle classes eeled into the interstices of this reticulation. This was pleasant as well as convenient, for here and there at any rate gold secured even glossier goods. Second-class titles, but still titles, second-class administrative offices, judicial and legal places could be obtained much more easily by wealth than by ability. The younger William Pitt, who was British prime minister in the last quarter of the century, remarked that any man who had an income of £10,000 a year should also have a title, and acted on that remark. Himself of middle-class origins, he is said to have blued more blood, and thereby paled all the rest of the blue, than any of his predecessors in office.

Yet, though it insinuated itself into existing society, capitalism violated its wonted habits and rigidities, first overseas—thousands of miles away from Europe—and then, and increasingly, at home. Ever since the discovery of the New World, and of the route to the wealthy east around the Cape of Good Hope, and the incessant penetrations inland that ensued, the European monarchies had found it difficult to supervise the doings, the comings and goings, of seamen and colonists, pirates and smugglers, bankers and importers, shippers and factors. The world had become too large and various and surprising, it presented too sudden opportunities and novelties, to be managed closely by a nagging metropolis. From the outset, a certain casualness, not to say freedom, characterized the relations among Europeans in the New World. They could not and would not rebel against the home governments but they behaved toward each other with a spirited informality strange to the old continent.

It was in the periphery of the European world that there was first defined an independent capitalist interest, which fitted but ill into the traditional framework of government and society. At home, the balanced and by now customary triangular association of aristocracy, monarchy and capitalism labored, though less spectacularly, under new strains. In the commercially developed countries there arose, alongside of privileged merchants and chartered companies, a considerable body of traders who found their enterprise checked and their profit limited by a system under which political favoritism was combined with economic operations. Merchants could not all be privileged, and so the hope of the outsiders lay in breaking that combination, in removing the monopolies and regulations that characterized mercantilism.

And then, slowly intensifying this anti-aristocratic interest, was the emergence of the most important economic factor of modern times—the discovery of the large-scale market for staple goods. Much of the older commerce and industry exploited the fancies, tastes and fashions of aristocratic—rich and artistically cultivated consumers. The interest of such capitalism naturally lay in the preservation of aristocracy, and this must mean a subordinate social position for the capitalist. It was the opening and expansion of the market for necessities—cheaper textiles, for example—that provided the opportunity for the independence and then the domination of the business man. There arose, in short, two quite different, and eventually competing, kinds of capitalism, with different attitudes toward the existing order.

These developments in western Europe and overseas made the position of the business man under the old regime somewhat awkward. He had unquestionably thrived, and had even risen considerably. He had in fact risen as high as he could by his own efforts and deserts. For his more moderate ambitions—a competence and a condescending social recognition—the atmosphere of aristocracy, official clergy, and especially absolute monarchy, was decidedly congenial. But if business was to extend to its furthest limits, if commercial ability and success were to entail social dignity and public power, if the contempt of aristocrat were to be shamed, it was not enough to reduce the more annoying political controls over the economy or to abate the rigidities of the old regime. It was necessary to recognize all ability, for one could not well claim recognition for mercantile talent alone. It was necessary to infuse into society new ideas and purposes, and into the state, a new policy and program.

But business was not imaginative or ingenious or disinterested enough to compass the criticism and the reconstruction that such a reformation called for. The world was too complex to be apprehended by the merely practical man who learns largely, and too much, from direct experience. Apart from the business man's awe of the existing social ladder and the blinding gloss of the prevailing arrangements, the largely agrarian character of Europe and America, and the consequent weight of the landed interest, made him wary of asserting a paramount influence. Nor were business men so generally liked or respected that they could call to their support other non-aristocratic elements. In short, business lacked the vision, the courage and the sympathy for a transformation of the old regime.

These qualities, in abundance, were supplied by the Enlightenment through its more articulate leaders and its more cultivated devotees. In a sense, the Enlightenment was itself bourgeois. It thrived in royal and aristocratic courts but it thrived more typically in

> Towered cities . . .
> And the busy hum of men.

But then culture has always found its most favorable channel in urban intercourse and activity rather than rural isolation. The great ages of letters and art have been associated with great cities: Athens, Alexandria, Rome, Florence, Venice, Paris, London. But while the city of ancient times and of the Renaissance hummed with landed lords as well as bankers and traders, the modern was more distinctively bourgeois.

The Enlightenment recruited a large proportion of its creative spirits from among the middle classes of town and country. Ability and talent are not hereditary, and so not aristocratic; they are nurtured by leisure, education and training, and these were available only to people of some substance. Voltaire's grandfather was a merchant, his father a lawyer; Montesquieu's father was a titled judge of middle-class origins; David Hume's and Edward Gibbon's owned a small estate; Diderot's was a prosperous cutler; and Rousseau and Beaumarchais were sired by watchmakers.

But it is not enough to say that they, and their kind, were bourgeois: for it was the wider-eyed and rebellious sons, and not the conventional and comfortable fathers, trained intellect and not business, that fertilized the Enlightenment. Often enough, they combined the habits of business and enterprise—Voltaire was all his life engaged in financial speculation—with literary and scientific pursuits. The fashion of the time commanded an interest in culture. The rich man who makes a virtue of his ignorance and coarseness, and yet is respected in the community, was yet to be born. It was natural therefore in that century that the man of business and the man of letters should be much closer to each other than they are now, and occasionally they were melted together in such magnificent embodiments as Benjamin Franklin. Franklin is the great prototype of the business man who takes a strong interest in learning, and of the man of learning who tries his hand at business and speculation. But this does not diminish the distinction between the social functions of business and intellect, but rather helps to explain the natural ease of their co-operation in that age, the openness of the one to responsible reflection and the practical effectiveness of the other.

The power of land, birth and money, of armed force, impudence, and numbers, are commonplaces; and the devotees of intellect and learning have never been distinguished, as a group, by the possession of any of these. Their sole advantage lies in the circumstances that the world cannot be understood, managed and governed properly—if we except the rare cases of genius—without the memory of past experience, the evocation of ideal inspiration, and the knowledge of various lands and civilizations that the intellectual and professional groups peculiarly represent and embody. In medieval times it was the clergy that performed the functions of teaching the young, guiding the populace, advising the powerful, supplying the chancelleries and administrations, and articulating philosophies of society and policies of government. The intellectuals are the modern clergy—without the theology, caste organization, privilege, and assured income. Often, and perhaps typically associated with the larger forces of wealth or numbers, they have striven, ever since the seventeenth century, for an independent influence in public affairs. They have made their voice heard in royal courts and aristocratic houses, in middle-class parliaments and, later, in proletarian factories and union halls.

It was in the eighteenth century that they began to rebel against the patronage of aristocrats. For the first time writers and artists could entertain the hope, though they seldom fully realized it, of acquiring a competence by their own exertions. A cultivated public opinion, and market for the products of the intellectual, were distinctly emerging. They could be reached by rulers and statesmen only through the intermediation of the writer and the orator; these could persuade and sway public opinion, but, turning around, they could also represent it and thus exert pressure upon the powers that be. An autonomous area was being staked out. It was the satirists and the philosophers, the poets, the wits, and the dramatists, who shamed the impudence of fanaticism, protested the iniquity of privilege, mocked the vanity of aristocratic pretensions, punctured the claims of absolutism, and aroused sympathy for the disinherited of the earth. Their contribution in the eighteenth century was the elaboration of a program by the use of which the dominant forces of aristocracy and monarchy could preserve by reforming themselves, or, alternately, if these failed, the critics from the ranks of capitalism, and later democracy, could assert a claim to dignity and power. They moved in the vast no-man's-land between the formal institutions of the old regime and a growingly self-conscious and articulate society with a certain lonely pride.

The justification of the great eighteenth century monarchies, as later of capitalism and socialism, rested eventually upon the claim that their policy coincided with the truest interests of mankind at large. Such a claim could be made good only by association with a culture that was not limited by its social origins nor exhausted by its social function. The Enlightenment was such an authentic culture; it contrived a power and persuasion, a grace and charm, that softened the egoism of vested interests and the egoism of the groups that challenged these interests.

Scarcity and Abundance
in Ethical Theory

❧ BY ABRAHAM EDEL
City College of New York

*A*LTHOUGH the destructive possibilities of the atomic age are at present uppermost in men's minds, there is a strong undercurrent of speculation about the constructive changes that atomic power will make possible in human life. The keynote of this speculation is the replacement of scarcity by abundance and control. It differs only in degree from the technological optimism that has characterized the past half century, but the difference is great enough to give the problem a central place in reflective thought. Neo-Malthusian pessimists may fear the rapidity of population growth and underscore erosion, devastation and wasteful exploitation of fundamental resources. But there are sufficient grounds for hope—if only war and self-willed destruction can be avoided—that abundance replacing scarcity will some day be the fundamental fact underlying all social, political and cultural life.

I.

One has only to study the history of man to see how thoroughly men's relations, institutions, feeling and ideas are permeated with the awareness of scarcity and the insecurity and strife that it entails. Moral philosophy is no exception. And while it is far too early to assess the detailed consequences of an abundance that is not yet and may not soon be achieved, it is not too early to reflect on the kind of role that abundance replacing scarcity can have in the formulation of ethical concepts and methods.

To assess the material conditions—social and organic—of ethical theory is a task that moral philosophers have been prone to neglect. It is well to be reminded by Morris R. Cohen of the immediate material bases of the very sense of values: "What makes it possible for us to carry on, instead of quitting as we can when we really want to, is not our guess as to the unknown goal, but rather the zest developed by our actual daily experiences, by our organic activities, by the light and warmth of the sun and air, and by the joys of human companionship. When the zest for life is really gone, all words of comfort or exhortation are vain. There is nothing to which to appeal. But wise reflection may fan the flame when it is low, illumine our labor, and increase the scope of our peaceful enjoyments."[1]

In the present study I should like to look very briefly at the historical role of the scarcity concept in ethical formulations, and then in greater detail at the kinds of changes in ethical constructions that its replacement by an abundance concept might involve. The underlying ethical problem of what constitutes the good life when it has abundance at its command—in short, the objects of ultimate value for mankind—is not our present concern. But the shift in what appear to be means and material conditions will prove to be far-reaching, and its consequences extend into unsuspected areas.

The guiding role of scarcity in the formulation of ethical theory is an old one, although its operation has frequently taken a disguised form. A world of scarcity has been so pervasive a fact that it is accepted as the permanent background of the ethical scene. The setting seems so immovable that little thought is given to its cramping effect upon the action that goes on within the human stage and blame is channeled on other factors in the field.

Plato's *Republic* furnishes a classic illustration. Socrates constructs an ideal society, the simple city of simple tastes. Glaucon brands it a city of pigs. So Socrates enlarges it, adds luxury services, embellishments, professions, and concludes: "The country, too, which was large enough to support the original inhabitants, will now be too small. If we are to have enough pasture and plough land, we shall have to cut off a slice of our neighbors' territory; and if they too are not content with necessaries, but give themselves up to getting unlimited wealth, they will want a slice of ours."[2]

War is unavoidable, and this necessitates a warrior-guardian

---

[1] Cohen, Morris R., *The Faith of a Liberal*, (New York 1946) p. 7.
[2] Plato, *Republic*, trans. by F. M. Cornford, p. 61.

group, out of which is elaborated the familiar Platonic class-structure and cultural regimentation. Plato, however, does not attribute the characteristics of his state to the foundation of scarcity, but to the desire for luxury and the passions of men.

In ancient moral philosophy generally the influence of scarcity is refracted through such condemnation of the passions or else through a restrictive ideal of self-sufficiency. These two approaches are united in Epicurean and Stoic theory. Epicurus contracts desire by simplifying tastes and so attains security and peace of mind. The Stoics cut off the spirit from worldly attachments. One of the central components in the stress on intellectual activity in all ancient philosophy is its self-sufficient character. Its domain is abundant and completely accessible. Thinking is the activity in which a man relies most on himself, needs least of the world, trespasses not at all on his neighbor. Thinking unites men just as competing passions for limited objectives divide them. Thinking allows a constant accumulation for all. Hence the intellectual life is a safe investment—it never is precarious or at the mercy of accident.

With the break-up of the mediaeval outlook and the growth of secular aims, the acquisitive passions acquire respectability. But even the positive pursuit of power reflects in a fundamental way the setting of scarcity. For attention is focussed on competition, and the "state of nature" is one of insecurity and the scramble for scarce goods. Hobbes is perfectly clear about the negative basis of the pursuit of power. When he endows mankind with "a perpetuall and restlesse desire of Power after power, that ceaseth only in Death" he adds: "And the cause of this, is not always that a man hopes for a more intensive delight, than he has already attained to; or that he cannot be content with a moderate power: but because he cannot assure the power and means to live well, which he hath present, without the acquisition of more."[3]

Even in so sophisticated a system as Kantian ethics, the insecurity of the natural world may be seen as a background. Kant's condemnation of the serpentine windings of utilitarianism clearly reflects the view that the consequences of action are in fact incalculable, so that security of judgment can be found only in the

[3] *Leviathan*, Part I, ch. xi.

attachment of morality to pure principle. And his very moral argument for the existence of God rests on the assumption that the natural and social world cannot be made to guarantee the unity of virtue with happiness, which is the *summum bonum.*

Only with the flowering of pleasure theory in the school of Bentham is the hold of scarcity both in its condemnation of the passions and in its basic insecurity reaction consciously broken. The difference between ancient and modern pleasure theory, it has so often been pointed out, lies in the shift from a pessimistic to an optimistic outlook. It was, of course, a shift grounded in the promise of trade and industry, in the accession to dominance of the commercial and industrial classes, and the vista of the whole globe as a source of growing wealth and happiness. Bentham can be liberal to all desires. If he allows that "quantity of pleasure being equal, push-pin is as good as poetry," it is because he thinks the world has room for both and more. Abundance is specifically included by Bentham as one of the ends of civil law. If security, the major goal, is provided by protection of property, then abundance needs no special urging.

Desires extend with means. The horizon elevates itself as we advance; and each new want, attended on the one hand by pain, on the other by pleasure, becomes a new principle of action. Opulence, which is only a comparative term, does not arrest this movement once begun. On the contrary, the greater our means, the greater the scale on which we labor; the greater is the recompense, and, consequently, the greater also the force of motive which animates to labor. Now what is the wealth of society, if not the sum of all individual wealth? And what more is necessary than the force of these natural motives, to carry wealth, by successive movements, to the highest possible point?

It appears that abundance is formed little by little, by the continued operation of the same causes which produce subsistence. Those who blame abundance under the name of luxury, have never looked at it from this point of view.[4]

Bentham's attitude toward abundance has two elements which are capable of leading in different directions. His fundamental this-worldliness, resting on a realization of the possibility of achieving increasing abundance, sweeps away the disparaging attitude toward desires which had thrived in a background of assumed inevitable.

[4] *The Theory of Legislation,* Ogden ed. p. 101.

scarcity. But his opposition to any organized or collective effort for achieving abundance and his general atomic individualism thwart the development of a fully self-conscious ethics of abundance. In fact his conception of human nature is capable of sustaining the same type of ethics as the older conception of passion as evil. For with competitiveness and desire for indefinite aggrandizement postulated, the older absolute scarcity is merely replaced by an inevitable relative scarcity.

The Marxist philosophers, taking an international perspective and making collective social action the center of their thinking, gained a fuller vista of the possible role of abundance. They were prompted to this by their view of history as the growth of freedom and their stress on the fundamental part played by the mode of production in determining the character of human life. Engels epitomizes this realization in his *Anti-Dühring:* "In a society in which the motive for stealing has been done away with, in which therefore at the very most only lunatics would ever steal, how the teacher of morals would be laughed at who tried solemnly to proclaim the eternal truth: Thou shalt not steal!"[5] And in similar fashion he greets the argument that the labor-time of the professional architect and the professional porter are equally valuable with a rejoinder that sweeps away the problem: "It is a fine sort of socialism which perpetuates the professional porter!"[6]

That the possibility of abundance is something seriously to be reckoned with in social and ethical formulations is now a common view. Some still hold to relative scarcity through competitive desire. Thus Roscoe Pound, in his *Social Control Through Law*, makes it a premise of law that "as the saying is, we all want the earth. We all have a multiplicity of desires and demands which we seek to satisfy. There are very many of us but there is only one earth."[7] But the consequences of nation devouring nation in the attempt to encompass the globe are now too sinister, and the pursuit of global conquest by any nation will thwart the very abundance for which it may hope. Thus the promise of tremendously increased abundance for all mankind is the only alternative to total destruction.

[5] Engels, Friedrich, *Anti-Dühring,* trans. by Burns, p. 109.
[6] *Ibid.,* p. 229.
[7] Pound, Roscoe, *Social Control Through Law* (New Haven 1942) p. 64.

II.

Serious objections will be raised in ethical theory to assigning a moral significance to the transition from scarcity to abundance. These merit at least preliminary consideration.

One objection comes from the dominant ethical tradition. "What has abundance to do with moral truth?" it will be said. "It may determine whether men have the means to carry out what is right, but how can it relate to ends, or be in any sense determinative of what is right or wrong?" In this view morality is regarded as the assertion of a set of truths which remain true whether they are applied or not.

Without entering here into a critical consideration of the nature of ethics, it must be recognized that even under the objection nothing prevents various truths from changing in relative "importance." The profound truths of one age may become the trivial truths of another age. "Thou shalt not scalp thy neighboring tribesman" once had tremendous relevance in America. No doubt it is even now a sound moral injunction. Nor is its content adequately disposed of by subsuming it under "Thou shalt not kill," which is still very pertinent. For scalping has a different social, psychological and ethical content; it differed from murder just as does our killing in warfare.

It should be noted further that the objector does not represent the unanimous verdict of the ethical tradition. A great part of naturalistic ethics does not make the sharp distinction of ends and means on which he rests his criticism, and would therefore readily admit a developed technique of preventing or transcending problems as an essential method of ethics.[8]

What is more, great or important means acquire moral quality in the very organization of human energy they make possible. When Henry A. Wallace, in his *Century of the Common Man* speech, offered the vista of a pint of milk a day for every child throughout the world, all the jibes of articulate reaction could not rob it of its spiritual quality as a symbol of the human love of the child and hope of the future.

A second objection hits at the very heart of the technique of

[8] See, for example, Dewey and Tufts, *Ethics,* rev. ed. (New York 1932) ch. x.

abundance. For the essence of an ethical approach in terms of abundance is to solve moral problems by transcending them. The objector will deny that this is a genuine mode of ethical solution: to manage to avoid facing problems is not to answer them, it is to be lucky rather than moral. Therefore he turns for ethical insight to the extreme case, the "marginal" situation, the choice which is individual and final, and cannot be subsumed under readily applicable general rules. For example, Jean-Paul Sartre, referring to the choices made by resistance workers in France under the Nazi occupation, says: "And the choice that each of us made of his life and of his being was an authentic choice because it was made face to face with death, because it could always have been expressed in these terms: 'Rather death than . . .' "[9]

This objection confirms as much as it refutes the underlying claims of an ethical approach in terms of abundance; for it focusses its special attention upon the unavoidable scarcities and insecurities of life. From the point of view of the moral economy, death is the scarcity of time, however much metaphysically it presents itself as the cessation of individual being.

A further assumption of the existentialist ethical analysis is the individualist character of morality. If, however, morality be regarded as social in its inmost nature, in the sense in which a language is social even when it occurs in a monologue or in reflection, then the marginal case presents no problem in principle. How a man should behave in the face of death, where sacrifice is desirable, how a man should assume creative responsibility in unique situations, are problems of concrete social evaluation. To focus them as primarily individual problems because the individual is the one who dies is to substitute psychology for morality. How a particular man deals with crucial situations enables us to judge the structure of his personality. Perhaps it is true that every man has his critical point, or breaking point, beyond which all moral quality disappears and there is simply struggle for survival—though for some the point is so low that death will first overtake them. And perhaps there is a correlation between a given man's critical point and the qualities of his moral feeling. But in principle to make this the central phenom-

[9] "The Republic of Silence," in *The Republic of Silence,* compiled and edited by A. J. Liebling (New York 1947) p. 498-99.

enon of morality is as if one studied language as primarily an expression of individual emotion just because one does not speak
unless one is "moved" sufficiently.

A third and more immediate objection at this point is the fear
sometimes expressed that the technique of transcending ethical
problems may adversely affect character. It is argued that if men
are not hardened in the school of ethical torment they will be softer
and unable to meet crucial problems, if they arise, without shock.
This is a serious question, comparable to the issue in bringing up
children as to whether the parents ought always to avoid saying
"no" to the child by skillful steering and reconstruction of situations
or whether they ought deliberately to allow some crucial negations
to arise in order that the child should not become "self-willed."

This type of objection is to some extent a reflection of the era
of scarcity itself. It has much in common with the claims that civilization makes men decadent. It seems to rest on the assumption
that an achieved abundance is itself insecure, so that men should
be ready for its disappearance at any time. But we do not now train
men in the habits of the frontier wilderness, on the assumption that
city life may suddenly vanish. So we must estimate realistically
whether an achieved abundance is a temporary windfall or genuinely secure. In general, the ultimate effect on character of particular techniques for transcending problems is itself a problem of experimental psychology. If a utopian abundance makes life too
easy and men in some definite sense "weak," then hardening processes can be incorporated into collective experience. At most, therefore, such types of objections provide certain cautions within an
ethic of abundance, rather than grounds for general rejection of
such an ethic.

III.

Just as scarcity connotes absence of means and precariousness
of realizing ends, abundance implies availability of materials,
knowledge and control. We are not speaking of magical fulfillment
such as Aladdin's lamp (or even Gyges' ring), but specifically of
existent technology, attainable security, and the scientific inventive-
ness which reasonably assures progress and increasing control. It is
not the static abundance of an agricultural community with rich
soil on which a plentiful yield of traditional crops is assured, but

the growing fields of applied physical science and social organization. Given such a background we may see at least three ethical consequences of abundance:

(1) It can prevent a scramble for scarce goods by providing enough of a given good for everyone's consumption. Thus it can remove many a basis for crime or strife.

(2) Where there are distinct and non-competing desires which nevertheless conflict because of a crowded field, abundance may remove the ground of the discrepancy and allow each desire separate and diverse expression. For example, if materials are sufficiently abundant so that apartments have sound-proof walls, many an obvious clash is removed, hence many an ethical controversy or legal complaint.

(3) Knowledge coupled with resources makes possible more long-range planning and development of character, hence anticipatory prevention of desires and attitudes that are a source of frustration and conflict. Abundance means a higher quality of educational system, greater individualization, attention to personal and emotional problems, remedial treatment of criminality where it occurs, and hosts of reforms whose type and beneficial effects have long been clear to educators, social theorists and practical commissions of experts, but whose extension has always been thwarted on budgetary grounds.

The way in which obligations, virtues and vices shift as we go from scarcity to abundance may be seen in greater detail if we take one illustration of an already accomplished transition. Water is a constant good both for drinking and washing. Yet how different are the duties and attitudes ethically relevant in a small community situated on a lake, in a larger community that imports its water as a commodity, and in a large industrialized city of today. In the first the essential problems are those of avoiding pollution. Rules are directed to the individual; they are simple but strict. Without special problems of transportation, with direct resort to the lake when a pump breaks down, there need be no borrowing of water, no rationing of supply. In the second case, however, the problems of water resemble very much the current case of milk. Given the old-fashioned water-carrier of many a European city of the past, the whole ethics of buying and selling, of property and theft, of quality of commodity, are immediately relevant. (If water cannot be diluted it can be polluted.) There is the ethic of charity, the virtue of gratitude; there is room for ethical problems of borrowing and of interest. And apart from all this there are additional calculations about the number of baths that can be afforded and the relative values of cleanliness and other achievable objectives with a given limited means.

In a modern city the issues have been completely changed. At first sight water may seem to have been removed from the domain of moral problems. Given public fountains reasonably distributed, as well as public lavatories, the quenching of thirst and cleanliness (except as the latter depends on living quarters, clothes, etc.) are open to all, and each may take according to his need, not according to means or as a reward for work. Nevertheless, although moral issues are screened by the impersonal character of the relationship, there are very definite virtues and obligations involved in a number of different areas. On the technical side there are problems of responsibility of technicians in care of reservoirs, in maintenance of transportation facilities, etc. These are the virtues of responsible workmen. There are all the obligations of a civil service system, an ethics of impersonal choice of personnel as against a partisan patronage system. There are problems of justice in fixing of wage-scales and conditions of work. From the point of view of supporting the system, different principles of taxation may be employed which raise quite different issues for consumers: water-meters and payment according to amount used, special water tax, or support of water system from general tax fund. That such differences involve moral as well as economic components may be seen in the discussions that centered around the Beveridge report on social security in England; it recommended financing partly through general taxation, partly through individual contributions in order to give the feeling of participation. (The whole issue of moral attitudes toward the general tax fund is well worth special study by moral philosophers.) Again, from the point of view of the consumer there are virtues of care and conservation involving fixing of leaking faucets, not wasting water, repressing of desire for a free flow in washing dishes as against use of a dish-pan and curbing length of showers when the mayor warns that the rainfall has been insufficient to re-plenish reserves. These are problems of education, although some of them may be removed in turn by the technique of abundance—for example, the familiar automatically closing faucets in public fountains so that the problem of care itself disappears.

The above by no means constitutes a complete treatment of the ethics of water-supply, but it is sufficient to enable us to offer pre-liminary generalizations about the typical direction of ethical prob-lems in a situation of achieved abundance:

(1) The problems involved tend to be viewed as whole-society problems, whether the mechanism of accomplishment be state en-terprise, co-operative enterprise or competitive enterprise. This en-tails, as a minimum, social regulation of standards from a point of view of broad social welfare.

(2) Insofar as maintenance of abundance or productivity is a central task, many virtues and vices, duties and responsibilities will be oriented toward this end. The whole moral tone of these rules will depend upon the importance of specific ends in the scheme of life. Care, for example, may very well acquire the moral tone that thrift once had, as our technological system becomes more complex and a single slip may produce a plane crash or an explosion.

(3) Problems of distribution of costs or burdens become fun-damental. These are in principle society-wide problems and not usually to be determined by the special character of the field alone. Issues concerning the price structure in a society and the desirable extent of social control through subsidies, price-fixing, etc., as well as the questions of taxation referred to above, illustrate these problems.

(4) The greater the abundance the more the principle of dis-tribution of the good tends to become "to each according to his need." This is clear in public drinking-fountains; in the modern theory of educational opportunity, and so forth. The judgment of need in the case of water is left to the individual, given complete abundance. This may be supplemented by guidance (as in health or vocational guidance). In such matters there may also be the democratic regulation of limits and standards, for example, of abil-ity to become a doctor, or of social need for doctors. Again, it must

be noted that water is a material quantitatively divisible, easily disposed of, and having uses by itself. Fresh problems of social relations would arise, for example, in an abundance of aeroplanes.

(5) If relative scarcity shows itself within a field of abundance, it may be dealt with by a sub-ethic of rationing, and does not entail abandoning the whole ethics of abundance. Numerous special principles require elaboration in such a sub-ethic. There are, however, limits beyond which the system itself collapses. Yet even here, from the point of view of the ethics of abundance, general orientation should be toward recovery of abundance by increased productivity. In this sense the ethics of abundance urges men to get together for the increase of the common good rather than regard as their central moral task the development of principles by which a limited good may be partitioned. Thus predatory habits are avoided by establishing the goal of abundance even in a period of scarcity. This is the point implicit in the common notion of replacing the struggle of man against man by that of man against nature.[10]

(6) The ethics of abundance provides no answer for situations of extreme scarcity. It does not itself tell men what to do in the typical text-book situation of two men on a log out at sea when one must let go or both will sink. It does, however, urge the manufacture of safer boats, the abolition of war and torpedoes, and the development of scientific techniques in advance for emergency situations—a life-belt for every man, inflated rubber life-boats, and so forth. In this sense the ethics of abundance is addressed to society rather than the individual alone, to educators and legislators and men who plan ahead. The situations of tragedy are not removed but the ethics that gives a central role to abundance aims to make them the exception rather than the type in terms of which moral principles are to be framed. In this sense the traditional preoccupation of ethical teaching with "individual" rather than "social" morality reflects the ethics of scarcity.

(7) In general, an ethics of abundance takes a positive rather than a negative approach to moral questions. It is less concerned with telling men what they must *not* do than with working out positive opportunities for harmonious human happiness. Thus its

---

[10] The ethics of abundance is to the ethics of scarcity as the abolition of the causes of war is to The Hague regulation of war practices.

interpretation of liberty will not be merely that social control over the individual is lacking but that determinate conditions of human welfare be brought into existence. Its interpretation of equality will not be merely impartiality of treatment and the absence of discrimination, but the effective release of all men's initiative and capacities. This same approach, ethically and psychologically, will characterize the handling of the traditional problems of social philosophy.

It should be stressed in conclusion that to realize the possible role of abundance in ethical theory is not merely to attempt a portrait of a possible future. For the acquisition of abundance may begin to function as a present goal, acting because it is so vast, as a standard by which many of our present virtues, vices, obligations and responsibilities may be assessed. Thus awareness of what is possible may become a driving force in the midst of the actual. The realization that a great part of our morality is grounded in scarcity and the expectation that the achievement of abundance and social self-sufficiency will release untold human energies, generating a veritable flowering of human values, are twin pivots in the reconstruction of a moral outlook today. And they illustrate amply the paradoxical truth of human life that attention to material conditions provides the only high road to general enhancement of ideal goods.

The Spiritual Life:
A Secular View

ᴥᵹ *BY IRWIN EDMAN*
Columbia University

*O*NE does not have to be a studious explorer of current tendencies among historians, men of letters, and philosophical or dialectical theologians, to have become aware of the current renaissance of other-worldliness and supernaturalism. Not, of course, that these were ever dead. It is a familiar provincialism among rationalistic minds that what is not vital to them is dead in the world. There are millions of pious communicants, millions more of merely nominal believers, who have remained unaffected by the doubts, the scruples, the denials, and equally untouched by the affirmations of the relatively small group of secular-minded philosophers in any, even in a rationalistic, era.

For a very long time, however, since Lucretius—one dares almost to say since Socrates—there have been serious and responsible thinkers who have thought it possible and necessary to speak and think of moral standards and spiritual values without recourse to the supernatural, without appeal to the sanctions of a theology or the support of a church. Since the beginning of the eighteenth century, this has indeed become normal practice among liberal minds of an empirical cast. Different as was their tone, Condillac in France and Hume in England illustrated this practice and this direction in the eighteenth century. John Stuart Mill gave eloquent and succinct expression to the same secular view of moral standards and spiritual values. His essay on *Utilitarianism* and his *Three Essays on Religion* are the classical places to find it for the nineteenth century. In the twentieth century, Santayana has treated the same themes from a not very different point of view, and so has John Dewey, whose *A Common Faith* is a vigorous statement of what one may call secular spirituality.

But the trend, insofar at least as the general educated public is concerned, is all the other way. Mr. Toynbee has, in the United States at least, won an enormous following, largely by deriving from or, as it would seem, imposing upon history a Christian coherence and a Christian meaning, a God-intended past and future. Mr. Reinhold Niebuhr has transposed all the questions of politics and morals, about which in secular terms he often writes so empirically, into the mystical language of a sense of sin and the possibility of grace as the *sine qua non* of intelligent moral and political action.

It seems to me urgently necessary at this time to reiterate the possibility and the necessity of addressing oneself to moral and spiritual issues in secular and this-worldly terms, and this for two reasons. The first is that a physical view of nature is now alone possible to many; the second is that these can only have a notion of morals or spirit in such a context.

This is not the place to marshal all the arguments for a conception of the universe that excludes teleology and admits of no divine origin or intention in things. It can here be only briefly recalled that so far as the conclusions of empirical inquiry are concerned, there are purely statistical regularities to be observed, stable recurrences which we call laws of nature. There is at least very considerable ground, if we take the scientific method seriously, for taking a non-theological metaphysic seriously also. As a matter of fact, that is what a great many nominal believers do also. Whatever their official beliefs, their day-to-day orthodoxy, so to speak, is posited upon faith in the deliverances of scientific inquiry. For all who live consistently in terms of such an empirical world, it is very difficult to entertain seriously views which conflict with the habits of mind engendered by modern science. Nor can they accept a metaphysic that seems to conflict with such habits. Such a metaphysic is pluralistic; it regards the nature of being in terms of the various ways of things; it envisages ends as the natural realization or fulfillment of unintended, unintentional processes, not as the achievement of purposes laid down in advance, by some beneficently designing intelligence.

Whatever significance these processes have, they derive their significance from and for some human interest or passion or some deliberate intention that has arisen as the technique of or the transformation of these passions and interests. These meanings and significances are eternal only in the sense that the structure of things and of human interests seem to be recurrent in their patterns. The permanence of values is another name for recurrence, not for perdurance or for eternity. And the naturalistically minded philosopher cannot find in the variety of meanings which the human psyche finds in the plurality of natural processes, any reason for believing that these meanings are somehow bound into one single or comprehensive meaning, nor can he believe that single and separate meanings or even a context of meanings can find validity only in their relation to some central and comprehensive significance called the meaning of the universe, any more than the values of a given painting to the connoisseur are bound up with the value of some cosmic painting of which one particular picture is simply an aspect or a phase.

To persons committed to such a general view of circumstances, there is a danger of a very real despair, of an aching sense of futility, if they are forced into the position of believing that without a theology, in which they cannot believe, without a church (to which they cannot adhere), their moral standards, their spiritual values, their ideals are vanity and illusion, and their pretended moralities a shamble. In such blackness, some have experienced suddenly a vision of God. There are uncounted others who, if they swallowed the theological critique of a world without God in it, while they persisted in being unable to believe in God, would have a vision only of the

> "dark tides of nothingness,
> Where all who know may drown."

For it is perfectly true, I think, that without something in some sense to be called "spiritual," life becomes a nightmare or a nausea.

Now the term spiritual has a persuasive and a glorious sound where it does not have a routine and homiletic one. By spiritual values, there is fair agreement (among men of very different cosmological convictions) that one denotes the ends which justify life, the ultimates which give life unassailable and unexpungable meaning. For thousands of years, it has been assumed in theological circles (it is largely assumed in them today) that these ultimates which give life meaning derive their sanction and their significance from a supernatural world. Men have always been diffident about trusting their finest impulses, their most elevated ideals. They have regarded their spiritual values, or been taught to regard them, as of no value whatever unless these had their sanction in a total and compelling realm of ideality. Virtually all Christian theory has held human purposes to be purposeless save in terms of one grand inclusive total purpose. Individual lives have been the mere buzzing of complex insects, without meaning save in terms of one over-arching meaning.

The meaning of spiritual values has been held to lie in the domain of spirit, and the ends of life have been conceived as negligible or trivial unless they have their status in "a world elsewhere." Thus spirit has been set over against nature, and in the term have been fused both a morality and a metaphysics. Empiricists and transcendentalists may agree about what some of the identifiable goods of life are. But they have a very different conception of what their locus, origin and validity consist in. To be spiritual for the transcendentalist consists in having a status in some hypostatized realm called Spirit or Being, a realm accessible to dialectic demonstration or sometimes to mystical intuition, but alone real metaphysically, and alone significant morally. Spiritual has thus an ambiguous status when used in moral and religious discourse. It is a name for what is ultimate in action and final for contemplation. But it is insinuated into the very terms that what is thus ultimate in action and final in contemplation is part of a domain of timeless essence, an integration of timeless essences in a cosmos that is a cosmos in the sense of being a coherent system of ideas, a context of logical forms. And somehow what is regarded by any human beings as ultimate in action or final in contemplation is supposed to borrow its ultimacy or finality from the alleged order or Logis which is identified as Spirit.

Whatever fulfills the absorbed and awakened consciousness is final for that moment of contemplation; whatever concludes, realizes, integrates action and is its conclusive as it is its concluding reward, is ultimate. A symphony comes to a finis although the music of the spheres does not end at that moment and though it is not proved to be part of that imagined and perhaps not impossible celestial harmony. An individual life may be defined in terms of certain ultimate goods, or the life of a whole society may be so defined. But it is in terms of the personal organization and circumstances of the individual psyche, in terms of the social conditions of a given culture that those ideals are lighted upon and rested in as terms of reference, as goals and social hypotheses for action. If they are to be called spiritual, it is because they seem to illuminate and clarify life, and thus to justify it, to render to a given person, to a given culture, clarity and intensity, to render life more alive and consciousness more aware. There is no clear gain whatever, no addition in meaning to spirituality, to say that the values in the light of which conduct is directed, or the ends to which it is moving, are parts of a realm of logical forms called Reality or Spirit or Being. Insofar as spiritual values exist, they exist as realizations of natural processes. It is only in a fit of metaphysical enthusiasm that these values are abstracted from nature into a realm called Spirit. The realm of Spirit is moral, not cosmological, and to insist that spiritual values relate to a metaphysical world is simply to hypostatize logic and then to materialize the hypostasis.

Modest limited partial meanings have been made to appear absurd. It has further been held to be a denigration of the spirit to assume that it is the flowering and the fruition of a fleshly creature in a physical or mechanical world that matters. Spiritual values, it has been held, belong to spirit, and spirit, in the theological tradition of the West, is identified with a bodiless soul and a spaceless, timeless eternity. St. Paul long ago, out of Hebrew myth, provided the Christian apparatus for libeling man's once-born nature. Ever since, original sin has been invoked to explain and to contemn man's natural equipment of impulse and desire; and man's own secular efforts, even his virtues, have been, as St. Augustine said of pagan virtues, at best splendid vices. It is easy, for saints as well as satirists, to pile up the evidence that man is a lustful, greedy, lying, earthbound creature, fated to live by violence and to die by damnation. On these terms, if man is to be saved, it is only by the entrance in him of divine grace, following upon his own recognition of his unworthiness. Consider Paul, Augustine, Niebuhr, and many writers less gifted but not without influence.

Not only is the individual human being condemned with the whole of human nature, but all of human history is dismissed as trivial or worse, save as the divinely arranged march of mankind toward the Kingdom of God. Otherwise, it is held that history is the record simply of the successive endings of individual lives, in themselves futile, and the final freezing or burning up of the earth or the death of the whole solar system—a sort of secular last judgment, a demonstration of the final futility of merely secular history. No less invidious things have been said about merely human standards of morality than have been uttered about attempts to define the spiritual in merely human terms. Quite apart from theology, there has been a logical uneasiness among many human beings about moral standards in a purely relative world. Theologians have jumped to insist that moral standards are hopelessly unauthoritative, if there is no absolute against which a relative standard may acquire a status. Otherwise, as Thrasmymachus says in the *Republic* of Plato: "Justice is merely the right of the stronger."

To those homesick for absolutes, what the empiricist calls social utilities in morals are merely brute expediencies; customary rules of conduct never are any more than the function of the ruthless survival of coarse powers in a wretched conflict of coarse rival interests. To the theologians, not only do relative moral standards seem merely relative, they do not seem in any sense moral at all. Many men besides Immanuel Kant have been suspicious of moral claims that have no "higher" warrant than utility. Sometimes the moral character of an act dramatically illustrates to the traditional religious moralists the opposition between the moral and the useful, as in the case of group martyrdoms. (Though even the most intransigeant theologians find some use in martyrdom, since "in the blood of the martyrs is the seed of the Church.")

Religious traditions have alleged to provide both a rock of absolute foundation, God, and his absolute commands—those of a God so completely pure spirit that his commands have a moral quality inherent in them. They are untinctured either by fleshliness, relativity or utility. Only in religion, it is argued, can morality be raised from the purely relative and the purely conventional and trivial, to the eternal, the exalted, the divinely good.

All this is familiar enough to anyone who has read Kant or

St. Paul, or their current more fashionable spokesmen. It would be idle to pretend that these familiar critiques of a purely relative and purely secular morality are beneath consideration. Obviously, they would not have been considered as seriously and as long as they were. I realize, no less than the next philosopher, that very considerable ingenuity has been expended on these arguments, and that very considerable adroitness is needed even to give pause to those who hold them. But ingenuity of dialectic does not hide the questions that are begged in many theological systems, and a secular point of view depends on verifiable data rather than on fine-spun dialectical demonstration.

Moreover, in addition to the impressiveness of centuries of argument, those who take a theological view of nature and man have a clear psychological advantage. They are effective through persuasion, not through logic alone. In the words, in the very tone of the words they have the winning power of centuries of accrued association, of symbols touched with age-old poetry, of familiar pieties, of the touching language of mystical devotion, of ceremonies at once elevated and rich with childhood memories.

Those, on the other hand, who have busied themselves in formulating the secular point of view, have rarely been poets and mystics, and even where they have been, they have felt that they had prior work to do. Broadly speaking, they have been intellectual entrepreneurs like Francis Bacon, or passionate assailants of religion like Lucretius, or of the church, like Voltaire. In more recent times, proponents of the secular point of view have been preoccupied either with controversial defense or attack, or with the minutiae or the drynesses of method. They have, as it were, let spiritual values go by default. They have left it to the angelic hosts, or to those who regard themselves as their agents, to have all the good songs, all the poetry of insight and idealism, or moral grandeur. Eager to avoid rhetoric, the secular-minded have forgotten the poetry of existence. The forms of, and images in which, the spiritual life is brought home to men have been neglected in the interest of the exact formulas of understanding.

The ends and values of life are what human beings experience them to be. It would scarcely be argued seriously, save by those with a theological axe to grind, that values would be values at all, save for the human beings to whom they are values. Values valued by no one would be the square circles of morality. Certain values or goods are not altogether dissimilar from generation to generation, but are regarded as paramount and ultimate by sensitive and reflective men and women. Upon some of these the secular and the theologically-minded often seem able to agree. The theist and the atheist, for example, recognize some of the same values in the non-Christian literature and art of ancient Greece. It is not generally denied by well-read bishops that even where theological language is used in Greek tragedy, it is flexible, tentative, metaphorical. The Greek gods are forms of expression of such natural forces as any empiricist would be ready to recognize. No one in Greek literature takes the gods very literally; no one but a Thomist would confuse Aristotle's God with the Christian deity, or Plato's with that of even a liberal canon of the Church of England.

Even theologians, I take it, are prepared to admit that human beings experience in art and in life what one may call moments of secular exaltation. These need not be, and often are not, in any way connected with or dependent upon any belief in a world elsewhere, or any commitment to any theology or any communion with a church. Human beings have sacrificed themselves with sublime detachment to ideals that could not in any way, save the most metaphorical, be called supernatural. Soldiers and scientists, teachers and doctors, social workers and government officials have devoted their lives sacrificially to the good of a group or a nation or mankind—although convinced that there was no eventual kingdom of God to which all mankind is moving. Men have been known to have a saintly love of all mankind, who, while they believed all men to be in their origin and their common hopes brothers, could not believe in any literal sense that they were children of God. In our own time, secular minds no less than believers, and possibly more optimistically than some of those, are concerned for the future of mankind which (should there be any future at all) would surely outlast their own short lives.

Pagans, no less than religious minds in our time, have experienced moments of sublimity—have, if one will, experienced "the sublime"—when confronted with imagined tragedy in art, or the actual tragedies of human beings in our own dreadful era, or the general human plight in any era. The beauty and the wonder of human nature have been loved by those who in no traditional sense believe in the soul or immortality. Men who do not think that in order to recognize—and forgive—human weaknesses, human beings must first be regarded simply as vessels of corruption, have experienced charity for human nature. Men have fought for the liberation and nurture of spiritual values without counting at all on a miracle of grace. Finally, generous minds and hearts have been able to interest themselves in the adventure of mankind, without believing that that adventure is endless, or that it adds up to a single meaning. They have felt it a sufficient challenge to action, imagination and thought to render life as rich with meanings as possible.

All these generous aspects of the secular imagination are clearly "spiritual" in character. They have been evidences to theologians that even the conscious pagan is willy-nilly a religious creature. I think what they mean is that natural man has spiritual possibilities, and the flesh comes to spiritual fruition. Such is exactly the point of this paper. This perishing earthly creature, man, for all his lusts, confusions, and weaknesses, is on occasion an artist, a hero, a saint. This is revealed unwillingly even by the most crabbed historians of mankind. But this is not to say that the hero, the artist or the saint needs a theology to explain him, or that he need have one—or that it need in either case be Christian. The values, devotion to which and absorption in which have made the artist, the hero and the saint, are not dependent on the belief of these men in a providentially arranged system of nature or a divinely purposed march of history.

Men born to perish have given their awed allegiance, their breathless adoration, to causes and things outside themselves. Sometimes they have given them to things other human beings have made, like the plays of Shakespeare or the symphonies of Mozart. Some of them have felt as imperative an obligation to do what was helpful to their fellows as others have felt obligated to do what was commanded by God. They have rallied to movements for peace and justice, without any belief in the fatherhood of God. They have felt that men are in the same boat, though the boat has no port marked out for it, and there may be no port at all. It would,

I think, be difficult to find one spiritual value or one spiritual manifestation, any moral discipline or moral standard within the domain of religious tradition, that has not equally been practiced outside the sphere of theologies and churches. Nor is there any reason to think that charity or hope, happiness or salvation, need to find their source or their support in the supernatural or in the arms of a church. Nature nourishes spirit as the soil sustains flowers. One need not look to a world elsewhere, and the bright gleams in the clouded history of mankind are there to prove it.

The Affirmation of Man

✒ BY HORACE FRIESS
Columbia University

GOETHE has a short philosophical poem on "The Divine" (*Das Göttliche*) which begins:

> Edel sei der Mensch,
> Hilfreich und gut!
> Denn das allein
> Unterscheidet ihn
> Von allen Wesen,
> Die wir kennen.

These lines are so simple, it is impossible to keep their poetic bloom in a close translation. But I will venture to express their thought in this way:

> Let man be human-hearted ever,
> High-minded and constructive his endeavor.
> Of all known creatures he alone
> Can choose this way to be his own.

I use "high-minded" for "*edel*," "constructive" for "*hilfreich*," and "human-hearted" for "*gut.*"

In their simplicity these lines have magnitude and a thrilling sureness of touch. The whole poem, indeed, is superb on the same counts. The poet, of course, does not need to explain his terms "*hilfreich und gut*," as a philosopher might try to do. Though, as a matter of fact, in his last stanza, he writes:

> Der edle Mensch
> Sei hilfreich und gut!
> Unermüdet schaff' er
> Das Nützliche, Rechte.

Philosophical reflection, however, can not avoid raising the question whether an illusory idealization of man underlies Goethe's

128

whole conception. Can man be expected to work for what is useful and right without tiring? Can his example in so doing give a real intimation of "the Divine," as the poem elsewhere suggests? Can man choose to be ever human-hearted, high-minded and constructive in his endeavor? It is no news that doubts have been raised on these points.

The affirmation of man is more than a theoretical concern. It has, as Aristotle says of "ethics," a practical interest. We are interested, not only in knowing "man," but in how we are to be members of the human race. The aim of this present essay is not to affirm a theoretical doctrine about man, so much as it is to assist in the practical affirmation of man. Its intention, therefore, is to discuss the bearing of a certain fund of ideas, rather than of a single thesis, upon the active enterprise of living more or less fully as men. The conduct of life suffers if its guiding ideas turn out to be unreliable or too wide of the facts. Some sceptical souls seek to avoid this by extending little credit in their strict economy of ideas. But too limited a supply of ideas will also subtract from one's earnings. It is best neither to be a dupe of illusions, nor needlessly to sacrifice real possibilities in one's heritage as a man. One wants neither to be fooled, nor to fall short as a half-real person.

Philosophers are particularly allergic to the thought of being deceived by illusions, yet, like all other men, they come by their illusions in ways that make these very difficult to expel. In so far as philosophers make it their business to question ideas, they are unusually favored to discover unreliable ones. But no one can thoroughly scrutinize every influence and relation affecting him. And the invalid ideas do not stand out of the mass with identification tags to invite inspection. They generally pass along in comfortable congruence, real or apparent, with wishes and habits and procedures that compose life's familiar round. Hence to discover illusions, especially when they are part of a man's more unconsciously molded patterns, usually requires some jolt to his existence.

Personal history grips even philosophers. They may come to know some eternal verities and to have genuine love of wisdom. But in meeting the common human challenge to affirm one's humanity amply and truly, to live fully and to see clearly, no one may expect to be more than partly successful. If there is such a thing as a perfect human life, it is something that includes limitation and error. There is no single doctrine or method that can guarantee a complete life and the seeing of it all truly. Personal fulfillment is always an individual sum. Each and all are limited to affirming, sifting, and testing specific matters selected in terms of their own lives.

Morris Cohen used to ask how certain contemporary philosophers could expect anthropology and sociology to become more scientific than metaphysics. The generic traits of being are within reach, he thought, of steady observation and analysis. But man's social and cultural life appears so contingent and variable as to remain, perhaps necessarily, a realm of conjecture. Probably no project of anthropological study can be more contingent than to explore the practical bearings of philosophical ideas, such as the present essay proposes to discuss. Certainly, by sifting my own experience with these ideas, I now expect only to locate a number of problems, and to suggest some hypotheses for their solution.

I.

The philosophical ideas that first reached me, and took effect, were mainly interpretations of man's moral nature and good. That teacher who gave me the customary academic "Introduction" had his students memorize certain key passages of Plato and Aristotle. One was the statement of Plato's that virtue is "a kind of health and beauty, and good habit of the soul; and vice is a disease, and deformity, and sickness of it" (*Republic,* IV, 444). Another was Aristotle's definition of "happiness" as "a complete life,"—"a life of activity in accordance with complete virtue, and sufficiently equipped with external goods, not for some chance period but throughout a complete life-time" (*Ethics,* I, 1101). These texts were far more to me than classic sayings learned at school. They had living significance, because they helped in transforming a home-spun, diligent energism, nurtured in my family, into a broader conception of human fulfillment. Two teachers especially, John J. Coss and Frederick Woodbridge, aided this realization by the attractive way they actually exemplified as well as professed these ideas. Their practice, as well as their conceptions, of the good life had richness and range. They were strenuously active, but with notable care for esthetic and theoretic as well as practical values. They were both fond of good living without being soft. There was a hearty and nourishing sense of humanity, coupled with great intellectual honesty, in what these men gave.

Two other teachers, Felix Adler and John Dewey, in the same years, brought many more ideas interpreting man's moral enterprise. The time was that of World War I. Adler and Dewey were both distinguished for active concern with forwarding community life in the spirit of modern democracy. Reinterpreting its universal and equalitarian perspectives, they both criticized the traditional individualistic canons. Their efforts in this respect did much to bring independent philosophizing into critical rapport with the socialistic movements of the age. The contrast in their mentalities also represented significant cultural issues. Felix Adler had a religious fervor of prophetic, transcendent cast; he implemented it intellectually with the aid of Kantian philosophy. John Dewey was as thoroughly dedicated to the development of experimental method and its human implications.

Transcendental and experimental concepts chased each other about in my thoughts. Some features of this encounter will be considered presently. But the main object at stake was an understanding of moral community, responsibility, and practical reason. The fund of ideas, congruent and divergent, which came to me chiefly from Aristotle, Kant, Felix Adler, and John Dewey, was focussed upon the interpretation and furthering of man's career as a social and rational being. To conceive practical reason as a reasonable concrete unifying of ends and means seemed more fertile than to regard it more abstractly as the pure form of universal law. But on such a view it remains problematic, one must admit, how comprehensive and universal practical reason, as a concrete unifying of ends and means, can be or can become. I could not answer, on this view, whether practical reason involves a general sovereign principle aligning all specific moralities in a single order of universal validity—and, if so, what that principle is.

Reflection on these philosophical questions did not take place in a great era of peace. Millions of people, like myself, lived through a great contradiction. We were brought up on benign teachings, in counsels intended to foster peaceful and reasonable co-operation.

But while we were at school, the world plunged into the most gigantic wars of history. The outbreak of World War I, in 1914, took almost everyone by surprise. It was only later, in the course of that war's aftermath, the revolutions and conflicts unleashed, that by historical review one became aware of a progressively mounting violence among the civilized nations—a trend which has not yet one fears, been arrested or reversed. In 1898 Moncure Conway asked Herbert Spencer for his advice about setting up an international arbitration tribunal to avoid war. Spencer replied:

> . . . in people's present mood nothing can be done in that direction. . . . Now that we have entered upon an era of social cannibalism, in which the strong nations are devouring the weaker, . . . there is a bad time coming. . . . The universal aggressiveness and universal culture of blood-thirst will bring back military despotism, out of which, after many generations, partial freedom may again emerge. (M. D. Conway, *Autobiography*, vol. ii, p. 448-49).

This dark foreboding at the very threshold of the century is all the more striking in being voiced by Herbert Spencer, whose "principles of sociology" taught that the growth of industrial society would promote peace among men.

Now, despite all evil in World War II, one may still hesitate to conclude that Spencer was wrong in his long-term predictions of progress, and right only in his dark sense of imminent regressions. The nineteenth-century dream of industrial man dispossessing military man may slowly prove to be more than a grand illusion. But it is not yet clear what the events of the 1930's and '40's have really done to man's sense of himself. It is not the sheer horror in those events, but their effect on men's sense and systems of responsibility that is in question. World War I came to my generation before we had reached an age of responsibility for public affairs. But now, as adults, we had to face our inability to check the further march to destruction and coarsening of life. What are our children inheriting? Can we really expect them to do better than we did, and to work through to a more humane world?

With such uneasiness prevalent, the gospel of repent and be saved no doubt meets a rising need. A sense of man's inveterate sinfulness and need of grace is freshly and genuinely felt. But can the concept of sin, even when reinforced with up-to-date insights, bring sufficient illumination and relief of man's manifold plight? The nails of compunction have perhaps been driven in a bit further by the special attention which Reinhold Niebuhr and other contemporaries give to "the children of light" and the sins of moralism. It is good to shake the subtler forms of complacency. Yet how thoroughly can man be brought to grips with himself—as he certainly needs to be—in terms of confession, fear and trembling, and the like?

It has been hard, during much of the recent past, to keep in mind man's works as *"edel, hilfreich, und gut."* I remember students in the 1930's coming to class gasping and unnerved, when some atrocious abuse of human beings had been proclaimed by a leader of state as public policy. To make a virtue of deliberate distortion was peculiarly upsetting to all engaged in seeking truth. The conception of man, as a creature signalized by practical reason, seems not to cover all the facts. On the other hand, to call him an old sinner may be too easy a way to balance the account. It seems important to make a more differentiated and fresh inventory of man's capacities, including his manifold excesses and ability to reach extremes in all directions. During the '30's I began to think, not for the first time, but more searchingly than before about crime, and madness, saintliness, virtuosity, and genius. I began to think of man as a creature "fearfully and wonderfully made" (*Psalms* 139:14), and as showing himself to be such, both in war and peace. Certainly I was living in a fearful, and in many respects a wonderful age. And I felt compelled to ponder man's bursting the familiar bounds of reasonable living in so many astonishing ways.

The word "wonderful" is here used primarily in a secular rather than in a religious sense. It refers to what is extraordinary, extreme, strange, and astonishing, whether or not such things and events be taken as signs of divine presence or supernatural power. When they are so taken, we have wonders or miracles in the usual religious sense. The distinction has particular, though not exclusive, bearing on such a category as saintliness. Everyday discourse often enough applies the word "saint" to persons regarded as of extraordinary or heroic virtue. In the traditions of religion, however, the saints must also be accredited with miracles. They are wonderful people, not only in a sense relative to other human beings, but in that they appear to have been visited extraordinarily by something of more than human power. These religious qualifications adhere clearly to pagan "heroes," such as Oedipus, Achilles, Orestes, as much as to the saints of more otherworldly religions.

Returning to the main theme, the capacity of man for excess and extreme achievement runs in all directions. In one mode or other it is actual or potential in the many as well as in the few. The mention of crime and madness does not imply that all instances of these categories are fearful and wonderful, though many are. From Herodotus down, history and narration are as replete with remarkable tales of crime and of madness as with the wonders of great virtuosity and genius. In these latter categories, the variety in our day ranges from an Einstein to the circus-performer, Unus, who has taken the trouble to learn to balance his body on one finger. All this excess gives the human world a far greater richness than practical reason has need for, or is well-prepared to handle.

The genius that gives man gas engines, nuclear fission, and so on, has a faculty, greater than crime or madness, for occasioning practical and moral difficulties. Tradition, in many climes, also holds that it is necessary for saints to get out of the home. Man's wonderful excesses are apt to outdo his moralities. They do not neatly fit the patterns, in which practical reason undertakes to unite ends and means. At the same time, man as moral and man as wonderful do not exist apart, but in complex interrelations. A wise lawgiver can be justly reckoned among the more wonderful of men. The saint and criminal, madman and genius, to exist in their several ways, have each to make a moral reckoning with the community, and sometimes they achieve high individual success in doing so. But more important still, the success of practical reason, as a community matter, clearly involves the relation achieved between what is extraordinary in people and their doings and the general system of ends and means.

The human scene must convince us, I think, of moral limitation, but not of man's moral failure. When the whole range of the propensities for the fearful and wonderful, existing not in the few alone but also in the many, is really considered, then the limited partial successes of moral organization and practical reason must appear impressive. They clearly constitute an essential part of the affirmation of man, though they do less than justice to what is in him. Practical reason, like government finance, is not generally bankrupt, though it is never caught up in giving everything its due. Again, like governments, our concrete systems of practical reason have been the moralities of partial communities rather than of all mankind. Expensive hot and cold wars have been more or less chronic between them. One day this condition might conceivably cease, and one moral system approve itself for all men, but it is far from clear that this will happen, or that mankind would achieve a more complete life if it did.

There appears to be more *itinerarium mentis* than argument and analysis in the course of these reflections. But they do contain a thesis, which can now be more succinctly stated. The enterprise of living fully as human beings, without failing through deficiency or overreaching through illusory aims, is the problem referred to as the affirmation of man. The thesis concerns how man is to be affirmed in view of his extraordinarily rich capacities, and at the same time his need of moral community and responsibility. One indispensable foundation of human fulfillment is a system of practical reason for unifying many different ends and means. But such moral systems can not be expected to accomplish all that may be done to affirm man. In the manifold excesses of man—in those of genius and saintliness as well as in crime and madness—there are obviously illusions which practical reason must condemn. But in these same excesses there are also truths which point to a fuller humanity, and which reflect illusions or at least limitations in the prevailing moralities. It is, therefore, a function of art and science, of religion and of ethical aspiration, liberally to explore all these realms, and to catch, if possible, the meaning for a more complete affirmation of man of many things considered foreign or even hostile to morality.

It may seem that the thesis as stated is exceedingly broad. It may seem that, for peace of mind, I am seeking a way to say "yes" to everything and anything. It may seem that no room has been left to distinguish a negating from an affirming of man. I do not plead guilty to such indiscrimination, though gladly, if I may, to the charge of broadness. In defense of the latter I might quote from Scripture: "I have seen an end of all perfection, but thy commandment is exceeding broad." (*Psalms* 119:96.) But it seems to me the thesis, for all its breadth, leaves room for at least two ways of denying man. One is by holding to a lifeless or killing, a no longer life-giving, moral system. The other is by a fanaticism which seeks to make a peculiar or special form of life generally normative. To help identify, warn against, and work against such deadly tendencies seems to me an ever-pertinent charge of philosophers.

II.

The bearing of these broad conclusions upon that fund of philosophical ideas mentioned earlier in this essay invites at least brief discussion at this time. The energistic ethics, associated with Aristotle, a doctrine of fulfillment in characteristic human activities, remains basically appealing and convincing. A young girl has told me, however, that Aristotle's definition of "a complete life" lacks singing quality. The criticism is very aptly taken of his rather staid accents, but an energistic outlook on life need not have this deficiency. The affirming as well as the lulling of activity often breaks into song. Simple work-songs of the fields sometimes carry a thrill that seems to connect with life's roots and core. Here is such a song from the Chinese *Book of Odes*:

> Ho, there! clear the weeds!
> Ho, there! stub up the roots of forest!
> Let your ploughs cleave the clods!
> Thousands of couples, go and hoe!
> There, to the valleys; there, to the heights!
> Here is the master and his first-born!
> Here are the younger ones, the children, the
>   helpers, and the journeymen.
>   (After Marcel Granet, *Chinese Civilization*, p. 141.)

One part of Aristotelean ethics, which I found difficult to evaluate, was the doctrine of virtue as "a mean between extremes." For a long while I puzzled over the place of moderation and prudence in personal conduct. But I did not see my way to a sufficiently inclusive view of the matter. Aristotle's making "the mean" relative to the individual seemed wise, but whether, even with this flexible provision, justice could be done with the concept to the moral states of sinners and saints remained doubtful. Is virtue never an extreme state? So perplexed, I regarded the doctrine of "the mean" as secondary and less universally normative than the central energistic and functional ideas of Aristotle. But now it occurs to me that a more inclusive and adequate estimate of this particular doctrine may be reached, if personal considerations are not allowed to obscure the social perspective. A whole community or society, one may venture to judge, could not draw the working norms of its moral life, without qualification, from extreme cases, such as saints or robber barons, for example. Ethics as a branch of politics must pay attention to the mean range of behavior in considering social standards. And yet not to this alone, for rejection and condemnation of extremes by the community can become impoverishing and perhaps even unsafe. Virtue, to conclude, does not have to seek a "mean" as its essence in all individuals, but there is an important sense in which, as a social norm, it is drawn centripetally around the middle ranges of conduct.

In considering moral questions from a social, as well as a personal, perspective, I was greatly helped both by Felix Adler and John Dewey. Both teachers strongly emphasized social ethics, and also the social character of personality itself. Both were concerned with the nature and growth of democratic community. But each placed his major emphasis upon different requirements. Dewey stressed the importance of everyone finding access to the means implied in an experimental social process. Adler sought to define or reconstrue an overarching ideal principle of membership in community, something functionally equivalent to Kant's categorical imperative or law for a realm of ends.

Idealistic philosophers have argued that without such a general sovereign principle moral judgment becomes arbitrary and opportunistic. The ultimate ideal foundations of practical reason, responsibility, and moral community, it is claimed, are neglected or even undermined by experimentalism. There is another side to the case, however. Attachment to general principles will also provide inadequate foundations for moral judgment, if attention is not given to those concrete and specific conditions, ends and means that experimentalism stresses. Moreover, in my own experience, I discovered that it is possible to become theoretically an advocate of experimental method without being seriously experimental in one's own thinking habits. Before ever meeting Dewey as a teacher, through reading *How We Think* and the *Essays in Experimental Logic,* the significance of his work as a methodologist gripped me immediately, but real assimilation of his ideas proceeded only very gradually. It took a long while, and several shocks, to perceive how precious few "complete acts of thought," in the Deweyan sense, I performed. More often my mental gait took me on rambles, *"aux vacances dans le ciel."*

The purport of these remarks is not to claim that general principles, *e.g.* those of Kant, have no earthly use, but that their use is not a simple matter of course. The use Felix Adler made of his modified Kantian principles of community was clear and definite enough. He thought it a crucial matter of principle "to lay the same equal stress on multiplicity as on unity, on diversity as on likeness." With the traditional emphasis in ethics on unity and universal relations, he sought to combine a coordinate stress on the unique and differentiated members related in community. The supreme moral law, as he interpreted it, is one of community in the sense of mutually furthering interaction between different natures and functions. The applications Adler made of these general ideas were critical of individualism, but also of single-tracked collectivisms that viewed society in any one dominant pattern. Family, school, vocation, state, and religious association were each and all regarded as essential organs for cultivating various indispensable relationships, but absolute sovereignty in the moral community was not claimed for any institution, person, or set of persons.

Morris Cohen always made abundantly clear, in his philosophical works, the leading significance he attached to the principle of conjoint search, and regard for both unity and multiplicity in all fields. I could not help observing, however, that in relating the principle to experience, he and Professor Adler went each his own way. There was nothing the least strange in such a divergence, but for me it cast certain philosophical lights and shadows anew. The overarching principle of diversity within unity involves some form of universal harmony, either immanent or transcendent. But what will appear in concrete cases, in the way of harmony, remains, of course, ambiguous. The principles of universal community, which men conceive, do not control history, or reveal the fate of conflicts in man's world with its many partial communities. General ideas soundly conceived indicate conditions and possibilities of achievement, but events remain ambiguous. The illusion of escaping conflicts by a metaphysical idea, or vision, of harmony should be transparent, however it may persist. Neither Felix Adler nor Morris Cohen was subject to this illusion; neither inferred from his metaphysical principles any absence or vanity of conflict in the human world. Both were long and hardy fighters in the human causes they so strongly espoused. Indeed, unpolemical temperaments might not easily come to terms with the martial qualities in these two men. But there was powerful medicine in the effort so to do. For surely, the affirmation of man would but limp along, if critical minds in every generation did not learn what to fight, and why, and how.

The good fight is clearly one of life's constant charges. Up to a point, it is a cost that adds genuinely to the value of its object. It is hard indeed to imagine how life would taste without the relish of struggle. But, for all that, one must admit the seasoning is rarely well-mixed. For many it comes too high and fiery. To fight in just cause, and not to mere exhaustion, certainly does belong to the affirmation of man. But the same can not be said of all the fearful mistaken battles against himself to which man is prone. This whole misery can not easily be swallowed as so much sauce to a good dish.

In fact, it seems almost frivolous to suggest that man's torn state could be taken that way. Today it seems once again fitting to face the old question how man is to stomach the dish of evil set before him. Would he be helped by taking more of the ancient "medicine of immortality" into his system? The fact that so much of the evil from which he suffers is self-inflicted persuades many that otherworldly medicine is indicated. The faults in man are so deep, they say, that he can not find a clear path to strength and to wholeness except by looking beyond himself, to some transcendent ideal, or natural law, or God. A sound and healing affirmation of man must be anchored in something greater and better than man.

In estimating this argument it is important to remember that otherworldliness takes many forms, and is not always supernaturalistic. The this-worldly world is the world of business, sport, fashion, and of social concern that most of us find is "too much with us" unless we have touch with another world too. The nature-lover, the contemplative, Spinoza and his intellectual amor, Morris Cohen "dispraising life," and many more can exemplify varieties of naturalistic otherworldliness. Again, there is great variety to be found in what is recommended, even within one religious tradition, as relation to a supernatural other world. It can be ecstatic experience, submission to an absolute Word, participation in rites and symbols of ultimate concern, rejection of the world, confession of dependence on divine mercy, and still other forms of reference to a transcendent source of salvation.

Arguments for otherworldliness often present some one form of it as the indispensable sovereign remedy for human ills. To me the really impressive evidence of its genuine and enduring value to man comes far more from the great variety of the forms that it takes. It does not seem unlikely that each of these many forms of otherworldliness can bear some weight of man's burden, and can give some true testimony as to his predicaments, longings, and sense of possibilities in a universe of unknown magnitude. But it does seem unlikely that the cure of all man's ills can come from exclusive faith in one otherworldly remedy, any more than it could from fanatic reliance on some this-worldly panacea. Philosophers must question also an indiscriminate swallowing of the whole pharmacopeia which assumes that man is just an empty reed or a bottomless pit. Therapy needs knowledge and an understanding regard for man, lest mistaken medicine merely aggravate his disease.

The role of otherworldliness in the affirmation of man is not a single equation. It varies as its many forms relate to man in his requirements as a creature of practical reason and moral community, and to his propensities for fearful and wonderful excesses. The facts of human existence in both these aspects are not to be dodged. For his own good, man surely must give searching heed to the larger world beyond him in which his life is set, yet he must not expect to find there the realization of what is distinctly human. What he finds there has meaning for his own affirmation only in its bearing upon human capacities.

To affirm man is to seek as clear vision and as complete life as we can through good and bad fortune. We should hope for friends, such as Moliere describes so well in *The Misanthrope,* who will do all they can to dissuade us from any desperate wishes to resign from the human race. In the sense of so teaching a firm allegiance to the human enterprise this doctrine is a form of humanism. But it does not imply any conception of man as stranger in a world either alien to him or empty of value save for his works. The affirmation of man is not well served by squinting at the larger universe that surrounds us.

Nature and the Human Spirit

BY SIDNEY HOOK
New York University

*T*HE present situation in human history is a challenge to philosophers to vindicate their traditional claim to the possession of a vision that can help integrate and enrich human experience. What is required of such vision is that it avoid arbitrariness and pretentiousness, and hold out some promise—however modest—of fruitful co-operation among those different peoples and cultures of the world which have a will to co-operate.

Viewed in the light of the history of philosophy, the great danger of all philosophical thought which goes beyond logical analysis of categories is not an excess of speculation—which has at least an imaginative appeal—but an excess of salvationary zeal. The great systems have made promises that they cannot possibly fulfill. For they have ignored the fact that the concrete issues which divide men and inspire conflict have their primary locus in economic, political, and national life. No philosophical vision or synthesis can provide viable answers to them in their own terms. It is well to admit openly that there is no royal philosophical road to social salvation, however it may be with the quest for personal salvation. And if by personal salvation we mean the achievement of a sane and dignified order in the life of individuals, recent history furnishes a grim but conclusive reminder that for the overwhelming majority of men this is impossible until a stable and more equitable social order has been introduced.

Nonetheless it is undeniable that philosophical attitudes have a broad even if indirect bearing upon the problems of human experience. To the extent that they mobilize human attention and effort along some lines and divert them from others, they have practical consequences even when they preach detachment and withdrawal. I am not here maintaining that any *specific* philosophical doctrines have logical consequences for specific problems

—in fact I shall be concerned to deny this—but only that certain basic points of view which express value judgments have a selective impact upon the variety of problems given at any moment, and on the possible approaches to these problems.

The position of this paper is that the philosophy of *naturalistic* humanism, which regards man as an integral but distinctive part of nature, as wholly a creature of natural origin and natural end, offers an adequate and fruitful basis for the social reconstruction which is essential for the emergence of patterns of human dignity on a world-wide scale. This view in recent years has been the object of sustained criticisms from various quarters which have called into question the self-sufficiency of man. Some years ago, adopting a phrase from Gilbert Murray's account of the stages of Greek religion, I referred to this anti-naturalistic movement as "the new failure of nerve." Since then it has taken on the proportions of a tidal wave in philosophy, theology, literature and the philosophy of history. Characteristic of its views are two beliefs: (1) that our time of troubles is primarily an historical and logical consequence of the abandonment of the religious and metaphysical foundations of Western civilization and of a shift to secularism; and (2) that what gives genuine happiness to man, and relief from the multiple alienations which fragmentize both personality and society, in the words of St. Augustine "is something which does not proceed from human nature but which is above human nature." And from these beliefs the criticism follows that naturalism in any form is incapable of doing justice to the actually experienced qualities of human life, particularly the nature of man's moral experience.

Before proceeding to a logical analysis of these criticisms a few historical remarks are in order. The notion that the decline of medieval supernaturalism gave rise to a secular naturalistic humanism which enjoyed the same position of authority and prestige as the philosophy it replaced is a legend that will no more bear examination than its countermyth which holds that the rise of Christian supernaturalism resulted not from the bankruptcy of pagan supernaturalism but from the alleged failure of Greco-Roman secularism. The life of a culture is expressed primarily in its institutions and the *institutional* history of Europe nowhere reveals the presence of a unifying humanistic secular philosophy to integrate with the heritage of the past the radical changes precipitated by war, scientific technology, and the expansion of the capitalist economy. On the contrary, the new tendencies of industrialization, urbanization, and nationalism were neither predicted nor prepared for by any philosophy, either supernaturalist or naturalist. They made their way in the teeth of the old traditions which were helpless to cope with them and which ultimately were compelled by the logic of events to make uneasy compromises with the historical situations they could not exorcise. The defenders of traditional supernaturalism systematically engaged themselves not so much with the social *problems* resulting from the uncontrolled expansion of the new productive forces in Europe as in a furious polemic against the humanistic striving to find the new social forms and institutions which, without aborting the burst of creative energy unleashed by the industrial revolution, would sustain through the operating institutions of a reconstructed society the dignity of all human beings.

One could make a far better historical case for the contrary view. To the extent that the dilemmas and tragedies of modern culture are attributable to ideological factors, a greater responsibility rests with a supernaturalist philosophy which was powerless to prevent the emergence of the tendencies it deplored or to give them a moral direction once they appeared, than to the chaotic multitude of doctrines—among which naturalistic humanism was the weakest—that sought, often by transparent rationalizations of sectional and class interests, to give some moral meaning and direction to the new social developments.

Nor in face of the assertion that the wars, revolutions, and bestial atrocities of our century are a consequence of the abandonment of the transcendent religious and metaphysical beliefs of the past, must we overlook the significance of the fact that those centuries when European culture rested on religious foundations were marked, once allowance is made for scale, by practices of persecution and extermination almost as inhuman as those committed by modern totalitarianisms.

1. But historical considerations aside, it is demonstrable that no set of metaphysical or theological statements by themselves en-

tail any specific empirical consequences about the life of man or the structure of human society. Without raising the questions here of the criteria of meaningfulness and verification of such statements, it is apparent that they are compatible with mutually inconsistent social beliefs and the most diverse social institutions. For example, the same set of premises about divine existence, immortality, the nature of substance and the self have been held by believers in feudalism, capitalism, and socialism, by democrats as well as by totalitarians. This indicates that belief in the first set of propositions is not a sufficient condition of belief in the second set of propositions. And we are all acquainted with principled advocates of democracy or dictatorship, capitalism or socialism who regard the metaphysical and theological propositions often offered in alleged justification of these institutions as either meaningless or false which establishes that belief in them is certainly not a necessary condition of social doctrine and action. Indeed, *logically,* with sufficient ingenuity, allegiance to any social system can be squared with belief in any metaphysical system whatsoever.

This has sometimes been denied by those for whom metaphysical and theological statements are value judgments in disguise. When challenged they retreat to the position that the validity of moral judgments rests upon transcendental truths of a metaphysical or theological nature. Not only does such a position destroy the autonomy of moral experience, it is exposed to the same logical and historical difficulties that we have noted above. To the extent that transcendental beliefs are disguised value judgments, the actual relation between theology and morals is obscured. For it is indisputable that far from morals being historically derived from theological beliefs, men have always created their gods in their own moral image. The voice that stayed the hand of Abraham as he was about to slay Isaac is identified as the voice of the true God rather than the false one or the Devil because of Abraham's prior moral insight into the wickedness of human sacrifice.

2. Any attempt to find a basis to improve the human estate by resort to a principle "above human nature" is doomed to failure because it cannot supply definite criteria to guide the construction of the programs of action required to meet the concrete needs, wants, and aspirations of men which are very much part of human

nature and in which the most pressing problems of a domestic and international character are rooted. Ideals and ends that are out of time and so lack a natural basis can never be brought into logical and causal continuity with the means recommended to achieve them, for all such means are temporal acts with temporal consequences. The result of postulating ends that are outside of time and of postulating principles above human nature is that the *choice* of means, without which ends cannot be realized or tested, is lamed at the outset. Freed from critical direction, human choice *professedly* oriented to principles above human nature, oscillates between the extremes of dogmatism and opportunism.

The proposal of naturalistic humanism is to approach the problems of men in their natural and social contexts and to test the validity of all theoretical claims, not by examining their presuppositions but by investigating their empirical consequences. In refusing to allow this concern with antecedent presuppositions to dominate intellectual activity, in pointing out that conflicting varieties of presuppositions are equally compatible with verifiable fact, the naturalistic humanists seek to give the criterion of fruitfulness the same standing in all inquiry as it has in inquiry in the natural sciences. There is no guarantee, of course, that human beings, endowed with variant as well as common needs, will agree upon consequences, but a great deal of human experience testifies that in some areas and in some periods this is possible, sometimes even normal. One of the most impressive expressions of that human experience is the existence of democratic communities in which to a large part a consensus of belief and action in respect to political institutions and processes has been established among individuals holding the most varied metaphysical and theological presuppositions. What is being suggested by this proposal to take consequences not presuppositions as a point of departure is that those processes of inquiry by which in some parts of the world idealists and materialists, atheists and theists, Catholics, Protestants, Jews and Mohammedans have been able to reach a community of working agreement be employed to explore all the empirical problems and difficulties that beset men today.

Where needs are common, there are as a rule much less differences among human beings as to what constitutes endurable or unendurable, satisfactory or unsatisfactory, resolutions of problems than there are over metaphysical or theological presuppositions. To wait upon agreement on first or last principles as a precondition for a solution of what may be called "the intermediate" problems of human experience is hardly a counsel of wisdom in view of the fact that there is no accepted method by which the conflict of first or last principles of this type can be settled, whereas objective methods of settling "intermediate problems" exist that can extend the area of *uncoerced* agreement among men. To be sure, the results won in the latter case are tentative and piecemeal but they make up in impressive number for what they lack in pretentious promise. It would hardly be an exaggeration to say that any attempt to make agreement on philosophical presuppositions a condition precedent for co-operative action would hopelessly divide the world and destroy the working unity established in many existing human communities.

The obvious retort to this is that naturalistic humanism has its own presuppositions. Certainly, but what I am urging here is not the acceptance of its presuppositions but of its program of orientation and work, a program which is justified by its fruitful consequences, and not by its alleged presuppositions. The argument avoids vicious circularity because at the outset it makes no other appeal than to the reasonable procedures recognized not only by philosophers but by all other men in their successful working practice in solving the problems that confront them in daily life.

It is in the light of those reasonable procedures that naturalistic humanism sees no warrant in experience for belief either in two separate worlds or two truths or two generic methods of reaching truths although it recognizes plural modes or levels of association and existence within nature, and a multiplicity of special methods and techniques which reflect the characteristic differences between the living and the non-living, the purposeful and the non-purposeful, the historical and the non-historical. Just as it refuses to separate man from society and society from nature, so it refuses to draw a sharp line of separation or opposition between scientific method on the one hand, and the reasonable procedures in the primary knowledge-getting activities of men struggling to control their environment, on the other. With the

development of instruments of measurement and the use of mathematical notation, science becomes more abstract, more systematic,
more precise, more complex. *But wherever a man had an idea
sufficiently clear to enable him to draw a logically valid inference,
the truth of whose conclusion he sought to test by controlled observation or experiment, he was proceeding—no matter how primi-
tively—in a scientific way.* His procedure was reasonable. The continuity between reasonable procedures in reaching conclusions about
matters of fact of everyday concern, and the procedures by which
we make the most esoteric discoveries in the advanced sciences cannot be breached without making the whole enterprise of science a
mystery. For every science starts from and returns to some of these
reasonable procedures.

It is in its allegiance to the continuity of scientific analysis
from field to field that naturalistic humanism differentiates itself
from all other varieties of humanism, and in its insistence on the
plurality and qualitative specificity of the different fields of experience that it differentiates itself from all other varieties of naturalism. It is not in virtue of any of its alleged presuppositions but
because it follows the lead of scientific method from its primal to
advanced stage that it holds that the occurrence of all qualities
and events depends upon the organization of a material system in
space-time, and that their emergence, development and disappearance are determined by change in such organization.

3. At first blush it would seem that the philosophy of naturalistic humanism would be regarded as not inadequate—in its intention, at least—to encompass the whole life of man. For it recognizes the complex natural interrelations of man—interrelations
made even more complex by his behavior as an historical creature
in time, with a developing society and consciousness which, within
certain limits, can influence the natural conditions of his existence.
But for historical reasons which I shall not here examine, such a
philosophy has been criticized for impoverishing human experience,
denigrating the human status in the cosmos, and closing the ave-
nues to new truths and insights.

The grounds on which such criticisms have been based are
many. But I limit myself only to three: (a) that scientific explanation is inadequate to what is distinctly human, (b) that it neces-

sarily entails 'reductionism', and (c) that even if everything else distinctively human could be shown to be accessible to scientific analysis, it is, and will remain, helpless before the facts and problems of moral experience.

(a) Scientific explanation consists in the subsumption under general laws of particular phenomena which have fulfilled certain initial defining conditions, thus enabling us to predict and sometimes to control events. To say, therefore, that scientific explanation cannot account for what is *uniquely* human is in one sense a truism, in another sense false. It is a truism in the sense that we cannot explain any unique event, not only in history but in physics. It is false, however, in suggesting that despite its uniqueness, a phenomenon cannot share common traits or relations with other unique phenomena. It is false further in suggesting that any trait which differentiates a class of phenomena from other classes, whether it be the mammary glands of mammals or man's rationality or sense of humor, cannot be correlated with material conditions of determination, physical or social. It is false in suggesting that scientific explanation is concerned with the totality of any event or even with one total event or that it pretends to finality or exhaustiveness in its account of any event or any aspect of any event.

The main question about human motives, for example, which are cited by Hocking and others as beyond scientific explanation, is not whether their existence can be accounted for in terms of laws about neural impulses or electronic movements. Although highly unlikely, this is not inconceivable. The question is whether determinate relations can be established between the occurrence, variation and intensity of motives and any changes in the historical, material space-time systems in which all individuals develop. A social or historical explanation of the operation of motives is entirely legitimate even if we do not understand very well its biological basis. In biology, for example, the laws of genetics are accepted as explanations of the facts of heredity although we cannot derive them from physical laws governing molecular phenomena. Yet it would be admitted that despite its lack of comparable exactness, biology is no less scientific than physics.

(b) This first criticism of naturalistic humanism is usually a preface to a more comprehensive indictment of scientific explanation as guilty of reductionism, of explaining away the very phenomena, particularly the consciousness of qualities, given in human experience. That some formulations of materialism in the past have given a superficial justification for this charge hardly extenuates this interpretation of modern naturalism. It is true that the language in which the *causes* of changes in qualitative experience is expressed contains terms which differ from those employed in the *descriptions* of human experience. But it is a complete non-sequitur to infer that therefore the existence of the qualities of human experience are rendered precarious in any way. The experience of qualities, whether it be the taste of sugar or the sense of awe, is irreducible as an experience. But it is not therefore inexplicable. Whether any particular naturalist is faithful in his descriptions is an empirical matter to be decided by controlled observation. And since the adequacy of his causal explanations depends in part on whether the experience in question can be reduplicated or transformed under certain conditions, it is literally absurd, if we take note of his procedure, to charge him with reductionism.

It is noteworthy that the charge of reductionism is rarely made against the physicist who explains variations in the distinctive properties of physical things, for example, their sound or color by variations in the quantities of qualities of another order. It is only when the distinctive qualities of human experience are explained that we hear the charge that according to naturalists man is "nothing but" this or that, "merely" a handful of salts in a solution of water, etc., despite the fact that he is proceeding no differently from the physicist who explains a snowflake in terms of certain laws of temperature and liquids without "reducing" the geometrical or esthetic patterns of snowflakes to such laws. It is appropriate to retort here that in virtue of its commitments to the logic of scientific method, naturalism proclaims that "Nothing is *nothing—but*" and "Nothing is *merely* one thing and not anything else."

It is hard to see how any scientific explanation of the qualities of the human spirit can in any way endanger these qualities, no matter how frail and exquisite they are. On the contrary, by revealing the structure of the material patterns in which they are enmeshed, they can, if we wish, be made more secure. Because it refuses to hypostasize these qualities and insists upon exploring their causes and consequences in the same spirit that it explores the qualities of the physical world, naturalistic humanism has from time to time provoked the hostility of those who feared that increasing knowledge might transform the world. Although such opposition asserts in argument that naturalism ignores the qualities of the human spirit, its secret hope is that materialism will ignore these qualities lest the power to control them be exercised in unacceptable ways.

In this connection two other points must be briefly touched upon. Insofar as mechanism is the belief that all human phenomena can be explained or predicted on the basis of the most general laws of physics, naturalistic humanism is not mechanistic. For it, variation, novelty and variation are not only undeniable facts of experience, it seeks to bring them about in different areas. And in virtue of its efforts, its failures as well as successes, it recognizes that many more things will occur than we can predict or control. It knows that human ideals and human volition, as well as knowledge of what transpired in the past, may enter as contributing conditions in redetermining the movement of events. The *same* antecedent conditions which determine objective alternatives do not determine the human perception and action which alter the probabilities that one or the other alternative will in fact be realized.

Nor is it true that according to naturalistic humanism only what can be observed exists. Both in science and common life many things may be reasonably inferred to exist from what is observed, and then confirmed by further observations. It does hold that where there is no evidence drawn from observed or observable effects, existence cannot be responsibly attributed. Otherwise the distinction between fact and fantasy disappears.

In the light of the foregoing we can now assess the paradoxical character of the criticism made by some critics of naturalistic humanism that "it blocks the paths of inquiry in that it seeks to settle by stipulation the very issue that we most need to be reasonable about if we can." And the ground for this criticism? In answer, we are told that "having committed themselves in advance to a position which identifies reasonable procedures with that which does not differ 'sharply' from that of the more developed sciences, they [the naturalistic humanists] will limit the scope of reasonable inquiry to what can be settled by the method these sciences employ."[1]

This charge rests upon a double confusion—one of interpretation and one of observation. It is not "reasonable procedure"—the basic pattern of inquiry—of which the naturalist says that it does not differ *sharply* from the more developed sciences but rather the techniques and body of knowledge which enable us to master our everyday affairs that do not differ sharply from the techniques and body of knowledge the sciences have developed. For *some* of the techniques and parts of the body of knowledge of the former are always incorporated in the latter. The reasonable procedure—which according to naturalistic humanists is emphatically not a special technique of any special science—is *identical* in every *formal* respect in every field in which we can lay claim to tested knowledge. How, then, can it serve as an obstacle to further inquiry, unless it is held that some disciplines have a basic pattern of inquiry quite different from that employed by critical common sense and science? What are these disciplines? What is this pattern? And what knowledge comparable in scope, reliability and capacity to elicit universal agreement has been won by it comparable to the achievements of other fields?

The error of observation in this criticism derives from the failure to note that the driving motivation of modern naturalistic humanism has been not to block but to open up the paths of inquiry into whole fields which until now have not been investigated scientifically—especially the social disciplines. Some, though by no means all, of the leading naturalists of our time have even been daring enough to suggest that this pattern of inquiry be extended into the field of values—and that judgments of value, although judgments about a different kind of fact from that investigated by the natural sciences, are subject to the same logic of confirmation as any other judgment of fact. Were the criticism that naturalistic humanists tend to block the paths of inquiry a just one, we should expect to find them opposing attempts to introduce

[1] *Cf.* Murphy, A., in *Journal of Philosophy*, vol. xlii, 413.

scientific methods into anthropology, history and economics on the ground that the methods and techniques of mathematical physics —"the more fully developed sciences"—were not applicable to them. But it is precisely the naturalistic humanists who, by distinguishing between the basic patterns of inquiry and the special techniques applicable to different subject-matters, have been trying to banish methodological purism.

(c) As far as the facts of moral experience are concerned, it is clear that we must distinguish between the causal explanation of moral qualities, and the proper analysis of those qualities. Naturalistic humanists differ among themselves as to the proper analysis of moral statements—some maintaining that they are commands without cognitive significance and others that they make a genuine knowledge claim. But it is certainly illegitimate to infer from the fact that one or another school contests the validity of a particular analysis of moral experience that it denies the existence of moral experience. That we experience moral obligation is a fact to be explained. What is denied by all naturalistic schools is that the explanation requires any transcendent ideal or power.

The most common objection to naturalistic humanism is not that it has no place for moral experience but that it has no place for an *authoritative* moral experience except one which rests merely on arbitrary preference, habit or force. In consequence, it is accused of lapsing into the morass of relativism despite its desire to discover inclusive and enduring ends which will enable human beings to live harmoniously together. The impression that relativism is entailed by every form of naturalism is reinforced by the refusal of current humanists to content themselves with the affirmation of general ends certified to immediate intuition and by their insistence that ends must be related to means and both to determinate conditions of trouble and difficulty in specific historical situations. This makes value judgments in the only form in which they count, "relative"—but "relative" not in the sense of subjective but rather relational. The opposite of "relative" is not "objective" but "absolute" or "unconditioned." This emphasis upon relational character reflects the dependence of value qualities, like *all* other qualities in nature, upon activities in process of objective interaction with each other. It should then be clear that the assertion "a value is *related* to a situation of concrete historical interests"—and the further assertion that "a judgment of value is warranted when reflection indicates that what is declared valuable promises to satisfy these interests," does *not* add up to the view that anyone can legitimately believe that *anything* is valuable in *any* situation. On the contrary. Inquiry into the relational character of values, their historical, cultural and psychological reference, aims to find reliable values to guide action, reliable because they have objective grounds.

The impression that because values are relational they are therefore subjective is the consequence of confusing two different problems. The first is whether values have objective status and validity; the second is whether in case of conflict, objective values and the interests to which they are related, can be shared, i.e., whether a new value situation can be constructed which will transform the conflicting values into a satisfying integrated whole.

One can hold to the belief in the objectivity of values without *guaranteeing* that agreement among conflicting values, all of which are objective from their own point of view, can be won. How far such agreement can be won cannot be foretold until actual investigation into the conditions and consequences of value claims in definite situations is undertaken—and this is precisely what naturalistic humanists propose to do instead of taking moral intuitions as absolute fiats subject to no control. The assumption that in any particular case agreement can be won, that an objective moral resolution of value conflicts is possible, entails the belief that men are sufficiently alike to work out ways of becoming *more* alike, or sufficiently alike to agree about the permissible limits of *being different*. Let us note in passing that an analogous belief is involved wherever there are conflicts about what constitutes any *knowledge* of fact. Without the assumption of identity or similarity, in whatever organic structures and activities are involved in communication, there can be no rational understanding among men. The unity of man as well as his rationality is illustrated most conspicuously in the body of common knowledge he has built up.

Rationality or reasonableness in conduct is the ability—which men possess—to envisage alternatives of action, to apply the test of observable consequences to conflicting proposals, and to accept or reconstruct these proposals in the light of consequences. The institutional expression of this rationality is the communal process of deliberation and critical assessment of evidence which alone makes possible a *freely* given consent. The willingness to sit down in the face of differences and reason together is the only categorical imperative a naturalistic humanist recognizes. And reliance upon the rules of the game by which grounded conclusions concerning concrete value judgments are reached is the only methodological absolute to which he is committed. This places authority solely in the untrammeled processes of inquiry and any alleged humanism, whether Thomistic humanism or so-called Soviet humanism, which places primary authority in institutions or dogmas, is guilty of the most transparent kind of semantic corruption.

Insofar as our age requires a unifying faith, it is clear that it cannot be found in any official doctrine or creed but rather in the commitment to the processes and methods of critical intelligence. Just as science made its way without an official metaphysics or theology, so it *may* be possible to build up a body of social science as a guide to action independently of the plural *over-beliefs* which its practitioners entertain provided only that those beliefs do not encourage the erection of non-trespass signs to inquiry about man and all his works.

In the nature of the case the philosophy of naturalistic humanism cannot promise what the facts of human involvement with nature rules out as unlikely. But within the range of possibilities it promises so much that it is wilful romanticism to demand more. It does not deprive human beings of their responsibility but rather brings home to them their own responsibility, within the constraining conditions of nature and social traditions. By nature man is a creature who can make his own history. But he did not make the world in which that history is open to him. Because he did not make the world is not a valid ground for the belief that any other species did—natural or supernatural. Nor does it follow that because he refuses to worship any supernatural power, that he must worship the human pretenders to such power like Hitler or Stalin. Man in fact relies only on his own natural and human resources even when he claims to rely on other resources.

Once men realize this then the chances become better—not certain—that these resources will be sufficient to develop a dignified human existence in a just social order. We need not repine that we are not gods or the children of gods. The politics of despair, the philosophy of magical idealism and the theology of consolation forget that although we are not gods, we can still act like men.

Pacifist Ethic

and Militarist Virtue

~§ BY HORACE M. KALLEN
The New School for Social Research

$\mathcal{M}$ORE than one hundred and sixty years ago, in the same year the American people added the Bill of Rights to their new constitution, the people of France, by shattering the Bastille, started in Europe the struggle to bring peace and freedom to the common man, which had been started in America on July 4, 1776.

This more than a century and a half has consisted of years of recurrent wars, each costing an ever greater price in blood and sweat and tears. The world is long in the "cold" phase of the most recent of these wars, which has been called a war for survival, a war for the Four Freedoms, a war for a new world, a war for democracy. In this phase, former allies are present enemies; the union imposed by a common foe has become a battle over the power and rule to be nourished by his defeat. A "united nations organization," devised for the purpose of supporting and defending international peace, is employed as a theater for the reciprocal paralysis of common action to that end. For Americans, although the opponent has changed, the issue is the same. This Second World War, going on Third, was the eighth of the major wars which the nation has waged, beginning with the War for Independence—one about every twenty years. The fear that hot war must follow cold rides us like an incubus, assaulting our civil liberties, frustrating the national reason, deprecating the national resources of might and knowledge, diverting the national attention from growth to "defense."

It is therefore worth while to inquire whether the conventional antithesis between peace and war is valid, whether in fact the programs of pacifism and militarism are mutually exclusive.

I.

During the hot war I met many pronounced pacifists. They were by no means all of a kind. Their preferred ways of rejecting war and cherishing peace, together with the diverse justifications of their preferences, divided them into denominations. Some were companies of men and women who from their depths felt: "I cannot kill. I'd rather die than kill." Others evinced less irreducible motivations. Each confronted the power of the society whose requirements of military service he was set to deny, lacking any power of his own with which to make his denials effective. He had only his personal will not to yield. Perhaps because all these pacifists did so confront insuperable odds in a critical time, they gave the impression that they felt they were not as other men, that they were invested of a special virtue, wherein they were blessed, and through which, no matter what might happen, they infallibly expected practitioners of this virtue to inherit the earth. "Other men" were all men not pacifists, therefore men inwardly, even though innocently, corrupt because they acquiesce in war and violence and therefore men not worthy to be succored when subject to assault by foes insatiable beyond any appeasement. Did the embattled peoples of the British Commonwealth, with their backs to the wall, stand alone confronting Hitler and his savage hordes? The peace-lovers were to keep apart, perhaps in tears, and let the foe have his way with his victims. In the eyes of some, God had searched out British iniquity in India, in Egypt, and in Ireland and Hitler was but the scourge of the Lord's justice! Did the government of the United States seek by arming to defend the unarmed nation's peace from the open threat and hidden conspiracy directed against it by Hitler and Hirohito? It was the duty of the peace-lover to denounce and condemn it. He saw the nation as corrupt with injustices against the poor, the meek and the lowly. Let government devote itself to correcting those injustices instead of war-mongering and filling the pockets of "merchants of death." Does it now call *Alert!* against the Communist assault on free society? This peace-lover accuses it of intolerance, imperialism and exploitation. In his sight, the aggression of Hitler and Hirohito was, and the aggression of Stalin is, a justifiable aggression springing from their needs; they were, they are, "have-nots"; give "have-nots" what they demand, and they will keep the peace, at least, "in our time."

Such is his conviction today. Such, before December 7, 1941, had been the gist of the public sentiment of such vocal princes of peace as Charles Augustus Lindbergh, Robert Maynard Hutchins, Gerald Nye, Charles Coughlin, Burton K. Wheeler, Philip LaFollette and Hamilton Fish. Their successors of 1951 have a new look but speak similarly. They must not, of course, be confused with the quiet companies of those who, though they die for it, simply refuse to kill. Yet all own a common mood and expression which suggest an undiminished phariseeism and an unreduced aggressiveness. Without raising the question of the sincerity of the different sects and preachers of pacifism, it is needful, hence, to examine a little the underlying ethic of pacifist doctrine.

The word "pacifism" is a compound word. Its Latin roots are *pac* and *fac;* they mean "pact" or "agreement," and "make." *Pac* grows into pax, that is, "peace," of which the primary dictionary meaning is *bargain* or *agreement.* By first intention then, pacifism is peace-*making.* It presupposes war and conflict. It is a theory and practice of intervention in disputes, whatever the degree, with the view of binding the contending parties to a contract of reconciliation. Thus, the mediaeval "peace-gild" was a member of an association of such gilds formed for the purpose of mutual defense of their separate rights and liberties. Later, *peace* came to mean not preventing aggression or contention but refraining from contention altogether; and pacifism came to mean, not enforcing peace, but refusing to fight. In discussion, to "hold your peace" is to keep silent, regardless of provocation; in war, it is to refuse to fight, regardless of aggression.

The pacifism which refuses to fight is usually espoused on religious grounds. Adherents to such pacifism are men with a conscientious objection to taking *human* life in any way, but not, as a rule, animal or vegetable life. I have known some conscientious objectors who were vegetarians, like Gandhi or the Buddhists, but none whose objection to taking life as such led them to starve themselves to death, or even to suffer vermin to feed on them, as do Yogi saints.

Most of these pacifists were content to enjoy their daily three square meals cooked from the flesh of animals killed for the purpose of feeding them. The faith of such believers draws the line only at killing, or contributing to killing, *homo sapiens*. It rests their hope of salvation on not-killing other men. In order to refrain from war they will endure any hardship, they will accept martyrdom. Rather than kill other men they will willingly submit to being killed themselves. Such pacifists are honest and consistent. So far as they are personally concerned, theirs is a victorious pacifism. By yielding their lives and not their principles, they defeat their enemy, who does not want to take their lives, but does want to take their principles and put his own in their place.

But if such pacifists desire the survival and spread of their principles, they succeed, by accepting martyrdom, only in defeating their own ends. By dying for their principles they abandon their principles, for they leave their principles without a defender. They leave the warriors and the believers in war without anybody to oppose them, thus the masters of the world.[1]

Of course, pacifists of this persuasion are not known to have existed in Nazi Germany or in Japan, and if they did exist did not long survive. Nor, according to Inside Germany Reports, were even sudden pacifists on the battlefield or their relatives at home permitted to survive. According to the Reports, *the German command had posted notices in many places informing soldiers that if they commit suicide, their families at home will receive suitable punishment.* For the Nazis, also peace by suicide was out. There is no evidence that Stalin's Communists hold a different view, and there is considerable evidence that they emulate the Japonazi practices. Absolute pacifists are phenomena of the free countries, where they may count on the extreme unlikelihood of martyrdom being imposed on them. Their heaviest punishment is likely to be confinement in prison, where they may live safely and not discontentedly upon the bounty of the society whose principles they condemn and whose struggle for survival they repudiate. That

---

[1] There is a widespread legend that "the blood of the martyrs is the seed of the church." Historic inquiry does not confirm this legend. On the record, war and the threat of war have been prominent instruments of conversion, and inquisition and persecution potent checks upon misbelieving.

such an existence is morally parasitical can little affect the kind of faith which leads to preferring the status of parasite to killing other men.

In the next degree of intransigence were the pacifists who declined the hazards of the battlefield but not of the hospital, the cornfield or even the munitions factory. So long as they are not personally required to kill, their consciences are satisfied. Indeed, many were disposed to enter the Red Cross, or the Friends' Service Committee and to minister to the wounded, help heal the sick, and serve the needy on both sides of the battle line. Although such non-partisan cheering of both parties in a war might seem to impartial observers like helping prolong the iniquity of war rather than to shorten it, the attitude leads those who take it to claim that they are men of peace, not embattled on either side. Whatever such activities may involve emotionally, practically they make every person who engages in them as precisely a contributor to warfare as any munitions worker or any member of a repair corps in a tank or aviation unit. If war be iniquitous and killing be crime, every such pacifist is guilty of the iniquity and an accessory to the crime. Ethical consistency would require pacifists of this order to join the absolute pacifists. Practically the situation does not, at least in free countries, call for ethical consistency. So long as it enables the pacifist to *feel* pacific, his requirements seem to be satisfied.

Finally, there are the pacifists who are most vocal and can dispose of power. They reject not war as such, but certain specific wars which they declare to be unjust. Such missioners are peace-mongers. They are opportunistic pacifists, to whom pacifism is not an end, a faith, but a military or political means. America First had many recruits from such pseudo-pacifists. The peace-mongerings of the fascist priest, Charles Coughlin, of American Communists before Hitler attacked the Soviet Union, and since Stalin has begun his cold war against the Allies without whose aid he could not have withstood Hitler's assault, are cases of malicious pacifism of this kind. Morally it is tantamount to war-effort on behalf of the other side; practically, it comes down to providing aid and comfort for the enemy. One American term for this kind of pacifist is Copperhead. Totalitarian governments extirpate him wherever they find him; free societies permit and endure him up to certain limits as part of the eternal price of freedom.

This last type of pacifism, being in fact a means of warfare, may under certain circumstances gain its ends. On the other hand, the other types, being genuinely dedicated to the achievement and upkeep of peace, are consistently self-defeating. They either insure the persistence of war by abandoning the world to the warlike or by contributing in unwarlike ways to the waging of war. Their will-to-peace is not guided by realism and implemented by intelligence. Realists about peace do not reject war as an instrument of peace. They go back to the first intention of the word "pacifism." They recognize that peace is a contract, that it always takes two to keep the peace and only one to break it, that hence peace-making is meaningless without peace-enforcing, that peace-enforcing implies the power of war and the threat of war as an implement of peace. Realistic pacifists recognize that only those can keep the peace who are ready to fight for it. They understand peace, in consequence, not negatively, as rejecting war, but positively, as a pact or bargain so made that the might of all the parties to the bargain can be mobilized against a breach of it by any. Only pacifism of this kind can avail toward a sure and lasting peace the world over. Morally, it involves caring enough about peace to be willing to fight for it.

A pacifist who is not ready to fight for peace assures the persistence of war either by contributing in non-combative ways to the waging of war, or by abandoning the world entirely to the warlike. Short of accepting death for refusing to fight, the pacifist must be an accessory to the fighting or a parasite on the fighters. For while it takes two to keep the peace, let me repeat that it takes only one to make a quarrel. Any individual, any group, can turn aggressor, anywhere, at any time; and hot war begins at the point where the aggressor is no longer appeased and endured but resisted and opposed with force beyond words. The record shows that peace is not the opposite of war and separable from it. On the contrary, that aggressors shall be restrained and peace prolonged requires always the threat, and sometimes the act, of war. Once more, in a word, peace, to be preserved, must be enforced. As Thomas Jefferson, then President of the United States, wrote to Madame de Stael in 1807: "When wrongs are pressed because it is believed they will be borne, resistance becomes morality."

II.

I wish now to discuss what this relationship of war to peace implies for those who assert that war is the be-all and end-all of our existence and the highest perfection of human culture, what war implies for those to whom heaven is Valhalla. There is reason to believe that just as the religion of the pacifist commits the believer in peace to the waging of war, so the religion of the warrior commits the believer in war to the ways of peace, that it assimilates peace to war as one of the components of war.

This observation need not be taken on a level merely of abstraction and dialectic. It is confirmed, I think, by the case of the late Mohandas Gandhi, and by observations made by that connoisseur of war, Ernest Hemingway, in his introduction to a volume of "the best war stories of all time," which he edited.[2] The notion that Gandhi was actually waging war challenges, of course, the conventional image of this devotee of the *Bhagavagita*, admirer of Tolstoi, and perennial reader of Thoreau's argument *On Civil Disobedience*. "But if thou wilt not carry on this righteous warfare," the Lord admonishes Arjuna in the *Gita*, "then wilt thou, casting away thine own duty and thine honor, incur sin."

On the record, Gandhi kept himself sinless for half a century. The singularity of his warlike genius is evinced by the weapons and strategy of the war he waged. In this he was not as other warriors. War, in the words of the classical writer on war, von Clausewitz, "is an act of violence for the purpose of compelling the enemy to do what we will." But Gandhi undertook to compel his enemy to do what he willed by acts of "non-violence" and "civil disobedience." As he employed "non-violence" it worked the same effects as violence, and his "non-cooperation" exerted a force the equivalent of organized military co-operation. But can this be called waging war? I think it can, and without prejudice, if we distinguish in the Gandhian record professions from practices, attitudes from consequences. Those of our world who look upon

[2] *Men at War. The Best War Stories of All Time,* edited with an introduction by Ernest Hemingway (New York 1943).

the late Mahatma as an apostle of peace regard his words and
works but disregard their violent consequences in the works and
ways of his followers, partizans and foes. Also Hitler, also Stalin,
certainly on the record of their sayings, might have been described
as pacifists; and indeed, they kept consistently referring to themselves as lovers of peace upon whom war has been thrust by
opponents who wickedly refused to give him what they wanted
when he wanted it, and thus forced them, poor saints, to take it
for themselves with arms. Stalin is still successful at it. Hitler, indeed, also employed "non-violent" means to compel "the enemy"
to do what he willed. But Hitler's legend did not divide his words
from their consequences. We recognized them as instruments of
warfare. We knew them as offering violence to men's minds and
hearts. We saw them first passing over, into, then combined with
violence against men's flesh and bones. We called them "psychological warfare," even as today we call much of Stalin's cold war
"psychological."

Now Gandhi was our generation's Old Master of psychological
warfare. He may be said, indeed, to have developed and per-
fected it as a political instrument, with techniques fitted to the
folkways and mores of his land, and to the religious professions
and political preferences of western liberals. Scion of a family of
officials in the service of a local princeling, the Mahatma-to-be
went to London to study law, and there, a mere Vaishya, was so
snubbed by both British and Brahmans, that he withdrew from
all but the most necessary social contacts. Returned to India, still
desirous of a career in accord with the family tradition, Gandhi
felt himself cut off from such a career after a rude and stupid
British official from whom he had asked a favor ordered a servant
to lay contaminating hands on him and throw him out.

"I pocketed the insult," Gandhi wrote in his autobiography, and
the subsequent record suggests that it was an insult beyond redress.
"Pocketed," suppressed, apparently forgotten, the insult must
nevertheless have continued to rankle. Become a lawyer, practicing before the Bombay High Court, business took its victim, in
1893, to South Africa, where the wounded spirit saw the shame
and suffering inflicted on him personally multiplied a hundred
thousand times. He identified himself with the sufferers from the

conscienceless indignities, untouchables included, and made himself their defender. The philosophy and cultural economy of the Hindus now became to him the paramount good of existence while the faiths and works of the West, with certain exceptions, became the paramount evil. Gandhi's whole aim of life was now to wage war against this evil until his country was purged of it—especially of evil's incarnation and carrier, the British *raj*. For his personal rule of life he took the ascetic discipline of the Brahman *sanyassin*. For his land and people he sought to abolish what industrialization had been already achieved and to stop all extension of it. He preached the restoration of pre-industrial economy. He exalted Hindu medicine above Western. But he did call in a western surgeon when he needed surgery. Although he acquiesced in the worse than useless reverence for cows, he sanctioned the elimination of sacred monkeys. Sufficient as might have been his hatred of industry, he could exact contributions of money earned by it to serve his causes.

To implement his aggression against the faith and works of the West, Gandhi employed the ideas of the Westerner Thoreau and the techniques of the western organization of laborers known as the I.W.W. They consist of refusing to participate in the activities of the political economy; of a withdrawal of co-operation from field, factory and hall of government, and of compelling the enemy by such withdrawal to submit to one's will. Hunger strikes are similar means of coercion. The civil disobedience and non-cooperation Gandhi called *satyagraha,* the hunger-strike *dharana.* In Gandhi's use of them, both were much enhanced by a certain religious aura. The western parallel for them would be the ecclesiastical excommunication and interdict. On the record, their overarching purpose was less to bring to the miserable peoples of India freedom or peace or better living, than to drive the British and *all* they stood for out of India.

The Brahmana doctrine and discipline thus implemented enabled the offended man to turn his impotence into a weapon of aggression against the British in a warfare which he never after relaxed. Gandhi never made even an interim peace with them in his heart. It is common knowledge that Sir Stafford Cripps offered the All-India Congress even more than they had ever asked for and that Gandhi prevented acceptance. He set what was then an impossible price. "Had Gandhi willed it," wrote Mr. Raman[3] in 1943, "a settlement could have been reached in March with Sir Stafford Cripps." It looks, from the record, that for the old offense he could accept nothing short of the supreme expiation: the elimination of the offender. Gandhi made his requirement explicit in the rationalization of it which he wrote in his *Appeal to the British:* "Let them entrust India to God, or in modern parlance, to anarchy." In other words: Out with the British—no matter what price in life and suffering and slavery the Indian multitudes pay! And have they not paid? Are they not paying? And was not Gandhi helpless to stop the payment he exacted and received, except as peace in India be *enforced?* His last message to the Congress Party was that it become a semi-military organization "although subscribing to non-violent principles."

Nor had Gandhi confined his psychological warfare to the British. He had used his *dharanas,* often rationalized as "penitential," against Hindu industrialists and Hindu monarchs who would not do his will; against the opposition within his own party; and in order to overcome party-division and trends toward deliquescence. With few exceptions, his non-violent initiatives brought violent consequences[4] as he well knew they would. Annie Besant denounced Gandhi as the cause of the slaughter of Malabar.

In the degree that the initiatives of Gandhi's non-violent warfare won victories, they won them not because the power he attacked was weaker than he, but because, for almost half a century the British *raj* had conducted itself according to rules and by methods which conceded his right to fight and acknowledged the human pertinence of his party's desires and aspirations; and because, hence, it submitted to the give and take of the struggle and looked forward to a conclusion in which each shall gain something and none shall lose everything; such a conclusion as Sir Stafford had offered. The warfare of the *raj* was not total but civilized—that is, its premises and goal were the state of peace. But in his unreconcilable heart, Gandhi was waging total war. He was making its issue *all or nothing;* unconsciously, he kept

[3] Raman, T. A., *What Does Gandhi Want?*
[4] Raman, *op. cit.,* throughout 101-13.

forcing the contenders toward the alternatives: *oust or be ousted, kill or be killed.* The British had always had the power but never the will to rub out the whole Congress movement. Gandhi counted on that ethic to the limit, and events have validated his expectations. The British *are* out of India, but obviously, from their choice, not his force. They could have stayed and if the lives and limbs of Indian multitudes are a consideration, perhaps should have. Had Gandhi been fighting a tribe like the Russians or the Nazis or the Japanese, whose wars were murderous predation and not combat, the will would have anticipated and perhaps even outrun the power. Long before this, there would have been no Gandhi, no Congress, no Pakistan, no independent India, and a decimated and enslaved land would have been mobilized under the taskmaster's lash to struggle for a cause it does not share with a people against whom it has no grievance; to make a wasteland and call it peace.

That kind of peace is not peace, but destruction. Ultimately, it is destruction and death for the victor no less than for the vanquished. If, like Helmuth von Moltke, you envisage war as "a part of God's world order," ordained to save that divine arrangement from materialism; if war is your religion; if you believe that the peak and ecstasy of life are reached only *in* combat and *through* combat, then the continued presence of a foeman worthy of your strength and skill is the indispensable condition of your reaching that peak and experiencing that ecstasy. If you abolish the condition, you condemn the warrior in you to death. In the warrior's heaven, Valhalla, which is the symbolic immortality of battle, both vanquished and victors rise to fight again; and victory is ever a chance and never a fate. To the degree that you hold the warlike life to be the best life, you commit yourself to the preservation and equal prosperity of your enemy. Neither you nor he seeks each other's slaughter; each seeks superiority in a struggle where the victory of one must never be such as to prevent the other from fighting again. Such a victory would defeat the victor. For lack of an enemy his strength would decay, his spirit corrupt. His excellence is a function of his struggle, and he needs his enemy as he needs his breath. Thus war is co-operation as well as competition. To survive, it can never be total; as it destroys, it must recreate. Indeed, to metaphysicians like Nietzsche and Emerson, to moralists like Ruskin and Spengler, this was of war's essence. Men live, they think, for

> The stern joy that warriors feel
> In foemen worthy of their steel.

Ruskin urged that war is a game expressing the full personal power of the human creature: "when well-played, it determines who is the best man"; and Justice Oliver Wendell Holmes told his fellow-veterans of the Civil War, those men who "were gentle; they cared nothing for their lives," that they had "felt and still feel the passion of life at its top."

To experience that passion, you must, having conquered fear, caring nothing for your life, still remain alive.

> Nor war's wild note nor glory's peal
> Shall thrill with fierce delight
> Those hearts that never more may feel
> The rapture of the fight.

III.

Something of this sentiment emerges also from the confused assemblage of tales and stories with which Ernest Hemingway thought he could show how men have fought and died.

Significantly, the most revealing tale for this fighting writing-man, who is a veteran of World War I and of the betrayed Spanish Republic's war to keep its people free, is *The Red Badge of Courage* by Stephen Crane, who had never seen a battle. The entire meaning of the experience of battle seems to rest in a sort of initiation, seems to turn on being blooded, on undergoing the baptism of fire, and being thereby freed from fear. Hemingway, speaking for himself, says that he felt at first that he couldn't be killed. Then he was wounded, and after that he felt that he had survived the worst, that now death had no terrors. He sums up the resulting outlook with a quotation from Shakespeare: "By my troth, I care not: a man can die but once: we owe God a death . . . and let it go which way it will, he that dies this year, is quit for the next." But we find the same attitude in Hamlet, overruling his own monitions of death: "We defy augury. . . . If it be not now, yet it will

come. The readiness is all." To me, the mood's ultimate expression is
the Virgilian line cited by Justice Oliver Wendell Holmes to friends
who came to congratulate him on his ninetieth birthday: "Death
plucks at my ears and cries: Live, for I am coming."

The idea is that death is the permanent contingency of all living
and its inescapable end; that the struggle to live which we call
peace is not less beset with the termination of death than the
struggle for mastery which we call war. Hemingway put the tales
by which he illustrates that struggle in a frame of reference made
up of sentences he had chosen from Carl von Clausewitz's *Vom
Kriege*. He calls that Prussian analyst of Napoleon's campaigns
"the most intelligent writer on the metaphysics of war," and gives
this writer's sentences the effect of texts upon which the appended
tales are glosses. The texts thus serve as a summation of the meaning of the tales.

And what is this meaning?

That war is a mode of human intercourse, like business and
politics, although not like the arts and sciences. That it can be
well-fought only as men develop courage as well as wisdom concerning dangers; a courage not the body's indifference to hurt
merely, but also the spirit's resolution to endure and not yield but
conquer; but also the mind's knowledge and skill, without which
the blind animal drive cannot become human determination and
insight. Even so, the fortunes of battle often rub out the wisest
generalship, the highest private intelligence. Uncertainty attends
every step to the very last. Chance events may falsify every expectation; unforeseeable changes may disrupt the surest plan or balk
the cleverest improvisation. The simplest action may develop inner
friction in the most unexpected places, and the frictions may compound. To overcome these inherent dangers and insufficiencies of
war and battle, each man has in the end but the resolution of his
own character and the security of his own knowledge, the fighting
faith which overrules his defeatist moods, holds him staunch and
unyielding against repeated disaster and is the inner ground of
victory at last.

The idea that this describes the ways of war more than the ways
of peace seems to me a conventional illusion created by wishful
thinking and deficient observation. That the description does not

apply to art and science seems to me entirely false. I recall Ralph
Waldo Emerson having written in his *Journal*:

Heaven takes care to show us that war is part of our education as
much as milk, or love, and is not to be escaped. We affect to put it all
back in history, as the Trojan War, the War of the Roses, the Revolutionary War. Not so; it is *your* war. Has that been declared? Has that
been fought out: And where did Victory perch? The wars of other people and of history growl at a distance, but your war comes near, looks
into your eyes, in politics, in professional pursuit, in choices in the street,
in daily habit, in all the questions of the times, in keeping or surrendering the control of your day, and your horse, and your opinions, in the
terrors of the night, in the frauds and skepticism of the day . . . *Your
independence!* That is the question of all the present. Have you fought
out that? And settled it once and again, and once for all, in the minds of
all persons with whom you have to do, that you and your sense of right
and fit and fair are an invincible, indestructible somewhat, which is not
to be bought or cajoled or frightened away? That done, the victory in-
scribed on your eyes and brow and voice, the other American freedom
begins instantly to have some meaning and support.

I recall William James describing what makes a life significant:

I was speeding with the train toward Buffalo, when, near that city, the
sight of a workman doing something on the dizzy edge of a sky-scaling
iron construction brought me to my senses very suddenly. I perceived
that I had been steeping myself in pure ancestral blindness, and looking
at life with the eyes of a remote spectator. Wishing for heroism and the
spectacle of human nature on the rack, I had never noticed the great
fields of heroism lying around me, I had failed to see it present and
alive. I could only think of it as dead and embalmed, labelled and cos-
tumed, as it is in the pages of romance. And yet there it was before me
in the daily lives of the laboring classes. Not in clanging fights and
desperate marches only is heroism to be looked for, but on every railway
bridge and fireproof building that is going up today. On freight trains,
on the decks of vessels, in cattle-yards and mines, on lumber-rafts, among
the firemen and policemen, the demand for courage is incessant; and the
supply never fails. There, every day of the year somewhere, is human
nature *in extremis* for you. And wherever a scythe, an axe, a pick, or a
shovel is wielded, you have it sweating and aching with its powers of
patient endurance racked to the utmost under the length of hours of the
strain. . . . These are our soldiers, thought I, these our sustainers, these
the very parents of our life.

And I feel impelled to add to this what must be apparent to
anyone who knows that in times of peace and times of war alike,
the casualties of industry outnumber the casualties of battle; that

wherever men are *working* together in a dangerous work, the common task and the common safety call out the so-called military virtues. There, too, are the quick obedience to orders, the gathering of personal energies to a peak; the liquidation of fear in ordered action so that the feel of the performance absorbs the sense of its danger; and lastly the swift voluntary filling of a place made empty by an accident or death. But—

I recall likewise what the late Justice Holmes said to law students at Harvard:

> Only when you have worked alone—when you have felt around you a black gulf of solitude more isolating than that which surrounds the dying man, and in hope and in despair you have trusted to your own unshaken will,—then only will you have achieved. Thus only can you gain the secret isolated joy of the thinker . . . the subtle rapture of postponed power, which the world knows not because it has no external trappings, but which to his prophetic vision is more real than that which commands an army.

From within then, the farmer in his fields, the worker in his factory, the sailor on his ship, the intellectual in his study, needs the same resolution, the same staunchness, and the same fighting faith as the soldier at the front. And they need them the more in order to endure the routine and boredom into which the critical urgency of struggle breaks like a liberator.

"War, when you are at it," says Oliver Wendell Holmes, and every soldier will confirm him, "is horrible and dull." Most of it calls for an occupational routine with its own attendant changes and chances not less creative nor less productive than peace. Indeed, some say, much more productive, and continue to make unkept promises of abundance of good things born of the war-time's needs for peace-time use. War but reorganizes the aggregations of conflict and co-operation which we call peace and adds to the usual processes of production and consumption and creation and destruction, another set, whose goal among civilized combatants is not to loot and enslave or to destroy the enemy but to disarm and master him, to prove in fair and open combat, who, as Ruskin says, is the better man. Like peace, it has its abominations.

For it is true that the primary lusts and perversions of spirit which peace-times diffuse and check and police, war-times con-

centrate, release and encourage. Civilized armies, however, seek
to deviate as little as possible from civilian ways and works in
their morality and their morale. Sometimes, soldiers tear loose
from those ways and works, like civilian lynch-mobs in the South,
or in any other region of the world one inspects. But these aberrations to sadist madness are judged as aberrations and sharply
condemned. It is denied that they are in any way a legitimate
part of the institution of war; they are but parasites on it, as on
those of peace. And is not the denial deepened and confirmed by
the present effort to extend the rules of war by placing genocide
among other forms of violence and destruction, as a criminal violation of the law of nations?

If war, as ideal and as fact, be what its interpreters and defenders say it is, then the recent struggle of mankind against the Nipponazis of Europe and Asia, although described as total war, was
not war. It was a struggle for survival of the same sort that we
make against any irrational cataclysm of nature, such as earth-
quakes, tidal waves, floods, or plagues like syphilis or leprosy.
East and West, the Nipponazis had magnified and refined sadistic
aberrations into institutional techniques. They did not simply
wage war, they practiced murder and destruction without ruth,
without law. Both by their faith and their works, they had wilfully made themselves as different from humanity as are the
spyrochites or the germs of leprosy. If mankind would not kill
them they would kill mankind.

That their success must later destroy them, as success does
any parasite which kills the host it lives on, was not envisaged by
their Rosenbergs and their other oracles who exalt the warrior's
life as the best life. They and their type merely *say* that war is their
end, but they employ it only as their means. As the trials of Nazi
industrialists no less than of their military men reveal, they did
not live for war, they lived for loot. They were not warriors. They
were incapable of the courage which is wisdom concerning dangers, nor could they feel the stern joy that warriors feel in foemen worthy of their steel. They evaded such foemen, and regularly
attacked those only whom they believed weaker, and without help
against their cruel voracity. Yet a ghost of their outlawed humanity
haunted even the Nazis. This was a certain respect for the ways of

peace. They kept protesting that they were peaceable men whose people were forced at the end of the First World War to plead to a guilt of which they were innocent. They protested that their intentions were pacific at the moment that their aggression was most murderous and destructive. And they pleaded that all the sadist abominations they committed were acts of defense to which their victims compelled them. At the time of writing, the Russians are taking their own turn at this practice, and improving upon it.

Hypocrisy? Cunning? Not entirely. In part this duplicity also testifies to the restless shade of an unburied humanity haunting the torture chamber which their totalitarian doctrines and disciplines had made of the German and Japanese lands and stalking behind the iron curtain of the Soviets. The dropping of that curtain testifies to it. But most of all it seems to me confirmation from an unexpected quarter of the view that peace and war are not contrasted opposites but different varieties of a similar species; that the virtues and vices of men at war differ from those of men at peace neither in degree nor in kind, but only in occasion; that just as it is impossible to maintain peace without fighting for it, so it is impossible to wage war without the co-operative enterprises of peace. Provide the qualities of men which war enchannels and gratifies with other occasions, no less adequate than war to yield the same incommunicable experience, the same feel of "the passion of life at its top," and war will be displaced as the horse is displaced by the motor, displaced because another thing can do the same job better.

Emerson recognized this fact long ago and wrote it down. "The man-hood [he meant by "man-hood" the warrior's virtue] that has been in war must be transferred to the cause of peace, before war can lose its charm or peace be venerable to men." To date, however, none of the multitude of moral equivalents for war, able to win this manhood to a fighting faith, has achieved the adequate allure. The way of war endures, one among many other ways men take or come to, seeking the passion of life at its top.

Consequently, that peace is most quickly broken which shuts out war and the threat of war. That war degenerates into blind destruction which shuts out peace and the co-operations of peace, for it kills both combatants instead of sustaining each in battle and enabling victory for one. This is why, in wars of religious aggression—such as was the presently dormant or "cold" world-wide civil war—men cease to be human and for their faith's sake make of themselves ravening beasts. That peace lasts longest which incorporates into its own structure the actualities of war and the threat of war. That war is shortest which is honestly waged as an event in the organization of peace and in order to keep the peace. Lasting peace needs, for its maintenance, the readiness to fight in its behalf.

And hence, free men cannot be educated for peace, unless they are at one and the same time educated also for war. That peace shall last, the men of peace must learn the science and the art which, in the great John Milton's definition, shall enable them "to perform justly, skillfully, thoughtfully and magnanimously all the offices, both private and public, of peace and war."

A Note on Emergence

✑ BY MAURICE MANDELBAUM
Dartmouth College

*I*T IS my purpose in this note concerning the doctrine of emergence to formulate a theoretical position which has not previously been explicitly formulated.[1] A clear indication of the nature of this position may, I believe, be of some help in clarifying the substantive issues which are raised whenever the problem of emergence is discussed. In this belief lies the appropriateness of including this tentative note in the present volume: whatever is written in the hope that it may lead to a clarification of fundamental philosophic issues may properly be dedicated to the lucid and inquiring spirit of Morris R. Cohen.

I.

It will be useful to note at the outset the distinction which Lovejoy has drawn between existential and functional emergence.[2]

To believe in *existential emergence* is to believe that during the course of time there have come into existence qualities, objects, or events of a type not previously present in the world, and that knowledge concerning the specific nature of such novel types of existents could not have been derived from a knowledge, however complete, of the nature of what previously existed.

To believe in *functional emergence* is to believe that the modes

---

[1] It is perhaps suggested in ch. 4 of Edel's *Theory and Practice of Philosophy* (taking p. 59f. and 61 conjointly), but it is not there developed as a single consistent position.

[2] *Cf.* "The Discontinuities of Evolution," in *University of California Publications in Philosophy*, vol. v, especially p. 178f.; and "The Meaning of 'Emergence' and Its Modes," in *Journal of Philosophical Studies*, vol. ii, especially p. 173ff.

It should be noted that my use of these terms is not wholly congruent with that of Lovejoy, but a discussion of the differences would not be in place here.

of functioning exhibited by existents of different types are, in some cases, ultimately and irreducibly discontinuous, so that no single set of laws could be adequate to explain the characteristic functions of all types. Such functional discontinuities may either be held to be due to the emergence of novel types of existents, or they may be held to be due to the presence of "levels of organization" among existents, regardless of whether these levels are novel or were always present in the world.[3] Where temporal novelty is stressed, the doctrine of functional emergence consists in the belief that the behavior of new types of entities cannot be adequately described through special applications of those laws which were adequate to describe the functioning of previously existing entities; where levels of organization are stressed, the doctrine of functional emergence consists in the belief that each higher level of organization possesses modes of functioning which cannot be adequately described in terms of laws which are applicable to the functioning of entities on lower levels. In either case, a belief in functional emergence consists in the claim that there is an ultimate pluralism in the laws which are adequate to describe the functioning of different types of existents.

What the concepts of existential emergence and functional emergence have in common should now be clear: both claim the non-deducibility of that with which they are concerned. Existential emergence claims that the existence of novel types of quality, objects, or events would not have been deducible from a knowledge, however complete, of the previously manifested nature and properties of existing entities. This non-deducibility of novel existents is usually referred to as "unpredictability." Functional emergence, on the other hand, claims that the laws which are necessary to explain the characteristic modes of functioning of some existents are not deducible from the laws which are adequate to explain the modes of functioning of other types of entity. This non-deducibility

---

[3] For an example of the rather widespread tendency to give a non-temporal definition of emergence, stressing the whole-part relationship, *cf.* Hempel and Oppenheim: *Studies in the Logic of Explanation* (*Philosophy of Science*, vol. xv, p. 146ff.). *Cf.* also the origin of the concept of emergence in Mill and Lewes, and Broad's definition—*The Mind and Its Place in Nature*, p. 61—which does not utilize any temporal terms.

of particular laws is most usefully designated as "irreducibility."[4]

Now, it is to be noted that while the doctrine of emergence usually involves the claim that reality presents examples of both existential and functional emergence, it is theoretically possible to hold that there are functional emergents but no existential emergents, or that there are existential emergents but no functional emergents. In the first case one would be denying that any genuinely novel existents arise in the course of time, but would be claiming an irreducible pluralism in the types of law necessary to explain the functioning of existing types of entities. In the second case one would be admitting the existence of unpredictable novelty in the universe, but would be claiming that the laws which explain the manner in which these novelties function, once they exist, are reducible to the laws which explain the manner in which all other existents function, being merely special applications of these more general laws. It is this second (apparently paradoxical) position which it is my aim to elucidate.

II.

Let us now connect Broad's useful distinction between transordinal, intraordinal, and ordinally-neutral laws with our present distinction between existential and functional emergence.[5] What Broad means by a transordinal law is a law stating a relationship between diverse types of existents, for example, between a novel property and the conditions which are always concomitant with its presence. By an intraordinal law Broad means a law which is not reducible to ordinally-neutral laws, and which serves to explain the mode of functioning of a given type of existent in terms of its characteristic organizational (or "novel") properties. By ordinally-

---

[4] In Henle's critique of the use of the concept of "unpredictability" in discussions of emergence (*cf. Journ. of Philosophy,* vol. xxxix, p. 486-93) no distinction between existential and functional emergence is maintained. It appears to me that his argument would not be valid with respect to existential emergents, whatever may be the case with respect to functional emergence. What he terms the "logically unrelated" is, I believe, primarily a question of functional emergence, and I should prefer to use the term "irreducibility" in this connection.

[5] *Cf. The Mind and Its Place in Nature,* p. 77ff.

neutral laws Broad means whatever laws apply to the modes of functioning of all existents without restriction as to type.

We may say that if *all* laws are ordinally-neutral the theory of emergence is false so far as functional emergence is concerned. It would also be false in so far as existential emergence is concerned, unless the coming into being of novel entities or properties is subject to *no* law. The latter position, that emergents arise independently of all natural necessity, has sometimes been attributed to those who believe in emergence, but it is not in fact widely held, nor is it a position which possesses much to commend it. We may therefore safely say that if *all* laws are ordinally-neutral the theory of emergence is false.

The theory of functional emergence holds that there are irreducible intraordinal laws, the existence of such laws being in fact the essential contention of this doctrine. It is to be noted, however, that the conception of intraordinal laws only refers to the question of what laws are adequate to explain the functioning of entities of a given type: to deny the existence of irreducible intraordinal laws is to deny functional, but not necessarily existential, emergence.

What Broad terms transordinal laws are, in essence, laws of existential emergence. It is their purpose to state a relationship between a given novel type of quality, object, or event and the conditions which are invariantly and necessarily correlated with its existence. To hold that there are such laws is not to deny that the phenomenon in question is novel: it remains unpredictable (*i.e.,* non-deducible) on the basis of any knowledge afforded by the nature of what previously existed. What the belief in transordinal laws involves is the dual contention that novel existents of specific types arise only under certain specifiable conditions, *and* that the connection between these existents and their necessary conditions is a connection of "brute fact," the existence of the novel phenomenon not being deducible from the previously existing conditions by means of any ordinally-neutral law. Therefore, the existence of a non-deducible transordinal law would prove existential emergence, but it would not, in itself, tell us whether the theory of functional emergence is also true.

III.

Utilizing these distinctions I should now like to present two considerations concerning existential and functional emergence. These considerations are not, of course, sufficient to decide the substantive question as to whether the emergent doctrine in any of its forms is true: they may, however, be of use in lending some weight to the particular position which it is the aim of this paper to formulate.

It would seem to me that no philosophic theory can deny that in the course of time there have occurred in nature genuinely "augmentative or transmutative events."[6] To do so would be to deny what is known of the earth's history. If, for example, we examine the nature and characteristics of living things without a prejudice born of opposition to the supposed existence of intra-ordinal laws, we cannot, I believe, fail to admit that there have arisen objects with properties which previously existing objects did not possess.

Granting the existence of such properties, the so-called reductionist must, I believe, also grant that there are transordinal laws: to deny such laws would be to hold that these properties bear no necessary relation to the conditions with which they are invariably associated. This, as we have seen, would be precisely the position which he charges—usually unfairly—that the believer in emergence upholds.

But if one grants that there are transordinal laws which state a connection between a property not formerly present (or not present at all levels) and the conditions under which it appears, such a law would not be deducible from ordinally-neutral laws. This follows necessarily from two facts: first, a law which aims to state such a relationship must contain the property in question as an inexpungeable term; second, such a property is, by definition, different from any property common to all existents, *i.e.*, it itself is not "ordinally-neutral." Therefore, no transordinal law would be reducible to ordinally-neutral laws.

It is this line of argumentation which leads me to conclude that

[6] This phrase is Lovejoy's: *op. cit., Journal of Philosophic Studies,* vol. ii, p. 169.

existential emergence, as defined above, is a fact. Contained in this
conclusion there is, so far as I can see, nothing which is not compatible with an unbridled acceptance of the ideals of scientific
explanation.

On the other hand, it appears to me to be far from certain that
that there are any irreducible intraordinal laws. While it is doubtless possible to formulate specifically biological and psychological
laws which are descriptive of organic and human modes of functioning, it is conceivable (as I shall later show) that these laws are
but special applications of ordinally-neutral laws. Whether or not
this is the case is an empirical problem, and the empirical evidence
which is available is inconclusive. However, there is one problem
inherent in the assumption of irreducible intraordinal laws to which
I should like to direct the reader's attention.

The doctrine of functional emergence, it will be recalled, holds
that the modes of functioning exhibited by existents of different
types are, in some cases at least, discontinuous, so that no single
set of laws could be adequate to explain the modes of functioning
of all existents. Intraordinal laws are formulated to explain those
modes of functioning which are characteristic of novel types of
existents or of specific levels of organization. But it is to be noted
that in the traditional interpretations of the doctrine of emergence
the number of such types or levels is limited, the discriminated
number usually ranging between three and six. At the same time
it is usually admitted that finer discriminations can be made.

This situation I find disturbing. It would appear that once we
admit the existential emergence of novel properties, or concentrate
on the differences in the levels of organization represented by existing entities, we find that important discriminable differences are
extremely numerous. To hold that there are as many irreducible
intraordinal laws as there are novel emergents (or as there are
differences in levels of organization among existing entities)
would, I believe, be false: there appears to be far more unity in
the ways in which entities function than one could then expect.
But if, on the other hand, one seeks to limit the number of intraordinal laws to cover only broad bands of phenomena (*e.g.*, matter,
life, mind), the discriminable novel properties or levels of organi-

zation within each of these bands is left unexplained by the intra-ordinal laws, and presumably also by the ordinally-neutral laws.

This difficulty concerning the possible number of irreducible intraordinal laws has been rather frequently noted, but it has not, I believe, been adequately solved by those who believe in functional emergence. The question is, of course, an empirical one, and if the theory of functional emergence were true no final answer could be forthcoming until all intraordinal laws had in fact been discovered. But the inconclusiveness of my argument with respect to the question of how many irreducible intraordinal laws there may be does not furnish an excuse for the failure of the theory of functional emergence to provide an answer to the other facet of the same problem: when one intraordinal law applies equally to two discriminable novelties, by means of what type of law can we explain the differences in their characteristic modes of functioning? For example, if (as Broad suggests) irreducible intraordinal laws are necessary to account for the organic function of reproduction, by what means other than postulating two different intraordinal laws can we account for the functional differences represented by a sexual and sexual reproduction? In short, the upholder of functional emergence is caught in a dilemma: either he will introduce so many supposedly irreducible intraordinal laws that the degree of systematic unity which we find in nature will be inexplicable, or he will confine attention to relatively few types of irreducible modes of functioning and leave unexplained the observable differences within each of these modes. It is for this reason (buttressed by what I believe the recent history of the sciences to have illustrated) that I am doubtful as to the claims put forward on behalf of the theory of functional emergence.

IV.

The position which I therefore propose as worthy of consideration is that there arise in the course of time entities possessing novel, emergent properties;[7] that the transordinal laws linking such

[7] For the sake of convenience in exposition I shall at this point assume that all existential emergents are temporally novel, neglecting the possibility that there were eternally existing differences in levels of organization.

properties to the conditions upon which they depend are not deducible from ordinally-neutral laws; but that the latter are nonetheless adequate to explain the mode of functioning of all existent entities, intraordinal laws being but instances of them.

The apparent paradox contained in this position—*viz.*, that there are genuinely novel properties, but that the behavior of entities possessing these properties is explicable in terms of the same laws which hold of all other entities—disappears when we consider the differences and the connections between transordinal and intraordinal laws.

A transordinal law takes a particular mode of functioning as a datum, and correlates it with the occurrence of events which are invariantly copresent with it. But since the datum is, by definition, a novel element in existence, it differs in character from the events which are claimed to be invariantly connected with it. On the other hand, an intraordinal law attempts to explain a characteristic function through correlating one novel property with another: it is not concerned with the conditions underlying the existence of these novel properties, but with their functional interrelationships.

Now, each novel property is (theoretically) capable of being connected with events which are not novel by means of a transordinal law. And such non-novel types of events, it is generally admitted, are related to one another in ways describable through what are termed ordinally-neutral laws. It is therefore conceivable that we could state every so-called intraordinal law as a special case of ordinally-neutral laws, by "translating" the relationship between novel properties into a relationship between the conditions found to underlie each of them. In making such a translation we should not be guilty of any "reductionist" fallacy, for what is in question in an intraordinal law is not the existence of particular novel properties but the determination of relationships among them. I therefore believe it legitimate (in principle) to hold that the invariant connections which are formulated in so-called intraordinal laws may be but special cases of ordinally neutral laws: when novel properties are expressed in terms of their invariant non-novel correlates, ordinally-neutral laws would then state precisely those functional relationships which are to be found on the emergent level. In this sense intraordinal laws could be said to be deducible from ordinally-neutral laws whenever we have an adequate knowledge of the relevant transordinal laws.

Applied to the field of organic and mental phenomena the position which I have suggested would mean: first, that in the course of time entities have arisen which possess properties such as cell-division and cognition which were not the properties of any previously existing entities; second, that such properties are correlated with specific physical-chemical constituents or forms of organization, such correlations being formulated in terms of transordinal laws; third, that we may formulate "intraordinal" (*i.e.*, specifically biological or psychological) laws, stating relationships between one novel property and another; but, fourth, that while transordinal laws are not deducible from ordinally-neutral laws (since they contain as data novel properties), the intraordinal laws are, in principle, thus deducible through the mediation of transordinal laws.

V.

That the position thus stated is in fact correct cannot be claimed on the basis of empirical evidence: our knowledge of the transordinal laws connecting specific novel properties with underlying conditions is too limited to permit us to judge whether all intraordinal laws are expressions of the ordinally-neutral laws which have been (or may be) discovered. But advances in biology seem to show that this position is not implausible, and there may be grounds for the belief that a similar development is also occurring in psychology.

Whether or not his position is correct (as I believe it to be) it deserves formulation as one possible answer to the problems posed by the concept of emergence.

Notes on Civilization in Historical Perspective

◆§ BY RALPH MARCUS
University of Chicago

*T*HE last book that Morris R. Cohen himself seems to have got ready for the press was *The Meaning of Human History*, published by the Paul Carus Foundation a few months after his death in January 1947. Like all his works it is noteworthy for its learning, acuteness and healthy common sense. If in some ways it is less impressive than his earlier writings, the reason is probably that during the last few years of his intellectually strenuous life his health had suffered too greatly to permit of his refining and broadening his criticism of current theories of history.[1] In the brief study here offered as a tribute to the memory of a great philosopher and humanist I shall present a few by-products of a projected work on the history of theories of the origin and nature of civilization. Most of these notes deal with problems which Morris Cohen has discussed, though sometimes only casually, in his *The Meaning of Human History*.

I. THE EXTENT OF RECENT LITERATURE ON THEORETICAL HISTORY

Cohen begins his book with the unelaborated observation that "the Philosophy of History is certainly the most neglected province of philosophy." Here he is probably alluding to the kind of systematic philosophy of history that is found in the Hegelian tradition. If, however, we broaden the sense of "philosophy of history" (in which, incidentally, Cohen seems to include the methodology of

---

[1] This may be the reason for the absence in *The Meaning of Human History* of any reference to Arnold Toynbee's *A Study of History* and other recent works of this kind.

history) and extend it to cover the related fields of universal history and the history of civilization,[2] we see that there has been a considerable amount of literature on the subject produced during the last quarter of a century not only by historians, anthropologists and sociologists but also by philosophers and theologians. It is, of course, not surprising that great numbers of intellectuals should be concerned about the meaning of human history and the nature of civilization in view of the fact that our civilization is obviously in the process of radical change. What is surprising, however, is the large number of books and monographs which have recently been published by scholars and thinkers who have hitherto been concerned with other than general historical problems. Among these philosophers of history[3] are W. F. Albright, John Boodin, Martin Buber, Kenneth Burke, Ernst Cassirer, Christopher Dawson, John Dewey, James Feibelman, Gerald Heard, Sidney Hook, Karl Jaspers, Eric Kahler, Arthur Liebert, Karl Löwith, Lewis Mumford, Reinhold Niebuhr, F. S. C. Northrup, Jose Ortega y Gasset, Max Scheler, Albert Schweitzer, V. T. Stace and Paul Tillich.

II. THE HISTORY OF THE WORD "CIVILIZATION"

In touching on the problem of the origin of civilization Cohen reminds us[4] that

The term "civilization" was apparently never used in any language before the middle of the eighteenth century. Dr. Johnson refused to put it in his dictionary. Its appearance in the dictionary of the French Academy dates only from 1798. The term "Kultur" is also apparently a late introduction into the German language.

[2] For a useful discussion of the distinctions which may be made between several sub-fields of general history see Jan Romein's "Theoretical History," in *Journal of the History of Ideas*, vol. ix (1948) 53-64. Romein reminds us (p. 55) that the term "theoretical history" was used by Dugald Steward in 1793 to denote what other writers of the same period called "hypothetical, ideal, conjectural, natural or generalized history." He suggests that we "briefly imagine theoretical history as a central square surrounded on its four sides (a) by what in the eighteenth century was sometimes called theoretical history; (b) by what nowadays is known as the philosophy of history; (c) by the technique of historical research, which is often miscalled historical method; (d) and finally by what might be named practical, as distinct from theoretical, history."

[3] A selected list of such works is given in the Appendix to this paper.

[4] P. 230-31.

The word "civilization" thus embodies a modern appraisal of what distinguishes, in degree, at least, the things that we regard as our highest attainments and sets them apart from the attainments of more primitive peoples. Literally the term "civilization" means the making of cities or of city-life. The terms "urbanity" and "polished" are earlier terms for the complex of factors which distinguish city-life.

These statements are substantially true but somewhat misleading because they ignore the linguistic antecedents of the rather recent term *civilization*. In reality this term is only a slightly modified form of a word which goes back to Roman antiquity, this, in turn, being the translation of a still older Greek term.

It was probably from the Oxford Dictionary that Cohen got his information about the first appearance of *civilization* in English. There we read:

> 1772. Boswell, Johnson xxv. On Monday, March 23, I found him preparing a fourth edition of his folio Dictionary. He would not admit *civilisation* but only *civility*. With great deference to him I thought *civilisation* from *to civilise* better, in the sense opposed to *barbarity*, than *civility*.

But the difference between *civilization* (the American spelling of *civilisation*) and *civility* is only one of specific difference within a genus. In the 17th century *civility* and *civil life* or *civil society* were used by Bacon and Hobbes and other philosophers in the same sense as that which *civilization* has for us. The phrase "civilise their barbarous natures" occurs in a play by Massinger, written in 1631. *Civilité* was used in the sense of *civilization* by French writers of the 16th century.

All these words are derived from the Latin *civilitas*, which had the same meaning as our word *civilization*, at least as early as the 5th century C.E. Writing at that time, Cassiodorus (in his *Variae* 4. 33) remarked that "The true sign of *civilitas* is the observance of law. It is this which makes life in communities possible and distinguishes man from the brutes." According to the *Thesaurus Linguae Latinae*, another writer of about 500 C.E. complimented a Roman noble on having been educated by Greece in "the lap of *civilitas*."

Although I have not chanced to find *civilitas* used in this sense in Latin writings of the republican era, there can be little doubt that the Romans of that period would have given it that meaning if they had not already been used to other forms derived from the primitive base. Certainly Cicero is thinking of what we call "civilization" when he writes (*De Re Publica* i. 32), "Quare cum lex sit civilis societatis vinculum." Here incidentally, we can see the origin of the 17th century English phrase "civil society" in the sense of "civilization."

There can be little doubt, however, that the various Latin derivatives of *civis* and *civitas* were largely used to render the corresponding Greek terms, *polis, politeia* and the like. Our Greek lexicons are at fault in not recording the meaning "civilization" under the word *politeia,* together with its usual meanings, "citizenship," "form of government," "constitution" and "commonwealth." There are several examples of *politeia* meaning "civilization" in the works of Philo of Alexandria.[5] This also seems to be the meaning of the term in a fragment from the writings of the Stoic philosopher Chrysippus, who says that *politeia* is the proper rearing of men in community."[6] Nor would it be fanciful to find this meaning in Plato's use of *politeia* in *The Statesman* 271 E and in Aristotle's in *Politics* i. 2.

Apparently the civilized peoples of the ancient Near East had no corresponding terms but that they had the concept of civilization is hardly subject to doubt. As far back as the 3rd millennium B.C.E. the Sumerian and Babylonian writers of the Gilgamesh and Uttu poems had a clear consciousness of the cultural differences between savages and themselves. According to these ancient writings men acquired what we should call "civilization" when the gods taught them to plant grain, raise domestic animals, build houses of mud-brick and carry on similar activities.

This rapid sketch of the history and, so to speak, prehistory of the word *civilization* has, I trust, made it clear that this 18th century term is the direct descendant of a word with the same meaning which was used in classical antiquity.

[5] *Quaestiones in Genesin* ii. 2 and iv. 47 (retranslated into Greek from the Armenian version).
[6] von Arnim, J., *Stoicorum Veterum Fragmenta* iii. 81, Nr. 332,
ἡ δὲ ἐστι τροφὴ ἀνθρώπων καλὴ κατὰ κοινωνίαν.

III. THE GROWTH OF CIVILIZATION IN EARLIER PHILOSOPHICAL HISTORICAL LITERATURE

If a person of average education were asked what stages led to the formation of civilized societies and what general traits distinguish them from savage and barbarous societies, he would probably reply that favorable racial or environmental factors were the causes of development from savagery to civilization and that the main characteristics of civilized society are settled life in towns and cities, the division of labor, the existence of a leisure class devoted to art and science, a relatively stable political organization and the rudiments of a literary tradition.

Our hypothetical person of average education would probably be surprised to learn that many secondary traits of civilized society are to be found in the most primitive societies known to us. According to George P. Murdock's study, "The Common Denominator of Culture,"[7] there are some seventy-five traits of culture which are found among peoples of all periods in all parts of the world. These include a good many that most of us are accustomed to think of as peculiar to civilization. Among them are age-grading, calendar, dream-interpretation, ethno-botany, hygiene, inheritance rules, mythology, numerals, population policy, status differentiation, surgery and trade.

But to return to the average man's idea of what constitutes civilization—if we have rightly reported his view, it does not differ greatly from the views held by educated persons during the past few millennia. We saw above that the direct ancestor of the word *civilization* existed in classical antiquity and that the concept of civilization was even older. Now we shall see that the prevailing modern concepts of how civilization arose and what its chief characteristics are are merely variations on ancient themes.

We shall therefore make an extremely rapid survey of philosophical-historical literature and briefly notice some of the older theorists who attempted to trace the stages of society leading to civilization. In this survey we shall not concern ourselves with the further problem of progress vs. degeneration or that of the differ-

[7] In *The Science of Man,* edited by Ralph Linton (New York 1945) p. 123-42.

ence between "chronological primitivism" and "cultural primitivism."[8]

We have already noted that the Sumerian and Akkadian literature of the 3rd millennium B.C.E. shows awareness of some of the traits that distinguish urban from nomadic society, and that it accounts for the technological changes by explaining that men were taught new skills by the gods. The Israelite writers who set down the traditions of the patriarchal age were probably influenced by contemporary prophetic teaching to idealize the semi-nomadic past of their people and to condemn the features of urban civilization associated with Canaanite polytheism. One might, however, be justified in taking the Hebrew adjective *tam*, applied to Jacob, to mean that he was "civilized" in contrast to his brother Esau, the hunter. But this is meager evidence, and it is safer to refrain from drawing definite conclusions about Israelite concepts of civilization from the scanty material to be found in the Hebrew Bible.

Much clearer is the developmental scheme found in the ancient Indian doctrine of the four Yugas or world-periods. According to the *Vayu Purana*, material culture became much more complex in the second world-period. Whereas men had originally got food from trees, they now found their supplies exhausted through greed, and being afflicted by heat and cold, began to take shelter in caves. Thereafter they measured out towns, cities, villages and smaller dwelling-units, cultivated plants, established the four castes, created systems of law and sacrifice and, in a word, produced a civilization.

The Greek and Latin sources are still more detailed and explicit on the subject of the origin and growth of civilization. For a fairly complete collection of these sources the reader is referred to Lovejoy and Boas' *Documentary History of Primitivism*, mentioned above. We shall here glance at only a few of the most influential writers.

Hesiod, possibly drawing upon Indian-Iranian tradition,[9] has

[8] These terms are used by Arthur Lovejoy and George Boas in *A Documentary History of Primitivism and Related Ideas* (Baltimore 1935).

[9] For attempts to prove the thesis that there was Oriental influence on early Greek thought see R. Reitzenstein and H. H. Schaeder, *Studien zum antiken Synkretismus aus Iran und Griechenland* (Leipzig 1926); H. G. Güterbock, *Kumarbi, Mythen vom churritischen Kronos* (Zürich 1946); Franz Dornseiff,

touched on the subject of technical advance in the Prometheus story and the Legend of the Ages in his *Works and Days* 47-201. Unfortunately, it is difficult to reconstruct from these passages a clear-cut outline of the change from primitive to civilized society. A clearer picture is given by Aeschylus in his revision of the Prometheus story in *Prometheus Bound* 447-506.[10] Among the arts which the culture-hero proudly claims to have taught primitive men, "who had been buried in the ground and lived like little ants in the recesses of sunless caves," were the building of houses, the knowledge of astronomy and the calendar, writing, the domestication of wild animals, navigation, medicine, divination and the working of metals. A briefer list of skills is found in the version of the Prometheus story attributed to Protagoras in Plato's dialogue of that name, 320c-323a. In these early Greek sources we have only the beginning of what might be called a philosophy of civilization.

More systematic and philosophical is the account of the growth of civilization in Plato's *Laws* iii, 676-687, which Lovejoy and Boas think "is perhaps the Platonic passage which had most influence in the subsequent history of primitivism." [11] Here we have a brief sketch of the development from what we should call Stone Age culture to the stage of urban civilization. Plato shows how the

---

"Altorientailsches in Hesiods Theogonie," in *l'Antiquité classique* vol. vi (1937) 230-44. For a study of Hesiod which is not concerned with possible Oriental influences see Teggart, F. J., "The Argument of Hesiod's Works and Days," in *Journal of the History of Ideas,* vol. viii (1947) 45-77. Teggart does not believe that Hesiod set out to show that "the history of mankind was a process of continuing degeneration." Lovejoy and Boas, *op. cit.,* p. 196, hold that the Hesiodic version of the Prometheus story "is favorable to chronological but adverse to cultural primitivism."

[10] On the significance of the Prometheus story for Aeschylus and his contemporaries see Kitto, H. D. F., *Greek Tragedy, a Literary Study* (London 1939) p. 64, n. 1, "I have discussed the interpretation of the trilogy in the *Journal of Hellenic Studies,* 1934, p. 14 ff. In brief my suggestion was and is that Aeschylus presented a contest between Zeus (= Power, Order) and Prometheus (= Intelligence). Both have to concede something and assimilate something before they are reconciled in the later perfect cosmic order of Zeus. Such an evolutionary theme explains the prominence given to the evolution of civilization in our play, and it accords very well with the evolutionary theme which becomes prominent in the *Oresteia.*" So also Plato (according to L. A. Post, cited by Kitto), in *Epist.* ii, 310e-311b, suggests that Prometheus and Zeus were thought by the ancients to be symbols of wisdom and power.

[11] Lovejoy and Boas, *op cit.,* p. 162-64.

advance in technique was accompanied by a change in social organization. When he speaks, in 678b, of *poleis* and *politeiai* as the final stage of society, we are justified, I think (see above, section II) in rendering *politeiai* as "civilizations."

Aristotle, in *Politics* 1252, assumes that there were three stages of social development: family, village and city. He is only incidentally concerned, however, with the material elements of the various stages, and he does not furnish us a connected account of the change from primitive society to civilization. More interesting, from our present point of view, is the Aristotelian philosopher Dicaearchus, who wrote in the late 4th century B.C.E.[12] He sums up the views of earlier ethnographers as positing three stages of society: the primitive stage of food-gathering, the pastoral stage (in which war was introduced) and the agricultural stage (in which came the beginning of private property and class distinctions).

An eloquent account of the growth and appurtenances of civilization is given by the Epicurean philosopher-poet Lucretius in *De Rerum Natura* v. 771-1457, a passage much admired, though criticized for impiety, by Giambattista Vico.[13] The various elements, chiefly of material progress, enumerated by Lucretius, with occasional digressions on the abuses of civilization,[14] are the discovery of fire and the art of cooking, the founding of cities by kings, the distribution of lands, the discovery of gold, the appointing of magistrates, the formulation of laws, the development of speech

[12] *Apud* Porphyry, *De Abstinentia* iv. 1.2, translated by Lovejoy and Boas, *op. cit.*, p. 95-96.

[13] See Fisch, Max H., and Bergin, Thomas G., *The Autobiography of Giambattista Vico* (Ithaca 1944) p. 36, 41.

[14] The problem of Lucretius' divergence from Epicurus' view of historical development is briefly discussed by Lovejoy and Boas, *op. cit.*, p. 222, 239-40. See also the judicious treatment of this problem by Margaret Taylor, "Progress and Primitivism in Lucretius," in *American Journal of Philology* vol. lxviii (1947) 180-94, esp. p. 194, where she writes: "It is within this framework and in the light of the concept of the final good that we find a limited truth in the assertion, often repeated and often challenged, that some concept of progress is found in Epicureanism. . . . Lucretius himself frequently dwells on the darker side of the picture. But that he would have exchanged the knowledge and the security which civilization had brought for the life of savage or primitive man is surely inconceivable in the light of his own ideals. His very diatribes against contemporary society are the more bitter because man fails to avail himself of the happiness within his reach. It remains within his reach so long as the world shall last."

"through nature, need and use," the beginnings of religion and belief in gods through dreams and visions (one is reminded of Tylor's theory of animism), the working of other metals, with copper yielding to iron, technical improvements in hunting and war, the manufacture of clothing by spindle and loom, advances in agriculture and horticulture, the making of musical instruments, the sailing of ships, the contracting of treaties, the invention of writing and the formation of literature—"all these arts were learned by practice and the experience of man's eager mind." Though he does not divide man's progress into a number of well-defined stages, Lucretius apparently accepts the earlier known scheme of the development from primitive to pastoral and then to agricultural and finally to urban or civilized society.

Leaving the philosophical historians of antiquity with an apology for the brevity of our stay with them, we may just as briefly visit two culture-historians of the Middle Ages, Saint Augustine in the West and Ibn Khaldun in the Near East (culturally speaking, since the latter actually lived in North Africa).

In writing the *De Civitate Dei* Augustine was motivated by much the same feeling about an impending transformation of society as is found among the philosophical historians of our own day, although modern thinkers have a much longer perspective of history to contemplate and therefore probably (but not certainly) have a more accurate estimate of the degree of change that was taking place in Augustine's lifetime than did he himself.

For Augustine the great historic change took the dramatic form of the plundering of Rome ("the eternal city") by the Goths in 410 C.E., in which Christians as well as pagans suffered severely. Reflecting upon the vicissitudes of temporal society, Augustine felt it his duty to persuade his contemporaries to place their hopes of happiness in "the city of God," that is, the Church. Unfortunately for our present purpose, his concept of the historical development of mankind was so thoroughly determined by the scriptural account of Israel's divinely guided past that whatever he had learned from Greek and Roman philosophers—which, of course, was a great deal—is fairly well concealed in the interstices of the elaborate structure which he built to scriptural specifications.

Augustine has several schemes of social and political development. One is the twofold division of history into the period before the diffusion of the Gospel and that after it. Another takes the form of a biological analogy: the youth of mankind was the period of Nature, its maturity the period of Law, its old age the period of Grace. This is a sort of theological counterpart of the tripartite scheme which we have found in the Greek sources.

That Augustine was, however, aware of secular theories of man's advance from savagery through nomadism and agriculture to urban civilization seems to be indicated by his incidental remarks in chapters 15-17 of Book XIX. Here he reminds us, on the basis of Scripture, that "the first holy men were shepherds rather than kings." This may, to be sure, be merely an echo of conventional Stoic and Neo-Pythagorean ideas of the shepherd as a symbol of the ideal ruler, as in Homer. More revealing of the secular philosophy underlying his theological interpretation of history is the passage in which he enumerates, as illustrations of "the necessities and accidents of human life," cattle, grain, wine, oil, wood, coinage, navigation, war and marriage—a list which suggests that he considers these things typical of civilization as opposed to primitive society.

This briefest of surveys of earlier theories of civilization[15] will close with an abstract of the views of the remarkable Ibn Khaldun, a Muslim philosopher of history, who flourished in the latter half of the 14th century and wrote a Prolegomena (Arabic *Muqaddamat*) to the history of North Africa.[16] His "new science" (the phrase inevitably reminds one of the title of Giambattista Vico's great work) consisted of the use of the comparative method, the study of environmental factors and social-psychological analysis. On the assumption that the urban population of North Africa had

---

[15] For a selection of western medieval philosophies of history arranged on the plan of the volume by Lovejoy and Boas mentioned above see Boas, *Essays on Primitivism and Related Ideas in the Middle Ages* (Baltimore 1948).

[16] This abstract of Ibn Khaldun's views is based on the study by Kamil Ayad (a Muslim of North Africa), *Die Geschichts- und Gesellschaftslehre Ibn Khalduns* (Stuttgart and Berlin 1930). Of particular interest is Ibn Khaldun's doctrine of "*aṣṣabiyya* (from the Arabic root "*aṣṣaba* "to bind together"), which may be translated as "feeling of kinship." It is akin to the doctrine of "consciousness of kind" which was taught by Franklin Giddings, one of the pioneers of sociological research in this country.

once lived as nomads, Ibn Khaldun reached the conclusion that all cultural states were the result of a developmental process.

He regarded it as the task of "the new science" to study human society in its various forms of material and spiritual culture from savagery to civilization. After surveying the problems of methodology, he treats the history of mankind in six sections as follows:

(1) a. The necessity of the adopting of social life by all men.
    b. The distribution of the various races on the earth, and the climatic zones.
    c. The influence of climatic and geographical conditions upon human culture.

(2) Nomadic life as the first stage of cultural development, after savagery, among all peoples (herein is included the agriculture of semi-nomadism).

(3) The state; its rise, its varieties, its decline.

(4) On cities and urban life as the last stage of cultural development.

(5) Crafts, industries and arts.

(6) The classification of the sciences; literature.

Regarding the clan as the most important social-political unit, Ibn Khaldun traces the parallel development from patriarchal society, ruled by a chief chosen from a large and noble family, through the stage of peoplehood (*'umma*), ruled by an aristocracy, to the final stage of urban culture and kingship.

This admittedly elliptical survey may suffice to establish the fact that the prevailing theory of the successive stages of society from savagery to urban life was also the view that prevailed among ancient and medieval philosophers of history. It seems clear, moreover, that many ancient and medieval thinkers agreed on the whole with modern thinkers about the nature of the most important material and spiritual traits that distinguish civilization from earlier stages of human society.

IV. SOME REMARKS ON TOYNBEE'S PHILOSOPHY
OF HISTORY

One of the significant social phenomena of the present time is the great popularity of the one-volume summary of Arnold Toynbee's impressive *Study of History*. One may venture to suppose that if Morris R. Cohen had left us a critique of Toynbee's six-volume work, he would have detected the hidden strains and stresses in its majestic structure. Following the example given us by Cohen in his penetrating criticism of other philosophers of history, I shall point out some of the weaknesses, as they seem to me, of Toynbee's argument.[17]

Toynbee uses the formula of "challenge and response" in attempting to account for the origin and the preservation or disintegration of various civilized societies.[18] He tells us that Egyptian ("Egyptiac"!) civilization was created by certain North African groups who met the challenge of a changed environment by settling in the swamps of the Nile valley when the fertile soil of North Africa was dessicated as a result of the northward shift of the Atlantic cyclone belt. In contrast to these adventurous proto-Egyptians, other groups in the same area chose the line of least resistance and followed the African game animals to the tropical Sudan and there continued their old way of life, which is still followed by their descendants, the modern Dinka and Shilluk.

This explanation of the rise of Egyptian civilization is good so far as it goes. But curiosity leads us to ask what made the proto-Egyptians more adventurous than the ancestors of the Dinka and Shilluk? Why did one group accept the challenge of a changed environment, and the other group decline it? Toynbee raises the problem but does not attempt to solve it (perhaps because he is less adventurous than the proto-Egyptians). He merely remarks with regret that the reaction of the actor to the ordeal is a quantity which remains unknown to the would-be calculator.[19]

One of the most persuasive sections of Toynbee's book is the discussion of the racial and environmental factors in the development of societies. The author has undeniably done a good job in exposing the weaknesses of theories which attribute the origins of civilization or other stages of social development exclusively to race or to environment.

---

[17] I shall try to avoid duplicating the points made by P. Geyl in his critique of Toynbee in "Toynbee's System of Civilization," in *Journal of the History of Ideas*, vol. ix (1948) 93-124.

[18] P. 69-73 of the abridgement by D. C. Somervell (New York and London 1947), which is more generally accessible than the six-volume work and suffices for our purpose here.

[19] Toynbee-Somervell, p. 68.

The essence of both theories is the correlation between two sets of variables, in the one case, character and physique, in the other case, character and environment, and this correlation must be proved to be fixed and permanent if the theories founded on it are to be established. Under this test we have already seen the race theory break down, and we shall now see that the environment theory, though less preposterous, will fare no better.[20]

It will not, I hope, seem hypercritical to say that Toynbee is at fault in not taking into consideration further aspects of the correlation between race or environment and the form of culture. One necessary condition for establishing such a correlation is that there must be enough people living in a particular environment to have a form of culture which is capable of development *überhaupt*. This condition Toynbee seems to overlook when he points out that certain areas like the Argentinian pampas or the Australian grasslands have not produced nomadic societies of their own, as have the Eurasian and Afrasian steppes.

A second shortcoming in Toynbee's discussion is, I think, his failure to recognize that in any correlation of character and environment the reaction between the two may bring about a change in environment as well as in character. That is to say, the environment has a partly subjective nature. Two groups of people may live in the same area or in similar areas without (subjectively) having the same environment, since one group may regard as essential certain elements in the environment which the other group regards as unessential. Perhaps a linguistic analogy would be helpful here. The same sound, regarded as a physical and physiological phenomenon, may exist in two languages but in the one language it may be part of the linguistic pattern and so constitute a phoneme, while in the other language it may be incidental and extraneous to the linguistic pattern and therefore may not constitute a phoneme.

Among errors of judgment relating to certain civilizations which Toynbee may not unfairly be accused of having made, there is one which should be of special interest to readers of this volume since it concerns the Jews. First of all, Jewish readers, even if they are trained and objective historians, are likely to be annoyed by Toynbee's statement that the Jews are "a fossilized remnant of

[20] Toynbee-Somervell, p. 56.

Syriac society." It would not be difficult to show that the Jews are neither fossilized nor a remnant of Syriac society. But this is hardly necessary since Toynbee himself grants that the social philosophy of Zionism "has already been justified by its results." In that case, of course, the Jews can scarcely be described with any accuracy as "fossilized." As to their being a remnant of Syriac society, Toynbee himself must have doubts on that score. On different occasions he represents the Jews as the "internal proletariat" of three different societies—the Babylonian, the Syrian and the Hellenic. Perhaps one of the reasons why Toynbee is confused about the origin and nature of Jewish culture is that he has mistakenly assumed that "Judaism actually took shape 'by the waters of Babylon.' "[21]

V. TOWARD A MODERN VIEW OF CIVILIZATION

In view of Cohen's apparent commendation of the "institutional approach" to history it may not be inappropriate to present here a theory of historical perspective which is largely based on this method of determining the extent of change undergone by human society as a whole in advancing from savagery to civilization.

This theory is, very briefly, that man has now reached a transitional period between the third and fourth great stages of his career since his appearance as *homo sapiens.*

Taking the phrase "historical perspective" to imply the partial replacement of biological by cultural forces, I think that the following scheme comes near to a just appreciation of the great social-economic stages of human society and the measures of their duration (for convenience and brevity I have omitted the periods of transition).

Stage   I.   Tribal-hunting (paleolithic and mesolithic).
Stage   II.   Village-agricultural (neolithic and chalcolithic).
Stage III.   Urban-prototechnical (*ca.* 3000 B.C.E. to *ca.* 1900 C.E.)
Stage IV.   Ecumenical-neotechnical (*ca.* 1900 C.E. to *ca.* 3000 C.E.?)

[21] Toynbee-Somervell, v. 427.

Appendix

THE following list of books published during the past twenty-five years (1926-1950) on theoretical history, universal history, the philosophy of history and the like, is not meant to be exhaustive or even comprehensive. It is merely intended to suggest how widespread has been the interest in these subjects among contemporary philosophers, theologians, social scientists and even journalists. The list does not include works on historical method or on historiography as such. A few of the books here mentioned are new editions or translations of works first published before 1926. Not having been able to consult some of the books here mentioned I may inadvertently, on the strength of some other scholar's reference or review, have included some works that do not strictly belong to such a list. On the whole I have been most interested in noting down books which have received some attention in popular reviews. (Some long titles have been abbreviated.)

1926

E. H. Goddard and P. Gibbons, *Civilisation or Civilisations: an Essay in the Spenglerian Philisophy of History.*

F. S. Marvin, *Science and Civilization.*

Lynn Thorndike, *A Short History of Civilization* (2nd ed. published in 1948).

W. M. Tozzer, *Social Origins and Social Continuity.*

1927

H. Schneider, *Die Kulturleistungen der Menschheit* (Eng. translation published in 1931).

Harold Peake and Hubert Fleure, *Corridors of Time,* vols. 1, 2 (6 vols. published to date).

1928

Roland B. Dixon, *The Building of Cultures.*

A. L. Rowse, *Science and History.*

1929

G. Elliott-Smith, *Human History.*

Albert Schweitzer, *The Philosophy of Civilization.*

Max Scheler, *Menschheit und Geschichte.*

1930

J. Huizinga, *Wege der Kulturgeschichte.*

M. Maus, *Les civilisations, élements et formes.*

1931

John Dewey, *Philosophy and Civilization.*

Hugh P. Vorules, *The Quest of Power from Prehistoric Times to the Present Day.*

1932

Harry Elmer Barnes, *Can Man Be Civilized?*

Robert Briffault, *Breakdown: the Collapse of Traditional Civilization.*

1933
G. Elliot-Smith, *The Diffusion of Culture.*
A. A. Goldenweiser, *History, Psychology and Culture.*
Fritz Kern, *Die Anfänge der Weltgeschichte.*
1934
Arnold J. Toynbee, *A Study of History,* vols. 1-3 (vols. 4-6 published
    in 1939).
H. G. Wood, *Christianity and the Nature of History.*
1935
Alfred Weber, *Kulturgeschichte als Kultursoziologie.*
1937
Kenneth Burke, *Attitudes Toward History.*
N. Elias, *Ueber den Prozess der Zivilization* (1937-1938).
James Harvey Robinson, *The Human Comedy.*
P. A. Sorokin, *Social and Cultural Dynamics* (1937-1941).
1938
Christopher Dawson, *The Kingdom of God and History.*
Charles Seignobos, *Essai d'une histoire comparée des peuples de l'Europe.*
1939
John E. Boodin, *Man in His World.*
C. Delisle Burns, *Civilisation: the Next Step.*
1940
William F. Albright, *From the Stone Age to Christianity.*
1941
V. Gordon Childe, *Man Makes Himself.*
Gerald Heard, *Man the Master.*
Reinhold Niebuhr, *The Destiny of Man* (1941-1943).
Jose Ortega y Gasset, *Toward a Philosophy of History.*
1942
Hans Kohn, *World Order in Historical Perspective.*
V. T. Stace, *The Destiny of Western Man.*
T. W. Wallbank and A. M. Taylor, *Civilization, Past and Present.*
1943
V. Gordon Childe, *What Happened in History.*
Eric Fischer, *The Passing of the European Age.*
Sidney Hook, *The Hero in History.*
J. Huizinga, *Im Banne der Geschichte.*
Erich Kahler, *Man the Measure.*
Geza Roheim, *The Origin and Function of Culture.*
Lynn Thorndike, *Man and His Works.*
1944
Ernst Cassirer, *An Essay on Man.*
W. W. Howells, *Mankind So Far.*
A. L. Kroeber, *Configurations of Culture Growth.*
Harold Laski, *Faith, Reason and Civilisation.*

Bronislaw Malinowski, *A Scientific Theory of Culture.*
J. Pirenne, *Die grossen Strömungen in der Weltgeschichte.*
Karl Polanyi, *The Great Transformation.*
1945
Ellsworth Huntingdon, *The Mainsprings of Civilization.*
Sir Arthur Keith, *Essays on Human Evolution.*
Hans Kelsen, *General Theory of Law in the State.*
Paul Tillich, *The Interpretation of History.*
1946
Grahame Clark, *From Savagery to Civilization.*
R. G. Collingwood, *The Idea of History.*
James Feibelman, *Theory of Culture.*
R. Latham, *The Quest of Civilization.*
Arthur Liebert, *Der universale Humanismus.*
F. S. C. Northrup, *The Meeting of East and West.*
P. Van Schilfgaarde, *De Zin der Geschiedenes* (3rd ed.).
1947
Morris R. Cohen, *The Meaning of Human History.*
P. Laviosa-Zambotti, *Origine e diffusione della civilta.*
P. A. Sorokin, *Society, Culture and Personality.*
Jakob Taubes, *Abendländische Eschatologie.*
1948
Martin Buber, *Between Man and Man.*
H. D. A. Major, *Civilization and Religious Values.*
Paul Schrecker, *Work and History: An Essay on the Structure of Civi-
    lization.*
Arnold Toynbee, *Civilization on Trial.*
L. L. Whyte, *The Next Development in Man.*
1949
V. Gordon Childe, *History.*
Karl Jaspers, *Vom Ursprung und Ziel der Geschichte.*
Karl Löwith, *Meaning in History.*
Reinhold Niebuhr, *Faith and History.*
Leslie A. White, *The Science of Culture.*
1950 (Incomplete)
Sterling Lamprecht, *Nature and History.*

Evidence in History

BY RICHARD McKEON
University of Chicago

THE PROBLEM OF INCOMPLETENESS OF EVIDENCE ILLUSTRATED FROM THE HISTORY OF IDEAS DURING THE MIDDLE AGES

"The facts of history do not change. What has happened cannot 'unhappen.' Nor do competent historians ordinarily differ where the evidence is sufficient to warrant a definite conclusion. It is when evidence is inadequate, as in the early history of the Jews, that different writers reconstruct different pictures of what they think must have happened."—Morris Raphael Cohen

THE problems of method in history, notwithstanding the natural tendency to distinguish facts from their interpretation, are problems of relevance as well as of fact. The problems of historical evidence which bear on discovering and demonstrating what took place cannot be separated wholly from the problems of historical interpretation which bear on reconstructing in argument how or why it took place. If problems of method are restricted to problems of fact, historical method may be thought to be conditioned only by a subject matter which the historian, in guise of scientist, must investigate objectively. The facts with which historians deal, however, are not atomic entities possessed of proper and fixed characteristics. If they were, evidence could be treated in quantitative terms, and the problems involved in treating the few facts available when evidence is "scarce" would be the same in kind but simpler than those involved in presenting the multitude of facts discoverable when evidence is "abundant."

In general, evidence is abundant in modern history and scarce in ancient history. Historians have worked for centuries on the common core of information concerning antiquity. Some new facts have become available, both from the discovery of literary materials and the interpretation of material remains, but even in the treatment of old familiar documents historians seldom find that the subject matter has been treated adequately by their predecessors. The examination of problems and the proof of conclusions in the argumentative portions of historical narratives and in the documentation of footnotes is sometimes encumbered, and sometimes motivated, by criticisms not merely of the methods by which other historians were led to ignore or misinterpret data but more simply of their views and reconstructions of the past. The arguments and reasons which bind the facts into plausible account are inseparable from the discoveries and demonstrations which establish the facts, and the controversy concerning whether or not history is a science is complicated by the assumption usually made when scientific method is applied to history that science consists simply in the collection of facts.

The calculation of evidence available and the balance of its probabilities implies some determination of what constitutes evidence and relevance. Once his subject matter has been delimited, whether by tacit preconception or explicit definition, the historian may use "scientific methods" for the collection of data, for induction and generalization, for the estimation of probabilities, or even for the formulation of principles. He may state his basic laws or assume them as common truths in no need of explicit formulation or adapt them from one or more of the sciences, from economics, sociology, anthropology, politics, psychology, physics, biology, geology, or cosmology. His treatment of evidence, thereafter, may resemble the statistical interpretation of curves and tendencies, the social, biological or psychopathic diagnoses of symptoms, or the philosophic reconstruction of causes of events, tempers of ages, or cycles of birth and destruction. The historian who treats happenings and times in one fashion, however, is faced not only with the problems involved in his data but also those presented by the opposed methods and different data of historians who approach the same period and related occurrences on other assumptions. The economic historian must find at least a problem in the data and methods of the historian who delineates the morphology and physiognomy of ages or the historian who traces the causal influences of political actions or, if such data and methods seem too far removed, at least in those of the economic historian of another persuasion, classical or Marxist. The problem of evidence is involved not merely in the interpretation of commonly accepted data, but in the correlation of apparently irreducible differences of data found in different interpretations and thought acceptable on different grounds and in the estimation of incommensurate weights of importance and cogency assigned to them. In the treatment of the latter problems, methods of inquiry and proof, in which history is similar to science, are subordinated to methods of persuasion or dissuasion, edification, or even exhortation and imprecation in the interests of utility or salvation, in which history, continuing an old tradition, is a branch of rhetoric, or literature, or politics, or theology.

To speak of scarcity of evidence or abundance of evidence is to concentrate on one of these two aspects of historical method in an effort to reduce it as far as possible to quantitative terms. Evidence is scarce when the historian fixes his attention—frequently as a consequence of historical or scientific interests which came into vogue since the time he studies—on a period and a place, or on events, or a group or class of persons or an aspect of their activity or association concerning which he can find little or no information. This paucity of evidence is due sometimes to the fact that no direct record was kept at the time, although the facts can be reconstructed partially on indirect evidence. It is sometimes the result of the deliberate or accidental destruction of documents or monuments which might have supplied the details of information sought. Whether the evidence never existed or whether it is known or thought to have existed but to have been destroyed, the paucity of evidence is part of the historical situation itself. It is often the result of a conviction, at the time of the events recorded or in the interim since their occurrence, that in the transactions of life, viewed either for the purposes of control of practical action or for the purposes of record in the memory of man, such information was insignificant or pernicious. Historical accidents apart—and theories have not been without their influence in determining historical accidents—paucity of evidence reflects recorded or unrecorded differences of theory between those who preserved the data and

those who later seek it. For an ancient writing to have survived,
accident and chance apart, it must have excited interest at regular
intervals to ensure the continuous preparation of new copies or the
preservation of old. Evidence is abundant when neither the
passage of time nor the theories of men have eliminated data or
limited their possible interpretation. When evidence is abundant
the intrusion of theory by the historian is less easily detected, since
it is often a theory similar to that according to which the data were
assembled and arranged for preservation. Historians may, when
that is the case, differ both in interpretation of data and in selection among indefinitely various data. Incompleteness of evidence,
however, unlike scarcity or abundance, is not a quantitative term,
and the problems of evidence which it raises may be used to
uncover the non-quantitative and theoretic aspects of other considerations of historical method and historical inquiry, including
those related to scarcity and abundance of evidence. Incomplete
evidence is not, as might seem to be the case, midway between
scarce and abundant evidence, for evidence may be complete
enough to be probative in spite of the fact that it is scarce, or
incomplete although abundant. A further question, which has no
bearing on quantity, must be asked to determine for what purpose
or relevant to what problem the evidence is complete or incomplete.

The intellectual history of the Middle Ages and particularly the
late Middle Ages abounds with illustrations of the interplay between these two aspects of the problem of historical evidence.
Evidence is scarce concerning the development of ideas during the
period, although an abundance of documents is known to exist,
unpublished or inadequately edited, partially reported or recorded
only by *incipit* or vague catalogue description, difficult to assemble
or interpret without paleographic techniques which are not common even among historians or without historical and scientific
knowledge uncommon among paleographers. While both aspects
of historical evidence—the qualitative and the quantitative, the
theoretic and the material—are present in any use or treatment of
arguments and data, the two sets of problems may occur in three
possible combinations, and evidence may, therefore, be thought
incomplete in three senses.

In the first sense, evidence is incomplete when documents or information that might have been recorded are missing. The historian must then reconstruct the probable contents of documents— with as little distortion by the intrusion of his own theories as possible—from documents which discuss missing materials from other points of view, or documents influenced by lost documents, or documents probably similar to such records or concerned with similar matters if earlier documents never existed.

In the second sense, evidence is incomplete when documents which exist but have been neglected, and which can be made available only slowly and with difficulty, become important to the interpretation of a period or movement. Evidence is incomplete in this sense, not because of something that has happened to the documents, but because of something that has happened to the interests and theories of the historian and his contemporaries. The whole scope of the history of political theory, of logic, physics, metaphysics, and literary criticism, and of philosophy in general, during the late Middle Ages is illustration of incomplete evidence in this sense. Interest in these aspects of this period of intellectual history is recent—less than a century old in the case of the most venerable forms of interest in medieval thought, not much more than two decades old in the case of the most sprightly—for the philosophy, science, and theory of the Middle Ages had prior to that change been passed over with slighting examples borrowed by one historian from another and with judgments which echoed the Renaissance expressions of distaste and contempt, whereas more recently the historian has studied manuscripts or has impatiently awaited the publication of new editions of scientific and philosophic works previously unquoted and often unsuspected.

In the third sense, evidence is incomplete not because documents are missing or because documents have been neglected, but because historians have re-examined and revised their views, and as a result new and more satisfying interpretations are superposed on data which no longer seem to support the earlier conclusions. Evidence is known to be incomplete in the first sense by an inference from documents to documents, in the second sense by a theoretic insight which is supported by the examination of documents, but in this third sense the inadequacies are apparent primarily from the opposition of historical theories, and one or the other interpretation becomes meaningless when the theoretic positions of the historians engaged in the dispute are forgotten. Thus, peculiar problems—like the recurrent disputes concerning the decline and fall of the Roman empire, the continuity of the empire, the relation of the Papacy to the empire, or the very question, whether or not the "Middle Ages" is a properly designated and accurately defined period, with the consequent tendency for the traditional darkness to set in later and to be dispelled earlier in the pages of each succeeding historian—can be understood only if the language of the historian is compared with the language of disputes in progress in political theory, philosophy, science, and technology at the time he conducts his historical inquiries into the past. Such problems are frequent in the history of the Middle Ages—though not more frequent than in the history of other periods—in spite of the impatience of historians who tend to dismiss them with unhistorical expressions of surprise that anyone should have fallen into the earlier errors or have made the distinctions of other historians and with philosophical intimations, which purport to be grounded in history, that the problem is not real. Yet when the grounds on which evidence is thought to be incomplete are examined, such problems are found to be involved in all historical inquiry, even in those apparently solid investigations which are thought to proceed wholly according to the indisputable evidence of documents and monuments.

Evidence is incomplete in its simplest and least sophisticated form when the lack of a document or group of documents is apparent to the' unaided reflection of common sense by the evidence of other documents. Thus, in the history of municipal institutions and in the history of universities in the Middle Ages the characteristics and contents of lost documents may frequently be reconstructed from existing information without appeal to elaborate theoretic postulates. Since the early charters of the important cities exist only rarely, discussion of the institutions of those cities or even the official form of the regulation of those institutions is based on probabilities and on the charters of *villes-neuves*. Since the early charters of the oldest universities frequently do not exist, or since we have reason in many cases to believe that university practices grew up earlier than the first charters which regulated them and often in different forms than is specified in the regulations, historians infer from later to earlier charters, from official regulation to probable practice anterior and posterior to the statutes, as well as contemporary with them, following no other guide than documentary data and the analogy of other and similar academic processes. The lacunae in evidence which is incomplete in this sense can be filled in only by the discovery and study of missing documents, and the validity of earlier inferences can be tested conclusively only by the authority of such documents. Thus, in the brilliant example of Denifle's publication, in 1887, of the 1317 statutes of the University of Bologna together with additions to the statutes of 1347,[1] the edition is prefaced by a long study which corroborates and supplements earlier conjectures concerning the relation of the newly published statutes to the more familiar statutes of 1432 and to those of Padua, Perugia and Florence which, with the statutes of Lerida (ca. 1300), had previously been the basis for information concerning the early institutions of Bologna.[2]

When such processes of inference are applied to the texts of intellectual history the conjectured lacunae take on a second dimension of variation, for the texts may themselves be the result of practices regulated by statutes. Thus, when Glorieux undertook in 1925 to study the history of the use of quodlibetal disputations at the University of Paris,[3] he found that the earliest statutes in which they are treated in detail, those of 1335 and 1366, set up the quodlibetal disputes among the tests imposed on bachelors for admission to the licentiate. On the other hand, we have numerous texts of quodlibetal questions as they were actually disputed at the University of Paris, most of them between 1260 and 1320, composed not by students but by regent professors, and indeed all the most famous philosophers and theologians of the earlier period seem to have prepared such questions. The incompleteness of evidence is in this case symmetrical, for we have no university statutes which take

[1] Denifle, H., "Die Statisten der Juristen-Universität Bologna vom J. 1317-1347 und deren Verhältniss zu jenen Paduas, Perugias, Florenz," in *Archiv für Literatur- und Kirchen-Geschichte des Mittelalters*, vol. iii (1887) 196-408.
[2] *Cf.* Rashdall, H., *The Universities of Europe in the Middle Ages*, ed. F. M. Powicke and A. B. Emden (Oxford 1936) vol. i, p. 173-74.
[3] Glorieux, P., *La Littérature Quodlibétique de 1260 à 1320*, vol. i (La Saulchoir Kain 1925); vol. ii (Paris 1935).

cognizance of the institution for the earlier period when professors undertook the questions, although we have numerous examples of the disputations themselves; conversely, for the period during which we have explicit indication of the place and function of the exercise in the administration of the university we have no texts of questions. Glorieux therefore argues plausibly that the questions began as solemn functions of the university exercised by the masters, but were, by a process not without analogues in academic life, gradually added to the duties of students as prerequisites for degrees, and that they were first recognized explicitly in the regulations of the university in the latter guise.

Incompleteness of evidence in this first sense, in which documents are alone or primarily in question, involves, although in inconspicuous proportions, the interpretative and inferential ingredient which determines incompletenss of evidence in the second sense. The transition is therefore gradual from the search for documents previously unknown to the study of documents previously ignored and neglected though not unknown. Thus, despite the spread of interest during the nineteenth century in the persons and doctrines of men suspected of, or condemned for, theological error or heresy, their works in many instances have been published only in recent years, and the early reconstructions of their positions from the propositions enumerated in their condemnations have only subsequent to such publication been rectified and extended by study of the documents which furnish the basis and context of the propositions condemned. When Renan published his *Averroès et l'Averroïsme* in 1852, he treated Latin Averroism of the thirteenth century primarily by listing propositions condemned in 1270 and 1277 and by quoting from Thomas Aquinas' treatise against the Averroists; yet he knew that manuscripts of Siger of Brabant existed, and in one brief sentence he even generalized vaguely concerning one of Siger's unpublished treatises.[4] The influence of Arabic philosophers on thirteenth-century Latin thought has been recognized, partly because of the suggestions of Renan, as one of the keys to the intellectual problems of the Middle Ages, and the works of the Latin Averroists have slowly been published. Man-

[4] Renan, E., *Averroès et l'Averroïsme, Essai Historique* (Paris n.d.) p. 271-78, and esp. 272.

donnet's revolutionary study, in 1899, of Siger of Brabant and Latin Averroism in the thirteenth century was based on his own and Baeumker's publication of considerable fragments of the works of Siger. In 1922 Ehrle, and in 1924 Grabmann, published information concerning further newly discovered manuscripts of Siger of Brabant to which Grabmann added data concerning Siger's even more legendary colleague in condemnation, Boethius of Dacia. In 1931 and 1942 still more fragments of Siger's work were published by Van Steenberghen, and in 1937 a brief work of Boethius was published by Grabmann. The task is still far from complete either with respect to the publication of known manuscripts or with respect to the possible discovery of unsuspected manuscripts, for, to cite only one instance, Grabmann has pointed out that we have no trace of commentaries of Siger on Aristotle's *Ethics* or *Politics* although we have the testimony of Pierre Dubois (*De Recuperatione Terrae Sanctae*, sec. 132) that he heard Siger lecture on the *Politics*.[5] In much the same fashion the most definite indica-

---

[5] Mandonnet, P., *Siger de Brabant et l'averroïsme latin au XIIIe siecle*, 1st ed. Collectanea Friburgensia, fasc. VIII (Fribourg, Switzerland, 1899). In the second edition in *Les Philosophes Belges* the texts are published in vol. vii (Louvain 1908) and the study in vol. vi (Louvain 1911). Cl. Baeumker published *Die "Impossibilia" des Siger von Brabant* in *Beiträge zur Geschichte der Philosophie des Mittelalters* II, 6 (Münster 1898). *Cf.* his "Zur Beurteilung Sigers van Brabant," *Philosophisches Jahrbuch*, XXIV (1911) 177-202, and his "Um Siger Von Brabant," *Ibid.*, 369-81 and 517-19. *Cf.* also Ehrle, F., "Nuove proposte per lo studio dei manoscritti della scolastica medioevale," in *Gregorianum* III (1922) 198-218, and Grabmann, M., "Neu aufgefundene Werke des Siger von Brabant und Boetius von Dacien," in *Sitzungsberichte der Bayerischen Akademie der Wissenschaften, Philos. Klasse*, 1924, 2 (Munich 1924) and his "Neuaufgefundene 'Quaestionen' Sigers von Brabant zu den Werken des Aristoteles," in *Miscellanea Francesco Ehrle, Scritti di Storia e Paleografia* (Rome 1924) vol. i, p. 103-47. More recently Grabmann has continued his studies of Averroism in "Der Lateinische Averroismus des 13. Jahrhunderts und seine Stellung zur christlichen Weltanschauung. Mitteilungen aus ungedruckten Ethikkommentaren," in *Sitzungsberichte der Bayerischen Akademie der Wissenschaften, Philos.-hist. Abt.* (1931) and "Studien über den Einfluss der aristotelischen Philosophie auf die mittelalterlichen Theorien über das Verhältnis von Kirche und Staat," *ibid.* (1934). In the latter article the reference to Pierre Dubois (p. 46) occurs. F. Stegmüller edited *Quinque Quaestiones Morales* and *Sex Quaestiones Naturales* of Siger in the *Recherches de Théologie Ancienne et Médiévale*, vol. iii, in 1931. F. Van Steenberghen added to the list of previously unpublished manuscripts and to the interpretation of their significance in his two volumes, *Siger de Brabant d'après ses Oeuvres Inédites. I, Les Oeuvres Inédites* and *II, Siger dans l'Histoire de*

tion we had of the doctrines of Nicholas of Autrecourt was the list
of propositions condemned by the faculty of the University of
Paris in 1348 until two of his works were published, one in 1908,
the other in 1939.[6]

The shifts of interest which reveal incompleteness of evidence
in this sense can be described best, not by listing the names and
times affected, but by stating the convictions which caused their
neglect and the opposed convictions which have led to their
renewed study. We know relatively little concerning the intellectual movements of the late twelfth and early thirteenth centuries,
because that was a period engaged in the translation and assimilation of the works of Aristotle, and the doctrines of the men who
first assisted in that labor seemed for purposes of the technical
disputes which followed its consummation, incomplete, inaccurate,
irrelevant, and in error on many points of theology and philosophy.
There were Dominicans teaching at Paris and at Oxford before
Albertus Magnus and Thomas Aquinas and contemporary with
them. Yet we have only second-hand reports of the doctrines and
descriptions of the manuscripts of Roland of Cremona, Hugo of
St. Cher, Peter of Tarantaise, Bombolognus of Bolognia, Romanus
of Rome, or Richard Fischacre.[7] There were Franciscans teaching

l'Aristotélisme (*Les Philosophes Belges*, vols. xii and xiii, Louvain, 1931 and
1942). W. J. Dwyer published Siger's *De Aeternitate Mundi* (Louvain 1937);
Ph. Delehaye, his *Quaestiones super libros Physicorum* (*Les Philosophes
Belges*, vol. xv, Louvain, 1941); and C. A. Graiff, his *Quaestiones in Meta-
physicam* (Philosophes Médiévaux, vol. i, Louvain, 1948). Grabmann's edition
of Boethius of Dacia appears under the title "Die opuscula de Summo Bono
sive de Vita Philosophi und de Sompniis des Boetius von Dacien," in *Mittelalterliches Geistesleben* (Munich 1936) vol. ii, p. 200-24. The publication of
these manuscripts has been accompanied and followed by discussion and controversy concerning their authenticity, interpretation, and significance.

[6] *Chartularium Universitatis Parisiensis*, ed. H. Denifle and A. Chatelain,
vol. ii (Paris 1891) 1041 and 1124, p. 505 and 576-87. Lappe, J., *Nicolaus
von Autrecourt, Sein Leben, Seine Philosophie, Seine Schriften*, in *Beiträge zur
Geschichte der Philosophie des Mittelaltres* (edition of portions of the correspondence of Nicholas) (Münster 1908) VI, 2. O'Donnell, J. R., "Nicholas of
Autrecourt" (edition of the *Exigit Ordo Executionis*) in *Mediaeval Studies*,
vol. i (1939) 179-280.

[7] *Cf.* Geyer, B., *Die patristische und scholastische Philosophie* (Berlin
1928) p. 398-400; Grabmann, M., "Forschungsziele und Forschungswege auf
dem Gebiet der mittelalterlichen Scholastik und Mystik," in *Mittelalterliches
Geistesleben* (Munich 1926) 36-38.

at Paris before Roger Bacon joined the Order or Bonaventura started his studies there, and other Franciscans were engaged on philosophical and theological questions in Oxford. Yet the critical edition of the *Summa Theologica* of Alexander of Hales was undertaken only in 1924 and the fourth volume completed in 1948, after its editors had struggled with almost incredible textual and critical difficulties, and problems concerning the authenticity of many parts of the work are still unresolved. The projected critical edition of Duns Scotus seems indefinitely postponed by similar problems of text and authenticity. We have only a poor modern edition of one of the works of John of La Rochelle, and with only rare exceptions we are dependent on manuscripts or early printed editions of the writings of Adam Marsh, Thomas of York, John Pecham, and Richard of Middleton.[8] The edition of the *Opera hactenus inedita* of Roger Bacon reached its sixteenth fascicule in 1940. The interests and attitudes of philosophers of the second half of the century not only determined the state of the materials preserved from the preceding period, and thereby set the problems which existing documents and knowledge present, but give plausibility to judgments of the character and the alleged confusions of earlier discussions which have been continued by historians who do not share the conviction that fidelity to theological principles or accuracy of interpretation of Aristotle are pertinent critical canons, much less grounds for historical consideration or silence.

The same judgments, implicit or expressed, determined the fate of much of the philosophy and theology of the twelfth century. The theories of many writers, formulated on the basis of little more than a slight knowledge of the logic of Aristotle, fell into disuse in later disputes and inquiries which depended on increasing knowledge of Aristotelian metaphysical, scientific and moral doctrines. In addition, the suspicion of heresy touched many doctrines at points at which the issues and dangers were only later defined. The work of an influential theologian like Peter Lombard, which was to become one of the bases of theological education during the next few centuries, had first to be rectified, and many of the theo-

[8] *Cf.* Geyer, B., *Die Patristische und Scholastische Philosophie*, p. 382-86, 396-97; Grabmann, M., "Forschungsziele und Forschungswege," p. 32-34; Sharp, D. E., *Franciscan Philosophy at Oxford* (Oxford 1930).

logical speculations of a dialectician like Peter Abailard, which were widely influential after his death though he was not always quoted by name, were condemned despite the effort of influential disciples to rectify them. The shifts of interest which have returned Abailard's work to prominence are no more directly dependent on historical facts or use of historical methods than the fidelity to theological principles and the accuracy of Aristotelian interpretation, which cut short his reputation, were related to his historical merits or his historical influence. Even apart from the morbid and romantic interest which has attached to the story of his life, the motives of the renewed interest in his career have little relevance either to his doctrine or the history of their influence. Cousin, in his edition of the previously unpublished *Sic et Non* and the *Dialectica* in 1836, celebrated him as one of the two great philosophers of France. Later his works have been instanced as episodes in the development of freedom of thought or as the beginning of the scholastic method. Only recently has it been possible to consider his doctrine in the context of movements of thought contemporary with his development: two of his logical works were published for the first time between 1919 and 1933, and one of his theological works was published in 1939.[9]

The historian of the intellectual movements of the fourteenth and

[9] *Ouvrages inédits d'Abélard pour servir à l'histoire de la philosophie scolastique en France.* Ed. V. Cousin (Paris 1836) p. v-vi: "Abélard et Descartes sont incontestablement les deux plus grands philosophes qu'ait produits la France, l'un au moyen âge, l'autre dans les temps modernes; et cependant, il y a douze années, la France n'avait point une édition complète de Descartes, et elle attend encore une édition complète d'Abélard. . . . J'appelle de tous mes voeux, je seconderais de tous les moyens qui sont en moi, une édition complète des oeuvres de Pierre Abélard. Si j'étais plus jeune, je n'hesiterais point à l'entreprendre, et je signale ce travail à la fois patriotique et philosophique à quelqu'un de ces jeunes professeurs, pleins de zèle et de talent, auxquels j'ai ouvert la carrière, et que j'y suis avec tant d'intérêt." The *Logica "Ingredientibus"* was published in three fascicules of the *Beiträge zur Geschichte der Philosophie des Mittelalters*, vol. xxi, under the editorship of B. Geyer: 1, "Die Glossen zu Porphyrius" (1919); 2, "Die Glossen zu den Kategorien" (1921); 3, "Die Glossen zu περὶ ἑρμηνείας» (1927). Geyer published "Die 'Logica Nostrorum Petitioni Sociorum'" in fascicule 4 of the same volume of the *Beiträge* in 1933. H. Ostlender published *Peter Abaelards Theologia "Summi Boni"* in volume xxxv of the *Beiträge* in 1939. Moreover, a number of writings of other twelfth-century authors, including some that show the marks of the Abailard school, has been edited.

fifteenth centuries faces problems of inadequate evidence in which the relation of theories to the discovery or creation of lacunae is easily discernible. As the judgments and silences of late thirteenth-century philosophers put a termination on the study of the doctrines of the prior one hundred years, so the criticism of Renaissance humanists and early modern philosophers for a long time determined the intellectual history of the late Middle Ages. It has continued to be presented as the period of subtle logic-chopping which ruined logic, stupid traditionalism which all but destroyed religion, and excessive rationalism which made the scientific use of reason impossible, until stage by stage historians began to find in it the beginnings or the paradigms of modern social, economic, and religious institutions, the anticipations of modern science, and most recently the first steps of the innovations of modern logic.

Great collections of documents of political theory and political controversy were published during periods in which the oppositions expressed were still living issues or recent memories. But since the publication of the monumental editions of Goldast, Schard, Gratius, Brown and others, only occasional works, previously unpublished or long unedited, have been printed. Editions of two of the works of Marsilius of Padua appeared in 1922 and 1928, but two others must be consulted in editions of the eighteenth century or earlier. Several unpublished works of William of Ockham have been edited during the last twenty-five years, and in 1940 the first volume of a projected critical edition of his political writings was issued. There are no modern editions of the political writings of men as important as John Gerson, Robert Grosseteste or Agostino Trionfo, and the names of other contributors to political theory seem obscure, despite the importance of their doctrines or their influence, because of the inaccessibility of their works.

Many excellent editions and collections of the theological treatises of the late Middle Ages were published, in like fashion and for like reasons, from the fifteenth to the seventeenth centuries. Theologians who advanced or combatted innovations could usually find an editor, for the heretics of one tradition were counted among the defenders or anticipators of another and might be subjected to further study on either grounds so long as the issue was debated.

But critical editions have not been lavished on theologians between the times of St. Thomas and Luther. The best editions of the collected works of Duns Scotus and Suarez are highly imperfect nineteenth-century reproductions of seventeenth-century editions. The works of John Gerson and the theological writings of William of Ockham, including his *Commentary on the Sentences* and his *Quodlibetal Questions,* must be consulted in incunabulum editions. The publication of editions of the works of Meister Eckhart and Nicholas of Cusa was interrupted by the war. Modern collections of editions and re-editions of theological texts stop short of the late Middle Ages. The excellent critical editions of the *Corpus Scriptorum Ecclesiasticorum Latinorum* of the Vienna Academy are devoted almost wholly to the Patristic period, and even the convenient though uneven collection of reprinted texts of Migne's Latin Patrology does not extend beyond the twelfth century. The great collections of documents of the later period are devoted to the statement of doctrines and disputes, the formulations of the papal curia or the deliberations of theological bodies, and only incidentally to the works of the theologians.

The national collections of documents concerned with the histories, or even the prehistories, of individual nations are of a later date and often continue to the present day the effort to preserve the past of a people, to make available the grounds for celebrating its extended history, and to afford expression to its nationalistic pride. Collections of medieval literary texts, when they began to appear, followed similar national lines under the impulse of linguistic differences, and the interest in medieval philosophy took its beginnings from present-day theological movements and has therefore extended only slightly and occasionally beyond the study of the thirteenth century. There has never been a corpus of scientific, or logical, or metaphysical writings of the late Middle Ages, and the historian interested in those speculations, which were very prominent at the time, is dependent almost entirely on manuscripts and early printed editions.

The study of medieval philosophy and the publication of medieval philosophic texts were sporadic until the nineteenth century. Then pioneers like Cousin, Hauréau and Picavet edited some manuscripts and reported the contents of others. The encyclical letter of Pope Leo XIII and the variety of religious forces that led to the construction of neoscholastic philosophy turned the attention of able scholars to the study of St. Thomas Aquinas. The emphasis tended to fall on the thirteenth century and on the theological ramifications of philosophy even in the essays and editions of the *Beiträge zur Geshichte der Philosophie des Mittelalters,* initiated in 1891, and in the later *Archives d'Histoire Doctrinale et Littéraire du Moyen Age,* started in 1926. Such enthusiasms as were expressed about philosophers who flourished before or after the thirteenth century—the discovery of the beginnings of freedom of thought and skepticism in Abailard, the affinity which Hegel found to his own dialectic in Nicholas of Cusa, the foundations for modern science which Pierce constructed from, or the theory of meaning which Heidegger referred to, Duns Scotus, the anticipations of the truth which semanticists and logicians have found in Peter of Spain, William of Ockham, and Albert of Saxony, and, in general, the controversy of the nominalists and realists which constitutes the stock construction referred to the twelfth and fourteenth centuries—contributed little to the scholarly study of medieval thought and were often difficult to relate to the doctrines and tendencies expressed in medieval texts.[10]

Contemporary developments in the ideas of theoretical physics were reflected in Pierre Duhem's re-examination of the early history of science and his discovery of predecessors and anticipators for Copernicus, da Vinci, Galileo and their contemporaries. Different attitudes toward Duhem's enterprise in seeking anticipations of scientific theories in commentaries on Aristotle and on the Sentences of Peter Lombard have developed in later inquiries into the history of medieval science. Haskins found little evidence that authority hampered the free use of reason seriously during the Middle Ages; Thorndike explored the close affinity in the developments of magic and experimental science; Sarton argued that positive knowledge must be separated sharply from superstition and magic and discounted alleged anticipation of scientific truths in

---

[10] Twelfth century philosophic texts have received more attention since the foundation of the *Spicilegium Sacrum Louvaniense* (Louvain 1922 ff.) and the *Publications in Mediaeval Studies* (Notre Dame, Indiana, 1936 ff.), while *Mediaeval Studies* (Toronto, Canada, 1939 ff.) has published some very important twelfth and fourteenth century texts.

theological writings. Haskins and Thorndike have greatly increased our knowledge of manuscript sources. The historian of science must work largely with manuscripts and earlier printed editions, for unlike philosophic texts the works of scientists were seldom reprinted in theological or national collections, and there is a dearth of modern critical editions of medieval scientific texts.[11]

The analogies of modern symbolic logic have turned favorable attention to those aspects of formal and verbal analysis in late scholasticism which Renaissance humanists criticized most violently. The recent upsurge of interest in the history of medieval logic is one result. Yet the growing tendency to discover striking anticipations of more recent theories has been based on a few recurring generalizations which are difficult to test in the absence of reliable texts. The conception and formulation of logic was profoundly influenced by the *summulae* of logic which were used as textbooks in the thirteenth century and which determined the nature and contents of much of what has since passed for the "Aristotelian" or "traditional" logic; yet texts of the *summulae* were very difficult of access until recently. William of Shyreswood's *Introductiones in logicam* was printed for the first time in 1937 and his *Syncategoremata* in 1941; the *Summulae logicales* of Peter of Spain was printed frequently in the fifteenth and sixteenth centuries but no new edition was brought out for several hundred years until 1947; the manuscripts of Lambert of Auxerre have been studied, but no edition, ancient or modern, has ever been prepared of his works.[12] Very important changes were introduced into logic

[11] *Cf.* Thorndike, Lynn, "Prospectus for a Corpus of Medieval Scientific Literature in Latin," in *Isis* vol. xiv (1930) 368-84. The first three volumes of such a *corpus* with the publication of Thorndike's editions of *The Herbal of Rufinus* (Chicago 1946), *The Sphere of Sacrobosco and its Commentators* (Chicago 1949) and *Latin Treatises on Comets between 1238 and 1368 A.D.* (1950).

[12] *Die Introductiones in logicam des Wilhelm von Shyreswood*, ed. M. Grabmann in *Sitzungsberichte der Bayerischen Akademie der Wissenschaften*, 1937, heft 10; O'Donnell, J. R., "The Syncategoremata of William of Sherwood," in *Mediaeval Studies* III (1941) 46-93. Besides the edition of the *Summulae logicales* prepared by M. J. Bochenski (Turin 1947) a translation of part of the work into English has been made on the basis of incunabulum editions by J. P. Mullally, *The Summulae Logicales of Peter of Spain* (Notre Dame 1945), and editions have been published by M. Alonso of his *De Anima* (Madrid 1941) and his *Commentary on the De Anima of Aristotle* (Madrid 1944).

in development of the inquiry into the properties of terms, initiated in the *summulae,* and in reaction against that inquiry, in setting the foundations of "speculative grammar," in elaborating the "combinatory art" and in ingenious adaptations of the Aristotelian logic to the problems presented by these tendencies in logic. Yet there are no modern critical editors of the great fourteenth- and fifteenth-century logicians.

Both of the first two varieties of incompleteness of evidence, the simple lack of documents made apparent by other documents and the need of unused documents made apparent by change of theory reflect the influence of the third kind of incompleteness by which historical theories suffer seeming refutation irrespective of the material evidence by which they are bolstered. No follower of Spengler or any of the numerous historians who have divided the history of mankind into ages need be disturbed if the characteristics of a period seem contradictory, for he must take as axiom that every age retains vestiges of the old and develops anticipations of the new; no evolutionary historian engaged in tracing the progress of human institutions need hesitate because of interruptions of barbarism and degradation, for progress can always be found to continue in some phases of human activity despite its cessation in others or we may be reminded that the ages, or indeed the whole, of recorded history are fantastically short on the scale of human evolution and biological adjustment; no economic or social historian need pause to consider the niceties of contradictory moral, intellectual, esthetic, or spiritual phenomena, for they can all be reduced to the economic or social conditions from which they originate or even to the psychological states which they reveal or the linguistic forms in which they are discussed or the moral or religious impulses which they express.

The whole study of the Middle Ages is set in a frame determined by such modern recurrences or persistences of ideas for which the justification has been forgotten, and evidence concerning the characteristics of the Middle Ages is complete or incomplete dependent on historical hypotheses which are almost wholly independent of facts alleged simply as facts and unweighted by hypotheses. Historians during the Middle Ages usually cast their narratives, when their accounts extended beyond annals and the chronicles of

particular events, in a scheme of six or seven ages on the analogy
of the days of creation or of the succession of four empires in
fulfillment of the prophecy of the Book of Daniel. History was
the tale of a progress and a struggle to which Christianity and
eventually the last judgment were peripety and culmination. After
the fall of man and his redemption by Christ there was no lapse
or need of a middle period in the progress to redemption. Both
schemes—of ages and empires—and various combinations of them
persisted far into modern historiography; but after the Renaissance,
opposed schemes reflecting changed political, religious, and artistic
interests all required a middle age: if the German emperors are
thought to resume the tradition of the Roman Empire, there is
an interval to be accounted for before the pretensions of the papacy
are finally put down; if the humanists recapture the purity of
Ciceronian Latin there is a stage between antiquity and the Renaissance marked by the unmistakable characteristics of *media
Latinitas;* if primitive Christianity is re-established after the corruption of the organized church the lineaments and limits of the
intermediate period are clearly determined; the historian of art
can supplement these stories of "middle ages" by introducing the
concept of a freedom from limitations gradually recovered in the
Renaissance, and the historian of ideas can build out the concept
of freedom by finding that an earlier preoccupation with God and
the other world is superseded by the discovery of man and nature.
The large coincidences of these accounts conceal the differences
of conceptual bases on which they are constructed and overshadows
the other "middle ages," based on similar grounds, such as Francis
Bacon's conception of "civil history" in which the middle consists
of "the state of Grecia and the state of Rome; the histories whereof,
occupying the middle part of time, have more ancient to them
histories which may by one common name be termed the antiqui-
ties of the world: and after them, histories which may be likewise
called by the name of modern history."[13] The middle period may
be viewed as a culmination between two periods of slighter achievement, rather than a decline between two periods of enlightenment,
both in the case of Bacon's "two exemplar states of the world for
arms, learning, moral virtue, policy, and laws," and in the case

[13] *Advancement of Learning* Bk. II, ii. 6.

of the more conventionally marked "middle ages" viewed in the light of recent scholarship in the history of science, logic, philosophy, political institutions, and cultural achievements.

Historians do not refute the basic theories of such histories, but in the enthusiasm of discovering that other ideas can be used to organize historical facts and render them intelligible, they do forget earlier theories and seek factual and documentary refutation for the interpretations consequent on them. The concept of the Middle Ages ceased to be a convenient device when political history was dissociated from the aspirations of the Germanic emperors. It became an intrusion in tracing the history of social and economic institutions, and a paradox when the historians of medieval philosophy evinced a disturbing tendency to prove that the philosophy of the Renaissance was negligible and that the philosophy of the seventeenth century was a development or even a degradation from high speculative achievements. Finally, in the history of technologies, great advances in most of the economically important techniques are known to have been achieved during the Middle Ages, and the most revolutionary changes took place during the darkest period of what had been the Dark Ages. It has become difficult to bear in mind the reasons which originally led to the designation of the "middle ages," and the term is retained more frequently because it is conventional than because it is convenient.[14]

The incompleteness of the evidence available to the medieval historian of ideas consists, on the material side, in a serious scarcity of texts, which is the consequence, on the formal side, of the prejudices of past generations counteracted by the enthusiasms of the present. He seldom has modern critical editions; frequently he can make use of early printed editions, but they involve uncertainties of reading and they are not easy of access; occasionally he can use reports of the contents of manuscripts prepared by modern scholars, but they are rarely adequate guides without

[14] For a historical survey of the fashion in which the "middle ages" has been treated by historians, *cf.* Falco, G., *La Polemico sul Medio Evo* (Turin 1933). For a survey of the history of technology during the Middle Ages, *cf.* White, L., "Technology and Invention in the Middle Ages," in *Speculum*, vol. xv (1940) 141-59; Sarton, G., *Introduction to the History of Science*, vol. iii (Baltimore 1947) p. 140-45, 704-36, 1122-26, 1539-64.

supplementary consultation of the manuscripts; ultimately the study of intellectual developments during the last centuries of the Middle Ages depends on the renewed study and publication of manuscripts. The situation is only slightly different in different fields of study and reflects in each the history of past interest in those fields.

The difficulties on the formal side, which are seldom noticed until a later generation criticizes the emphases and prejudices of earlier historians, result from the same causes as determine the scarcity or abundance of texts. Ideas may operate as historical causes determining the fate of documents and other sources of information; they may operate as instruments of inquiry and interpretation in the search for documents and the interpretation of their meaning. The errors of interpretation which resulted from theological, ecclesiastical, nationalistic, or philosophic presuppositions can be rectified when the documents survive, but their effects on the state of the formation available to us are sometimes irremediable. On the other hand, we seldom notice that our own approach in inquiry and interpretation depends on similar presuppositions or we suppose that their consequences are wholly beneficial. Dominant preconceptions can usually be detected in intellectual history by the tendency to discover anticipations of ideas usually supposed to have originated much later or, as part of the same process, to refute attributions of ideas and influences mistakenly made by other historians. It is easy to assemble diverse and even contradictory interpretations and judgments concerning the development of theological or political theory or concerning any other field in which doctrines have been studied for a long time. Thus, Marsilius of Padua has been treated first as a defender of the empire against the papacy, then as one of the originators of the doctrine of popular sovereignty and of the modern conception of freedom, and finally, in recent studies, as an exponent of totalitarianism. The tendency to discover anticipations of modern doctrines in the disciplines in which interest is recrudescent—in science, logic, and metaphysics—is likewise a sign of the zeal of the historian who sometimes debates his points surreptitiously with his subject and sometimes makes the position of his subject, as he sees it, his own in debate against other historians.

The differentiation of these three types of incompleteness of evidence is of particular importance to the intellectual historian of the late Middle Ages, since his study borders on fresh fields which have been opened precisely because earlier judgments of the physics, the logic, the metaphysics and the political theory of his period seem ungrounded. The utility of the distinctions to him, however, suggests the need of like distinctions in other fields of history and their applicability to all problems of historiography. It would be foolish to suppose, after the basic ideas of earlier historical inquiry are seen to be inadequate, that new directions are undertaken without comparable presuppositions and that, unlike previous assumptions, they stand in no need of isolation and examination. On the material side, the statement of such presuppositions affords the only possible criteria to guide editors in the enormous task of filling the lacunae in texts short of taking the fact that a manuscript has never been edited to be in itself sufficient reason for publishing it. On the formal side, the examination of presuppositions is even more important not only to the discipline of history but to related disciplines which history may supplement and to the life of man which it may enrich. The premises and conclusions of historians have been disputed by other historians, and the judgments of persons, periods, and events have been indefinitely various and will doubtless take on further variety whether historians become scientific (since there are many sciences by which they may be inspired and many applications of any given science) or practical (since many golden ages have been envisaged as pragmatic tests at the beginning, middle, or end of the line historians trace).

Yet, despite such multiplicity of judgments, history is not committed to an arbitrary relativity. On the contrary, if the principles of history are checked not only against the best evidence of the science or speculation to which they are relevant today but by the conscientious reconstruction of the speculation to which they are applied, history may approach both accuracy in the estimation and understanding of the past and precision in the statement and testing of its assumptions. Intellectual history is a dialectical process: at worst it is a dispute in which the historian victimizes a dead opponent; at best it is a discussion in which understanding of the past may contribute to the understanding of the present and may even suggest forgotten analyses which will rectify errors of the present. We do not understand the past nor can we apply the lessons of history to the present by searching out traces of the present in the past: to praise Ockham on the basis of misinterpreted texts for having anticipated the modern doctrine of many-valued logics is as far from historical accuracy and justice as to dispose of the Aristotelian physics with the observation that Galileo had discarded it. If the history of science and logic is to be written, the criteria must be stated and the analysis of materials must be scientifically explicit. Otherwise we trace the history of possible applications of our prejudices and we degrade alike our own convictions and the theories we measure against them; and even if we write history in which the presuppositions, unlike those of intellectual history, are not of the same order as the materials, we can be scientific in a fashion suited to the task of history only if, in addition to borrowing from the sciences devices to treat materials, we learn to submit the principles of history themselves to scrutiny.

The Field of Cosmology

BY MILTON K. MUNITZ

New York University

*T*HE central problem of cosmology, that of understanding the structure of the universe as a whole, is both an ancient and a persistent one. Each culture and age has proposed its own answers. Philosophy, religion, and science have each undertaken in some fashion or other to deal with the problem. Taken together, these efforts may be regarded as ministering to an ineradicable desire—one that stems primarily from man's possession of a sense of wonder—to understand the world in which he lives.

At the same time, however, the manner of statement of the problem, the very meanings of the terms used in its formulation, the special motives we may have for posing it, and the methods we may use to solve it, are all intimately bound up with the distinctive character of these several traditions and intellectual sources. A variety of patterns of thought and methods of approach is superimposed, though not in any mechanical way, upon our native human curiosity and serves to channel its expression. The first fact that confronts us, therefore, in any attempt at precisely identifying the field of cosmology—its subject matter, problems, methods and goals—is the welter of terms used and the apparent confusion and conflict in meanings assigned to the key concepts involved. This situation exists even apart from linguistic differences and philologic considerations, however important these indeed are. On the one hand, terms like "Universe", "World", "Cosmos", "Nature", "Reality", "Being", taken to designate the subject matter of which an account is given, and on the other, "theory of the Universe" (or of "Nature", "Reality", "Being"), "theory of the Heavens", "cosmology", "cosmogony", "cosmography", "metaphysics", as terms for the accounts themselves, are used with anything but unanimity in the literature and history of the subject. In some cases, indeed, some of these terms (in both groups) will be used interchangeably; in others, some will be subordinated as parts of a whole. Further differences set in with the use of qualifying expressions as in "a universe", "plurality of worlds", "created universe", "physical universe", "metaphysical cosmology", "scientific cosmology", and the like. Finally, "cosmogony" or "cosmology", in being assigned to one or another of the domains of mythologic speculation, philosophy, or science will have different evaluations placed upon its worth in accordance with the intellectual predilections of a given author of school of thought.

All this is, in a sense, quite natural. There is no reason, certainly, why we need expect anything else, if we bear in mind the fact that terminology, when garnered from the entire history of thought, reflects the gropings and shifts, the growths and controversies that characterize that history. There is no single, univocal meaning to cosmology, simply because its various characterizations reveal differences in philosophic, religious or scientific outlook. Descriptions of its domain are sensitive to and reflect the several positions in these areas or such stages in their development of which they are capable. All that one can hope to do at the outset, therefore, is to point out what forms this has taken, and then to go on and indicate wherein progress may be presumed to lie; and, since "progress" implies the use of some standard, to declare what that standard is. The conception of what cosmology is, in other words, is a function of the growth of the discipline itself. If this appears to involve circularity, then the circularity is at any rate neither vicious nor unique. It is characteristic of the progressive and self-corrective character of responsible thought itself.

I propose, then, in what follows to attempt to indicate something of the variety of conceptions of cosmology and what type of progress in principle as well as in fact may be recognized in its development. In the light of this discussion we shall be led to notice the special significance which attaches to current scientific investigations in the field, the materials and problems which they present, and the opportunity they offer for the fruitful co-operation between philosophy and science.

I.

In attempting to take into account the various ways in which cosmology has been conceived, attention to the broad relations which subsist between mythology, metaphysical speculation and science proves to be convenient and helpful. The first significant form, considered both historically and logically, in which cosmological speculation appears is that of myth. Here is the seedbed out of which grow what we call theology, science, and philosophy. It itself undergoes a rich and varied development, so that the finished product, poetically expressed, exhibits a degree of coherence and creative imagination which are not to be found on a truly primitive or savage level of life. While the general excellence in the results naturally vary, numerous illustrations of such poetic cosmologies and cosmogonies are available in the anthropological accounts and literary remains of most primitive peoples. This is not the place in which to undertake any detailed analysis of this fascinating field. We need but recall, however, two striking and influential instances of the way in which poetic myths directed to cosmological speculation have left their indelible imprint upon the heritage of western ideas. The *Theogony* of Hesiod and the account to be found in *Genesis* contain between them the structure of ideas upon which subsequent thought established much of its foundation. They exhibit the activity of imagination which is the primary faculty at work in man's first efforts at understanding the world.

In its essence, myth consists of a dramatic interpretation of the world in terms of familiar human experience. The variety of creation myths and their account of the relations between natural forces and objects illustrate the projection into the world itself of categories borrowed from the immediate arena of human activity.

The very notion of a cosmos, as a single unitary order encompassing all phenomena, is a chief concern of early Greek philosophy. Tradition generally assigns the first use of the term in the broad signification to Pythagoras.[1] The conception however, if not

[1] *Cf.* Diogenes Laertius, viii, 48.

the term, is already present in Anaximander. But even beyond this earliest of philosophers one can trace the notion of a universal Law and Destiny into the roots of mythology itself. For the notion of *Moira* or Fate which we find, for example, in Homer and Hesiod, is of an order at once moral and inviolable that controls the activities of the gods no less than of men. As such, however, it is one which is evidently a projection and generalization of the pervasively controlling moral and legal structure embedded in social life. Indeed the original meaning of the term "cosmos" reflects this human origin since it signifies at first simply the fact of a community of human beings living under law. Myth here reads into the very constitution of the world the legal apportionment of those necessary and just bounds which no being may dare to transgress.[2] In a similarly obvious way biological, especially sexual categories, are made to function on a cosmic scale. The generative process as the outcome of the union of male and female becomes analogized in the various myths concerning the origin of particular beings through the union of heaven and earth as mediated by love. Or again, the imagery borrowed from the sphere of art and craftsmanship, as in Plato's *Timaeus,* provides still another major source of categories. The elaboration of these instances or their multiplication need not be undertaken here. The important fact is that such myths are to be accepted and valued for what they are. It is only later, more sophisticated thought that undertakes to judge through the use of literal standards their relative inadequacy or naivete. Originally, however, myths were not created or adopted in the face of available alternatives. They represent, rather, the honest and serious effort at understanding the world in such terms and on the basis of such experience as were available. The vigor and imaginativeness which such products embody, moreover, were precisely those qualities necessary for the emergence of self-critical philosophy and science.

But if myths are clearly symbolic devices, so essentially are religion and science. Wherein, then, are to be found their differences? Myth, as a vehicle through which the world is interpreted in terms

---

[2] *Cf.* Jaeger, W., *Paideia*, vol. i, p. 155; same author's *Theology of the Early Greek Philosophers*, p. 35f.; Cornford, F. M., *From Religion to Philosophy*, chs. i, ii.

at once dramatic and familiar, represents a fusion of attention to the subject matter described and of the human experience of the subject making the description. To go beyond or transform myth into something literal results in the emergence of theologies or sciences, depending on how this process takes place. Religion as it is normally conceived and practiced involves a failure in properly differentiating and interpreting the sources and uses of the concepts it employs in describing the world and man's place in it. At its best it is significant poetry. Actually, however, the development of theology and religious cosmologies arise from the literal interpretation and elaboration of primitive myths in such a way that belief is had in the real existence of entities referred to by the myth. Metaphors become hypostatized realities. When Zeus, for example, is treated as a poetic symbol for the familiar heavens that surround us, we can appreciate the image of such a heavenly ruler. When, however, Zeus is taken, not as a symbol for the heavens, but as a being, himself existing in and ruling over the heavenly bodies, we are in the presence of a myth converted into a religious dogma. Imagination is then reduced to superstition; significant poetry is turned into spurious physics.[3] It might be protested that developed theology has deliberately shunned literalism and crude anthropomorphism. Allegory, it will be claimed, must be taken for what it is. But this is generally only half the story, for behind the allegory one finds characteristically retained a literal belief in entities like God, souls, Heaven, and the like. These are no longer as in honest poetry mere symbols for what is open to public experience in a natural world, nor is literal belief in them to be tested directly by confrontation with that world. Our "knowledge" of them requires the use of some non-empirical technique, whether it be blind faith, revelation, mystical insight, or unquestioned authority. In this direction man betrays and forfeits the exercise of his essential rationality.

On the other hand, we may take pains to separate out (what primitive mythology has neither the sophistication nor interest in doing) what in our descriptions of the world refer to those traits of our subject matter which can be universally and publicly confirmed, as contrasted with those elements which are borrowed from

[3] *Cf.* Santayana, G. *Reason in Religion,* ch. iv; *Reason in Science,* p. 8-14.

dramatic fancy and a variable, subjective experience. In this direction lies science in its emergence from the stage of myth. Science, too, becomes the use of literal symbols as a means of providing a faithful record of what it observes. The language it uses is shorn, however, of all dramatic and moral overtones. Its method is controlled by attention to systematic rigor and empirical confirmation. Instead of taking Zeus, now, as a being whose existence is on a plane with the heavenly bodies, it is to the structure and behavior of the heavenly bodies themselves to which attention is directed. Scientific discourse becomes a way, at least by intention, of transparently expressing the intelligible relations of a subject matter by reference to the traits it is found to possess.

In the light of these elementary distinctions, we are enabled to recognize a fundamental principle of classification of approaches to cosmology that go beyond the stage of mythology. One takes religion as its guide, the other science.

I shall use the term "metaphysical cosmology" to represent that mode of approach which operates under the influence of some form of theology and exhibits a general disregard for the tentative, empirically grounded and self-corrective method of science. (While the term "metaphysics" itself has enjoyed a notorious variety of usages, some of which are even antithetical to the above, the sense which is here selected is justified at once by its wide employment and the numerous illustrations which it covers.) Similarly, that orientation which takes science as its guide may be designated by the term "scientific cosmology." Philosophy has throughout its history oscillated between the influences exerted upon its activities by religion and science. "Philosophical cosmology," consequently, is a term that has no special significance. Rather, philosophical analysis in one direction of its interest has been used to develop and support either metaphysical or scientific cosmologies. It remains to point out with respect to the above distinctions between the approaches to cosmology through myth, metaphysics, and science, that they represent idealized types. Actually when we examine the variety of historical examples in some special period or in the writings of individual authors, we discover that they embody one or another of these approaches in varying degrees. One may thus find shreds of science in "metaphysical" systems, and remnants of metaphysics in "scientific" ones. It is the task of criticism to discriminate and evaluate these elements when they appear in a total product.

The metaphysical orientation to cosmology, the range that discipline is alleged to have, and the elaboration of particular theories in it, are basically determined by the manner in which one finds a literal projection made into the structure of reality of selected features of human experience and the consequent, generally non-empirical methods by which the resulting beliefs are upheld. In the broad sense of the term "moral," that in which it signifies all that makes up the scheme of values, ideals and aspirations of men, we may say that metaphysics consists essentially in a moral interpretation of reality. It reads into reality (and then claims to have found it there already) what lies closest to the heart. Man literally creates a God in his own image, gives Him a cosmic status to serve as the sanction for his own pursuits, and thereby finds comfort in one form or another for pursuing such goals and adopting such standards as he has already set for himself. The nature of the God or gods so created—even though they will not always be called by that name—their relation to the world and the souls of men, these are matters which are solved differently by various metaphysical systems, although the underlying motive and method are everywhere the same. Plato's doctrine of an eternal realm of intelligible Forms set over against the domain of sensible and transitory particular facts, the Hebraic-Christian belief in a transcendent Deity who creates a world *ex nihilo* to provide a setting for man's attainment of salvation, the variety of pantheistic philosophies with their belief in an immanent Deity, whether interpreted in a temporal, evolutionary, dialectical form, or a static one, or again in any of these cases whether cast into a materialistic or idealistic framework, all such systems are illustrations of the same metaphysical method. In basically dualistic systems as in Platonism and supernaturalism the field of cosmology will be restricted to the description of the world which, as a copy or handiwork of the realm that transcends it, possesses a secondary and derivative ontological status. In monistic or pantheistic systems—in Stoicism, Absolute Idealism or dialectical materialism, the locus of generative or sustaining values is to be found in the field encompassed by cosmology itself. The power that works for the right or the good is coextensive with the structure or development of the world.

Along with all such exhibitions on a grand scale of the pathetic fallacy one generally finds a method used consistent with such wishful thinking to support its claims. Since a candid inspection of the facts reveals no such forces at work as the metaphysics would have us believe in, resort must be had to some "higher" or "more reliable" method than critical common sense or science makes available. These latter, it will be claimed, are adequate enough in "their own spheres," but to determine the essential nature of reality, one must go behind or beyond publicly confirmable evidence to find the truth. One must have faith, or trust in some authority, or source of revelation, or a Reason altogether different from the normal faculty of intelligence with which men are equipped. Such subterfuges and abasements in methodology, moreover, frequently seek the very support of scientific results in upholding their own total system of ideas. Yet despite its outward adoption of such scientific facts, the net outcome is one which acquires no greater credibility as a result of their inclusion. For metaphysical systems of cosmology that "take over" scientific theories do so without actively participating in the method which leads to those results, either by contributing to fresh developments or by critically examining the old. Instead of recognizing the tentative character of scientific theories, they either take these as ultimate truths or seek to assess their adequacy in terms of some antecedently adopted set of dogmatically fixed principles. Such systems frequently, therefore, either become repositories of scientific beliefs which have outgrown their justification or, on the other hand, regard themselves as beyond the range of influence of the shifting advances of science. St. Thomas and Maimonides used Aristotelian "physics" with no essential modifications. The Stoics adopted some aspects of Ionian physics without materially contributing to their development. Or, finally, in our own day, theologians and metaphysical dogmatists (even when these are "scientists") use the current news-bulletins of science to support views which can lay no claim to having been developed through the very method whose results in some particular area it seeks to evaluate. Thus E. T. Whittaker, in his anxiety to uphold the dogmas of traditional Christian theology, grasps at the alleged proofs in modern scientific cosmology of a creation and finds in the second law of thermodynamics or the theory of the expanding universe support for such a doctrine.[4] Dean Inge, Eddington, Jeans, and a host of others are guilty of exactly similar travesties. Nor is the case any better when, for example, J. B. S. Haldane decides to cast in his lot with the views of Milne in cosmology because they are, in his opinion, in greater consonance with the metaphysical truths of dialectical materialism than are the views of Einstein and his followers.[5]

Finally, it may be remarked that for all its value and success in establishing the antinomial character of dogmatic metaphysical cosmologies and hence their futility, Kant's critical philosophy need not be taken as the final word on the subject. For despite its strictures on transcendental metaphysics, Kant's own approach exhibits in more than one direction precisely those faults he would find in other systems. The phenomenalistic, even psychological, treatment of space and time, his interpretation of these "forms" in absolute Newtonian terms, as if no other were possible, and the residual interest in championing a faith in God, freedom, and immortality though beyond the limits of scientific determination—all these set Kant's work within the same broad framework of a metaphysical approach to cosmology. If, on the other hand, much of Kant's philosophy should still provide fruitful clues in the theory of knowledge, the significance of these needs to be established, and their meaning and validity determined in the light of a careful examination of the scientific materials developed since Kant's own day. Only by making such a fresh examination can we hope to avoid the easy claim that all our problems have already been settled in this or any other system of philosophy.

The development of the conception of scientific cosmology and contributions to its domain roughly parallel the development of science itself. The first significant appearance of science in early

[4] Cf. *Space and Spirit* (1946); *The Beginning and End of the World*, (1942).
[5] Cf. *Marxist Philosophy of the Sciences;* "A New Theory of the Past," in *American Scientist*, vol. xxxiii (1945) 3, 129ff.

Greek thought marks one stage in and conception of cosmology. Here we find the effort made through the use of bold, imaginative hypotheses at understanding the fundamental principles and causes in terms of which all the diverse facts of natural existence could be rationally explained. The cosmological speculations of the early Ionians and the pluralists reflect at once the virtues and the limitations present in that effort. We find there a clear conception of a universal order, a knowledge of whose properties would enable us to fit the multitude of facts into their proper relationships. Such specifications as to what this order is, whether it be the selection of some single element of fire, air or water, or a generalized "atomic" theory, are to be valued not merely because they illustrate this goal of total comprehension but even for their anticipation of what subsequently were recognized to be fruitful types of explanation. Nevertheless these speculative efforts could not but be inadequate. They were founded on meagre evidence and limited experience; they were not formulated with sufficient rigor and mathematical detail. The ideal which they represent, however, may be taken as expressing the persistent goal of all science, the attainment of a complete and systematically integrated body of knowledge concerning the totality of phenomena. From time to time in the subsequent history of thought, one finds not merely the sense of what this ideal is, but similar attempts at capturing and embodying it in some set of fundamental principles. The speculative enthusiasms to which the notions of evolution or of Newtonian mechanics were subjected in modern thought as possible keys to the structure of the universe as a whole readily suggest themselves as illustrations. All such doctrines fail for the same reason; they are founded on too narrow a base of verified fact to support the extensive use to which the hypotheses are now put. They presume to generalize dogmatically about those areas and the traits of those subject matters to which the original, and within its own range possibly valid hypothesis, no longer finds a genuine applicability.

We may recognize a second typical approach to and conception of scientific cosmology that stems from the advance of science in specialized disciplines. Following the first flush of excitement of early Greek speculation, men began to lay siege patiently and piecemeal to the several areas of natural fact. The emergence of the individual disciplines of astronomy, biology, psychology and the like, were now guided by the construction of theories relevant to those individual domains and supported by the accumulation of observational evidence as was to be found with the use of available instruments and techniques. Important achievements in this direction were of course already made in Greek and Hellenistic thought. At the rebirth of science in the modern era, the physical sciences as the first to win a secure footing served to guide the conception of cosmology and the construction of particular theories in that domain. This has taken two forms. On the one hand, we find a recurrence to the kind of speculation we noted above, but this time with an important difference. Instead of attempting to encompass the totality of natural phenomena, cosmology becomes confined to an account of one "segment" or "level" of existence, that, namely, which is comprised under the heading of the physical—in its modern rather than Greek signification. One illustration, of many, that may be selected of this approach to and conception of cosmology is to be found in the celebrated work *Cosmos* (1845-1862) of Alexander von Humboldt. Humboldt identifies the subject of his investigations as "the science of the cosmos," "physical cosmography" or "physical description of the universe." It omits from its purview "the higher spheres of the organic world in which is comprised the human species in all its varied conformation, its creative intellectual power, and the languages to which it has given existence."[6] The principal subdivisions of its study are, in his own terminology, "Uranography" and "Geography," the former dealing with the sidereal portion of the physical universe, the latter with the terrestrial.[7] The outcome, however, for all its interest in the formulation of unifying principles, remains at best a laborious compendium of accumulated results with no actual systematic integration accomplished. The method employed keeps it from rising above the level actually reached in his day in the studies of astronomy, geology, and

[6] I, 369; Bohn Library ed.
[7] *Cf.* I, 40, 47, 53.

physical geography. The growth of cosmology was not to be found in such a premature grouping of the results of a selected number of the physical sciences![8]

Meanwhile, the development of physics and astronomy led to a conception of cosmology which was in some ways less ambitious. The introduction of the use of the telescope brought within range of more detailed observation the various bodies in our solar system. Also the overwhelming success of Newtonian mechanics provided the theoretical tools with which the motions of the planets could be exactly understood. Corresponding, therefore, to this level of precise astronomic observation and the area covered by the theory of gravitation, cosmology came to be identified primarily with a treatment of the structure and genesis of the solar system. Newton's own discussions on "The System of the World" and the cosmogonic speculations of Laplace, to take but two representative examples, exhibit this more restricted conception. Neither Nature as a whole, nor the domain of all physical fact, nor finally even the astronomic universe as a whole are taken as the subject matter for cosmology in this special sense. Science deals here with what it can actually handle. It is clear, of course, that this conception of cosmology, even though guided by available theory and experience, is nevertheless, this time, too narrow in scope. The solar system, after all, no more than the earth, is the entire universe. But a broadened conception of scientific cosmology which could actually make progress in the investigation of the stars and such other heavenly bodies as exist beyond the confines of our solar system had to wait until the weapons were forged with which one could securely extend the range of inquiry. These weapons were actually developed in increasing numbers and with cumulatively important results in the nineteenth century. Astronomy secured the use of more powerful telescopes and the use of the spectroscope. These now provided observational data about the relative distances and chemical composition of the stars themselves. Also, on the side of physical theory, the development of thermodynamics and electromagnetic theory pro-

[8] Significantly, Humboldt's contributions were to be found in the narrower sphere of geography itself, where he suggested fruitful hypotheses and made significant empirical observations based on his wide travels.

vided additional conceptual tools to those of mechanics with which to interpret the data of observation. The "universe" to which attention was now directed consisted of the vast swarm of stars to which our own solar system belongs. Its structure and properties —questions as to its uniqueness, shape, distribution of matter and motion in it—became the subject matter of investigation. Important steps were made in obtaining relevant information to help in answering in part some of these questions. But even these advances were soon to pale into insignificance as compared with the strides which have been made by astronomy and physics since the turn of the present century. We are in possession today of a sense of what the astronomic universe as a whole is, in which the system of stars comprising the Milky Way (the galaxy to which our own sun belongs) has become itself but a speck. From the vantage point of this tremendously widened conception of the cosmos in contemporary science, the field of cosmology can now be described as in the following brief statement by R. C. Tolman:

> For the scientist the problem of cosmology lies in an attempt to describe and understand the structure and behavior of the physical universe as a whole, looked at from a large-scale point of view which considers the average distribution and properties of the matter and radiation of which the universe is constructed, but neglects local details such as the structure of our own earth and solar system, or even the particular arrangement of stars in our own galaxy. Indeed the scale of view is so large that the contents of the universe are in some ways treated like a fluid with the stars taking the place of atoms and the galaxies or nebulae playing the role of molecules.[9]

The recrudescence of interest in cosmologic problems in this comprehensive astronomic sense was once more occasioned by fundamental changes in physical theory and important extensions of observational data. The traditional modern picture of the world in Newtonian terms was challenged, beginning at the turn of the present century, by the new approaches of relativity and quantum theory. The use likewise of high-powered telescopes, aided by the much improved techniques of photography, revealed the existence of objects and phenomena not hitherto observed or correctly understood. Contemporary scientific interest in cosmology may thus

[9] *Science,* vol. lxxv (1932) 368.

be said to date from 1917 with the appearance of Einstein's first paper dealing with the application of general relativity to the problem of the structure of the universe as a whole. Since then the development of relativity in its various forms has been applied to the cosmologic problem and a number of solutions proposed. Also since 1924 the first well-established observational evidence concerning the existence and nature of the extra-galactic nebulae has been accumulated and provides the empirical data to be used in verifying the alternative theories put forth. These investigations are not only, relatively speaking, extremely recent ones, but from the point of view of the long and uncertain career of cosmologic speculation perhaps the most important milestones in its achievements. Whatever may be the outcome of these investigations, however much they may be superseded by as yet unforeseen innovations in theory or observation, the fact remains that it is to them to which we must turn if we would avoid the shoals of sterile metaphysical controversy or the narrow confines of outworn scientific views themselves.

II.

A responsible and comprehensive treatment of cosmologic problems from a present-day, scientifically oriented point of view, demands attention to at least three different levels or types of evidence; that, first, which is derived from observational astronomy, second from physical theory, and third from philosophic analysis. It is the complex character of this enterprise, the defiance of neat segregations into isolated disciplines of separate interests, that accounts at once for the extremely difficult and hazardous character of any attempt one might make at a total treatment, yet at the same time also explains in good part the inadequacy of so many attempts when undertaken, whether in philosophy or in science, with an innocent disregard of the materials to be found in the other's domain. The significance of current cosmological inquiry and the way in which considerations derived from these several sources are involved in the pursuit of that inquiry may now be briefly indicated.

1. The observational approach to cosmology is that of the astronomer. By the use of powerful telescopes, especially the 100

inch reflector at Mt. Wilson, and through the work of men like Hubble, Humason, and Shapley, information is available today based on photographic and spectroscopic analyses concerning the extra-galactic nebulae out to a distance of something like 500 million light years. (It is expected of course that the use of the 200 inch telescope on Palomar Mountain will vastly increase the range of observation and provide fresh data by means of which some difficulties at present unresolved will find their solution.) The presently observable region of the universe, a sphere whose diameter is some 1,000 million light years, may be taken as the empirical "sample" of the astronomic universe as a whole. It is constituted of vast swarms of nebulae or galaxies[10] many of which in turn are enormous agglomerations of stars in a general way analogous to our own Milky Way—the galaxy to which our own solar system belongs. The first significant step in the positive empirical identification of the realm of the nebulae—"the particles" of which the universe may be regarded as composed—consisted in the establishment through new and reliable criteria of distances of the fact that the nebulae lay at enormous distances beyond our own galaxy. Aside from the data connected with the problem of the evolution of nebulae and their classification as to types, two significant observational results emerged from the general reconnaissance of the observable region of the nebulae.[11] The first is the fact that, generally speaking and on the basis of the sample so far observed, the distribution of nebulae in space is uniform. If the volume of space considered is sufficiently large, there does not appear to be any thinning out, any clustering, or any special grouping of the nebulae into some super-system. A second, more startling and at the same time more perplexing conclusion relates to the phenomenon of the red-shift in the spectra of nebulae. This has been formulated by Hubble in a law which establishes a linear relation between such red-shift and the distance of the nebulae. When the red-shift is

[10] The terms "extra-galactic nebulae," "galaxies," "nebulae" will be used synonymously. They are in any case to be distinguished from what, unfortunately, are also called nebulae, clouds of dust and gas, that form part of the structure of these more comprehensive systems. These latter are not immediately relevant to the cosmological problem and will not be referred to here.

[11] *Cf.* Hubble, E., *Realm of Nebulae* and *Observational Approach to Cosmology.*

interpreted as a Doppler effect, it is taken as indicative of a recessional velocity, and the interpretation of Hubble's law therefore leads to the conception of an expanding universe. The more distant the nebulae, the faster they recede from the point of observation, while the "nearer" nebulae are "running away" with correspondingly smaller velocities. The final interpretation, however, of this as well as other facts disclosed by observation and the extrapolation of observed data to yield idealized models of the universe are matters of theory.

2. The theoretical approach to cosmology involves the development and application of general physical principles in terms of which known observational data could be interpreted. The functions of theory here, as in any other empirical domain, are those of systematically organizing accumulated data, directing fresh research, and thus in general aiding in extending the frontiers of our knowledge. In contemporary cosmology two main groups of physical theory have been developed. One, originally an off-shoot of relativity theory, was initiated by Einstein himself in 1917 and was carried forward by a group of investigators including Lemaitre, Friedmann, de Sitter, Robertson, Tolman and others. The other is associated with the ideas of E. A. Milne of Oxford and his followers and is designated by the name "kinematic relativity." This second approach, developed since 1932, arose as a critical reaction against the conceptual framework adopted in Einstein's relativity theory and seeks by a reexamination of first principles, to interpret and extend the range of observable data in a way which it considers philosophically more acceptable.

Both sets of theory agree, in a general way, in the adoption of a principle that corresponds to the observed fact of the uniform distribution of nebulae. This fact of observation is extended and generalized in a way which is characteristic of a basically relativistic approach. In general, the problem faced in relativity physics is that of formulating the transformation equations that preserve the invariance of physical laws in changing from one frame of reference to another, where such frames of reference are in relative motion to one another. When applied to the special cosmologic domain, the relativistic approach involves the adoption of a principle according to which the description of the universe as a whole when made from the standpoint of some body (for example, a nebula) in the system will be the same as that made from the point of view of other bodies in the system. The principle asserts that the universe on the grand scale will give a similar appearance from whatever position in it that it is observed. This involves at once the surrender of any preferential body, frame of reference, place, or point of view. There is no absolute center, no absolute boundary to the universe.

The systems of relativistic cosmology that derive from Einstein's approach involve the application of the theory of general relativity. This is grounded in the assumption that the space-time geometry of any region and of the universe as a whole is determined by its material content and is expressed by Einstein's gravitational field equations. The solutions to the cosmologic problem according to classic relativity fall into two main groups: (1) the homogeneous, isotropic and static models and (2) the homogeneous, isotropic, and non-static models. The first solutions offered by Einstein and de Sitter in 1917 fall into the first group. These were subsequently abandoned. Einstein's original model failed to account for the observed fact of the red-shift and de Sitter's model failed to recognize the finite density of matter in the actual universe. A general solution of a non-static variety was first suggested by Friedmann in 1922 and later more accurately formulated by Robertson in 1929. This laid the foundation for the theoretical deduction of a number of models of the universe among which the expanding universe of current discussion was included. One of the tasks of observational astronomy, by no means as yet completely fulfilled, is that of supplying the data by which the several constants involved in the equations could be specified and thereby provide a basis of choice from among the variety of theoretic possibilities offered.[12]

Milne's early investigations beginning in 1932 and summarized in his *Relativity, Gravitation and World Structure* (Oxford 1935) were attempts to account for the fact of expansion, assuming the red-shift to be a velocity effect, in terms of kinematic considera-

[12] *Cf.* Tolman, R. C., *Relativity, Thermodynamics and Cosmology*, ch. x; Robertson, H. P., "Relativistic Cosmology," in *Reviews of Modern Physics*, vol. v (1933) 62-90.

tions solely, without employing the gravitational solution, dynamic theory, or philosophy of geometry contained in general relativity. His more elaborate approach developed within the past several years now makes it clear, however, that by adopting the notions of kinematic relativity it is possible to formulate a variety of possible models of which again the expanding universe will be but one illustration. The basis of choice from among these, according to Milne, is the scale of time adopted in original clock-graduation measures rather than arbitrary geometric decisions. According to the choice made one can describe the universe with equal consistency as either (a) finite in spatial extent, expanding, with a definite epoch of creation and embodying a flat euclidian geometry or (b) as infinite in spatial extent, non-expanding, with no epoch of creation and embodying a hyperbolic non-euclidian geometry.[13]

The way in which, therefore, the expansion of the universe of nebulae is interpreted, whether indeed the red-shift is to be taken as a velocity recession or is due to some other fact, and the specific character of the system of mechanics employed—all these are matters which are subject to different analyses in the current theory according to the nature of the basic assumptions made. The present state of physical theory is one of active exploration of suggestive leads with no unanimity prevalent.

3. Unless one takes philosophy to be already equipped with a set of eternal and absolute truths and as therefore quite independent of the piecemeal shifting advances of the sciences, it cannot but be part of the genuine philosophic interest to co-operate with science in the forging of those concepts and principles which will serve to advance our knowledge. Conversely, in present-day cosmologic discussions the occasion and the need for philosophic analysis is everywhere to be noted. That the labors of the astronomical observer and mathematical physicist need to be supplemented by philosophy is recognized on the whole by scientists themselves.

Traditionally as well as at the present time, the questions that

---

[13] Milne's recent investigations have been presented in a variety of technical papers; for a convenient summary see his articles in *Astrophysical Journal*, vol. xci (1940) 129; *Proc. Royal Soc. Edin.* A, vol. lxii (1943) 10; *Journ. London Math. Soc.*, vol. xv (1940) 44; also *Kinematic Relativity* (Oxford 1949).

have occupied the forefront of interest in characterizing the universe as a whole are those which relate to its spatial and temporal dimensions. With respect to its spatial extent, is the universe finite or infinite? Does the universe as a whole have a specific shape? When considered from the viewpoint of its temporal career did the universe have a beginning or was it always in existence? Is it destructible or indestructible? The order that is the cosmos, when conceived as a spatio-temporal order, has inevitably and persistently posed these familiar alternatives. It would of course be both naive and erroneous to assume that in asking these questions one finds in every case either clear or univocal meanings attaching to the concepts employed. The fact is that both in the asking of the questions as well as in the efforts at answering them, or for that matter even in refusing, as in Kant's critical philosophy, to undertake or expect answers, one finds certain assumptions made and concepts employed which together constitute some particular theory, whether crude or sophisticated, as to the nature of space and time, as well as some particular conception of the physical universe to which these are applied.

A theory of space and time is thus an integral aspect of cosmology. In the establishment of such a theory there are two broad and interdependent tasks that need to be performed. One is technical or scientific, the other philosophic. Looked at in a wide perspective, the terms "space" and "time" may serve as convenient designations for what is encompassed in certain types of measurement. One whole set of problems connected with the making of such measurements concerns the definition and exact formulation of various species of measure-numbers, their expression in certain abstract mathematical laws, the manner in which these may be calculated, systematically ordered, and the conditions specified for translating one into another. This is the task of pure mathematics. The interpretation and application of these calculi through suitable and clearly specified operational procedures is the task of empirical science in its use of these abstract languages. In carrying through this enterprise, however, there is inevitably present a controlling set of assumptions as to the manner and significance of what is accomplished. To make explicit, critically examine, and justify the use of these assumptions is the task of philosophy. It is concerned with an understanding of the relation of mathematics to empirical science and of scientific knowledge itself to the subject matter which it seeks to express. To have some reasoned account of these matters is to have a philosophy of science, a theory of knowledge. In the pursuit of cosmological inquiries, the influence of philosophical considerations as they bear on the adoption and use of space-time theories has emerged in contemporary discussions no less than in the past.

Is the construction of "homogeneous" cosmological models one which is guided simply by mathematical convenience and present-day observational support—a tentative empirical hypothesis in short—or is there some rational necessity that no other is possible? Is the determination of the curvature of space something which hinges upon empirical data, sufficient to fix the nature of the physical space that exists, or is every "application" of a geometry arbitrary and at the disposal of the observer, a matter of "convention"? How, moreover, are space-measures connected with time-measures? Does the use of a four-dimensional geometric language as in Einsteinian relativity adequately express their relationship or is it the case that in some clearly demonstrable manner time-measures are the more fundamental? If the latter, for example, what is involved in such priority? When reference is made to "a beginning" of the time sequence, to "creation," what precisely do these terms signify? In the construction of cosmologic theories is it necessary to proceed through the application and extrapolation of such physical laws as have been verified in some limited domain, or can independent, original principles be formulated for the universe as a whole which have these other laws as special consequences? Is there some limit to the rational deducibility of empirical laws such that at some point reference must be made to the given for the determination of particular quantitative functions, the value of particular constants, or is it possible for all laws of physics to be logically derived from an intuitively established axiomatic base? Is it possible in the latter case to find this base in the very process and possibility of acquiring knowledge for some conscious organism? Is it the case that there are some meaningful questions about the universe as a whole which refer to matters that indeed transcend the domain of scientific decision?

These are but some of the questions briefly formulated, that one finds actively discussed in the current literature of cosmology. Most of the questions have been stated with reference to the basic cleavages that separate relativistic cosmology from the kinematic approach. In any case the issues on the surface have a familiar ring when one recalls the disputes strewn across the pages of the history of philosophy. One may use convenient labels like "conventionalism vs. realism," "empiricism vs. rationalism," "phenomenalism vs. transcendental metaphysics," and the like, to identify the type of issues at stake. The writings of men like Einstein, Milne, Hubble, Tolman, Lemaitre, Eddington, Robertson, and others will be found to fall into one or another of these camps. It is clear, however, that what is involved concerns neither the acceptability of particular observational data nor the mathematical adequacy of certain deductive chains of reasoning. The issues rather concern the views held with respect to the relations between the data and the mathematics—in short, they involve, ultimately, fundamental principles in the theory of knowledge. The primary and constructive task of philosophy (whether performed by "scientists" or "philosophers" is simply a manner of names) is that of clarifying the points at issue and making critical evaluations of the merits in different positions. This task, however, is one which it would be fatal to regard as either "optional," "a matter of taste," or of "private opinion." Rather it is crucially essential to the pursuit and advancement of the discipline itself. Without it, the accumulation of observational materials and the refinement of mathematical techniques lose their relevance. Philosophical questions are thus not outside of or superimposed on scientific ones; one cannot decide not to include them within the scientific framework, *for they are already there.*

In the pursuit of cosmology as briefly outlined above, one has at the present juncture of man's intellectual resources, as at no time in the past, the materials with which to undertake the most difficult, persistent, and fascinating of all problems. That a rich field of co-operative enterprise awaits further development in which philosophy and science have their distinctive yet related roles to perform is the main point I have sought to establish.

Reflections on the Casual Character
of Modern Physical Theory

✑ *BY ERNEST NAGEL*
Columbia University

*R*ECENT developments in physical science have made evident
the limitations of the theories of classical physics as universally adequate systems of explanation. These developments have
also brought under critical scrutiny the validity of many time-
honored principles of scientific inquiry. Chief among these is the
classical view that the aim of science is the discovery of the causal
orders in which the events of nature occur. It is frequently maintained, on the strength of contemporary innovations in physical
theory, that the assumption of such orders is no longer warranted,
and that the ideal of a universal science of physics whose laws and
theories possess a strictly deterministic form must be relinquished
as inherently unrealizable. It is with some of the issues involved in
these claims that the present paper is concerned.

The problem which the advance of physics has made acute is
not the traditional one, much discussed by philosophers, concerning the correct analysis of the meaning of "cause," as this word is
employed in familiar practical affairs. Whether the casual relations
encountered in these latter contexts are further analyzable, whether
at bottom they indicate some kind of necessity or identity, or
whether they can be rendered in terms of regular though contingent sequences of events, are alternative views that are irrelevant to
the debate stimulated by quantum physics. The current problem
is generated by the successes of a comprehensive physical theory
which is apparently non-deterministic in its structure, and which
is allegedly incompatible with the assumption of an underlying
causal pattern for the interactions of the elementary processes
postulated by it. In consequence, the questions that require

answers are the precise sense in which classical physics is deterministic while current subatomic physics is supposedly not, and the import of recent theoretical innovations for an adequate view of the nature and aims of science.

Accordingly, since classical mechanics is the generally acknowledged paradigm of a deterministic theory, and since the language of current discussions of determinism is heavily indebted to mechanics for many of its distinctions, I shall first offer a brief account of the nature of determinism in this branch of physics. I shall next generalize a technical notion occurring in mechanics, so as to provide a tool for analyzing the structure of other theories in physics. And finally, I shall argue that though quantum mechanics does indeed exhibit important differences from classical physics, the former is indeterministic only in a somewhat Pickwickian sense, and that the present situation in physics does not necessitate the wholesale rejection of the category of causal determinism.

I.

Viewed formally, the theory of mechanics is a set of equations which formulate the dependence of certain traits of bodies in motion on other physical properties. The equations of motion in their Newtonian form assert the dependence of the time-rate of change of the momentum of each "mass-point" belonging to a given physical system—*i.e.*, of each body whose spatial dimensions can be neglected—upon a definite set of other factors, such as the distance of the body from other bodies, their relative masses, and the like. The equations are often said to express causal laws, even though the word "cause" does not occur in them, because they assert that the time-rate of change of a certain magnitude (the momentum of a mass-point) is a definite though generally unspecified function of various other physical properties of mass-points. And for similar reasons a similar locution is frequently employed in other branches of physical science.

A closer examination of the fundamental laws of motion shows them to be linear differential equations which in their general formulation contain an unspecified function, the so-called "force-function." Two important consequences directly follow from this. Before the equations can be applied to a concrete physical problem, the force-function must be specified for the case at hand; that is, a specific assumption must be made concerning the detailed form of the dependence between the time-rate of change in the momentum of a body and other parameters of the physical system to which it belongs. And secondly, since the equations can be used in concrete contexts only in their mathematically integrated form, the values of the constants of integration—two for each body, namely its initial position and initial momentum—must also be assigned. It is a truism that neither the specific form of the force function nor the values of these constants can be deduced from the general theory of motion, and that in principle they must be obtained on the basis of an independent experimental study of the physical system under consideration. Each concrete use of the fundamental theoretical equations of motion thus requires two supplementary assumptions.

Some brief remarks on each of these is now in order. In general, the form of the force-function will vary from case to case, though it is possible to classify these cases into comprehensive types and to prescribe a force-function for each type. For example, the Newtonian theory of gravitation consists in the assumption that the change in the momentum of a body belonging to a system of bodies is a function only of the masses and the mutual distances between members of the system. In point of fact, the force-function employed in many of the familiar applications of the equations of motion is specified in a manner analogous to the Newtonian hypothesis, in so far as it does not contain the time-variable explicitly. Indeed, though there are numerous cases for which the time-variable enters explicitly into the force-function (as in the case of damped vibrations), it is commonly assumed that the explicit presence of the time-variable can in principle be eliminated if the initial system of interacting bodies is suitably enlarged by including other bodies into it. For reasons that will be presently apparent, what is called the "principle of causality" (as distinguished from special causal laws) is in fact usually construed in classical physics as the maxim that should the force-function for a given physical system contain the time-variable explicitly, the system is to be enlarged in such a manner as to allow a specification of the force-function in which the time-variable does not appear.[1] And it is a matter of historical fact that in the main the search for such enlarged systems that do not coincide with the entire cosmos has been successful.

A physical system satisfying the condition that the force-function does not contain the time-variable explicitly possesses the important characteristic that its total mechanical energy is constant in time. But such a system has an even more arresting feature, namely, that what is called its "mechanical state" at one time completely determines its mechanical state at any other time. By the mechanical state of a mass-point at a given time we must understand its position and momentum at that time, where the position and momentum of a particle are said to be the coordinates of mechanical state or the mechanical state-variables. Analogously, the mechanical state of a system consisting of n mass-points is the set of values of the coordinates of state of each constituent particle. The mechanical state of a system of bodies whose dimensions cannot be ignored and which, in addition to translatory motions, may exhibit rotations, is defined in a similar manner.

The notion of mechanical state is an important one, and its significance can be conveyed with the help of an idealized example. Suppose S is a system of bodies completely isolated from all other systems. Members of S exhibit various traits (such as mass, distribution in space, motions, etc.) which can be described with the help of a fixed and finite set of predicates "P," "Q," "R," etc. If the specific form of these traits for each member of S were known at a given time t_0, we could say that the state of S is known for that time. Suppose then that at time t_0, S is in a state describable as P_0, Q_0, R_0, etc., that the state of S changes with time, and that at time t_1 S is in a state describable as P_1, Q_1, R_1, etc. Next imagine that S is brought back into the state it originally possessed at time t_0, that it is then permitted to change of its own accord, and that after an interval t_1-t_0 it once more exhibits the state describable as P_1, Q_1, R_1, that is, its state is once more what it was at time t_1. A system which always behaved in this manner would be one in which its state at one time uniquely determined its state at any other time.

Let us now complicate this abstract example. Suppose that in

[1] *Cf.* Silberstein, Ludwik, *Causality*, p. 69 ff.

addition to the preceding it is possible to establish a set of general laws L which enable us, given the state of the system S at one time, to deduce the formulation of the state at any other time. It would then be theoretically possible to predict the state of the system at any time, given the state of the system at some initial time. On the other hand, if the number of predicates needed to characterize the state of S were very large, it would not be feasible practically to formulate the state or to discover the laws L. Let us therefore assume that there is a small subset in the total set of predicates required to characterize the state of S completely—for example, the subset consisting of the two predicates "P" and "Q"—which is a sufficient basis for defining the remaining predicates or for formulating general laws connecting the predicates in the subset and all the others. On this assumption, a knowledge of the specific nature of the traits expressed by the predicates in the subset enables us to conclude to the specific nature of the remaining traits of members of S, and therefore to the state of S. Accordingly, the laws L need only formulate the connections between the traits in the subset at one time and these traits at any other time, in order to enable us to infer the state of S at any time, given the traits in the subset at some initial time. Under the circumstances, therefore, it will be useful to amend slightly the original meaning of "the state of the system S," and to stipulate that the relatively small number of predicates in the subset will characterize the state of S.

The relevance of this abstract example for the analysis of mechanics is perhaps obvious. Physical bodies exhibit various properties which are the special concern of the science of mechanics and which may therefore be called "mechanical properties." Moreover, all the mechanical properties of a system at a given time are in effect specified, if for that time the properties formulated by the mechanical coordinates of state are known; for example, if the position and momentum of a mass-point is given, its kinetic energy can be readily calculated. Accordingly, given the laws of motion and the specific form of the force-function, together with the mechanical state of the system for some specified initial instant, the mechanical state of the system for any other time—and therefore the full complexion of its mechanical properties—is uniquely determined.

It is this feature of the laws of classical mechanics which is the basis for characterizing the theory of mechanics as "deterministic." Certainly it is this feature that Laplace had in mind when he declared in a well-known passage that for an intelligence acquainted with the positions of all material particles and with the forces acting between them "the future as well as the past would be present to its eyes." For Laplace as well as for most of his 19th century successors, a satisfactory physical theory was one which conformed to the norm exhibited by analytical mechanics. Their ideal for physics was a theory which is deterministic in the sense that it employs a definition of physical state quite like that of classical mechanics, and that it makes possible, given an initial state of a system, the calculation of a unique state for any other time.

II.

Some further comments must now be added to this brief account of mechanics, so that the notion of physical state, thus far developed only for this science, may be extended to other branches of classical physics.

(1) It requires only passing mention that classical mechanics like any branch of inquiry is concerned only with a limited set of physical properties. The laws of mechanics can in fact explicitly deal only with those changes in physical systems which are expressible in terms of the mechanical coordinates of state in the manner indicated previously. At the same time, it is worth stressing that though classical mechanics is a deterministic theory, it is deterministic specifically and exclusively with respect to the mechanical states of system. Thus, given only the initial positions of a set of bodies, or given only the initial kinetic energy of such a system, mechanics does not enable us to calculate the positions or the kinetic energy for any other time. Again, the laws of mechanics assert nothing about electro-magnetic properties, and cannot be used to calculate variations in the magnitudes of such properties, however much may be known concerning the initial mechanical state of a system of bodies or concerning the forces operating between them. Quite clearly, then, a non-sequitur is involved in Laplace's dictum that "nothing would be uncertain" for an intelligence possessing a requisite knowledge of mechanical states and

forces. His claim can be regarded as warranted only if it is understood to mean that a sufficiently vast intelligence, knowing the mechanical state of the universe at one time, would be able to calculate the *mechanical state* of the universe at any other time. In brief, the determinism of classical mechanics is relative to physical states specified in terms of the mechanical coordinates of state.

(2) It is also important not to overlook the simple yet frequently ignored point that mechanics as a physical theory is not a descriptive account, whether partial or complete, of the actual course of events. For not only is that theory relevant only to certain selected phases of things—all discourse is selective in this sense. That theory expresses only a framework of abstract relations, and it is formulated with the help of notions that are defined as ideal limits of hypothetical observations rather than in terms of anything that is experimentally identifiable. For as already noted, the fundamental laws of mechanics must be supplemented by two distinct types of information before they can be put to actual use: by a special assumption concerning the forces involved in a given system, and by information concerning the initial mechanical state of the system. Moreover, and this is of particular importance for the present theme, classical mechanics is formulated as a set of differential equations, so that in consequence it is the "instantaneous" coordinates of mechanical state that are required to be known in the application of the theory. However, instantaneous positions and momenta are never experimental data, for actual observation can ascertain the positions and momenta of bodies only during some non-vanishing interval of time.

The determinism characterizing mechanics must therefore be understood as holding only relative to the *theoretical* specification of mechanical state, according to which the coordinates of state are *instantaneous* positions and momenta. It is quite a different issue, not capable of being settled merely by analyzing the formal structure of mechanical theory, whether initial positions and momenta of bodies *as measured experimentally* uniquely determine positions and momenta *similarly* measured at any other time.

This last point requires some expansion. The classical coordinates of mechanical state are instantaneous individual coordinates: each individual mass-point is assumed to possess an instantaneous position and momentum, and the predication of such positions and momenta does not in principle rest upon any statistical assumption or procedure. On the other hand, in experimental practice one never encounters anything that *literally* satisfies the conditions defining a mass-point, even if in the interest of applying theoretical analysis one may treat as "points" bodies whose dimensions are small when compared to the distances separating them. Again, the positions and momenta assigned to bodies on the basis of actual measurment are obtained by studying the behavior of bodies over some non-vanishing interval of time; and in consequence, experimentally evaluated positions and momenta are never instantaneous. Indeed, from the standpoint of the *theoretical* requirements for the coordinates of mechanical state, the values obtained for these coordinates by experiment are *average* values which involve some *statistical* assumptions. Thus, if the velocity of a body is ascertained by measuring the distance it moves during one second, from the standpoint of theory the value so obtained is simply a mean of the "instantaneous" velocities the body possesses during that second. Classical physics tacitly assumes that the temporal interval involved in measuring the coordinates of state may, in principle, be progressively diminished without limit. Nevertheless, this assumption is clearly not fully congruous with the facts of experimental procedure; for however refined techniques of measurement may become, they cannot yield instantaneous values but only what, from the perspective of theory, are merely statistically defined functions of such values. To be sure, there is a well-known procedure for bringing into concordance the theoretical definition of mechanical state with the magnitudes for coordinates of state obtained by overt measurement. But this procedure is based on the theory of experimental errors, and involves the adoption of statistical hypotheses concerning the frequencies with which various experimentally ascertained magnitudes occur. In any event, the fact remains that the relations of dependence which mechanical theory asserts can be ascertained to hold between properties whose experimentally determined magnitudes, from the standpoint of theory, are statistical coefficients.

It is sometimes concluded from considerations such as these that even classical mechanics is not a deterministic theory and is only approximately one. It has been maintained, for example, that if the mechanical state of a system is specified in "observational terms," the laws of mechanics assert no more than relations of probability or statistical correlation between states at different times. On this view, the formulation of the laws of mechanics as strictly universal statements represents simply an idealization, an idealization justified because the coefficients of probability are close to the maximum value of 1, so that the discrepancy between the true value of the probability and this maximum can be neglected in practice.

But this conception of the matter is based on the assumption that all theories, and the theory of mechanics in particular, are simply generalized descriptive formulations of the actual sequences of events encountered in experience; and some reasons have already been stated for questioning such an assumption. Moreover, and for the present paper this is the central point, the view under consideration appears to confound two issues which need to be kept distinct: the question as to what is the *logical structure* of a given theory, and the question as to the relevance of an abstract theory to observational data and the degree of agreement between the theory and experiment. It is hardly more than a truism to maintain that classical mechanics is "indeterministic" or statistical in nature, if the claim rests on no other grounds than that the experimental confirmation of classical mechanics involves the use of statistical procedures and that experiment confirms it only approximately. For any quantitatively formulated theory viewed from this standpoint is "indeterministic" and statistical: the experimental measurement of physical magnitudes such as velocity always yields a "spread" of values, and no law asserting a relation of dependence between continuous variables is in absolutely precise agreement with data of observation. Nonetheless, when a theory is analyzed for its logical structure, it may possess features that can be properly labelled as "deterministic" with respect to some *theoretical* definition of physical state. And if classical mechanics is so analyzed it is without question a deterministic theory relative to the theoretical definition of mechanical state.

(3) But it is time to remind ourselves that mechanics is not the only branch of classical physics, and that mechanics is not the only

physical theory with a deterministic structure. Moreover, even a cursory survey of other branches of physical science provides evidence for the conclusion that there are other ways of defining the state of a physical system than that employed in mechanics. However, the task of exhibiting these alternative ways requires attention to much technical detail, and it will not be attempted here. Instead, a short list will be constructed which will present in a schematic way definitions of physical state alternative to the one adopted in mechanics. The list does not pretend to be exhaustive, and it undoubtedly suffers from oversimplification. But in spite of its faults it may make clear the existence of genuine alternatives to the mechanical definition of physical state, and thus provide a helpful perspective for viewing current discussions of the causal character of a quantum theory.

Let us note once more that the mechanical state of a system is defined in terms of the instantaneous values of two coordinates for each mass-point belonging to the system, each coordinate being the magnitude of a property that is meaningfully predicable only of individual mass-points. Since the number of such particles is always finite even if it is large, the mechanical state of a system as a whole is thus specified by a finite number of values of the state coordinates.

The classical definition of mechanical state therefore involves distinctions which immediately suggest a way for classifying alternatives to it. In the first place, a physical state might be defined with the help of an *infinite* rather than a finite number of values of some set of parameters. Such a definition is in fact employed by so-called "field theories," and in particular by electromagnetic theory, which requires the state of an electro-magnetic field to be specified by the values of two vectors at each point (infinite in number) of the field. In the second place, instead of defining a physical state in terms of *instantaneous* values of state coordinates, the definition might require the values of state parameters at *several* distinct instants or *during* some continuous temporal stretch. This is the alternative mode of defining physical states adopted by theories devised for handling the phenomena of magnetic hysteresis and metal fatigue, and in general is typical of what is sometimes called "hereditary mechanics." And in the third place, a physical state might be defined with the help of certain *statistical* rather than *individual* coordinates. This is the alternative adopted in certain portions of statistical mechanics and, as will eventually appear, in modern quantum mechanics.

There are therefore at least three pairs of alternative requirements which may be used in defining the physical state of a system: the state may have to be specified with the help of either a finite or an infinite number of values of certain coordinates; the values of the coordinates may be instantaneous or involve reference to some non-vanishing duration; and the state coordinates may be individual coordinates or statistical parameters. Accordingly, since there are no relations of logical dependence between alternatives belonging to these different pairs, there are at least eight specifically different ways in which the state of a physical system might be defined. However, only a few of these eight ways appear to have been employed in the history of modern science.

It follows in any event that it is an error to suppose that a theory can be deterministic only if it employs the mechanical definition of physical state. Neither electro-magnetic theory nor the theory of heat flow, for example, defines the notion of physical state in terms of the positions and momenta of particles, and yet each of these theories is deterministic in the same general sense as is classical mechanics: each of these theories establishes a unique correspondence between the theoretical definition of state at one time and the state at any other time.

This conclusion is perhaps obvious and even trivial. For it does not appear to be possible[2] to specify in detail what is the appropriate definition of physical state for a given domain of phenomena until one is in possession of an adequate theory which is deterministic relative to some definition of state. Indeed, the very meaning of "physical state of a system" entails the conclusion that whenever one can specify what is the physical state for a given system, there is available a theory which is deterministic with respect to that physical state. What is not trivial in the above conclusion is that in point of fact theories having a deterministic form, but not employing the mechanical definition of physical state, have been used successfully in several branches of natural science.

[2] *Cf.* Frank, Philipp, *Modern Science and Its Philosophy*, p. 53-60.

III.

What light do these various considerations throw on the alleged acausal nature of modern quantum theory? Physicists with years of specialized training and experience are not in agreement on this matter; and a layman who ventures to discuss it risks committing first-class blunders. But even if blunder has not been avoided in the following quite general remarks, they may succeed in bringing into focus central issues in the analysis of quantum theory.

Whether quantum theory is formulated with the help of the Schrödinger wave-equation or the Heisenberg matrix algebra, it successfully accounts for a vast range of phenomena by adopting assumptions concerning processes interior to atoms. As in the case of all theories which postulate sub-microscopic entities, the empirical evidence supporting the various assumptions of quantum theory is indirect and is obtained through experiments conducted in familiar macroscopic domains. In this respect there is nothing novel in quantum theory.

The feature of modern quantum theory which has precipitated acute debate over the status of the principle of causality in recent physics is the deduction from its fundamental assumptions of the Heisenberg Uncertainty Relations. The formula which expresses one of these relations is: $\triangle p.\triangle q \geqq h$. Since "$q$" and "$p$" are usually construed as the coordinates of position and momentum of electrons, protons, and other subatomic elements, "$\triangle q$" and "$\triangle p$" represent the dispersion of values or the "error" obtained in ascertaining the values of these coordinates by measurement. Accordingly, the above formula is commonly interpreted to assert that the product of the accuracy with which the simultaneous position and the momentum of a subatomic element can be measured is constant. It then follows that if one of these coordinates is measured with great precision, the value of the conjugate coordinate becomes quite imprecise; and in particular, if the position of an electron is ascertained with a high degree of accuracy, so that $\triangle q$ is practically zero, then the range $\triangle p$ is practically infinite, so that no determinate value can be assigned to the momentum of the "particle."

It is the occurrence of such Uncertainty Relations within modern quantum mechanics that is held to mark the indeterministic character of that theory. For since the simultaneous positions and momenta of elementary particles cannot be ascertained with unlimited precision, so the argument often runs, the laws of quantum mechanics cannot establish a unique correspondence between positions and momenta at one time and positions and momenta at other times. But since quantum theory does make it possible to calculate the probability with which a particle has a certain momentum when it has a certain position (and vice versa), that theory has an inherent statistical nature though it fails to conform to the requirements of a strictly deterministic theory.

Before examining this fundamental thesis, it will be desirable to consider briefly some of the "explanations" and "interpretations" that have been proposed for the Uncertainty Relations. But we can dismiss as irrelevant the suggestion advanced by some physicists, philosophers and theologians that the Uncertainty Relations express the operation of some sort of "free-will"; and we can likewise dismiss as unilluminating the conception according to which the Uncertainty Relations are evidence for some "radical indeterminism" and "objective chance," where these expressions signify substantival agents of change.

A more sober and prima facie plausible account of the Uncertainty Relations is that they express the relatively large but unaccountable modifications in certain features of subatomic elements, resulting from the interaction between these elements and the instruments of measurement. Heisenberg declares, for example, that though when dealing with large-scale phenomena the effect of instruments of measurement upon the objects measured can be neglected, simply because the magnitudes of the disturbances thus produced are relatively small, in the case of subatomic physics

the interaction between observer and object causes uncontrollable and large changes in the system being observed, because of the discontinuous characteristic of atomic processes. The immediate consequence of this circumstance is that in general every experiment performed to determine some numerical quantity renders the knowledge of others illusory, since the uncontrollable perturbation of the observed system alters the values of previously determined quantities.[3]

An alternative interpretation of the Uncertainty Relations maintains that they require us to abandon the hope of explaining "all

[3] Heisenberg, Werner, *The Physical Principles of the Quantum Theory*, p. 3.

phenomena as relations between objects existing in space and time." The ultimate ground for the failure of the principle of causality in subatomic physics, so proponents of this interpretation urge, is the impossibility of describing subatomic processes in terms of spatio-temporal notions that are adequate only for macroscopic objects. As Heisenberg puts the matter:

> There exists a body of exact mathematical laws, but they cannot be interpreted as expressing simple relationships between objects existing in space and time. The observable predictions of this theory can be approximately described in such terms, but not uniquely. . . .[4]

He therefore proposes the following alternatives: Either we continue to describe subatomic processes in familiar spatio-temporal terms, but at the price of abandoning the possibility of giving causal explanations for those processes; or we retain the possibility of providing such causal explanations, but at the cost of forswearing the interpretation of mathematically formulated causal laws in familiar spatio-temporal terms.

In spite of the high authority supporting these interpretations of the Uncertainty Relations, they are not fully persuasive. Thus, the plausibility of the first-mentioned interpretation is somewhat diminished if it is noted that the Uncertainty Relations are not obtained from a consideration of the experimental facts of measurement, but are simply the consequences of the fundamental assumptions of quantum theory. Thus, the disturbing effect of instruments of measurement on what they measure is well recognized in classical physics, without requiring the adoption of any Uncertainty Relations; for in classical physics the extent of such disturbance can be calculated, at least in principle, with the help of established physical laws. But on the present interpretation of the Uncertainty Relations the central point consists in denying the possibility of calculating such disturbances even in principle, because these latter are the outcome of "uncontrollable changes." There does not, however, appear to be any direct evidence for such uncontrollable changes. Accordingly, if the Uncertainty Relations are accepted, they must be accepted not because of the fact (known in classical physics) that measuring instruments interact with what they measure, but because those Relations follow from the assump-

[4] *Op. cit.*, p. 64.

tions of quantum theory. Moreover, these Relations set no limits upon the precision with which, say, the coordinate of position of an electron may be measured. In spite of the supposed interaction between electron and measuring apparatus, the coordinate of position is in principle ascertainable with absolute precision. It cannot be the occurrence of such interactions which makes impossible the absolutely precise determination of position and momentum simultaneously.

The second interpretation of the Uncertainty Relations, according to which these Relations set limits upon the explanation of subatomic processes in terms of spatio-temporally localizable objects, does raise an important point, though the manner in which the interpretation is formulated obscures the main issue. The point which requires attention is that when electrons, protons and other postulated elements of subatomic physics are described as "particles" or "waves," these latter characterizations are used only on the strength of certain analogies. Can it be perchance that these elements cannot be described in spatio-temporal terms, not because spatio-temporal notions are not adequate for subatomic processes, but simply because electrons, protons, etc., are not particles or waves in the familiar and established senses of these terms? This is a suggestion which is at least worth exploring, and in what immediately follows it is proposed to examine the language of quantum theory more closely, in the hope that thereby the allegedly acausal nature of the theory will appear in clearer light.

(1) The subatomic entities postulated by quantum theory are frequently described in a language generally used to describe the mass-points of classical physics. The use of this language thus leads directly to the supposition that the subatomic particles possess both determinate positions and velocities at any time. However, in consequence of the Uncertainty Relations one is also compelled to say that the simultaneous position and velocity of such a particle cannot be determined with unlimited precision. Accordingly, the language employed in discussions of subatomic particles seems to imply that while such particles really do possess absolutely determinate positions and momenta at any instant, it just happens that we cannot possibly discover what their simultaneous values are —although the particles do have certain determinate properties,

the simultaneous values of the magnitudes of the properties are inherently inaccessible to human knowledge.

Such a conclusion, were it really necessitated by the facts, would require at least the partial abandonment of the ideal of verifiability which dominates modern science. It is essential to recall, however, that the conclusion depends on characterizing subatomic entities as particles. At the same time, it is only certain formal analogies with the classical conception of particle which lead physicists to employ the particle language in connection with these entities. These analogies, as is well known, are not complete and break down at various points. Physicists are keenly aware of the failures in the analogies, and have felt compelled to amend the particle language used to describe subatomic processes by supplementing it with the language of waves travelling in media. However, the language of waves like the language of particles has been introduced out of considerations of analogy between certain processes familiar from classical physics, and the structure of processes associated with subatomic entities; and as in the case of particles, the wave analogy also breaks down at various crucial points.

Let us therefore keep in mind what the actual situation in quantum physics is like. The fundamental assumptions of quantum theory are expressed with the help of a highly complex mathematical formalism, and once the conditions for applying this formalism to concrete empirical material are specified the content of the theory is contained in that formalism. Nonetheless, it is heuristically advantageous to express the content of the formalism in other ways, for example in terms of more or less visualizable models patterned after more familiar types of physical processes; and in the attempt to do just this, physicists have been led to employ the language developed in connection with the classical notions of particles and waves.[5] At the same time, the formally stated

[5] Consider the following account, contained in a standard textbook on quantum mechanics: "Our store of direct knowledge regarding the nature of the system known as the hydrogen atom consists in the results of a large number of experiments—spectroscopic, chemical, etc. It is found that all the known facts about this system can be correlated and systematized (and, we say, explained) by associating with this system a certain wave equation. Our confidence in the significance of this association increases when predictions regarding previously uninvestigated properties of the hydrogen atom are

equations of quantum mechanics must be taken to define *implicitly* the various subatomic entities thus postulated, however else these entities are construed; and whatever further characteristics may be associated with these entities, these latter must satisfy the formally expressed conditions or relations of the equations of the theory. Accordingly, the various consequences which are logically derivable from the fundamental equations of the theory—and in particular, the Uncertainty Relations—must be taken as constituting *partial definitions* of what these entities and their properties are.

Thus if certain measurable traits of electrons, to which the names "position" and "velocity" are assigned, must satisfy the conditions stated in the Uncertainty Relations, then these traits in spite of their names must be clearly distinguished from what in classical physics is understood by "position" and "velocity" of "particles." For although in quantum theory the parameters "q" and "p" are *called* the coordinates of "position" and "momentum" of "particles," these words are obviously being employed in unusual senses. According to the usage associated with them in classical physics, a particle has a determinate position and simultaneously a determinate momentum. On that usage it is simply nonsense to say that a particle has a definite position but no determinate momentum, or vice versa; for the meanings of the words are so interrelated that nothing can be said to be a particle which does not possess a determinate position and momentum. It follows that when

subsequently verified by experiment. We might then describe the hydrogen atom by giving its wave equation; this description would be complete. It is unsatisfactory, however, because it is unwieldy. On observing that there is a formal relation between this wave equation and the classical energy equation for a system of two particles of different masses and electrical charges, we seize on this as providing a simple, easy, and familiar way of describing the system, and we say that the hydrogen atom consists of two particles, the electron and proton, which attract each other according to Coulomb's inverse-square law. Actually we do not know that the electron and proton attract each other in the same way that two macroscopic electrically charged bodies do, inasmuch as the force between the two particles in a hydrogen atom has never been directly measured. All that we know is that the wave equation for the hydrogen atom bears a certain formal relation to the classical dynamical equations for a system of two particles attracting each other in this way." Linus Pauling and E. Bright Wilson, *Introduction to Quantum Mechanics*, p. 56.

the formalism of quantum mechanics is interpreted, and electrons are introduced as particles which are precluded by the theory from having determinate values simultaneously for both the properties symbolized by the "q's" and "p's," then either an electron is not a particle in the customary sense of the word, or these symbols cannot refer to positions and momenta in the customary senses of these words.

It is thus simply not the case that certain crucial expressions as used in quantum theory denote the identical traits of things which those expressions signify in classical physics. And outstanding physicists have often called attention to just this point,[6] even if they have not always made the best use of their insight. The use of the language of classical physics in the context of subatomic research is unquestionably valuable, for it calls attention to important analogies and so suggests fresh directions for inquiry. But the use of that language can also be a handicap, in so far as it prevents its users from recognizing important failures in analogy and therefore encourages them to raise misleading questions.

The point under discussion will perhaps be reinforced if we recall another historically important adaptation of old language to new contexts—that which occurred when the word "number" was extended from its use in connection with cardinal and ordinal integers to other kinds of mathematical "entities." As is well known, various operations were first developed for the cardinals (*e.g.*, addition, multiplication, and their inverses), and with their help cer-

---

[6] For example, von Neumann declares that it would be entirely meaningless to distinguish between a term p.q and a term q.p, if these are construed in the sense specified by classical mechanics. J. von Neumann, *Mathematische Grundlagen der Quantenmechanik*, p. 6. Heisenberg notes that the "uncertainty relation specifies the limits within which the particle picture can be applied. Any use of the words 'position' and 'velocity' with an accuracy exceeding that given by the Uncertainty equation is just as meaningless as the use of words whose sense is not defined." *Op. cit.*, p. 6. And Schrödinger remarks, in commenting on the indeterminacy which quantum mechanics ascribes to material particles, that "On a little reflection it will be clear that the object referred to by quantum mechanics in this connection is not a material point in the old sense of the word. . . . It should neither be disputed nor passed over in tactful silence (as is done in certain quarters) that the concept of the material point undergoes a considerable change which as yet we fail thoroughly to understand." Erwin Schrödinger, *Science and the Human Temperament*, p. 71-2.

tain properties of these numbers were defined (*e.g.*, being a perfect square, being odd or even, etc.). Presently, however, the use of the word "number" was extended so as to apply to the ratios of cardinals (usually represented as fractions); for definite operations can be introduced for the ratios of integers which are closely analogous to the operations upon cardinals themselves. Thus, ratios can be "added" and "multiplied," and these new operations exhibit formal patterns which—up to a point—are abstractly the same as the patterns that are exhibited by cardinal addition and multiplication. Nevertheless though the ratios of integers possess many properties that are analogous to those possessed by the cardinals, there are also properties characterizing the latter which are simply not defined for the former. Thus, the property of being a perfect square can be significantly predicated of both cardinals and ratios of cardinals; but the porperty of being odd (or even) is not defined for the ratios. We are thus unable to answer the question whether $\frac{2}{3}$ is odd or even; but our inability stems neither from an insufficiency in our knowledge nor from any inherent inaccessibility of properties of ratios—it stems simply from the fact that expressions like "$\frac{2}{3}$ is odd" have no defined sense. And what has just been said in brief about ratios applies with no less force to other entities that have been introduced in the development of mathematics and in the so-called extension of the "number concept" —for example, to matrices and to the failure of the commutative law for matrix multiplication. If anyone views this failure as a paradox, on the ground that the "essential nature" of multiplication requires it to be commutative, he needs to be reminded that the fact is a paradox only because the word "multiplication" is borrowed from one context (in which the operation it names *is* commutative) and then used as a designation for a quite distinct (though in some respect analogous) operation in another context.

In a similar way the quantum-mechanical use of the words "position," "velocity" and "particle" in connection with subatomic elements is to be viewed as an extension of their use in classical physics—an extension that depends on there being certain formal analogies between the mathematical formalism of quantum and classical mechanics. At the same time the actual sense of these expressions in their newer context of usage must be construed in terms of the restrictions imposed upon their possible meanings by the fundamental equations of quantum theory. And since the formal prescriptions which are imposed by quantum and classical physics are different, what these words mean in quantum mechanics is clearly different from their original meanings. To maintain that if we knew enough or had better experimental techniques we might obtain the precise simultaneous values for the "position" and "velocity" of electrons, is to overlook the capital point that in quantum mechanics these expressions are so defined that whatever is designated by them *must* satisfy the conditions stated in the Uncertainty Relations.

(2) It follows from what has now been said that quantum mechanics cannot rightly be characterized as an indeterministic theory merely on the ground that the Uncertainty Relations play an integral role in it. For if the above considerations are at all cogent, it is invalid to conclude that the "positions" and "momenta" which these Relations declare to be conjugately uncertain, are identifiable with traits of particles which classical mechanics declares to be subject to a deterministic order.

But another and independent point requires to be made. The view that quantum mechanics is indeterministic rests on the assumption that this theory, like classical mechanics, specifies the physical state of a system in terms of the coordinates of position and momentum. If this assumption could be safely made, there would be at least prima facie reason for the conclusion erected upon it. For since it is impossible to specify at any time the simultaneous instantaneous values of position and momentum for a subatomic "particle," it is obviously impossible to calculate a unique value for these coordinates for some other time.

However, it is just this assumption that requires to be examined: for even if quantum theory is not deterministic with respect to a state description defined in terms of "positions" and momenta," it does not follow that it may not be quite deterministic with respect to a different state description. And in point of fact, inspection of the formal statements of quantum mechanics does show that this theory does not employ a state description like that of classical mechanics, but that with respect to a mode of state description adopted by the theory it is deterministic in form. The heart of the matter can be stated very succinctly: If quantum theory is considered in its wave-mechanical formulation, the state description adopted by the theory is defined in terms of a certain function, the so-called Psi-function. Moreover, the wave equation has the important property that given the value of this function at one instant and assuming that the boundary conditions for the equation remain fixed, the equation assigns a unique value for that function for any other instant. Quantum mechanics is therefore deterministic with respect to the quantum-mechanical description of state.

Nevertheless, it is not possible to interpret the quantum-mechanical state description in terms of any visualizable model of physical processes. In particular, neither a picture in terms of the motions of classical particles, nor one in terms of the behavior of classical waves, can be used to give a satisfactory "intuitive" or "physical" interpretation for the Psi-function. Just in what way the quantum-mechanical formalism is employed for analyzing and bringing into a system various classes of experimentally ascertained phenomena is a difficult technical problem, far beyond the scope and competence of the present paper. In rough outline the matter appears to be somewhat as follows. The Psi-function is itself complex (in the technical mathematical sense), but the square of its amplitude is of course real (again in the strict mathematical sense). Moreover, the square of this amplitude can be associated with the probability that the electrons for which the Psi-function is the state description occupy a certain region and possess energies of specified magnitudes. The numerical value of this probability can be estimated from experimental data, though these data do not establish a unique value for the Psi-function itself. Accordingly, though quantum mechanics is deterministic with respect to the Psi-function, this function does not possess a direct experimental significance; experiment is capable of ascertaining the initial value of the amplitude of this function, but not the initial value of the function itself. Moreover, both the data that must be supplied to work the wave equation for any concrete case, as well as the physically significant consequences that can be derived from that equation, have a statistical form. For this reason, though quantum mechanics is deterministic with respect to the Psi-function as the state description, it is nevertheless maintained by outstanding quantum theorists that quantum theory is "in the nature of the case indeterministic, and therefore the affair of statistics."[7]

But it is perhaps worth emphasizing that when the amplitude of the Psi-function is interpreted as a probability—as the relative frequency with which certain types of elementary processes occur —a definite model or picture of physical changes is still being employed. Taken by itself this is not objectionable. However, the model may become an obstacle to understanding if it leads us to suppose that certain properties of electrons and the like, conceived on the pattern of classical particles, are inherently unknowable because of the alleged "indeterministic" nature of the postulated elements. For we must not lose sight of the basic point that though quantum theory is interpreted in terms of some physical model, the equations of the theory do establish unique correspondence between what, from the standpoint of the model, are average values of the magnitudes of properties characterizing the elements of the model. When it is said, for example, that a single electron has some specified configuration or behavior, what needs to be understood by such a statement is that a certain parameter, characterizing the statistical distribution of the properties of a large class of electrons, possesses a certain value and is associated with a certain coefficient of dispersion. And in any event, the equations of quantum theory are so constructed that the value of such a parameter and of its associated dispersion coefficient at one instant uniquely determine the corresponding values of these coordinates at any other instant. It is clear therefore that in terms of the model employed in reading the equations of the theory, the initial data that need to be supplied in applying the theory to a concrete case are interpreted in statistical terms. It should not therefore be surprising or appear paradoxical that all the conclusions obtained with the help of the theory from such data also require to be construed in statistical terms, and do not supply information about any individual member of the statistical aggregate. It would be surprising and paradoxical if the outcome were otherwise.

The remarks of the preceding paragraph are not intended as an argument for some such conclusions as that, since quantum

[7] Born, Max, *Atomic Physics*, p. 90.

mechanics is deterministic with respect to a statistically specified state-description, there are no important differences between quantum and classical physics. Such a conclusion would be quite incongruous with the known facts, and such a conclusion is not intended. The point of those remarks is to suggest that when quantum theory is characterized as "indeterministic," a tacit interpretation of the formalism of the theory in terms of the behavior of postulated statistical aggregates is being made, while at the same time the use of state descriptions defined in terms of statistical coordinates of state is employed as the sole ground for the characterization. However, if the above analysis of alternative ways for defining the state of a physical system has any merit, that characterization ignores a feature of quantum theory that is at least as central as the one it so emphatically notes.

IV.

The belief that subatomic processes are acausal has been often used as the foundation for the further claim that causal laws for macroscopic phenomena cannot be validly affirmed. The argument for this conclusion appears to be as follows. Macroscopic objects are complex structures of subatomic ones; hence the properties possessed by the former can occur only under conditions specifiable in terms of the arrangements and behaviors of the latter. But the behavior of subatomic objects is, by hypothesis, acausal, and the laws formulating this behavior are statistical; hence the interrelations and behaviors of macroscopic objects are also acausal, and the laws formulating them must be indeterministic. Various further consequences have been drawn from this conclusion, among others a number dealing with questions of human freedom and responsible action; but this aspect of the matter will not be pursued here any further.

One premise in this argument—namely, that the laws of quantum physics are indeterministic—has already been examined at considerable length, and has been found not to be fully warranted. However, even if this premise is granted, the argument is less than conclusive; and the remainder of the present paper will attempt to show why it is not.

A tacit assumption in the argument is the view that if a complex is analyzable into a structure of constituent elements, whether these be absolutely or only relatively "simple," the elements are in some special but not altogether clear sense more "ultimate" than or "metaphysically" prior to the complexes. What is perhaps meant is that no property or character has an indisputable place in an account of nature unless such a property can be predicated of the elements into which complexes may be analyzed. But if this is what the assumption means, it is a difficult one to warrant, and there is much to be said against it. Indeed, if the properties which macroscopic objects manifestly possess could be counted among the genuine features of nature only if their more elementary constituents possessed them, there would be no point in developing theoretical explanations for the behavior of macroscopic objects in terms of their elementary parts—for in that case the elementary parts would simply be diminutive duplicates of the macroscopic objects, and would possess all the traits whose very explanation is being sought. In point of fact, when a comprehensive body of theory makes intelligible the behavior of gross objects in terms of microscopic and submicroscopic elements, special laws must be assumed which connect the manifest traits of complexes with certain other traits of the elements; and the presence of such laws would be fatuously absurd, were not the traits of complexes not possessed by their elementary constituents as genuine features of the world as the traits of the elements are assumed to be.

It must also be noted that the phenomenal traits of gross objects do not correspond in a simple one-to-one fashion with the traits and distributions of subatomic elements. Indeed, the central idea in the statistical laws of modern physics is that to a given trait of gross objects—for brevity, let us refer to such trait as a "macro-state"—there corresponds a large number of theoretically possible and distinct combinations (or "micro-states") of the elements. According to classical statistical mechanics, for example, a given state of temperature of a gas corresponds to the mean kinetic energy of the molecules of the gas: the given macro-state thus corresponds to any one of a large number of alternative distributions in the molecular velocities, these alternatives being subject only to the condition that the mean kinetic energy be the same for each. Even if the subatomic elements exhibit only statistical regularities and are not subject to strictly deterministic laws—so that the occurrence of a given micro-state does not uniquely determine some *one* micro-state for another time, but is compatible with the occurrence of *a number of distinct* micro-states at that time—it does not therefore follow that the *macro-states* corresponding to these alternative micro-states are necessarily distinct. In short, though the laws connecting micro-states may be statistical in their structure, the laws connecting the macro-states that correspond to them may nevertheless have a strictly deterministic form.

If these remarks have merit, it follows that the determinate orders in which observable phenomena are found to occur when observable conditions for their occurrence are instituted, are not placed in jeopardy by researches into subatomic process. Such researches certainly enlarge our knowledge through the discovery of hitherto unnoticed factors upon which the occurrence of observable phenomena depends. But the discovery that subatomic processes do not exhibit the same modes of interconnection as do the macroscopic objects of which they are constituents, does not disprove the orders we have established for the latter or reduce them to illusion.

The Absolute and the Non-Absolute in Scientific Knowledge

BY F. S. C. NORTHROP*

*S*EVERAL years ago Morris Cohen and I were discussing Einstein's theory of relativity. Finally he summarized our common conclusion as follows: "One must believe in absolute knowledge and at the same time not believe in it."

When Morris Cohen said we must believe in absolute scientific knowledge he was, if I interpreted him correctly, referring to the meaning of what is asserted in verified scientific theory. When he was saying that at the same time one must not believe in absolute knowledge he was, if my interpretation of him was again correct, referring to the degree of certainty in the verification of the absolute knowledge which is meant. In short, scientific knowledge is absolute with respect to its meaning but not absolute with respect to the certainty of its verification.

Failure to keep this elementary distinction in mind leads to many prevalent erroneous conclusions. Many philosophers and scientists, noting that the verification of scientific knowledge is never absolute, conclude that what is meant and asserted in the propositions of scientific theory thus verified is also not absolute. This confuses the non-absoluteness of verification with the non-absoluteness of meaning.

The same confusion occurs also in connection with ethical theory and normative theories in the social sciences. Those who are attempting to determine and to verify scientifically normative ethical, legal and economic principles, which are absolute in the sense that they are valid for everyone, are often criticized, even by defenders

* The author is gratefully indebted to the Viking Fund for a grant which makes this and other research possible.

of experimental naturalism in ethics and the social sciences, for aiming at something which, if achieved, would be evil, since it would give rise to the absolute certainty with respect to one's beliefs which tends to produce intolerance, dictatorship and an inquisition. This, again, is to confuse absoluteness of what is meant so far as normative propositions are concerned with absolute certainty concerning their verification. Only absoluteness in the latter sense can produce the aforementioned evils.

It is important to note precisely in what factors of scientific method this non-absoluteness with respect to the certainty of verification has its basis. As Albert Einstein has noted, and Morris Cohen was well aware, it centers in the deductively formulated character of the theories of Western science and in their *indirect* method of verification.[1] *What* is affirmed in the scientific hypothesis or deductively formulated theory is absolute with respect to meaning in the sense that it is invariant for all observers and frames of reference. In the general theory of relativity Einstein achieves such absoluteness of knowledge without any conditioning restrictions of observers, standpoints, or frames of reference. The postulates of his general theory of relativity and his famous tensor law for gravitation are postulated as holding always for all observers and for any frame of reference, Galileian or non-Galileian. Thus what the theory means and what, when experimentally verified, it asserts to be the case is absolute.

It is only with respect to the certainty of the verification of this theory that at the same time we must hold it to be not absolute. This follows because in the method of verification we verify the theorems of the theory, not its postulates. When this verification occurs, we say that the theory is true or, more precisely, that it is confirmed. In saying this we are asserting that an absolute with respect to meaning is confirmed; hence the first part of Morris Cohen's statement. But since the verification is indirect, the logical fallacy of affirming the consequent is committed. The logic of indirect verification is as follows: If what the postulates of the theory

---

[1] See my *Logic of the Sciences and the Humanities,* ch. viii, especially p. 146-47 (New York 1947); also "Einstein's Conception of Science" in *Albert Einstein: Philosopher-Scientist,* ed. Paul A. Schilpp, vol. vii, Library of Living Philosophers, Inc. (Evanston Ill. 1949).

assert to be absolute is the case, then the theorems X, Y, and Z follow. Experiments show the theorems X, Y, and Z to be the case; therefore, what the postulates of the theory assert to be absolute is the case.

The significance of the presence of the fallacy of affirming the consequent in the verification of a scientific theory is not that it forces us to regard the theory as false, since the very logic involved in the fallacy assures us that the theory has been confirmed; its significance, instead, is that it tells us that even though we know that the theory is verified, we must realize that the connection between the experimental facts and the assumptions of the theory is not one of formal, logical necessity and hence does not permit one to regard the theory which is absolute with respect to its meaning, to be verified with absolute certainty. Hence Morris Cohen's dictum: We must believe in the absolute [so far as what scientific knowledge means is concerned], but at the same time not believe in the absolute [so far as the certainty of its verification is concerned].

This combination of absoluteness with respect to the meaning of scientific knowledge with non-absoluteness with respect to the certainty of verification of that absolute meaning is extremely important for another reason. It permits the formulation of a new and improved doctrine of toleration.

The distinguished contemporary British historian G. M. Trevelyan has pointed out,[2] that while many people previous to Locke believed in toleration when they were in minority religious or political groups, only to fail to practice it when they became the majority, and whereas others, such as Henry VIII, Elizabeth and Cromwell when he came into power, believed in toleration on instrumental grounds because they wanted a strong nationalistic England and saw that intolerant religious wars defeated that end, John Locke was one of the first, if not the first, to conceive of toleration as a positive good in itself, as a moral end rather than merely an instrumental means. Then it becomes something to be believed in and practiced when one is the majority in power as well as when one is a minority group out of power.

[2] *English Social History* (New York 1942). See also my *Meeting of East and West* (New York 1946) Chs. iii, iv, viii and xii.

Notwithstanding its unique merits, John Locke's doctrine of toleration has exhibited serious weaknesses. It depends upon a theory of the basis of human beliefs, largely introspective and private in character, which only certain Western thinkers affirm. Thus its basis lacks sufficient universality. This lack of universality has unfortunate practical consequences. Not being affirmed as a matter of basic principle by certain Western groups, such as the Roman Catholics and the Marxist Communists, it gives the latter groups, an unjust advantage over people who do affirm it. Non-believers in the Lockean basic principle of toleration appeal to it only when they are in the minority and reject the principle when they become the majority party or power.

A second weakness in the Lockean doctrine of toleration arises from the fundamental principle on which it rests. This principle is that any opinion is to be given as much weight as any other opinion merely because somebody believes in it. Such a basis tends to keep alive outmoded and scientifically disproved beliefs.

The location of the grounds for toleration in the indirect method by means of which any knowledge of the Western type is verified, places the doctrine of toleration upon a much sounder basis. Being grounded in the *method* of obtaining knowledge, rather than in the mere individual act of believing, a basis for toleration is provided which holds through the different theories to which the method of inquiry may lead one. Also, the indirectness of the method of verification engenders the openness of mind to new hypotheses and to alternative theories which is the essence of a tolerant attitude, while at the same time not giving the same weight to beliefs which have been shown by scientific methods not to be confirmed as to beliefs which have passed this test. Thereby, disproved and outmoded beliefs are eliminated.

Furthermore, when the distinction between absoluteness of meaning and the non-absoluteness of the verification of that meaning is kept in mind, a doctrine of toleration thus grounded in the scientific method of indirect verification encourages toleration, while at the same time fostering the universality with respect to what is meant necessary to avoid the breakdown of an effective public opinion and chaos in society. Without the latter absoluteness of meaning, generated by free discussion and scientific inquiry which leads to agreement with respect to what is believed, the majority opinion requisite for an effective democracy is not present. If the meaning of scientific knowledge as well as the certainty of the verification of that meaning is relative rather than absolute, then a plurality of minority opinions, parties and social groups which cannot agree sufficiently to form an effective government is the inevitable result, as was the case in democratic Germany before Hitler and as threatens to be the case in contemporary France. In short, the distinction with reference to human knowledge between absoluteness of its meaning and non-absoluteness of the certainty of its verification is as important practically for politics and democratic processes as it is theoretically for science, philosophy, and the theory of knowledge.

The Growth Imperative

✍ BY H. A. OVERSTREET
City College of New York

$\mathcal{N}$ OTHING is harder to come to with a fresh mind than something that is taken for granted but not really understood. This applies to the concept of psychological growth. Everybody knows that he has to grow up psychologically; and everybody thinks that he knows what growing up means. Does he not go to school? Does he not learn to read, write and figure? Does he not learn about Europe, Asia, Africa, and the rest? Does he not learn a vocation and the art of governing a family? In the process of learning all these, he feels that his child-mind grows into the mind of a mature adult.

Thus psychological growth is taken for granted by everyone, precisely as physical growth was once taken for granted. But most of us are as ignorant of what is needed for psychological growth as we once were of what was needed for physical growth. In olden days, we knew little of what our bodily requirements were. Now, however, we have learned so much that we are able to build up our bodies in ways impossible before.

New knowledge about psychological growth has likewise come —largely out of the laboratories of psychologists and the case studies of psychiatrists, but also out of the researches of social scientists into the life of societies. This knowledge has not yet—like vitamin knowledge—become widespread and readily applied. When it does, we may look forward to a time of building up our psychological powers with as brilliant success as we are now able to build up our physical powers.

I.

As William James pointed out long ago, even the best of us have not yet developed even a small fraction of the powers of the great human forebrain. These powers lie as yet untapped beneath the surface of our everyday engagements with life. It might well seem that our growing up from childhood to adulthood would be a process of bringing more and more of these untapped powers out into the open and into use.

On the contrary, the opposite all too frequently seems to happen. As we grow older, we tend rather to regress in our powers. William Sheldon, in his *Psychology and the Promethean Will*, speaks of average adulthood as a time of the "dying back of the brain." "The days of youth teem with fragments of living knowledge; with daring philosophies; morning dreams; plans. But the human mind at forty is commonly vulgar, smug, deadened, and wastes its hours. Everywhere adult brains seem to resemble blighted trees that have died in the upper branches, but yet cling to the struggling green wisp of life about the lower trunk."[1]

In short something seems to happen to psychological growth that ought not to happen. One would suppose that the growth-curve would mount steadily from infancy, through adolescence, and through all the adult years. It should be a process of up and up, with a continual increase of the individual's powers: a widening of horizons; a surer grasp of principles; a keener sense of fact and relationships; a continuous releasing of new powers not yet discovered. Instead, shortly after adolescence, the growth-curve begins to flatten out; and the individual who, presumably, should be growing up through his middle and old age into a greater and greater maturing of his powers and a greater and greater release of new powers into use, "settles down" into a fixated, a non-growing, and a relatively uninspired adulthood.

Why this curious reversal of the growth process that seems to be the fate of so many of us as we grow older? Is it something predetermined in our nature; something we cannot escape? Must we, in spite of our best intentions and most earnest efforts, stop our psychological growing in the years of our middle age and flatten out into adult dullness?

If this is fated—inevitable—there is then nothing we can do about it. We are compelled to look anxiously to middle and old age as a time of retracting our powers; of being less and less instead of

---

[1] Sheldon, William H., *Psychology and the Promethean Will*, p. 3.

more and more. But it may be that this is not fated. The dying back of our psychological powers may be due to our own ignorance of how to keep those powers alive and growing. Also it may be due to conditions in our world that discourage rather than encourage their growth.

Robert Frost has described one of his characters as a "decent product of life's ironing out." Had the life conditions in this man's case been different, he need not, one would suppose, have been "ironed out." He might have gone on growing into a rich and inspiring old age. Life conditions are all too frequently that way. By the sheer pressure of their demands—or terrors, or anxieties—they stop the growth in us.

But if this is what happens, then, obviously, the case is not hopeless: life conditions can be changed—if we know enough to change them.

Harry Stack Sullivan has written in similar vein that most of us, because of the tensions of life, are mere caricatures of what we might have been. Here again, the scientific thinker points to nothing that is fated, but to conditions of existence that arrest growth and turn us into creatures who are far less than we might be.

It is possible, then, to look upon adulthood with hopeful eyes. The "dying back," the "ironing out" are, indeed, real enough. In far too many cases adults do not go on growing into a stronger and wider development of their powers. They become arrested in their growth; prematurely fixated. Adulthood, in that case, becomes, as someone has called it, "adulledhood."

But apparently it need not be that way. We used to think, following the folk saying that you can't teach old dogs new tricks, that when people grow old they inevitably grow stiff and unresponsive in their minds, and that the time comes when they cannot go on mentally growing. In 1928, Edward Thorndike published his notable study, *Adult Learning.* In that study he showed that adults have the capacity to go on learning. The tempo may be slower, but the results in understanding are in most cases far greater than in the younger years.

Again, the case studies of psychiatrists show us that in many instances arrest of psychological growth occurs because of some childhood shock or misapprenhension that has lodged in the subconscious and has not matured into full understanding. The psychoanalytic process of lifting such an arrested fragment of a self into the full light of present consciousness starts the self growing again, with the result that the individual who was fixated in a kind of paralysis of childhood becomes again the growing man or woman.

Out of such psychiatric studies we have learned how tragically an arrest of mental and emotional development can affect the health and welfare of the individual; and how starting the growth process going again can restore the individual to health and well-being.

In every case where mental and emotional growth is stopped the individual becomes less capable as a human being. He may also become a dangerous human being.

Thus, where the individual stops the learning process too soon; where he is content to be "an ignorant old man"; or even an "ignorant middle-aged man," he becomes a breeding place not only of misinformation, but of wrong opinion, prejudice, suspicion, and hatred. The tragic antagonisms of the world come mostly out of the dark ignorance of men. Where men, by the millions, never develop into a mature awareness of the facts of their world; where their minds remain trapped in childish half truths, in rumor and innuendo, they are the soil for the growth of all kinds of noxious weeds.

Again, where the individual is arrested in his emotional development; where in the forties and fifties he is still emotionally a child—irresponsible, self-centered, wanting things for his own satisfaction, oblivious to others—he is a dangerous person to have around. Multiply such emotional child-adults by the millions and we have a civilization in which centering in oneself rather than in the common well-being becomes the ugly rule of survival.

The issue of our life, then, is to keep the psychological growth processes going: the growth of the mind into a fuller and clearer apprehension of its world; the growth of emotional life into a wider and more generous relating of the self to its world. Where the growth processes stop there is various tragedy: it may be merely a tragedy to the individual self—a flattening out into harmless dullness; or it may also be a tragedy to others—as when the ungrownup self, in ignorance, or in selfishness, or in both, plays havoc with the life around him.

II.

We discover, then, in ourselves a growth axiom: *Where there is a power that needs to grow, it must fulfill itself or become distorted.* The Latins had a maxim for this: *qui non proficit deficit:* who does not go forward goes backward; who does not grow deteriorates.

It is perfectly natural for a child to be ignorant. There is even something charming about it. His irrelevant prattle, wild guesses, amusing mistakes about what makes things click—all these create in us a warm affection for the child. This is so because the child's ignorance is coupled with an eager curiosity. The child actually wants to know; and pesters us with questions so that he may know.

But let there be a comparable ignorance in an adult; and it is no matter for warm affection. An ignorant adult is a monstrosity for the simple reason that in his adulthood this saving curiosity to know is usually absent. The child who does not know knows he does not know, and tries to know. The adult who does not know usually has no saving wish to know, because in his ignorance he thinks he knows.

Thus an ignorance which in the child was healthy has in the adult become something distorted and unhealthy.

The same is true about the egocentric absorptions of the child. We know that the child is born that way: that first he inevitably centers in himself. But even while the child centers in himself, he begins to have outreachings of affection, of interest in others, willingness to help others. We know that these will grow into a warm engagement with life. Hence, when, at times, the youngster settles down into a stubborn demandfulness, grabbing things for himself, we are not greatly worried. We know that this is only temporary and that if all goes well he will grow into the mature generosity that will link him with his kind.

But when we find in an adult, this stubborn demandfulness, this grabbing of things for himself, we are not so easy in our minds. Here something that was natural and even charming in the child has been fixated into an adult monstrosity. When the child sticks out his small hands to take things for himself, we know that in a moment or so he will be putting his arms around his mother or he will be carrying his favorite teddy bear over to the newly arrived guest.

We can tolerate the temporary self-centering, because we discern in the child the beginnings of an affection for others and a concern about their wishes.

In the self-centered adult, however, there is simply the self-centering. Unrelieved by a warm interest in others, it becomes an evil thing. Thus again, what was natural and even healthy in the child becomes in the adult something distorted and unhealthy.

There is also another reason why traits that seem altogether in place in childhood seem altogether out of place in adulthood. In childhood, the child's small understanding of the world is coupled with the child's small power: his small grabbing of things for himself is coupled with small power to grab. If, however, as the years go on, power is increased but understanding and generosity are not increased, we get the perverse situation where, in the adult, there is too much power and too little ability to understand the generous uses of that power.

We find this perverse situation in a family where the father, with a small, mean mind, exercises his adult power over his children; or in a business, where the employer, with a child's love of cruelty and a child's lack of understanding, tyrannizes over his employees; or in a public office, where the official, crassly ignorant or corrupt, uses his powers to bedevil those who come before him. Or the perverse situation may be found in the ordinary goings about of people, where, for example, the adult, with a mind inflamed by prejudiced hatreds, uses his adult power to spread misinformation and false opinion.

All adult life is characterized by the fact that in one way or another it *exerts an influence*. It helps to shape the conditions under which other people's lives have to be lived. If the possessor of such influence—and we all possess it—couples with his adult powers the mental and emotional immaturity of a child, there is usually the mischief to pay.

Arrest of psychological growth, therefore, is more than just an arrest: it is a distortion. It is more than just a harmless cessation: it is a misdirection.

Thus the person who has failed to mature his mental, emotional and moral self, because he goes on living and doing things—influencing people, commanding people, hiring and firing people, making speeches, voting, office holding—becomes a source of dangerous misjudgment and misapplication of his powers.

III.

What we have said of individuals applies likewise to societies and institutions. When they are arrested in their growth they become dangerous. The best test of a society or institution is to ask whether the powers in it that need to develop are growing healthily or are prematurely fixated. A fixated society or institution presents the same dangers as a fixated individual, with this important difference: whereas a fixated individual does damage up to the limits of his individual power, a fixated society or institution does damage to the extent of its vastly multiplied powers.

At the time of writing, we are witnessing a notorious case of societal immaturity that is endangering the whole structure of world peace. The Arabs, incensed at the possibility that the United Nations will solve the Palestinian problem by a division of Palestine into two states, are threatening to go to war if such a decision is made. The threat has all the bullying quality of a small boy who vows disaster if he does not have his way. "If you don't let me have a gun, you'll be sorry: I'll get even. I'll burn down the house!"

It is incredible that any member of the United Nations, having pledged its word to abide by the decisions of the body it has joined, should so expose its immaturity. But the Arabs are deplorably and dangerously immature. Note first of all their mental immaturity. In Egypt, 84 per cent of the men and 92 per cent of the women are illiterate. In Iraq, 85 to 95 per cent of the men and 97 per cent of the women are illiterate; in Syria, 62 per cent of the men and 80 per cent of the women are illiterate; in Lebanon, the figures are 56 per cent of the men and 77 per cent of the women.[2]

But the immaturity of the Arabs goes beyond illiteracy. "In Saudi Arabia and Yemen, slavery is recognized by law. In most of the Arab states, women are bought and sold." Here is moral immaturity. These people have not yet grown even to the minimum moral level of our age. "Infant and child mortality is record breaking. In Egypt and Iraq, half of the children die before they reach their

---

[2] These figures are from a memorandum submitted to the General Assembly of the United Nations by the *Nation Associates*, October 1947.

fifth year. In Iraq life expectancy is from 24 to 26 years. . . . Some 90% of the Arab population are afflicted with diseases that literally drain their lives." Here is social immaturity: the lack of any awareness of the need for public provisions for health and well-being.

"Governments are corrupt and subject to no real popular control . . . The tax system . . . helps to perpetuate the mass poverty . . . the land tax is paid by the peasant who works the field, not by the owner. This system helps to keep the working population enchained in debt and adds to the wealth of the small feudal landlord class." Economic and political immaturity.

Mental, social, economic, political, moral immaturity! And out of these there suddenly flares forth the emotional immaturity of a small boy who threatens dire consequences if he is not given his way.

This is one revealing example of the close connection between societal immaturity and our world troubles. Where a society remains fixated at all the childish levels, it becomes a perverse and stubborn opponent of the civilized sanities.

Germany, we now begin to realize, was likewise the victim of a dangerous immaturity; and because of this immaturity, it kept the world for generations from moving toward a rational peace. Germany's immaturity was that of a people bred to obedience. Obedience is what we require of a child: the Germans required it of themselves. It became for them the prime civic virtue, as it was their prime domestic virtue. Out of obedience they built the incredibly efficient military state, with its hierarchy of ranks on ranks of authority. In that hierarchy, each person knew whom he must obey and whom he had a right to command. The whole society was geared to command-giving and command-taking. When, in the depths of German despair, the hysterical command-giver arrived, the German people fell into line as docilely as sheep.

A people bred to obedience is incapable of practicing political maturity; for political maturity implies the power of initiative, of free thinking, of independent judgment and decision. In brief it implies the power of self-government. Even in their Weimar Republic the Germans proved themselves incapable of self-government. In fact, as the records show, they themselves, in vast majority, were bitterly opposed to a scheme of self-government. Powerful forces proceeded at once to tear down the republican structure and return the nation to its prior condition of obedience to authority. It is significant that among the returning soldiers a spirit of bewilderment prevailed. Fresh from the confusion of defeat, they found no government at home ready to make decisions for them, a government to whose decisions they could submit. Instead, they found one which asked them to decide for themselves!

We now know that the German people, for generations, had had little practice in the art of self-government: their whole society had been geared to command from above. Hence when, with the flight of the Emperor, the opportunity came to build a republic, they were too politically immature to do so. This immaturity of the Germans was prelude to world disaster.

The struggle of the world today is not one between good and evil. It is rather a struggle between various immaturities. It will be a long time before all nations and peoples grow into a high-level maturity of mind and spirit. Growing up takes time. In nation after nation and people after people, the maturity level is still so low that the achievement of a common understanding throughout the world —not to speak of a common practice—seems almost beyond possibility. The Arab who buys and sells his women, who draws up laws to enforce slavery, and who grinds the face of the peasant is a queer figure to talk with an Eleanor Roosevelt. Sitting in the same General Assembly, what can they possibly have in common? How can they build bridges of understanding between them? How can they draw up provisions for a sincerely United World?

In spite of the colossal difficulty, however, it still seems true that the way we are going at the problem is the mature way. We are giving immature nations and peoples (ourselves included) a chance to grow up by exposing their judgments and behaviors to one another and to public view. Children remain children most disastrously when they are only with children. Give children the chance to live with grownups and they soon take on the ways of grownups. If, among the nations and peoples of the world, there are the less mature and the more mature, the free and relatively friendly juxtaposition of them all is obviously the best means of enabling the less mature to grow to the levels of the more mature, and the more mature to go on maturing.

The United Nations, therefore, might be regarded as a practice place for maturing. It is not simply an instrument of politics but of psychological development. Given the good luck to survive, it will grow strong in the degree that the minds of its members move out of their obtuse and stubborn childishnesses into the grownup power to reason together. The United Nations may, in fact, become the proud agency whereby a new kind of political mind is created in the world: one that, with high sincerity and with a mature insight, works disinterestedly for the well-being of all peoples.

IV.

The economic order has been the happy hunting ground for the socially immature. It is the area in which it is taken for granted that people will naturally act with the self-regarding attitudes of children. When the businessman says impatiently, "But business is business," he is supposed to have delivered the proper reproach to social idealists. The economic order is an area in which getting the most and giving the least has come to be regarded not as an abomination but as good sense.

It is not so in religion. Here the expectation is different. The individual sees himself in a framework of reality in which his obligations to life beyond himself are manifest and urgent. Nor is it so in the family. Here, too, the expectation is different. It would be a curious parent who would say, brusquely: "My business as a parent is to get the most for myself." The family is a civilizing institution to the extent that each is for all and all are for each. Finally it would be a poor sort of citizen who would say "My aim as a citizen is so to vote and so to maneuver that I make things come my way." When he speaks in that manner we call him a politician.

These institutions—of religion, home, and citizenship—require of us the maturity of a caring about others. The astonishing thing about the economic order is that through history it has made no such requirement. It stands as the one area in life in which ungrownup attitudes have been publicly commended.

Consider again the Arabs. "In Yemen and Saudi Arabia slavery is recognized by law . . . In most Arab states women are bought and sold . . . The tax system helps to perpetuate mass poverty."

Here is a system that permits, nay expects, the flagrant overriding of the interests of other human beings. Here life is at the child-level where each who can grabs what he can for himself.

The Arabian feudal landlords who squeeze out of their peasants the last impossible coin are acquisitive in the most ego-centered and therefore immature sense of that word. They exploit up to the hilt. They use all their resources of personal power and control of legislation to turn wealth away from the masses into their own hands.

This is economics at the level of man's utmost immaturity. At that level his *self*-interest is entire. He is at the child-stage where imagination about the needs and rights of others is still completely undeveloped.

It is this kind of economic motivation that has spelled enormous misery for mankind. Most of human history, after our emergence from the tribal state, has been that of the concentrated effort of possessors of power to get the most for themselves and give the least. It is no pretty picture of mankind.

But here, as everywhere in life, growth is the saving way out. There is nothing in the economic order that condemns us to such immaturity as has made our economic history ugly with man's exploitation of man. Economic motives and behaviors—like all the rest of our motives and behaviors—have it in them to mature. They mature when they grow beyond the ego-centeredness that is typical of childhood.

A mature order of economics is one that has developed beyond the harsh exploitative stage of mere acquisitiveness into a mutuality-stage where the best success of all makes for the best success of each.

This is not visionary idealism but sensible fact. Contrast the economic philosophy of the heads of two large corporations (these men are alive and operative today; but they shall remain unnamed). The first feels that the success of his corporation must include the good of its entire working force, from top-manager to lowest-rank worker; that it must also include the good of its public. The whole corporation has been geared to this philosophy. The second pooh-poohs such a philosophy. He is proud of his hard-headed conviction that his only concern is the size of the profits his corporation makes and the secure mastery it has over its competitors.

The one corporation head has the imagination to envisage the needs and rights of all those who are in any way related to the economic processes within his corporation's control. The other remains at the immature level of the child's complete self-absorption and lack of imagination about anyone's needs save his own.

Most of the going economic institutions of today lie variously between these two levels. Those that are on or near the immature level have a way of excusing themselves by recourse to the term "self-interest." But the "self-interest" is itself susceptible of mature as well as immature interpretation. The key word here is "self." The immature economic mind conceives the "self" as does a child: meaning the immediate, self-contained entity that excludes others.

The mature person conceives the self as always in relation to other selves. There is for him no self that is a self by itself and for itself. Such a self would be a monstrosity. To be genuinely *self*-interested, the mature person would say, one must include others in one's interest since these others are genuinely part of the picture of oneself. Mature self-interest, therefore, does not exclude others but takes them within the compass of oneself.

In the case of the two corporations above mentioned, we note that the economic *system* is the same; but the *persons* who operate that system are different. In the one case, *because of the maturity-level of the person,* all the processes are geared to a wide consideration of the needs of all the people concerned; in the other, *again because of the immaturity-level of the person,* all the processes are geared to the most effective exploitation of all concerned.

This should give us a sense of how the vast amount of tragedy in our economic world, all through history, can be traced to the immaturity-level of the individuals who have been in economic power. It should also make us realize that the chief hope for an advance to economic health and sanity lies in the increase of those whose maturity-level is high.

V.

Every society and every institution is in the last analysis the lengthened shadow of man: maybe of one man; maybe of a half dozen; maybe of a million or more. It makes an enormous difference whether the shadow be that of a child-man or of a fully grownup human being.

Most of what has been tragic in human history has come from the child-men who have variously occupied places of influence and power.

Hence the *growth-imperative*. We cannot afford to have child-adults in power. But since every one of us—just because he occupies space and can say words and do things—exercises some power over others, we must shorten the sentence: We cannot afford to have child-adults.

Hence the growth-imperative for every individual, every institution and every society: *Find the powers that need to grow and beware lest there be any arrest in their development.* Where growth stops, danger begins.

History and The Social Sciences[*]

§ BY JOHN HERMAN RANDALL, JR.
Columbia University

*I*T IS well to start this examination of the relations between history and the social sciences with a confession. I have long been convinced that there is no such thing as "history," and for some time I have been coming to doubt whether there are any social sciences. These unfortunate facts might seem to leave me in the fix of Santayana, who is credibly reported to have asserted: "There is no God, and Mary is his mother." So any reader who hopes to find out from these pages something about the relation between these very dubious entities would be wise to skip them.

But fortunately, I am by profession a "philosopher"—in the technical and very Pickwickian sense. And I should certainly hate to achieve the distinction of being the first philosopher who ever stopped talking about any subject-matter just because that subject-matter does not happen to exist. So I am really in the same boat with the historians and the social scientists—there is no such thing as "philosophy" either. Consequently, we can all begin from scratch, and proceed from there. And just as Santayana, although he is convinced there is no God, can nevertheless be fascinating on the theme of theology without ontology, I want to begin by explaining why there is no such thing as "history," and why the social sciences are not "sciences," before going on to explore the very important relations between these non-existent disciplines.

I remember once long ago asking a friend what he was particularly interested in doing. This was in the morning of life, and we both had our ambitions. "I want to study history," he replied. "The history of what?" I went on to inquire—quite naturally, it seemed to

[*] The substance of this paper was given as a talk at Yale University on March 2, 1949, as the first in a series of Trumbull Lectures. Since the theme was always central in the thought of Morris R. Cohen, it seems appropriate to include these reflections, which derive so heavily from his own insights, in this memorial volume.

me. To my surprise, my friend was greatly perplexed at this simple
question. "Why," he finally managed to come out with, "I'm not
interested in the history of anything in particular. What I want to
go on and study is just history."

Now what this "just history" may be, that so many men seem
anxious to study, I have never been able to understand. It is easy
to observe that those devoted to it in the past have rarely been
agreed on just what it is; no two of the classic "historians" have
understood what "history" is in precisely the same way. And it is
hard today to avoid rival schools of "historians" vociferously debat-
ing just what kinds of material their "history" should include. We
have all been taught, I presume, that "history" is not merely or primarily past politics or past battles, but must comprehend a great
deal more than those very minor matters. Many tell us "history"
must include primarily facts about the economic institutions under
which men have lived. Others bid us study the great ideas that have
meant so much to those capable of appreciating their significance,
the ideas of science and philosophy. For some, it is the religion that
has organized and expressed the life of entire cultures that seems of
fundamental "historical" importance. Art and literature, those con-
summate expressions of what the past has been and has felt, have
their devoted followers. Still others insist that the true "history" is
of the beliefs and institutionalized habits of men, the beliefs which
the masses have actually entertained, and which have determined
the course of all men's social relations.

Now I can understand sympathetically a genuine interest in all
these things. I can indeed understand and share in an interest in
everything that men have done and thought and felt and made
during their long sojourn upon the earth. I can even understand
what used to be called "natural history"—though I find that today
what nature has done is not regarded as the province of the "historian," and enters therein, if at all, only if it has done something to
his "history"—usually in the first chapter. But I must confess I cannot understand even the meaning of the questions, which of these
many different interests should "history" include, and which should
it emphasize and make central? Nor, if "history" is to include all of
them, and is to be a complete record of everything that man has
achieved on this planet, can I see how "history" differs from the

entire sum of human knowledge. For everything that is has an historical aspect, and can hence be the appropriate subject-matter of historical investigation. Even mathematics, though it may deal with an order that is timeless and eternal, as a human enterprise is essentially progressive and historical in character.

For these reasons, we are told, "history" must inevitably be selective. I am inclined to agree, at least to the extent that I have always found it necessary to make a selection. But I have never understood why "history" has to. I am unable to see why a detailed study of Hannibal's campaigns is not perfectly valid "history," although I too know all the reasons why such study should not be inflicted upon the young. I have been amused to find that the historians of Columbia University, committed to the insignificance of military history, nevertheless imported an historian of military strategy as soon as it became apparent that military problems were about to become central. What should be taught to the young in the schools is a perfectly legitimate question, which demands its own answers; but this pedagogical question hardly delimits "history." I am not unacquainted with the familiar observation: "That used to be what history was considered, of course; but now it is only the history of military strategy." I am perfectly aware that "history" has itself enjoyed a history; and I flatter myself that I can with the best of them explain why different historians have been and still are interested in the histories of different things. But I must say that I can see no reason in the most complete understanding of why "history" has become what in practice it is today, for answering in one way rather than in another the question, "What should 'history' be and include?"

When pressed, historians will tell us that "history" selects from the record of the past that which gives us "understanding." I am perfectly willing to admit that that is just what historians actually do. To be sure, I have never yet found an historian who did not dwell lovingly on an immense amount of detail, not because it had any discoverable connection with the "understanding" of anything else, but simply because he was fascinated by it. I have never yet found any historian so puritanical as to be really bound by this pragmatic theory; nor do I ever expect to. But, granted the historian is trying to help us understand something else, it is still terribly difficult to find any plausible theory as to why what he selects does enable us to "understand."

One school of historians much in vogue today is very insistent that "history" should aim to explain why we are acting the way we are, and how we got into the mess we are in. The history of that mess does seem to me to be very important, and to illuminate what we should do about it. But I really cannot see why the history of our present mess is to be identified with "just history" in general. If it is, then the history of ancient Egypt, for example, will hardly be "history," for it seems to have made only a minor contribution to our troubles. This is a view I cannot accept, for I find Egyptian history fascinating. I cannot even regard it as the proper aim of "history" to account for how the Egyptians got into their messes; for their history seems to be about other things than messes, and is in fact largely irrelevant to them. And the same holds of the history of Greece. Despite the efforts of very able historians today, I am still not clear that the most important thing about the Greeks was their failures, though I hope I can point a moral as well as the next man. And though like their gods the Greeks were very human, I find that what interests me about them is not the way they resemble us, but the things they did that we cannot do. In any event, moreover, if "history" is really to explain why we are acting the way we are, I should think it would have to explain why we paint the kind of pictures we do, and compose the kind of music we write, and why we are puzzling our heads over the general theory of relativity. But that, I shall at once be told, is not "history"; that is the history of art or of music or of physics.

Ah! says another school, "history" helps us to understand where we are because it explains why things have been as they have. It makes clear the "pattern of the historical process." This seems a promising answer, until we reflect that it means that what "history" explains to us is "history" itself. And this is very puzzling and odd— *pace* Spengler, Toynbee, Sorokin, and other extremely speculative "positivists" who, in searching for a "pattern of history," for an "historical morphology," piously hope that they are being very "scientific" indeed—which is an act of faith rather than of knowledge. For it is clearly not history that enables us to understand history, but science—anthropology, psychology, economics, and the rest.

This wisdom as to the relation of the social sciences to history has been common knowledge for several generations. And the basic question remains: even if "history" could miraculously explain history, we should still have no light thrown on why we select the particular things we do to label "history."

There is of course a simple answer much in fashion today: "history" is really economic history. It is through the history of men's economic activities and relations that we can alone gain a genuine understanding of "history." But I observe that those who say this proceed to use economic history primarily to explain political history. What they are interested in understanding seems to be political struggles and fights; and they all point to further political battles in the future. I am inclined to agree that this is an excellent way to understand political goings on; and it certainly sheds a good deal of light on many other things as well. But I am still in the dark as to why it should be politics alone that "history" is trying to explain; and with the best will in the world I cannot see that economic history throws much light on many other things I want to understand —why, for instance, British thinkers have persisted down to Bertrand Russell in making the same initial assumptions as William of Ockham, despite the absurd consequences it has been shown in every generation those assumptions entail; or why and how the theory of quantum mechanics has transformed Newtonian science. The histories of such things seem intelligible without much reference to how men have made a living—to what a fashionable jargon calls the "relations of production." But perhaps "history" in general is merely what economics *does* enable us to explain. If that be true, it would at least simplify matters.

As a result of perplexing questions like these, I have been driven to ask whether there is any such thing as "history" in general. At present, I am convinced there is no such "thing." Nor do I know of any good reason why there should be men set apart as "Professors of History," or why there should be special "Departments of History" in our colleges and universities—except that I greatly enjoy and profit by what these men tell me, and am convinced that they ought to be supported in some way or other.

In any strictly rational organization of academic teaching, there would clearly be no place for any separate and independent "Departments of History." Rather, each department of knowledge concerned with a separate subject-matter would include members with a major intellectual interest in the history of that subject-matter, and of the intellectual efforts to grasp it. Of course, I am really not trying to be invidious. I believe there is equally no strictly rational reason for the existence of any separate and independent "Departments of Philosophy" in academic teaching. Every department should include members with philosophic imagination and horizons, and capable of philosophic analysis.

To be sure, however justified it might be rationally, I am not myself so addicted to the vice of pure reason as to have any immediate intention of starting such a purge. I am trying rather to emphasize certain fundamental facts about the nature of history. Everything in our world has *a* history, and the man who wants to understand any particular thing or field is well advised to inquire into *its* history. Everything that is, is historical in character, and has an existence that can be measured in time. And this historical aspect which any particular thing has and possesses is an essential part of what it is. But "just history" in general seems to have no meaning, unless it be taken as synonymous with knowledge as a whole. History is not a "thing" at all; it is not a noun, a "substance." It is rather a character, an adjective, a predicate. Or, put in somewhat more formal terms, "history" is not a distinctive subject-matter to be inquired into. It is rather at once a trait of all subject-matters, something to be discovered and understood about each of them; and a distinctive way of inquiring into any subject-matter—though by no means the only way.

And therefore I find no meaning in the questions: What should "history" include? What should "the historian" emphasize? There is no such thing as "history" in general, nor are there any men who are just "historians." Every history is *the* history *of* something, and every historian is trying to trace *the* past *of* something. In terms of that "something," it is not hard to discover what *its* history must include. The various strands so viewed fall into their proper perspective, once we have decided just what it is, the historical aspect of which we are interested in. The history of our science will then be one thing, and the history of our present mess a somewhat differ-

ent one; although in investigating either we shall often find ourselves concerned with the same factors that are in a different way
involved in the other. There is no "process of history" in general;
but every historian of anything will find himself discovering *the*
"historical processes" by which that particular thing came about.

Actually, of course, there does seem to be a need for "history"
in the academic curriculum, and for "historians"—just as there is
need for philosophy. Each interest in its own way can contribute
powerfully to the unification of intellectual perspectives. But this
need is pedagogical rather than strictly rational, and it is probably
best satisfied when neither historians nor philosophers remain isolated in separate "departments" of their own, but co-operate with
teachers whose interests are focused in other disciplines. But then—
of what academic "department" can this not be said?

On the basis of these facts about the nature of history, we can
now proceed to state certain fundamental relations between history
and the so-called social "sciences."

(1) For any understanding of the histories that things possess,
the social sciences are essential. The processes of change by which
anything human has come about are the proper subject-matter of
the social sciences, which distinguish those processes, and analyze
their structure, and how they co-operate with and interact with
other processes as they are found operating in the present. Every
history is full of "processes" at work: it exhibits a complex co-operation of processes interacting with each other. A particular history, to be sure, is not itself as a whole a "process." "Process" has
meaning only if it exhibits an invariant structure—only if that same
process can be repeated in various instances. A process, in other
words, is always an instance of a way of acting; and its structure
is a way of acting, a "law" or "universal." In contrast, "the history
of" anything is always a particular—it is always, as a whole, something unique and unrepeatable, something that is never an instance
of any repeated pattern. When we can say justly, "History is repeat-
ing itself," we mean we have found a "process" at work—a process
whose structure has been exemplified before.

The particular historical changes that have brought about the
state of anything whose history we are considering are to be

"explained" by drawing on the best available science of human behavior at our disposal—those sciences of cultural change in which certain patterns or constant ways of operating of human behavior have been arrived at through the experimental analysis of observed human behavior. The record of the past of course furnishes materials to these "sciences of cultural change," in the form of instances of the patterns of behavior that can be observed also in the present; and without this temporal dimension our knowledge of the way human nature functions would be exceedingly thin and provincial. But it remains inescapable that it is in terms of our present sciences of human behavior, such as they are—in terms of our anthropology, our psychology, our political science, our economics, our sociology, and the rest—that we must ultimately understand past human behavior, if we are to understand it at all.

"The history of" anything is always a particular, with a unique set of materials of its own, a unique set of human actors, and a unique pattern or structure of the action brought to bear on those materials. The sciences of the processes at work in histories will clearly not explain the presence of these particular materials in a history—institutions, ideas, and men—which are there in it to interact and change, within the unique limits set by those materials in each case. To explain the presence in a history of these particular materials, we have to turn not to the sciences of cultural change, but to tracing the histories of these materials back to those points where they were worked out and formed in their past.

A particular history is thus understood both in terms of the "origins" of its unique materials—"origins" which are themselves always unique histories—and in terms of the operations of human thought and action upon those materials—operations which are illustrations of the sciences of human operations, the social sciences. A history is understood, that is, in terms both of the "continuities" and of the "changes" it exhibits.

For these reasons, it is clear that historical inquiry is not strictly a "science." It includes and makes central this concern with unique materials—institutions, ideas, men, actions. Historical inquiry is thus an "art" or *techne* in the Aristotelian sense—it deals with particulars, but in terms of universals. This means, however, not that historical inquiry is less than a science, but that it is more—it is, as Morris

Cohen clearly sees, an "applied science."[1] There is a sense, of course, in which every science in the fullest extent of its functioning is an "applied science." On this view, a body of formalized theoretical principles and conclusions is not itself so much a "science" as it is one of the instruments in the functioning of a science.[2] In such a conception, which has everything to recommend it, history like medicine would be more rather than less scientific than mathematics or theoretical physics, just because it is an art to be practiced.

As an art, or an "applied science," history draws on all the social sciences—they are its essential instruments for dealing with the processes at work in histories. The theoretical "science" history employs, it is well to emphasize, is the subject-matter and the conclusions of the social sciences. Despite repeated attempts, men have never been able to discover any verifiable "scientific laws" of history itself.[3]

There exists a considerable body of evidence to support the position that there are discoverable patterns or "laws" of social change. In this complex field, we have not as yet arrived at any very precise or any very well-established conclusions. But there seems no reason to conclude that the inquiry after such laws should

[1] Cohen, Morris R., *The Meaning of Human History* (La Salle, Ill., 1947) p. 38: "History is applied science, as is geology, medicine, or engineering. The difference, however, is that while the engineer or the geologist knows precisely and explicitly what laws he is applying in order to explain the phenomena, the historian seldom explicitly states the laws of human events that he assumes. Yet implicitly he does make such assumptions."

[2] Dewey, John, *Experience and Nature* (Chicago, 1925) p. 161-62: "What is sometimes termed 'applied science,' may then be more truly science than what is conventionally called pure science. For it is directly concerned with not just instrumentalities, but instrumentalities at work in effecting modifications of existence in behalf of conclusions that are reflectively preferred. . . . Thus conceived, knowledge exists in engineering, medicine, and the social arts more adequately than it does in mathematics and physics. Thus conceived, history and anthropology are scientific in a sense in which bodies of information that stop short with general formulae are not."

[3] Cohen, *op. cit.*, p. 38: "Those who insist that history is a science in the same way in which physics is a science, often mean to assert that the subject matter of history is not the individual events but the laws or repeatable patterns of human behavior. Those, however, who do so, obviously confuse history with sociology. A science of sociology would be concerned with general laws and would leave to history the consideration of what actually happened in definite places at given times."

be ruled out as misdirected. There do seem to be patterns discoverable in such change. Naturally, since he has observed so many more instances than any of the other social scientists, it is the anthropologist who has carried this inquiry furthest, and investigated the complex processes of diffusion and invention and their consequences. Other social sciences have likewise discovered specific patterns of change—like the business cycle of the economists.

But these "laws" of social change belong to the dynamic aspects of the various social sciences, not to history itself. Such a "social dynamics," or "dynamic sociology," is clearly not the same thing as historical inquiry—though the latter eagerly uses and applies all that can be learned from it. The "science of social change" has different problems and procedures from historical inquiry. We may sum up the present state of the evidence, not despite the heroic attempts of Vico, Spengler, Toynbee, Sorokin, and the rest, but rather as a result of the recognized if not acknowledged failure of these attempts, that while there are discoverable patterns of the processes at work in histories, there is no shred of evidence for any "pattern of history" in general.

The results of this analysis indicate that evangelists like James Harvey Robinson and Harry Elmer Barnes are right—in principle. If he is really going to try to write the "history" of everything, "the historian" ought to know all the social sciences, and all the natural sciences and the cultural sciences as well. Very fortunately, there is no such thing as the "history of everything," and no such animal as "the historian," committed to such omniscience. The actual historical profession can more modestly select an historical subject for which it does possess something of the appropriate equipment. Any historian, obviously, should know the sciences of the particular subject-matter whose history he is undertaking to investigate. Not "the historian," but only "the philosopher," is really committed to the obligation to know everything. But then, the last man to be justly called "the philosopher" was Aristotle, who did.

Having made clear how, for any understanding of the histories that things possess, the social sciences are essential, we can now proceed to examine the second fundamental relation between history and the social sciences.

(2) For inquiry in the social sciences, a knowledge of history

is essential. This is true because the social sciences are fundamentally historical in character, in at least three basic ways: (a) their subject-matter is fundamentally historical; (b) many of the institutions they deal with have an essentially temporal and historical structure: they are human ways of acting that become unified only in the light of historically generated problems; (c) they necessarily employ methods of historical analysis—though by no means exclusively. I wish now to elucidate these three points.

(a) The subject-matter of the social sciences is fundamentally historical in character. That subject-matter is *human culture,* in the widest sense, as the anthropologist views it. The different social scientists select different aspects of human culture—aspects which are cut out from a common matrix. They are all exploring different perspectives on the same institutionalized behavior of men. This is true even of psychology, which is often considered to deal with "human nature." But "human nature" is nothing other than culture individualized and personalized. In reality, all the social sciences are merely different branches of a common "science of culture." The present division of labor among investigators is largely accidental, historically conditioned, and intelligible only in historical terms. Why, for example, are there "Departments of Sociology" in our institutions of higher learning? And where do they fit in with the other social sciences? Only the intellectual history of the last half of the nineteenth century could possibly give a rationale for a situation that is so rationally unintelligible.

Now human culture, the subject-matter of all the social sciences, is basically historical in character. Not only is it changing in time, and not immutable and eternal like the subject-matters of physics or chemistry, which seem to have remained unchanged during recorded history. Not only is culture historically conditioned, in that it always requires dating in time and location in place. Fundamentally, human culture is progressive and cumulative—it is a series of reworkings of materials inherited from the past, reworkings effected in the light of historically generated tensions.

This historical character of the subject-matter of the social sciences is the major difference between them and the natural sciences. There are, to be sure, natural sciences that are likewise historical in character—such as historical geology, paleontology, etc. The difference between the social and the natural sciences is consequently not the sharp opposition it was made in the German reflection on history and the *Geisteswissenschaften* during the last generation. This opposition, in Dilthey, Windelband, Simmel, Rickert, and others, has made their thought, despite its wealth of incidental insights, pretty confused and sterile. Rather, the social sciences and history have to consider an additional trait in their subject-matter—the trait of being "historical" in character, and of demanding in consequence historical treatment. The more abstract natural sciences, like physics and chemistry, can disregard this pervasive historical trait of the world, with its demand for historical knowledge. The social sciences simply cannot so disregard the historical character of all existence.[4]

Now every society or culture displays a number of distinguishable sets of complex social habits, of "structures" or "patterns" of institutionalized organization of habitual human behavior, institutionalized methods or ways of doing things. These sets include: (1) a technological organization—a set of habitual ways of turning natural materials to human use; (2) an economic organization—a set of habitual ways of controlling the technology of that society, and its fruits; (3) a political organization—a set of institutionalized methods for adjusting conflicts; (4) an intellectual organization—a set of habitual ways of believing about various objects of its experience; we commonly call this the folklore of that society, or, when it is systematically organized in terms of recognized standards, that society's science; (5) a religious organization—a set of institutionalized ways of acting, feeling, and even believing, holding that society together and expressing its common experience, by celebrating, consecrating, and clarifying its accepted values.

These sets of institutionalized social habits are channels or limits within which what men do in that society is carried on and

---

[4] *Cf.* Cohen, *op. cit.*, p. 40-41: "What is distinctive, then, about human history, is not its material, which is identical with the material of the social sciences, nor the critical apparatus that is utilized to search out this material and consists primarily of hypotheses borrowed from the sciences. What is distinctive is rather the focus or perspective which makes description or understanding of individual happenings in time and place central. Thus 'natural history' differs from natural science in that the former focuses on description, while the latter stresses theory, or systematic deduction from assumed principles or hypotheses. . . . History uses laws to explain facts."

human activities take place. They are not "forces"—they themselves *do* nothing. They are rather ways in which things are done. When for any reason men are led to act differently, then these ways of acting change—they are historically conditioned, we say. Like all habits, however, they have a very considerable inertia, and are changed only with great difficulty.

These "organizations" of socially institutionalized habitual behavior are sets of concrete ways of doing things, viewed *functionally*. They are selected from the total culture in terms of various distinguishable social ends. They are different ways of organizing men's habits to perform various kinds of function. Hence the same concrete activities of men will figure in several or even in all such types of organization—going out on strike, for instance, or leaving money to a church. Each such organization is really a perspective on all the activities of that society from the viewpoint of its distinctive social function. In part, each organization selects certain human activities as having a special bearing on that function. In part, it selects certain consequences of all, or nearly all, human activities.

Now, it is these functional organizations of human behavior that are the distinctive subject-matters of the different social sciences. And it is clear that as subject-matters they are all *historical* in character. They are temporally changing. They are historically conditioned. They are progressive and cumulative. They are "relative" and "limited to" a particular historical situation. And they all demand historical analysis.

This is true also of the subject-matter of psychology, "human nature." Human nature not only exhibits different powers in different cultures. It actually possesses a different constitution in different cultures. For "human nature" is not in any significant sense the wealth of possibility of response inherent in the human organism at birth, in the human "frame." It is rather the organization of the responses the human frame makes possible, the particular set of organized habits generated by the social institutions that are its primary environment. It is the organism, the human frame, that is constant and "original," not human nature, which is fundamentally historical, like the more specifically functional organizations of habits already indicated. Human nature is an "historical nature."

The human frame is extraordinarily plastic, before its organization into "human nature"—into a particular set of institutionalized group habits. It often seems that anthropologists have discovered every conceivable form of organization of human nature, in some culture or other. And human nature when so organized is extraordinarily tough and refractory. The toughness explains the fact of persistence, continuity, and tradition, where change has not been forced on human nature. The plasticity explains the novel behavior, when new ways of acting have been imposed—as by technology in our own culture, for example. This double fact makes plain, for instance, why the Russians are today still behaving in many ways as they always have, with their long tradition of Byzantine organization, despite the most drastic social revolution of all time. It also makes clear why no limits are set on the ways they will eventually display, by the ways in which we find, say, Americans now acting.

This illustration suggests that the powers of human nature—that is, of social institutions or group behavior—are revealed only in their operation under varied conditions. They are manifested only in history. But how those powers have operated in the past sets no limits on how they will operate in the future, with changed conditions in any one of the determining organizations, technological, economic, political, intellectual, religious, etc. History thus reveals much but teaches nothing about human nature. It explains why human nature is today what it is. It points to the factors and events that have organized it in the way we now find it functioning—and also to the factors and events that are changing that way and that organization. But history does not and cannot reveal what human nature will be.

(b) The social sciences are fundamentally historical in character, secondly, because many of the institutions they deal with have a structure that is itself essentially temporal and historical.

The simplest illustration of an "historical nature," that is, of something whose nature *is identical* with its history, and is definable only in historical terms, is a biological organism, like a seed we plant and watch unfold the pattern of its growth. The seed *is* its career in time; the structure of that career is temporal and cumulative, *time* enters into its very substance. Such a "career" in time can be traced from its very beginning; we can follow the development of what eventuates as a whole, of what emerges at the harvest. Similarly, the life of a man is just such a temporal "career."

Of such "careers" or historical natures we can tell the story. They lend themselves to the art of story-telling, of historical narrative. This art naturally selects its own appropriate materials. And past historians, having been great story-tellers, have chosen such "careers" as their subject-matter—episodes with some degree of dramatic unity, like the biographies of men, dramatic episodes such as wars, political campaigns and struggles, strikes, such dramatic themes as the rise of Rome or the conquest of Peru.

But the social scientist is usually concerned with more complex temporal structures or "historical natures," with societies, cultures, and institutions. These historical natures are likewise fundamentally historical in essence or structure, but they have no "career" as a whole, like the seed, that can be traced from its beginnings; for they are not wholes. A society or a social institution is not an "organism," despite the many attempts so to view them, especially in the heyday of evolutionary biological ideas in the last century. And all attempts to conceive an organism as a "society," like those of Leibniz, Diderot's "swarm of bees," Whitehead's generalization, have broken down in the face of the problem of accounting for that factor in a living organism which a "society" obviously does not possess—a unified "life" or "soul." A seed possesses what Aristotle called a "vegetative life," and an animal has a behavior as a whole. But a society has no "life," "mind," "soul," or "*Geist*"—it has no behavior as a whole. For it is not a "whole," a "totality." A society is not like a unified organism, but is more like a biological "religion"— like the lake Peattie describes in Oak Grove, Illinois, or like what the biologist means when he writes on "the natural history of the Plains region." A society, that is, is like a biological region, a group of interacting careers and histories, constituted by certain geographic and climatic limits.

Negatively, this means that there is no "career" of a society, with a single unified temporal pattern, like the career of the seed. Nor is there any unified "career" of a particular social institution— for such institutions are likewise not unities or wholes. Thus, there is no single "science" that has enjoyed a career in Western culture, like the career of the seed. If we ask, what was the career of "science" during the Middle Ages? we have to go on to ask, which "science" would it be? The symbolic science worked out by the Victorines? Or the Aristotelian science that gained a foothold in the universities in the thirteenth century? Or "our own" science? But "our" science did not as yet exist—though its "history" certainly takes us back to the Middle Ages.

Likewise, there is no discoverable "career" of medieval culture. For there were no "Middle Ages" until self-conscious "moderns" arose to criticize and fight and escape from them. There is also no career of "feudalism." For "feudalism" did not make its appearance—that is, men's action and thought were not taken as illustrating any unified political institution of "feudalism"—until the seventeenth- and eighteenth-century lawyers began to want to escape from certain features of their institutionalized political behavior, and proceeded to analyze those particular features of their "political organization" whose elimination formed their practical problem.[5]

Nor is there any discoverable "career" of "capitalism"; for "capitalism" did not exist—in the welter of confused and contradictory ways in which men have always acted economically—until men appeared who wanted to escape from certain of those ways, and proceeded to formulate a "capitalistic system" in the light of those features. It is notorious that the term "capitalism" was invented by the Socialists; and it is only in the last twenty-five years that it has been accepted as the name of something to be defended, in conscious reaction against socialistic attacks. The term "capitalism" was first used in English in 1854.[6] And Werner Sombart writes: "The concept of capitalism and even more clearly the term itself may be traced primarily to the writings of *socialist* theoreticians.

[5] "It was not before the eighteenth century that the custom arose of using for the designation of a whole system of social organization either compound expressions like feudal regime, government or system or, a little later, abstract substantives such as *féodalité* or feudalism. . . . The extension of the use of a word derived from a particular institution, the fief, which can scarcely be considered the central and only significant institution of feudalism, to characterize the social regime prevailing widely during the Middle Ages, . . . is mainly attributable to the influence of Montesquieu." Marc Bloch, in *Encyclopaedia of the Social Sciences,* vol. vi, p. 203.

[6] *Oxford Dictionary.*

It has in fact remained one of the key concepts of socialism down to the present time. Nevertheless, it cannot be said that a clear cut definition has ever been attempted. Even Karl Marx, who virtually discovered the phenomenon, defined only certain aspects of capitalism as the occasion required."[7]

Positively, these institutions which are so fundamental to social science are one complex type of "historical nature": they are ways of acting that have become historically unified in the light of historically generated problems. We may hence call them, in distinction from other types of historical nature, like the unities that possess a "career," "historical unifications." They all possess a "history," when we look backward from the focus of the problems they have generated. We can then trace factors in them back into the past, find the "sources" and "genesis" of different elements, antecedents that have led up to what has eventuated. We can trace the genesis of the problems in terms of which they have now become historically unified institutions. But there is no "career" of them, in the sense of beginning at the "beginning," or at any "beginning," or at any given point, and following the development of what eventuated as a whole. What has eventuated is not a whole, but a plurality of ways of behaving, interacting and generating unifying problems.

Societies and social institutions possess a complex, pluralistic structure of interacting habit patterns. They are not unified "wholes" or "organisms" with an organic structure. Rather, to borrow a current jargon, they are "an interpenetration of opposites." What belongs to that institution, and what "interpenetrates" it, is not known until the latter has become an "opposite"—that is, until it has generated a tension and a problem. Such institutions are "historical unifications" of behavior, selected by their historical development as structures and patterns with which the social

---

[7] Sombart, Werner, in *Encyclopaedia of the Social Sciences,* vol. iii, article on "Capitalism." Sombart goes on: "Neither the term nor the concept has as yet been universally recognized by representatives of academic economics. The older German economists and to a much greater extent the economists of other countries rejected entirely the concept of capitalism. . . . The term is not found in Gide, Cauwes, Marshall, Seligman or Cassel. . . . The works of Sombart are the first in which the concept of capitalism has been definitively recognized as fundamental to the system of economic thought."

sciences must deal. They do not merely possess an historical and temporal structure, like the seed, or the life of a man, or whatever exhibits a career. They are actually *created* as structures, as institutions, by historical processes. And they are intelligible only in the light of that history, through historical analysis, which singles out that historical structure from the complex facts and unifies it.

When so selected and unified, such historically generated institutions stand out against the confused facts. Consider the contrast between the infinitely complex mass of arrangements that succeeded each other during the Middle Ages, and the neat theory of the "feudalism" the eighteenth-century *philosophes* wanted to abolish completely. Or take the contrast between the welter of conflicting philosophical doctrines of the nineteenth century, and the philosophic naturalism we now see to have been emerging, and support. Or mark the contrast between the confused and contradictory ways of acting our culture displays today—its actual complex functioning, as the institutional economist would describe it— and the unified "capitalistic system" we can formulate in the light of the problems those ways generate.

Such historical unifications are intelligible only by means of an historical analysis. How much and what part of our present economic activities constitute "capitalism"? How much and what part of our present religious activities constitute "Christianity"? These activities are so manifold and confused, they exhibit so much "interpenetration," that no strictly contemporary analysis could avoid being arbitrary. Analysis of such institutions can become objective only by becoming historical. What is "essential" to capitalism or to Christianity is revealed only in the histories of our economic or our religious problems; it is clarified only when we see what has happened to saddle us with those problems.

In these problems, they have become genuine historical unifications, which have histories; and it is precisely these histories which made the unifications objective. No "earlier stages" are clearly distinguishable until problems have emerged. But those problems and their elements are then understood only in the light of "earlier stages" *of* those elements—stages which are quite objectively relative to the present form. Take "private property," for example. Only an historical analysis can determine what is "private property" today, and why. What private property, for instance, is represented by a share of non-voting common stock in a holding company for a bankrupt railroad mortgaged to the R. F. C.? It took an historian— Charles A. Beard—to find out who "owns" what in our railroads today.

(c) This is an illustration of the fact that, since their subject-matter is basically historical, and since many of the institutions they deal with are "historical unifications" created by history, the social sciences necessarily employ methods of historical analysis— though not exclusively so.

There is, in the first place, no such thing as "*the* historical method," or "*the* method of historical analysis." There are rather many different types of historical analysis, appropriate to different kinds of problems in different social sciences. These various types need careful analysis and distinguishing; but this is hardly the place to undertake it. It would require a year's course, or an entire volume, to deal even cursorily with all the problems involved.

Secondly, historical analysis is not of itself sufficient to deal with any problem in the social sciences. It must always be used in connection with other types of analysis—formal or structural analysis, and functional analysis. The latter is primary, and involves the others; though the reasons why are hardly pertinent to the present theme.

Here, I can only illustrate something of the relation between historical and functional analysis in the case of the very difficult problem of evaluation. Tracing the continuous history of a way of acting or believing—that is, of any institution—will disclose the specific function performed by that way or institution in the past. And it will reveal how well that way did its job. Such tracing of a history will not reveal the present functioning of that way, or its adequacy today. But it will illuminate the difference between past and present conditions, in which the institution has functioned and is functioning. And it will illuminate the consequent decline in adequacy of functioning—or even the changes in the very function performed.

This is why history is always relevant to an evaluation in the present, although it can never in itself furnish such an evaluation. To believe that it can and does is the "genetic fallacy," so justly condemned in our generation, in atonement for the intellectual sins of our evolutionary fathers. Since the genetic fallacy was so strongly castigated by Morris Cohen, a few general remarks may be in order on the sense in which the genesis of any belief is relevant to its validity, and the sense in which to appeal to origins is fallacious.

Beliefs are in fact, in the actual procedure of the scientist, judged to be scientifically "warranted," "verified," or proved to be "true," when they give a satisfactory solution to the specific problem to which they have been proposed as an answer. They are validated only when they have succeeded in doing what they were instituted to do. Beliefs, in scientific inquiry, are always designed to perform some determinate function. The objective criterion of their validity is the success of their functioning in the specific way in which they were designed to function. The question always is: Do they actually solve the specific and determinate problem they were designed to solve? This functional test is decisive. Whatever their origin, beliefs are ultimately validated by the way they function, not by the way they were generated.[8] To maintain that genetic considerations can of themselves validate or invalidate a belief, that the origin of knowledge is the test of its extent and certainty, is to commit the "genetic fallacy"—and it is a logical fallacy.

But in determining whether beliefs are functioning adequately so as to solve the specific problem they were worked out to solve, reference *to* that problem is obviously involved. In this sense, the standard of the adequate functioning of beliefs *does* involve the problematic situation from which they take their start. This genesis or origin can therefore be said to determine the specific problem the belief must satisfy in order to be warranted. It determines the context and the conditions in which the belief must function, and the nature of the function it must perform.

Thus any functional test of the validity and value of a belief does involve knowledge of the genesis of that belief, of its history.

---

[8] Dewey states this functional method precisely: "The function of consequences as necessary tests of the validity of propositions, *providing* these consequences are operationally instituted and are such as to resolve the specific problem evoking the operations." *Logic* (New York 1938) p. iv.

The functional method must include as a part of its procedure just such a "genetic analysis." Stated more fully, the functional method of verifying or warranting beliefs is a "genetic-functional" method. And as a matter of fact, every scientist, in reporting his conclusions or discoveries, does give a detailed account of just what he did to arrive at that outcome—his problem, his reasoning, his experiments, his findings, his interpretation. These genetic considerations are clearly relevant to the question of whether his conclusions are validated or warranted. To deny the relevance of this specification of the problem and context in which the beliefs were formulated, is to commit the "formalistic" or "structuralist" fallacy—and it is a logical fallacy. It is one which I am afraid Morris Cohen often committed, in theory at least. He failed to give due weight to genetic considerations, just because he was not enough of a functionalist in his thinking. His own method remains largely "intuitionist-structuralist," not "genetic-functional."[9]

In general, then, genetic considerations are always relevant to questions of validity and value, and are usually necessary. But the determination of the problem, what a belief must do, and the context in which it must do it, though a necessary condition of discovering whether the belief is valid, is unfortunately not a sufficient condition. Beliefs cannot be validated in terms of their origins alone, though they cannot be validated without reference to the problem in which they originated. Nothing can be judged in terms of its history alone, though nothing can be judged without reference to the function for which it originated.

This logical analysis of the procedure of validation and evaluation can be illustrated in the process of the evaluation of social institutions. For example, a famous remark of the late President Roosevelt ran: "The Constitution was devised for the horse-and-buggy age." This is an undoubted historical fact—though it raises questions in detail as to the history of transportation. Actually, the Constitution is more "old-fashioned" than the buggy, and was invented several generations earlier. This historical fact, however, does not indicate whether or not a "horse-and-buggy" Constitution is adequate for our own steamlined era—though it does suggest the

[9] For a fuller clarification of the meaning of these terms, see Dewey, *Problems of Men* (New York 1946) p. 416-18.

inquiry. Rather, when we today find that the checks and balances of the Constitution, its decentralization, etc., are not wholly adequate to our own political needs, and when we are hence forced to face the practical problems generated, the history of the Constitution makes clear why we are facing those problems. It focuses attention on the changed function we now require of our constitutional instrument. It reveals how well the Constitution performed in the past the functions which a functional analysis of our present situation may well indicate we can no longer afford to let it continue to perform.

The history of an institution is thus not in itself an evaluation. Nothing is good or bad merely because it has been—though familiarity is certainly a positive value. But history can make clear that a fresh evaluation is called for. And history provides many—though not all—of the factors necessary for that evaluation.

What has just been illustrated in connection with judging and evaluating is true of understanding in general. Nothing in the social sciences can be understood in terms of its history alone, though nothing can be understood without reference to that history. In general, we may state the conclusion of this analysis of the relation between history and the social sciences as follows: History cannot do its job without the social sciences, and the social sciences cannot do theirs without history. Each needs the other, but neither is to be confused with the other, or absorbed in or reduced to the other. Here are all the makings of a perfect marriage. What God hath joined together, let no man put asunder.

Science, Superstition and Precision

~§ BY PAUL WEISS
Yale University

THE WORLD OF COMMON SENSE

*T*HE world of common sense is a world frecked with mystery. The task of reason is to make it intelligible. At every moment we are confronted with the faint and the almost clear, the sensuous and the non-sensuous, the common-place and the surprising. Ours is a world which, pulsating with activity in one place, is almost quiescent in another. It is a mine of difficulties, a tissue of recalcitrant beings and problems. There are no clear finished truths to be found in it, awaiting merely the perceptive reader. Whatever exists points to and is inseparable from possibilities it would be desirable for us to realize or forestall. Each being in the universe raises questions by the very fact that it is a being among beings, a reality in time, the locus of a promise partly fulfilled and partly unrealized.

We, because we are both human and existent, cannot avoid facing and trying to answer the questions which we ourselves and everything else raise by the very fact of being. Our desire to be at home in our world makes desirable a knowledge of it. This in turn makes it desirable to possess answers to the questions which the world daily and everywhere presents.

The questions raised by nature are specific, and it is essential that we answer them on the level on which they are asked. Our very lives depend sometimes on our ability to know what this particular river is about to do, how this animal will spring, where this blow will fall, what the immediate response to the listener will be to the words we now utter. We cannot avoid specific issues; it is vital to our physical and mental health that we make an intelligent decision as to just how the particular problem we now confront

309

could be resolved most satisfactorily. But we then must deal with it not only as specific, here and now, but as general and universal.

There is no more satisfactory way of meeting the problems of daily existence than by resolving them here and now in such a way as to provide for all similar cases. It is good to know that this river will overflow and that we ought to get out of the way now; it is better to know in addition how any river might behave, and how to build dams so that there will be no further overflows. It is good to know that this animal is about to spring; it would be better if one could know in addition how other animals might act in similar circumstances, and how to domesticate them so that there would be nothing more to fear. The more practical a man, the more comprehensive his answer and the more is it designed to prevent similar problems from arising in the future.

This much perhaps would be granted by even the most ardent pragmatist and empiricist. They do not desire us to lose ourselves in momentary and local issues. They do not want us to blind ourselves to wider questions, so long as these are pertinent to the lives and well-being of men. They tell us to free ourselves from the particular situation in which we now are and to try to see our present problems as typical or revelatory of what else we might have to confront. But they are quick to remark that there is a point where generalized knowledge will cease to provide an answer to a host of related and specific problems and will instead become irrelevant to any. Just what that point is, they never say. They do not say where it is perhaps because they do not know where it is. And they do not know where it is perhaps because there is no such point.

It is merely an article of faith, it would seem, that there is a point at which general truths are irrelevant and useless. Such questions as whether or not there are fixed laws in nature, whether the future is already determined, whether causation is a universal phenomena, are highly general—cosmic in reach in fact. Yet they have relevance to what we are to do with the river and the animal. We can get along without such general knowledge for quite a time, but only if we are content to risk facing each problem only when and as it arises. But then we will be far from prudent, we will not be open to the teachings of experience, we will not be very worldly wise.

As common-sense men we must and do deal with items and problems of universal import. The more interested we are in specific items and problems, the more surely must we master the more general topics of which these are but specific cases.

To be most just to the concrete, we must be aware of what is abstract. To deal most adequately with the specific we must look to the general. The practice of the wisest men of practice is to encourage and make use of theory, to seek knowledge which can be utilized everywhere and always.

THE FIVE VIRTUES OF SCIENCE

General knowledge is indispensable. If we dismiss such knowledge we dismiss a good deal of science. Most scientific knowledge is general knowledge, describing not this fall, that stone or these trees, but falls in general, the nature of stones, the essence of trees, of which instances are to be found here and there. Most thinkers today would perhaps grant this much. What many would question would be the supposition that any other or more general knowledge than that provided by the sciences was possible or desirable. Were they right, any item of supposed knowledge which was outside the interest or reach of science would have to wait until science was ready for it, or must be denied significance.

At least five reasons might be advanced to justify the disposition to accept only scientific knowledge as worthwhile. (1) The sciences separate the superstitious and illusory elements in common-sense views from those which are objective and real, bringing order and system as a consequence into what we daily know. (2) They frame their assertions in precise and communicable language, thus stating what is definitely true or false and what can be communicated to every normal man. (3) Their assertions have predictive force, enabling all to check their truth, and where reliable, to anticipate the future. (4) Their truths are accepted by all competent workers, so that agreement and co-operation rather than disagreement or isolation is the order of the day. (5) Their truths have great utility, providing principles which enable us to improve our technology and resolve specific problems.

In contrast, philosophy, fine art, history, religion, and perhaps the "social" sciences seem to take common sense too naively or to produce schemes too alien to what we know in daily life; they seem to make use of metaphorical and private languages for which no objects can perhaps be found; they apparently do not predict nor provide an opportunity for checking their assertions; their practitioners are evidently at odds with one another as well as with almost everyone else; they do not succeed in offering truths which have any obvious relevance to living practice, to the world as daily lived.

Could the contrast be sustained and could it be made to cover the essential parts of science and the humanities, it would be reasonable to maintain that the only general knowledge that was desirable would be that obtainable by scientific methods, and which was compatible with or reducible to whatever else the sciences affirm. If it be true, however—and I shall try to make evident that it is—that the contrast cannot be sustained, that would not mean that there was no difference between the two kinds of inquiries, or that there was not great value in the kind of knowledge which science provides. In this essay I shall deal with only the first two of these supposed differences.[1]

SCIENCE AND SUPERSTITION

There can be little doubt but that superstitions which torture and distort the minds of many men have been punctured or dismissed by scientists. Men are constantly taking medicants which have been shown to have no medicinal value; they believe in schemes for beating games of chance, even though it can be rigorously demonstrated that these cannot work; they have an unwarranted fear of the number 13 to such an extent that skyscrapers built for balanced, scientifically and practically minded men have

---

[1] There are limitations to scientific prediction; successful predictions are sometimes made in history, sociology and politics. That scientists do not agree is evident from any issue of a scientific journal; that philosophers agree—perhaps too much—is the strong thesis of the sociology of knowledge. Finally, descriptive astronomy and the chemistry of rare earths have little or no utility, while art, religion and philosophy have made a difference to men's lives. It is along such lines I would argue that the last three features are not the exclusive nor the exhaustive characters of science. Science and non-science both have procedures and aims which are worthy and useful. It is a foolish view which would raise one above the other, except for some limited purpose which it was designed to satisfy more effectively than the other.

no story numbered 13 and no room with such a number—and this despite the fact that there is a thirteenth story and a thirteenth room which they happily occupy.

The illustrations are not important, and in any case they are but a sample of those available. Taken literally, such superstitions are tissues of fallacies and falsehoods. Taken metaphorically, or as they function in the lives of men, they often have much to say for themselves. Quite frequently, they express profound truths which ought never to be forgotten. It is well known, for example, that some savages erase the names of their enemies, burn them in effigy or stick spears into their replicas. Some of them—for there are fools and idiots in every society—might thereupon conclude that their enemies had been destroyed. But most of them seem to conclude that they themselves have thereupon become strengthened, or that the enemy, if he hears of the act, is weakened. Their view is sound. If you believe that a certain act will strengthen you, you are likely, after having performed that act, to have more strength than otherwise. The most conceited of men will soon be downcast if told often or forcefully enough that he is looking rundown—particularly when these statements are accompanied by some public act, testifying that we believe others agree with us.

The belief in the efficacy of an act occasionally makes it possible for the act to be efficacious; the very expression of an attitude sometimes converts an object into one which deserves the treatment that the attitude prescribes. If it were the intent of science to dismiss all superstitions, it would then be making the mistake of taking activities out of context and losing thereby the sense in which those superstitions express a truth. The superstitious man, of course, is mistaken in thinking—if he really so thinks—that the act in which he is engaged is relevant to the desired result, that it, in fact, produces it. He is not necessarily mistaken in thinking that the act will prove effective, since a superstition believed and acted on will often cease thereby to be a literal error to become instead a vital truth.

Until we have a scientific account which entirely explains whatever we are trying to understand, we cannot claim to have scientific reasons for supposing that some types of acts are always irrelevant for a given purpose, and that the performance of them for that purpose is the expression of a superstition. Since every act, every thing, every motion in the universe has some repercussion on every other, we have a clear right to term superstitious only those usages which invoke spiritual powers in the face of the fact that the occurrence could be fully explained without reference to them.

It is not a scientific truth, but a philosophic view, which is acceptable to the sciences, that nature is self-sufficient and that what goes on there is never affected by the decisions or activities of spiritual beings, whether they be human minds, angels, demons or gods. The scientists and the philosophers whose views sanctify science may be—and in the one instance of will are—mistaken in the judgment that there are no spiritual influences. Since it is not the business of science to say whether or not there are spirits, either inside or outside man, and since in its present state science confessedly does not understand how the mind works on the body, it cannot be science which can tell us if a belief in the efficacy of spiritual agents is really superstitious. To know that much we need reflection—a reflection which encompasses the whole scheme of things and makes evident to what degree nature is closed to mind and other spiritual forces.

There are facets of the world we cannot grasp and which we must understand by metaphor or attempt to control through communal ritual. If we say that we will reject or ignore them because they are not knowable through the senses or not known to the sciences, we will be bound to reject a good deal of science and a good deal of reliable experience. The electrons and protons, the positrons and neutrons, the curved space and the fields of energy, for example, on which so much of physical science rests, are not observed or even observable. It is true of course that they are intelligible, and that a belief in them might be justified on the basis of what we can observe. But it is equally true that spiritual powers are also intelligible, and that the data of experience leads to them, if not in the sense in which primitive and unreflecting men think, then in a sense which is a refinement of theirs. Common sense is crude science and crude philosophy; it observes carelessly and reasons loosely. But still it does observe and does reason and does come somewhere near the facts at which developed inquiry terminates. It is not a question of black and white, of superstition and stable belief, but of more or less, of incorrect assignment and sharpened, corrected judgment.

We are making incantations in the name of science when, in the face of direct experience checkable by every man, we deny that there are "frightening," "threatening," "intriguing," "tempting," "pleasing" things. The dark and unknown are frightening. We are urging a theory and not a fact when we say that they are calm or indifferent and that we, when frightened, project our fright into them. It is arbitrary to claim that all such characterizations express the result of a man's subjective attitude toward that which has no such nature, under any circumstance. Not only is the supposed act of projection not observable, but what we confront is confronted as calm or frightening before we have had time to reflect, project or construct. The dark presumably is not frightening when men are not present. Its character as frightening apparently presupposes a special attitude on the part of men. Whether this attitude makes the dark actually frightening or whether it merely enables one to know a dark that is frightening in itself is an open question. But in either case, the dark would be frightening, in the one case as something known and in the other as something knowable. We have no right to deny a frightening nature to the dark than we have to deny that a man is listening because he ceases to listen when a speaker stops talking.

If we rid ourselves of what is not sanctioned by science, we limit our horizon unnecessarily. In the last resort we make science itself impossible. In fact the very kind of evidence and observation which supports science is at the root of superstition as well. The evidences for science and superstition are at bottom one. It is common-sense evidence. If we reject this evidence we will have nothing on which to ground our scientific conclusions. The evidence for the existence of electrons and protons, for example, is provided not by the senses but by inferences drawn from the base of common-sense observations of such things as photographs, scales, light reflections, chronometers, etc. If we have no right to accept anything but the refined result of the sciences, the electrons and protons of advanced scientific knowledge, we will by that very fact have no right to the evidence which alone warrants the conclusion that there are electrons and protons.

We conclude that we cannot, we ought **not,** to look to science for the removal of all our "superstitions." A good number of them are grounded in beliefs beyond the province of science to test. Some of those which science might be tempted to puncture or dismiss intend a truth though they literally state an error, and ought to be refined rather than rejected. The kind of observation on which such superstitions rest must be acknowledged even by scientists to be indispensable, reliable and worth while.

On the other hand, philosophy and other non-scientific pursuits are in a position to acknowledge fields of data that science ignores and which some scientists are tempted to define as objects of superstition. Non-scientific subjects need not be superstitious. They can, no less than the sciences, free the beliefs of common man from error. They can take common sense seriously; they need not follow it slavishly. They can in fact, and with qualification ought to defend the world of common sense and science as well.

To know the meaning of beauty we consult the esthetitician; to know a proof of God we consult the theologian. To know the meaning of the unarticulated and mystical we should consult the ordinary man in his double role of artist and religious being. To correct the excesses of these and to bring them into harmony with whatever else we might know, we must have recourse to a view which lies behind all special inquiries and does not allow any one of them to obscure the light of the others. Such a view would not be a tissue of popular beliefs; it would look at them all from a vantage point which required these beliefs to be justified but not necessarily only by the means which the established sciences provide.

The observations of common sense are not to be accepted without reservation in any speculative or theoretical account. But they are not to be dismissed merely because they do not fit into some favored scheme. They are to be rejected only if they are internally incoherent or can be shown to be out of focus in the light of a substantiated system of all that could be true.

If we are to have stable and reliable knowledge, we must refine the crude knowledge of common sense. Science offers one way of doing this. But we should also make use of other means, particularly if we are to understand spheres of existence beyond the interest or reach of science. It is the task of both scientific and non-scientific inquirers to free us from crass superstition and error, the one doing it in one way, the other in another. Neither suffices by itself. Each needs the protection of the other in order to make sure that some of the things maintained by common sense ought to be eliminated, and some of the things unknown to common sense ought to be accepted because belonging to the whole of what is true and ought to be known.

A distinction between science and other inquiries cannot be maintained merely on the ground that one is and the other is not a means for freeing us from superstition or error. And so far as we can sustain the distinction on these grounds, we will find an exclusive devotion to science will compel a neglect of truths which ought to be embraced, of fields which ought to be investigated, of a kind of observation on which science itself depends for its evidence.

Both science and non-science are opposed to error. Both do much to free us from error. Both accept some common-sense data. Both deny themselves if they deny the data which warrants the other. A defense of the possibility and worth of science is in part a defense of philosophy and other inquiries as well. The converse is also true.

SCIENTIFIC PRECISION

"The language of science is precise and is available to all. Other subjects speak in metaphors and then with an emphasis and stress which varies the meaning from man to man." This contention, like the previous one, is not altogether justifiable. So far as what it claims is true, it shows that there is something more to be known than could be known by the methods of science; it points, in other words, to a conclusion opposite to that which it was intended to support.

Physics is not the only science. Nor are those disciplines which put their expressions in quantitative terms the only ones which are entitled to the designation "scientific." Chemistry is a science. So is biology, astronomy, geology. None of these is merely quantitative. The chemist remarks on the colors of his compounds, the botanist and the astronomer classify, the biological unit is the cell, the geologist has no hesitancy of speaking of faults in rocks. Each uses notions which have not been quantified completely. No one of them is so precisely expressed that no diversity of understanding is possible.

The language of the sciences is not as precise as it is popularly supposed to be. On the other hand, the terms and grammar of other subjects are not as loose as their critics say they are. It is possible for fellow-workers in non-scientific subjects to understand one another, to agree and disagree on a given issue, and it is possible for them to teach and communicate what they have discovered.

Where a topic is complex and has multiple facets presenting a host of problems, what is needed is not an expression which dissects it and arbitrarily limits the field, but a characterization which roughly marks it off from others and allows for the possibility of conquering it from many angles. Terms like "the historic past," "beauty," "truth," "substance" are not expressed in the language of the accepted sciences. Yet in their appropriate contexts they have an appropriate precision.

If we use only those terms which the sciences have made precise in meaning, reference and use, we will not be able to locate the common-sense world to which those terms ultimately refer. And if it is our business to deal with the world as experienced and with every kind of question it might raise, it would be wrong to prohibit the use of the very terms which, though metaphorical and in some respects vague and undefined, point to that world and no other.

The languages of the sciences are more precise than are the languages of other subjects, and particularly of philosophy. Scientists can now state more precisely than ever before what they mean by genes, electrons, elements, gravitation, etc. Philosophers seem to be just where they have always been. On questions relating to the soul, substance or divinity they seem even to be more incoherent and obscure than they were in the past.

Part of the advance in precision on the part of scientists is due to the fact that places where they could not obtain a desired precision were abandoned by them. Philosophers among others, on the other hand, have held tenaciously to a domain despite their inability to express what is true of it except by means of metaphor and analogy. The sciences abstract from the concrete, the individual, the private and substantial—and sometimes even from the sensuous and observable—to end with terms which are tissues of universals capable of complete and exhaustive analysis and definition. "Electron" means the same thing for a host of scientists in part because what is intended by the term is not a concrete entity but the universal "electronicity"—the character which all electrons share and perhaps exemplify in diverse ways. Like every abstract universal, "electronicity" is capable of sharp definition; but like every other universal it does not reveal anything about the individual natures and specific differences which distinguish one electron from another.

He who is willing to ignore the individual, indeterminate or substantial nature of beings can make his discourse in other fields as precise as that of the sciences. The classical economist is a case in point. He has few friends, not because he is too vague but because he formulates his principles and conclusions with too great a precision. What was wanted of him was not a knowledge of the way in which an abstract or ideal "economic man" might behave, but the character of a concrete economic process which could not be adequately accounted for by manipulating the economist's abstractions. A description of the exact course of individual events in the world requires the use of terms which are more flexible, more comprehensive and more emotionally palatable than those which the sciences employ.

LANGUAGE AND SCIENCE

It is an old saying that only what can be known through the intellect can be grasped in the same way by a multitude. Intellectual knowledge, it is supposed, is the only knowledge that is free from the limitations and individual emphases that the senses and the emotions inevitably impose on observed material. Since it is the intellect which knows universals and since it is only the intellect which can know them, it is only abstractly formulated truths which can hope for universal understanding.

The supposition is doubly questionable. Firstly, though the same universals can be known in the same way by many intellects, each intellect is rooted in an individual body and grasps things in a different way. The same content has a different meaning for each. Secondly, the senses and the emotions offer us content which is one with the content others confront. Both points require some elaboration.

All men may be able to understand the definitions and usages which the sciences give to their basic terms. But that knowledge alone will not suffice to make them scientists. The knowledge must be supported by common habits of response and work. The reason why scientific truths are universally intelligible is not because they are precisely formulated, or even because they deal with universals, but because scientists, despite the different weights which these truths have for them, are habituated to respond to them in common ways. In the same sense, the language of carpenters is universal, for even though they have no commonly accepted names or definitions for their tools, they use their tools in similar ways at similar times.

A truly universal language either presupposes a set of habits in the respondents which enable all of them to isolate a common meaning in diverse contents, or the use of terms in such a way that they prompt individuals to so respond to different meanings that the outcome is the same for each. Science follows the former procedure. Other subjects follow the latter; they use a universal language in that they say different things to different men with a corresponding difference of appeal, thereby enabling the different men to know a common truth.

There is a difference between the sciences and other subjects. The sciences use a cold language, a language about the nature of things as they might be when all human interests, preferences and insights are suppressed. The language of science expresses the least common denominator of knowledge, the aspect of things which anyone could observe at any time. It provides a minimum of content. Since some men are capable of noting things which others cannot, what the sciences report cannot be the entire truth, unless we make a cavalier identification of commonality and science.

It is not enough, however, to be concerned only with those truths which can be universally acknowledged. If it be true that science is interested only in that aspect of things which every man in principle can discern, we run the risk of denying the truths that men of genius and sudden insight can reach. Artists present truths in a guise which most men fail to see. That does not mean the artist is mistaken; on the contrary, those who take account of what the artist portrays learn truths they never knew or could have known.

There is a sense in which all men could be said to have a knowledge of things not expressed or expressable in the sciences. The senses and emotions provide them with content which, though differing from individual to individual in specific nature, is common and constant as vague and general. Though Tom may see red where John sees blue, both see a color and not a set of vibrations. If we ignore such content, we leave out the most reliable data we have about the nature of the real so far as it can be gleaned through perception.

The sciences are not as precise as they are supposed to be. Their language is not necessarily nor exclusively suited for universal communication. They are precise to some degree; inside the frame of special habits and customs, they speak a universal language. But a comparable precision and universality is evident in other disciplines as well. So far as the sciences, however, neglect or reject what cannot be made to conform to their ideal of a precise and communicable expression, other subjects must be brought to play on the facts so that full justice can be done to them. Supplementing the abstract, what is open to dispassionate thought, the quantifiable and duplicatable, is the concrete, the unique, the qualitative, what is open to men of insight. The truth is the two in one, only fragmentarily grasped in any inquiry whose reach is less than the whole of things.

PART THREE

Essays in
Jewish Culture

Gerhard Kittel and the Jewish Question in Antiquity

⤳§ BY W. F. ALBRIGHT

Johns Hopkins University

ON July 11th, 1948, Gerhard Kittel, youngest son of Rudolph Kittel, died of cancer in his sixtieth year.[1] This bald statement carries with it overtones of intellectual tragedy and spiritual damnation to those who know his story. For the deceased was a distinguished Protestant theologian, professor of New Testament at Tübingen and Vienna, and his father had been in his time the most eminent Old Testament scholar in Germany, whose Leipzig school led the way in pointing to a sound approach to biblical history. Yet he became the mouthpiece of the most vicious Nazi anti-semitism, sharing with Emanuel Hirsch of Göttingen the grim distinction of making extermination of the Jews theologically respectable.

The story of Kittel may seem to be an unimportant paragraph out of the nightmare history of the Nazi movement. Yet it is even darker and more menacing than the more flamboyant stories of Goering and Goebbels, since Kittel was a trained scholar and a Christian theologian. He was born September 23rd, 1888, and he grew up to be a delicate lad with aristocratic predilections.[2] He studied theology, becoming a New Testament scholar of promise,

---

[1] He was born in 1888, according to his own sketch in *Wer ist's*, not in 1889 as stated by Max Weinreich, in *Hitler's Professors* (New York, Yiddish Scientific Institute, 1946), p. 273. The latter volume is an admirable study of the available sources, and is invaluable to all who are interested in this sinister phase of history. The writer has found it exceedingly accurate as a rule, and has derived much help from it in preparing this article.

[2] This information was given me by Professor Georg Steindorff, for decades Rudolf Kittel's friend and colleague in Leipzig, as well as by other persons who wish to remain anonymous.

characterized by unusual breadth of preparation, including rabbinics. In fact his early work was distinguished from that of other New Testament students of his generation mainly by his emphasis on the importance of rabbinic studies. After becoming professor at Tübingen he launched a theological dictionary of the New Testament (1931——), which was interrupted by the war but is to be continued under different editorship. His own task in editing the dictionary was mainly one of organizing the contributions of others, which he did very well, so that the *Theologisches Wörterbuch zum Neuen Testament* rapidly became standard in its field.

When the Nazi movement came into power Gerhard Kittel immediately rose to prominence as one of its leading academic supporters and as one of its chief specialists on the *Judenfrage*. His first publication after Hitler seized power in 1933 was a little book, *Die Judenfrage*, published by a leading theological publisher that same year. When the official journal of the *Forschungsabteilung Judenfrage* of the Reichsinstitut für Geschichte des neuen Deutschlands was established in 1936 under the title, *Forschungen zur Judenfrage*, Kittel became its chief supporter; in fact his contributions to it during the nine years of its sorry life were several times as numerous as those of anyone else, aside from its editor, Walter Frank. He also contributed vicious articles to two other journals, *Die Judenfrage* (previously *Mitteilungen über die Judenfrage*), which began to appear in 1940, and *Archiv für Judenfragen*, initiated in 1943. His last contribution to the first of the three unholy sisters appeared in 1944, just before they suddenly expired. The content of these papers shows that there was no essential change in his public attitude toward the Nazi movement and the Jewish question up to 1943.

During this decade Kittel had, however, vigorously opposed Rosenberg and other extreme Nazi theorists who demanded the suppression of Christianity as well as of its Jewish parent, and had thus lost favor with the regime. After his transfer to the University of Vienna following the *Anschluss* in 1938, he is stated on excellent private authority[3] to have defended the religious value of the Old

---

[3] Especially an eminent German Protestant Old Testament scholar who wrote in detail to me, but wishes to remain anonymous, and an Austrian Catholic scholar whose letter I have read. Owing to the request of the former

Testament and to have deplored certain Nazi "excesses" in dealing with the Jews. None of this, however, was included in the articles that continued to appear until 1944. It must be remembered that the wholesale massacre of Russian Jews began almost immediately after the German invasion of Russia in the summer of 1941 and that the first gas chambers were installed in the concentration camp at Ausschwitz in the early autumn of the same year. While it took some time for the news of this ghastly program to percolate through Germany, virtually all Germans had some inkling of what was going on before the end of 1942. Yet there is no record of any protest of public nature by Gerhard Kittel, who continued for nearly two years longer to publish his inflammatory material.

At the end of the war Kittel was captured and sent to a camp for war prisoners in the French Zone of Germany. Later he was released and allowed to retire to the Benedictine Abbey of Beuren, where he resumed work on the *Theologisches Wörterbuch* already mentioned. Both from his prison camp and from the Abbey of Beuren he kept up a stream of statements and letters on his own behalf, several of which reached the present writer through private channels. In these documents he was undoubtedly sincere, but his very earnestness is more terrifying in its vision of abysses within the human heart than the diabolical crimes of the Nazi leaders themselves. Like other ex-Nazis and Nazi sympathizers with whom the writer has corresponded since the end of the war, Kittel was totally unable to admit any guilt of his own. Again and again he stressed the "fact" that his scholarly work had been absolutely honest and that there was nothing in it of which to be ashamed. He asserted that the Nazi party leaders had "betrayed" him by going farther than he had expected—first by promising to respect the religious values of the Old Testament and then rejecting them

---

that his long letter on the subject be kept confidential, it is impossible to quote in detail, as I should like to do. So much may be said: my correspondent and Gerhard Kittel became friends as young men and remained in close touch thereafter until the end of the war; my correspondent is firmly convinced of Kittel's honesty and of the fact that he did not really know what was going on in the concentration camps after 1941; at the same time he found it impossible to understand how Kittel could support the Nazis as he did and take such continuous part in anti-Jewish propaganda. In such cases a stranger can often judge more impartially than a friend.

and forbidding the teaching of them, secondly by promising to support Christianity and then trying to suppress it, thirdly by promising only to remove the Jews from their "dominant" position in German life and then proceeding to liquidate them as a people. Many German and Austrian theologians, together with a few English and American scholars, defended Kittel between 1945 and his death in 1948, assuring the world that he was sincere (which was unhappily true) and that the content of his antisemitism had been exaggerated (which was not at all true). Among these defenders were some of the leading intellectual figures in both Protestantism and Catholicism, including some eminent scholars who knew him well. The most startling thing about this situation is that these men were not Nazis, though a few of them perhaps sympathized too much with the latter as against their victims.

In these periodical articles Kittel campaigned against Jewish elements in Christianity (which he distinguished from "Israelite") and especially against the alleged Jewish threat to Germanism, finding a striking similarity between the effect of Jewish infiltration into Hellenistic-Roman civilization in the time of Christ and the same process within Christian German culture. According to him the relatively pure Israelites of the Old Testament, to which Christianity owed its historical origin, had been replaced by a world Jewry (*Weltjudentum*) which represented a confused mixture of heterogeneous elements (*Rassengemisch*). This world Jewry, against which the early Christians reacted, he considered as substantially identical with modern Jewry, both of them parasitic growths constituting a fatal danger to their respective host civilizations.

To be sure, Gerhard Kittel was not the only Protestant New Testament scholar to affiliate himself with the Nazi movement and to write in support of its Jewish policy. We may, however, discount G. Bertram of Giessen, who was a relatively minor figure. The third of this triad, Emanuel Hirsch of Göttingen, was in some respects even worse than Kittel, since he taught a new theology (accepted by many "Deutsche Christen"), according to which the Old Testament and much of the New had at most only a vague sentimental interest for Christians, and the will of the German state was binding on the conscience of every Christian, regardless of its morality in pre-Nazi Christian terms. Hirsch was a strange fanatic who had been a specialist in the existential philosophy of Kierkegaard at the same time that he was a strong German nationalist in the Hegelian tradition. After Hitler's triumph he developed an unholy fusion of the Nazi program with existential metaphysics and Neo-Marcionite theology, which enjoyed a brief vogue in German Protestant circles. Hirsch and Kittel were between them clearly responsible for much of the guilt resting on the German Protestant churches for their silence while the Nazis were carrying out the liquidation of the Jews. After all, the fact that they were sincere made them even more dangerous, placing them in the line of Saul of Tarsus and Tomas Torquemada.

In this paper the writer will analyze the last book by Gerhard Kittel, *Das antike Weltjudentum,* written in collaboration with Eugen Fischer.[4] The preface of the book is dated in April 1942, a fact which clearly shows that the authors were conscious of what their propaganda foreshadowed. Kittel's collaborator was born in 1874 and in 1918 he became full professor and director of the Anatomisches Institut at Freiburg in Breisgau. Nine years later he was called to Berlin as professor of physical anthropology at the University and as director of the Kaiser Wilhelm-Institut für Anthropologie, Erblehre und Eugenik. In 1934 he became rector of the University of Berlin, having become a Nazi some time before. The writer owes to an eminent European physical anthropologist,[5] himself a strong anti-Nazi, the following characterization (much abbreviated) of Fischer's work:

"Fischer had a thorough training in anatomy and in much of biology, he was an outstanding pioneer in human genetics and he combined originality with high scholarly standards according to all his strictly technical work. In his great many large and small papers (up to 1939, to my knowledge) on human morphology and genetics Fischer's generalizations and conclusions were always carefully considered and well supported by ample and sound obser-

[4] Hamburg, Hanseatische Verlagsanstalt, 1943 (= *Forschungen zur Judenfrage,* Band 7), 256 pp. with 225 figures in the text and a map). I wish particularly to thank Professor Ignace J. Gelb of the Oriental Institute of the University of Chicago for his kindness in lending me this book for over a year.
[5] His name is kept confidential at his request; I shall say only that he is one of the most distinguished living specialists in his field.

vations. His staff and pupils produced a mass of publications under his direction which represent further contributions of lasting value for the development of physical anthropology as a science . . . Sharply contrasting with all this are Fischer's activities in 'Eugenik,' that premature and hence unfortunate attempt to apply anthropology in politics, etc. . . . Fischer was no longer a well-trained scientist, but a dreamer (with a nightmare) who talks verbosely and vaguely of generalized topics of eugenics, race hygiene, racial 'psychology,' and the 'Rassenseele' without ever as much as mentioning any facts. He did use such terms as 'minderwertige Rassen' as early as 1913[6] but, as far as I can determine, did not take an active, public, part in forming and preaching national-socialist theories until about 1930, when he evidently became a popular lecturer in Berlin at the expense of his scientific integrity and international reputation. For instance, his *Rede bei der Feier—der Berliner Universität*—1933 . . . is as full of . . . nonsensical claims as his technical reports are full of worth-while facts and modest, sound deductions . . ."

Das antike Weltjudentum is beautifully printed, with superb illustrations and elegant binding—obviously intended for wide circulation as popular propaganda. Almost the entire letter-press (p. 9-108) was written by Kittel, only p. 109-114 coming from the pen of Fischer. Kittel expressly states that he gathered and annotated all the illustrations, which were then classified and "interpreted" from the standpoint of human genetics and anatomy by Fischer. It is quite certain that Kittel's point of view had not yet changed when he wrote the preface in collaboration with Fischer in 1942. Nor did it change appreciably in the following two years before the beginning of German collapse, since several offensive essays of Kittel's appeared between 1942 and 1944, the latest of them in Vol. IX of *Forcshungen zur Judenfrage,* whereas *Das antike Judentum* constituted Vol. VII of the same periodical!

This book is divided into three parts, which will be briefly described in the author's own words:—In the first part we have "facts and texts . . . just those that clarify this Jewish question of world Jewry [sic!] With one exception all the texts are drawn from the

[6] In the monograph which made his reputation: *Die Rehobotherbastarde und das Bastardierungsproblem bei den Menschen.*

millennium between Ezra and the Merovingian period. They are sometimes reproduced in brief digests of their content, but generally in translation. For the specialist it will be self-evident that the most 'correct' reproduction demands a certain freedom of rendering, especially in the case of rabbinic texts . . ." (p. 11).

In the second part, "the Egyptian mummy portraits of the Hellenistic-Roman period are for the first time subjected to a systematic analysis with a view to determining the extent to which they are portraits of Jews. If we have here, as we hope to prove, a relatively large number of certain portraits of Jews from antiquity, it is obvious that very important material for the earlier racial history of the Jews is thus made available."

The third part of the volume is devoted to a study of the anti-Jewish attitudes reflected by the alleged caricatures of Jews preserved in the museum at Treves (Trier) in the Rhineland. These form a group of terra-cotta and bronze statuettes attributed to the second or third centuries A.C.E.[7]

In Gerhard Kittel's *Einleitung* (written entirely by him) he says (p. 9, first paragraph): "No one who scrutinizes the modern Jewish question can fail to recognize—especially during the present fateful struggle of Europe[!] for existence—that of all its underlying sources the fact of a world Jewry that spreads out over the world and everywhere maintains its bases of operation from which it infiltrates through the political, economic and cultural life of the peoples, is the most threatening. Among the many problems which are raised by Judaism as a curious phenomenon of world history and which together constitute the Jewish problem, the fact of a world Jewry and its effects on its environment is by far the most sinister (*unheimlich*) in its implications for non-Jewish mankind." Kittel goes on to insist that this "extraordinary phenomenon" is not really new; it is, on the contrary, he says, a repetition and continuation of a similar phenomenon in Hellenistic-Roman times. Men have failed to recognize its menace, he writes, because "its peculiar characteristics were submerged or concealed for a thousand years, from the beginning of the Ghetto to Jewish emancipation and assimilation." From this statement it is obvious that Kittel was bitterly

[7] For details see G. Kittel (alone), "Die ältesten Judenkarikaturen. Die Trierer Terrakotten," in *Forschungen zur Judenfrage*, IV, p. 250-59.

hostile both to the democratic ideal of Jewish emancipation and to
the liberal idea of assimilation. Hundreds of pages written by him
since 1933 and especially since 1940 are devoted to the development
of this thesis of his.

Kittel then goes on to describe the chief characteristics of his
"ancient world Jewry." First, he writes, came its diffusion over the
Roman world, "from Assuan to the Crimea, from the Persian
Gulf to Spain, from Tunis to Treves, Cologne and Britain." However, this people was not really an energetic and creative "conquering and colonizing stock," but was "characteristically represented"
by the ancient *"Wanderjude,"* the "clever trader" (*der geschäfts-
tüchtige Händler*), the "opportunistic freedman" (*der einflusshun-
grige Freigelassene*). "Its task was not to create anything new, but
to control already existing forces and cultures."

Our author goes on to say (p. 10) that there was a "peculiar
double tendency" (a kind of polarity) which characterized Hellenistic-Roman "world Jewry." On the one hand it became assimilated to existing Graeco-Roman civilization, its members trying to
assimilate as completely as possible. On the other hand it became
a vigorous missionary religion, which proselyted enormous masses
of people (*ein riesenhaftes Proselytentum*). He points out that
these proselytes ceased to be Greeks or Romans [so Kittel] and
attached themselves to the Jewish national bloc as well as to
Jewish faith. At the end of this paragraph he bursts out into the
familiar pattern of Nazi antisemitism: "For this was the underlying meaning and the basic unity of that double tendency: assimi-
lative adaptation and absorption of converts were both means for
a single purpose—power!" In recent antisemitic parlance, the
sinister Elders of Zion utilize both international capitalism and
international communism as tools for their own gigantic conspiracy against the non-Jewish world. Any group which one dislikes
is damned if it does and equally damned if it does the opposite.
The fact that Kittel generally disguises such sentiments behind a
screen of specious learning does not in the least alter their profoundly illogical, undemocratic, and thoroughly un-Christian character.

Kittel then writes: "Whether a Jewish slave-woman with genuine
or forged letters is intermediary between the wife of the Roman

emperor and a Jewish princess; . . . whether the embassy of the
Alexandrine Jews uses the empress to ingratiate itself with the
emperor and works for the execution of the leaders of the anti-
Jewish party; or whether the Jews of Alexandria and Cyrene and
Cyprus take advantage of the fact that the emperor is elsewhere
occupied to kill hundreds of thousands of non-Jews in their fero-
cious uprisings; or whether . . . —always, in all periods, whether
in the first century or the twentieth, world Jewry means a dream
of sole power in this world and in the next!"

It should go without saying that such distortions of the story of
Josephus (regardless of whether his version happens to be right
or not) and such uncritical acceptance of the wildest exaggerations
are alone enough to disprove Kittel's right to be considered as a
critical historian. Philological knowledge and historical learning are
not enough; the trained historian is supposed to weigh his sources,
assign them to their proper categories, and refuse to pass judgment
on human motives. In these wild sentences Kittel violates the
fundamental canons of good history just as flagrantly as Father
Coughlin flouted the standards of honest journalism by the falsehoods with which *Social Justice* was crammed. Kittel's hatred for
the Jews was so intense and so distorted as to make him quite
incapable of justice. How his non-Nazi German contemporaries
could for a moment judge him to be well intentioned is hard to
understand. A fanatic may be honest and sincere, but he intends
the worst to all unfortunate targets of his insane dislike.

Kittel's selection of texts in the first part of the book shows
wide learning and the traditional *Akribie* of the trained German
scholar. His sample texts are well calculated to prove that Jewish
settlement was widespread in that age, and that many Jews were
slaves or freedmen, that there was much proselyting and a consequent mixture of peoples. Of course, the notion of ethnic mixture
carried with it for the Nazi an idea of decadence and plebeian
crudeness which is most distasteful. To the average American, on
the other hand, the melting pot is a process whose value has been
demonstrated again and again by the amazing energy and vitality
of our composite people. We are proud of the many nationalities
to which our ancestors belonged. Not so the authors of this book!

As the selection of texts proceeds, the author shows his preju-

dice more and more by limiting himself to passages which prove
his points, such as a careful collection of references to Jewish
assimilation (p. 49 ff.), to Jews in business and banking (p. 53 ff.),
to Jewish cheats and rascals (p. 58 ff.), to Jewish officials and
arrivistes (p. 61 ff.), to Jewish resilience after virtual destruction
[which becomes a crime against humanity with Kittel!], etc. As
we go on, the arbitrary character of the selections becomes more
and more evident, until the author closes (p. 92) with quotations
from Tacitus ("the disgusting people"), Ammianus Marcellinus
(attributing to Marcus Aurelius the statement that the Egyptian
Jews were more contemptible than the German and Sarmatian bar-
barians), the Greek Esther (quoting without comment what purported to be the [false] accusations of Haman against the Jews),
and finally quoting the following passage from the Babylonian
Talmud (Abodah Zara, 10b): "An emperor who hated the Jews
said to the grandees of his kingdom, 'If there is a swelling on anybody's foot shall he cut it off in order to save his life, or shall he
let it be and suffer?' They answered, 'Let him cut it off in order
to save his life!' "[8] It is perfectly obvious that Gerhard Kittel meant
to suggest the complete liquidation of the Jewish people, though
we may safely suppose that he would not have prescribed the gas
chamber and general massacre, but would have found some slower
and more conventional methods for attaining the same end if he
himself had been in power.

When such a learned but warped mind as that of Kittel joins
forces with an equally learned and equally warped scientific mind
to produce a book like this, we expect an intellectual monstrosity
to come into existence. And this is exactly what happens in the
second and third parts of the book. In the second part the two
authors combine efforts to analyze the alleged Jewish racial percentage in some eighty mummy portraits of the Roman period in
Egypt. When we consider that most of the artists were conventional
and distinctly unskilled in indicating features, and that all are *en
face* instead of in profile, the probability of success seems slight.
When we further bear in mind that Lower Egypt then swarmed

[8] Kittel should naturally have taken this with its rather beautiful continuation in the Babylonian Talmud. As it stands the quotation is grotesque and,
placed where Kittel puts it, horrible.

with Greeks, Anatolians, Phoenicians, Aramaeans, and Arab Naba-
taeans, as well as with Jews, and that we have no contemporary
Jewish portraits (labeled as such) for comparison, the prospect of
successful analysis becomes much slighter. However, the two
authors plunge rashly on, stopping only for frequent slurs—one portrait is said to show typical Jewish "insolence, not to say impudence" (p. 160). As a result of their collaboration they assert that
12-13 percent of the portraits from the Faiyum represent Jews, a
figure which agrees (*"eine besonders schöne Bestätigung"*) with
Kittel's independent estimate of the Jewish population of Egypt as
one-eighth of the total. This estimate is based on uncritical acceptance of a generalization of Philo (a million Jews in Egypt in his
day) with the guess of certain papyrologists that the total population of Egypt in the Roman period averaged eight million. This
entire part is a caricature of scientific archaeological and anthropological method, showing to what lengths the best minds will go
when obsessed by a perverse dogma.

If Part II is disconcerting, Part III is stupefying. Devoted to
"the oldest caricatures of world Jewry," if we are to believe the
authors, it features a homogeneous group of terra-cottas "found"
shortly before the Nazi regime at Treves (Figs. 151-157) together
with illustrative material from the Rhineland and other parts of
the Roman Empire.[9] Kittel tries to prove from his comparative
material that all such caricatures from the Roman period—generally
characterized by exaggerated, often hooked noses—represent Jews.
The improbability of such an inference is clear enough to any
scholar who bears in mind that such noses were far more typical
of Anatolians and North Syrians than of Jews in antiquity as today,
and that Graeco-Roman caricature tended to exaggerate the length
of noses and to treat them as beaks—much like modern cartoonists.

In any event, no experienced archaeologist can doubt for a
moment—unless blinded by prejudice—that the bulk (at least) of
the Treves figurines are recent forgeries. This combination of caricature with gross obscenity is typical of forgers of antiques. Notorious examples are the figurines made by Salim el-Qari and sold
by Shapira in the early seventies of the last century. Said to come
from Moab, they combined grotesqueness with obscenity, and for

[9] *Cf.* above, n. 7.

a time many scholars regarded them as reflecting the abominations of Baal-peor(!).[10] In the twenties of this century a family of French peasants manufactured an entirely different kind of grotesque and obscene figurines which enjoyed much success among less critical scholars until the "affaire Glozel" was wound up with the unmasking of the deception.[11] This incredible Treves mixture of circumcized phalli with grotesque heads has never been found in any systematic excavation under a reputable archaeologist anywhere in the ancient world, and not a single reliable record of such a find can be produced by Kittel. It is fantastic nonsense from start to finish, and the inclusion of such horrors in the book before us is final proof that Gerhard Kittel intended at that time, in spite of his subsequent story, to whip up hatred against the Jews in Germany to the last terrible orgasm. Even Torquemada left no such testament as this to his misguided followers.

This grim story is also the tale of all intellectual defiance of the Ten Commandments and the Sermon on the Mount. In many ways Kittel and Fischer typified European intellectual activity at its best, since the two men were leaders in their respective philological and biological fields. Surrendering to the devil of intellectual over-confidence, they plunged into the uncharted depths between their respective islands of special skill. Selling themselves to Satan, they abandoned the Judaeo-Christian tradition of the fatherhood of God and the brotherhood of man. Worshiping at the shrine of the ancient pagan gods of *Blut und Boden*, they adopted the mark of Cain as their perpetual badge of dishonor. And what happened in Germany can take place wherever the human intellect turns its back on the spiritual traditions which we have inherited from their sources in ancient Israel.

[10] See especially the convenient summary by Ch. Clermont-Ganneau, who unmasked these forgeries, in his delightful book, *Les fraudes archéologiques en Palestine* (Paris 1885).

[11] For the latter see the *Rapport de la commission internationale: Fouilles de Glozel,* published by the Institut Internationale d'Anthropologie as a supplement to the *Revue Anthropologique,* no. 10-12, 1927.

New Horizons

in Jewish History

⌁ BY SALO W. BARON
Columbia University

*T*HAT each generation rewrites all previous history and that it teaches history from ever new angles has become a truism. After the climactic catastrophe in the whole history of anti-Jewish persecutions and the rise of a Third Jewish Commonwealth our generation certainly has a most urgent need of complete reorientation and reinterpretation of the records of the past. Such reorientation has been under way for some time, but scholars and educators of our day are intensely groping for some new approaches which would make the Jewish past as meaningful to this generation of Jews, and particularly to its youth, as the interpretations of a Zunz, Graetz or Dubnow were to the successive generations of the Emancipation era.

ETHNIC OR RELIGIOUS HISTORY

To begin with, history itself has answered the old and trite question as to whether the Jews are merely a religious group or also a national or even racial entity. This question, which might already have agitated the minds of the first Babylonian exiles if they had been cognizant of modern terminology, has affected Jewish historiography much less than publicist discussions. Jewish historians, truly familiar with the record, could not escape the impact of this extraordinary blend of nationalism and religion which has always characterized the history of the Jewish people. Even if personally anti-nationalist and preaching amalgamation with their neighbors, as did Jost, Zunz and Geiger, they could not help treating the empiric manifestations of Jewish group life as something far transcending the accustomed definitions of a religious group.

Most of them have indeed written in terms of a history of the Jewish "people," rather than that of its faith. Nevertheless there was much confusion even in our historical literature in trying to fit the Jewish experience under the accepted general categories of nationality, religion or race.

History has now decided the issue. Not in the obvious sense that, through the formation of the new state of Israel, Jews had become a nation like any other nation, that they now possess the "normal" characteristics of state, territory and language, but rather in the opposite sense of underscoring the uniqueness of Jewish experience. To give a pointed example: Let us assume that three brothers born in Kiev now live respectively in New York, Kiev and Tel-Aviv. The New Yorker would appear in every public consideration as a member of the Jewish "faith," *i.e.* of one of 256 denominations counted in the latest United States census of religious bodies. From an equally formal point of view the brother remaining in Kiev would be classified by law as a member of a recognized national minority, one of the 180 national minorities given full recognition in the Soviet Union, according to the census of 1939. The third brother living in Tel-Aviv, finally, would recently have become a national of Israel with all the normal characteristics of a citizen of a national state. Either the Kiev or the Tel-Aviv brother could actually change his faith to Christianity or Islam and still remain a member of the Jewish ethnic minority in the Ukraine if he so desired, or of the Israeli body politic, possibly against his wish. It is in some respects a pure accident, then, which of the three brothers, who otherwise may have changed little of their mode of living or ideological outlook, now appears in the record as a religious or ethnic Jew and which as a member of the Israeli nation.

The very rise of Israel has pointed up the peculiar fact that for the second time in history a "colony" was founded without a motherland. What was theoretically considered a mere religious group has created a nation. That nation in turn will increasingly influence the Jewish religious evolution even if it should, as now seems likely, formally separate its state from its synagogue.

This evolution has merely served to emphasize the uniqueness of Jewish experience. From the outset it was futile to try to subsume it under categories borrowed from other experiences. There is no question that Judaism is a religion. Nor do we have to search for more religious books than the Bible or Talmud. And yet, neither Bible nor Talmud has a word for "religion." When modern writers had to find a Hebrew equivalent for this term as used in all western languages they had to choose expressions like *dat* or *emunah,* neither of which originally had that connotation.

Nor was the national experience of the Jews in any way typical. Until the rise of Israel they were devoid of state and territory for more than eighteen centuries. Even during the Second Commonwealth, they represented an extraordinary compound of ethnic and religious features. Although generally used to national religions and their continued existence after the loss of national independence, the ancients were puzzled and, according to individual tempers and experiences, attracted or repelled by this strange group. Speaking four years after the first Roman entry into Palestine (59 B.C.E.), Cicero fulminated: "Even while Jerusalem was standing and the Jews were at peace with us, the practice of their sacred rites was at variance with the glory of our empire, the dignity of our name, the customs of our ancestors."[1] At the same time he strenuously objected to their "sticking together" and their great influence in Roman assemblies. Several generations later, the historian Tacitus realized even more clearly the growing threat to the Graeco-Roman way of life from the expansion of Jewish (and Christian) beliefs and mores. Concerned chiefly with its political effects he spoke harshly of that "most despicable of nations" which no sooner captivated the heart of a proselyte than it made him forget his family and disown his country.[2]

Curiously, at that time there hardly existed any linguistic barrier between Jew and Gentile; the majority of the Jews in the dispersion spoke Greek, and almost all the rest Aramaic—two international tongues spoken by many peoples of the eastern Mediterranean world. In more recent centuries the ethno-religious characteristics of the Jewish people stood out even more sharply in a nationalistically and linguistically divided though religiously more funda-

1 Cicero, *Pro Flacco*, XXVIII, 69.
2 Tacitus, *Hist.*, V, 5. *Cf.* Johanan (Hans) Lewy's searching analysis of Cicero's and Tacitus' utterances on Jews in his *Ha-Yehudim le-or ha-sifrut ha-romit* (The Jews in the Light of Roman Literature) (Jerusalem 1943) reprinted from the quarterly, *Zion*, vols. vii-viii.

mentally united civilization. Certainly a people speaking several "Jewish" languages (Hebrew, Yiddish, Ladino and Bokharan), together with a variety of non-Jewish dialects, did not fit into any of the numerous definitions of ordinary national groups. "Race," finally, was clearly a pseudo-scientific term when applied to Jews, and yet the vast majority of Jews now living remember only Jewish parents, grandparents and other ancestors as far back as they can trace them.

In short, if the accepted terminology does not fit historic reality it is the terms, not the facts, which must be altered. The new historiography, too, and with it the new instruction in Jewish history must of necessity emphasize the extraordinary nature of the group which it tries to describe.

This is not a call to renewed boasting in the "chosenness" of our people, nor is it, on the other hand, a denial of such "chosenness." The doctrine of the "chosen people" is a religious belief and, as such, essentially "beyond history." Suffice it to remember that every great historic experience is unique. Has there ever been an historic evolution similar to that of the United States? There is absolutely no parallel for the rise of the British Empire or the Soviet Union. Certainly French history, or German or Italian history or, for that matter, the history of any great people has never been fully duplicated. Whether such uniqueness should be the source of national pride or even aggressive self-assertion is beside the point. The important thing is that it be recognized as being of its own kind and that its historic treatment not try to force it into patterns borrowed from other, essentially different lines of evolution.

LACHRYMOSE CONCEPTION OF JEWISH HISTORY

A new approach to the interpretation of the two thousand years of Jewish history in the dispersion has indeed been in the offing. It was not Graetz who invented the designation *Leidens- und Gelehrtengeschichte* (history of sufferings and of scholars) as the keynote of Jewish history during the last two thousand years.[3] The concentration on Jewish "martyrdom" and intellectual pursuits was

[3] *Cf.*, however, the serious reservations made by Graetz himself in the introduction to his *Geschichte der Juden,* V, 4th ed. (Leipzig 1909) p. xiv ff. (not reproduced in the English translation).

characteristic already of the ancient rabbis. Were we to read only the talmudic record or most of the medieval Hebrew letters we would know very little about the military exploits of Judah the Maccabee and his brethren. The very festival of Hanukkah was long celebrated only as a religious memorial to the rededication of the Temple with some more or less desultory liturgical references to the staunch faith of Mattathias and his sons. Mattathias himself was extolled more as a defiant martyr, who single-handedly destroyed an idol placed in his native Modin by the Syrian authorities, rather than as a guerrilla general. In fact, we have reasons to believe that the custom of lighting candles on Hanukkah fully developed in Babylonia and not in Palestine, where the Maccabean regime left behind many unsavory memories.[4]

For good historic reasons, therefore, the Maccabean heroes had already become the famous seven Maccabean martyrs of the fourth book of *Maccabees*, who suffered death meekly and without resistance. So deeply ingrained did the equation of "Maccabee" and martyr become among the Jews (and even more among the later Christians) that a story describing the miraculous redemption of Egyptian Jews from threatening danger was nonchalantly called the third book of *Maccabees*, although no person bearing the illustrious name of the Judean dynasty was in any way involved in these dramatic events.[5] As time went on "the sanctifying of the name of the Lord" became not only an exalted religious duty but also an eminent educational instrument of social control. This doctrine became so deeply rooted in the Jewish psyche and the majority of Jews and their leaders became so firmly convinced that their destiny was to be the eternally persecuted exiles and wanderers that already in the talmudic age many earlier changes in law were glibly ex-

[4] *Cf.* Louis Ginzberg's *Ginze Schechter* (Genizah Studies), 2 vols. (New York 1928-29) vol. i, p. 476; and Viktor Aptowitzer's "Untersuchungen zur gaonäischen Literatur," in *Hebrew Union College Annual,* vol. viii-ix (1931-32) 395 f. n. 43.

[5] These events allegedly took place under Ptolemy IV Philopator (221-204 B.C.), hence about half a century *before* the Maccabean revolt. Although the compilation of III *Macc.* is much younger and may possibly, but not very likely, have been prepared in the age of Augustus (*cf.,* e.g., Viktor [Avigdor] Tcherikover's interesting Hebrew essay on "The Third Book of the Maccabees as an Historical Source of the Augustan Period," in *Zion,* vol. x, 1944-45, p. 1-20), its author made no pretense of associating it with that revolt or one of its leaders.

plained as the result of a *sheat herem,* an alleged period of persecutions for which modern historical scholarship has been unable to
find any evidence whatsoever. Incidentally this mental attitude
was taken over also by the early Christians who likewise glorified
their martyrs and "witnesses" far above their leaders and fighters.
Yehudah Halevi was not altogether wrong when, in his famous
dialogue, he made the Jewish spokesman convince the king of the
Khazars that Jewish political powerlessness was no proof of the
inferiority of Judaism. Do not the other faiths (Christianity and
Islam), he asked, in their sacred Scriptures likewise extol their
great martyrs, rather than their kings and generals?[6]

For the last quarter of a century I have staunchly battled
against what, in 1928, I first called somewhat deprecatingly the
"lachrymose conception of Jewish history." The more I have thought
about it since, the more firmly I became convinced that this conception of history, overstressing the idea of Jewish historic martyrdom, neither squared with the facts nor was of service to our
generation. Our youth, in particular, whether in Israel, America,
or any other country of emancipation has been growing increasingly restive under a doctrine which seemed to condemn it to
unceasing persecution.

The persistence of such a doctrine, to be sure, under modern
conditions had its valid sociological reasons. The struggle for both
emancipation and Zionism, in particular, although from different
angles, postulated the painting of the past in the blackest possible
colors so as to contrast it the more sharply with the bright semi-
messianic future expected from the realization of either complete
equality or the restoration to the Jewish homeland. Nevertheless
educators, rabbis and publicists often sensed the impatience of the
young generation with the glorification of past sufferings, which it
at times resented as a morbid obsession. Certainly the spectacle
of an entire community like Mayence committing mass suicide in
order to escape the vengeance of Crusaders, or rather in order to
avoid paying lip service to another faith, carried little direct appeal
to the modern American football player or the equally secularized
Palestinian pioneer. Devoid of religious sentiment, he often viewed

---

[6] Halevi's *Kitab Al-Khazari,* ed. by Hartwig Hirschfeld (Leipzig 1887) I, 113
ff.; IV, 21 ff. (also in the English transl. by Hirschfeld, new ed., New York 1927).

such "excesses" of religious zeal with as little understanding as does a non-musical person while listening to the sound and fury of a modern symphony.

Unconsciously yielding to some such intellectual pressure, recent historians have begun placing new emphases upon the normal rather than the abnormal features of Jewish life. They even gave vent to a certain romantic nostalgia for the quiet serenity and happiness of ghetto life, as contrasted with the confusion and irreconcilable conflicts of modern society. Such reinterpretation was further aided and abetted by the new trends in general as well as in Jewish historiography. The more historical literature stressed social rather than individual approaches, the more significantly loomed the underlying socio-economic, political and cultural factors rather than individual occurrences, however dramatic.

Paradoxically, the rise of Israel may lead to a revival of the lachrymose conception of Jewish history under a new, even more dangerous guise. In order to sharpen the line of demarcation between the unhappy "exilic" centuries and the happy lot of the Jew living on his own soil, all life in the dispersion, even in the emancipated and fairly prosperous communities of the western world, is described as spiritually bleak and deeply tinged with physical insecurity and mental maladjustments. We may indeed witness a revival of the *Leidens-und Gelehrtengeschichte*. But unlike Graetz, Zunz or Krochmal, to whom the spiritual achievements of their ancestors, combined with the moral fortitude of the ancient and medieval witnesses to the faith, were a major claim to fame, in fact one of the main justifications for the continued existence of the Jewish people, the prevailing temper among some younger Israeli students of history and their followers in other countries may well lead to a blanket condemnation of the entire exilic past as an historic nightmare. In other words, the new history based upon the "normal" nationalistic, against the transcendent religious, values is on the way of restoring the lachrymose conception to its former position of pre-eminence, but not to its status as a profound rationale for Jewish survival.

How detrimental such an approach would be to diaspora Jewry's pride in its heritage, indeed to its self-respect, need not be expatiated here. It would, of course, be but the logical consequence

of the old doctrine of the "negation of *galut*." Indulged in a rather
academic fashion by some early Zionist extremists, this doctrine
has now, in the days of realization of the Zionist ideals, become a
great menace to Jewish survival and, as such, of great detriment
to the Zionist achievement itself.[7] For generations to come Israel
will need a strong and prosperous diaspora, just as world Jewry
will need a strong and prosperous Israel. Any theory of history,
therefore, which is likely to undermine the morale, perhaps to sap
the vitality of world Jewry will, whatever its short-range myopic
benefits, bring incalculable damage to the Jewish people and, indi-
rectly also, to its continued extraordinary contributions to human
civilization. Being unsupported, moreover, by any more detached
review of the historic record, it must be repudiated on scholarly,
as well as moral grounds.

GLORIFICATION OF PIONEER AND HERO

Much more vital, because constructive rather than negativistic,
has been the revaluation of the Jewish historic experience by the
new appreciation of the fighter and builder brought into Jewish
life by the modern Zionist and socialist philosophies. Ever since
the advent of Zionism, Hanukkah has become first and foremost the
festival of national liberation, and as such one of the most important Jewish holidays of the year. Because of its calendar proximity
to Christmas—apart from the very likely common Oriental origins
of both festivals—it has also served as one of the main vehicles of
good will in interfaith celebrations and has loomed large as a major
Jewish communal and family institution. No longer ideal personi-
fications of passive martyrdom, the Maccabeans, and particularly
Judah the Maccabee, have been exalted as the prototypes of fighting heroes who, through their remarkable warlike exploits, succeeded in winning complete independence for their people in the
face of all but impossible odds.

This glorification of the hero has reached ever new heights of
intensity during the Haganah's underground struggle against the
mandatory government and the recent war against the Arab in-
vaders. Adumbrated in the early exaltation of the memory of Trum-

[7] *Cf.* my observations on "Prospects for the Diaspora," in *New Palestine*,
vol. xxxvii (no. 20 of June 20, 1947) 143-46.

peldor, it has begun to displace even the glorification of the *halutz,* the pioneer builder in the wilderness, who for a long time represented the apogee of national and social efforts at rebuilding the wholeness of Jewish life on the basis of national freedom and social justice. Perhaps, when peace is definitely restored, the new pioneering endeavors, keyed to the tremendous scale of Jewish immigration, will resume their rightful place as the symbol of the strivings of the Jewish people for a new way of life. But whether as soldier or as pioneer the new ideal personality will be entirely different from the saint and scholar, the traditional embodiment of the highest virtues of piety and learning, combined with the ever present readiness for supreme sacrifice.

Such transvaluation of all values has already affected Jewish historiography and the teaching of Jewish history throughout the world. Especially Western youth has long ago begun to lose interest in ghetto culture and its literature. Gradually but irresistibly the latter's appeal to Jewish children and young adults was replaced by the new appreciation of the struggle for the homeland. Even the great catastrophe of European Jewry has, on the whole, failed to resuscitate the ancient exaltation of the martyr's meek surrender, but rather furnished in the Warsaw ghetto fighter another variant of the same ideal, the heroic resister to tyranny and degradation. This new attitude has long disturbed Hebrew and Yiddish teachers in this country, as well as in Palestine, who have found it very difficult to convey to children and adolescents the meaning of the life in the old Jewish community, particularly the East European *shtetl,* so vividly portrayed by the great writers of the nineteenth century. Even the more alert and imaginative pupils have evinced less and less interest in the world of Mendele or Peretz, Bialik or Sholem Aleichem. In this way some of the greatest literary achievements of the modern Hebrew and Yiddish renaissance have unfortunately become meaningless, or at best antiquarian reminiscences, for the vast majority of Jewish youth; more antiquarian at times than the legal decisions or homiletical sayings of the talmudic sages or the metaphysical and ethical doctrines of medieval thinkers.

This is not to convey the idea that for this reason the history of the last two centuries and their culture are to be studied less intensively than hitherto. In fact, we now have achieved a certain distance, and with it a modicum of historical perspective, to evaluate more fully and dispassionately the significance of the emancipation era. On closer examination it will be seen that, rather than being, as still is generally assumed, opposing historical trends, emancipation and Zionism have been deeply interlocked as complementary historical forces.[8] But it does mean that the modern chapters in most Jewish historical textbooks have become quite obsolete. There has already been much too wide a gap between the songs of the *halutzim,* the *"hora"* and the speeches of Israeli leaders, which have become part and parcel of the curriculum of most Hebrew schools, and the traditional teaching of Jewish history with its stress on personalities and modes of living, which are strange and meaningless to our youth.

We shall not be surprised, therefore, if in the coming years and decades more and more books and articles will be written describing the activist and "heroic" features of the rich and multi-colored Jewish past. To cite a few random illustrations: Recently engaged in the study of the revolution of 1848, I have come across some noteworthy examples of Jewish heroism hitherto unsung by poets or historians. The German-speaking peasantry of Alsace, dissatisfied with the existing economic conditions, gave vent to its atavistic anti-Jewish feelings and began attacking one Jewish community after another while southern French peasantry, not having Jewish scapegoats around, more appropriately attacked the landowners. On this occasion Rabbi Nordmann of Hegenheim organized a Jewish self-defense. With a quickly improvised force of four platoons totaling eighty young men he beat back the attackers, bent on easy pillage but not prepared to face a regular battle. He then proceeded to the offensive, seized some of the ringleaders and turned them over to the authorities.[9]

[8] Such a more detached re-examination of the record reveals that already during the revolution of 1848, which in many ways constituted the "political debut" of the Jewish people, Zionist and emancipatory ideas often appeared side by side. *Cf.* my recent essay on "The Impact of the Revolution of 1848 on Jewish Emancipation," in *Jewish Social Studies,* vol. xi (1949) 246 ff.

[9] *Archives israélites,* vol. ix (1848) 217. *Cf.* my "Revolution of 1848 and Jewish Scholarship, I" in the *Proceedings of the American Academy for Jewish Research,* vol. xviii (1949) 8 f.

Such instances could be multiplied indefinitely. Long before Russian Jewry, forewarned by the pogroms of 1881, proceeded to the systematic organization of a *haganah asmit* (this name was given to the Jewish self-defense in the crucial years 1903-05; *cf.* e.g. the remarkable appeal issued by Ahad Haam after the Kishinev massacres and published twenty-five years later by one of its co-signers, Simon M. Dubnow[10]) Jews often individually and collectively put up a fierce resistance, although the record of their battles impressed contemporary chroniclers and later historians much less than the meek acceptance of their divinely ordained suffering by the "martyrs." The unflinching martyrdom of the 1,500 Jews of Tultshin may well be replaced now by the story of their preceding successful defence of the city against the Cossack assailants until their betrayal by their "noble" fellow combatants.

Nor has sufficient attention been paid to the individual heroic exploits of innumerable Jewish fighters in the various western armies during the emancipation era. Few of us remember, for example, the figure of the small Jewish businessman from Mississippi whose name, Fronthall (Max Frankenthal), became proverbial for extraordinary courage among his Confederate comrades.[11] Even the story of the Jewish members of the various robber bands, avoided like a pestilence by our apologetically-minded Jewish historical literature, is likely to yield many dramatic clues for truthful, if somewhat romanticizing, narratives. One need not be surprised if the new search should yield Jewish counterparts to Robin Hood, Schiller's *Raüber,* the Sicilian *Maffia* and those other legendary fighters for freedom, who had to resort to extra-legal means when law itself was abused by men and classes in power. Just as the *biryonim* of besieged ancient Jerusalem have found modern defenders among such nationalistically-minded historians as Joseph Klausner,[12] a complete marshaling of the available evidence for

[10] Dubnow, "Ahad Haam's Secret Circular" (Hebrew), in *Hatekufah,* vol. xxiv (1925) 416-20.

[11] Cohen, Henry, "A Modern Maccabean," in *Publications of the American Jewish Historical Society,* vol. vi (1897) 31-37.

[12] *Cf.,* in particular, Klausner's essay on John of Gischala and Simon son of Giyoras in his *Ke-she-umah nilhemet al herutah* (When a People Fights for Freedom), 3d ed. (Tel-Aviv 1944) p. 295-330.

medieval and modern Jewish outlaws will undoutedly add to the
lights, as well as the shadows, of Jewish history.

Even greater rewards await the narrator of the long and varie-
gated story of Jewish pioneering. In our day of easy communi-
cations it is difficult fully to grasp the hazards and discomforts
accompanying every medieval and early modern sea journey and
most of the travel by land. The pioneering efforts of early medieval
Jewry which went into the backward lands of France, Germany or
England in quest of ever new opportunities, and thus not only acquainted the nobility and peasantry of those countries with some
of the fruits of the most advanced civilization of the day, but also
taught them new methods of cultivating the soil, building houses
or healing the sick, have never yet been told with the necessary
attention to the tremendous psychological adjustments which settlement in western Europe involved to the average citizen of an
Arabic-speaking country. One merely has to exert one's imagination
slightly to envisage the risks taken by the Jewish traveller who
penetrated the dark forests of western and central Europe at a time
when, according to the law of the land (*jus albinagii*), any for-
eigner found on the road was a legitimate prey for highwaymen
(often called "nobles"), unless protected by some specific decree
of a more powerful monarch.[13] For an Oriental, even Spanish Jew
of the tenth century to settle in western Europe was a transition
far more drastic and perilous than that of a German refugee in our
day settling in Paraguay or New Caledonia. Did not an eleventh-
century Muslim judge of Toledo, Ṣa'id Al-Ṭulayṭuli, advance the
following biological explanation for the inferiority of Arab Spain's
Christian neighbors beyond the Pyrenees?

Because the sun does not shed its rays directly over their heads [the
judge wrote] their climate is cold and atmosphere clouded. Consequently their temperaments have become cold and their humors rude,
while their bodies have grown large, their complexion white and their
hair long. They lack withal sharpness of wit and penetration of intellect,
while stupidity and folly prevail among them.[14]

[13] *Cf.* further illustrations in my "Jewish Factor in Medieval Civilization," in
Proceedings of the American Academy for Jewish Research, vol. xii (1942) 1-48,
and especially p. 18 ff., 24 ff.

[14] Sa'id ibn-Aḥmad al-Ṭulayṭuli, *Tabaqat al-Umam* (Classification of Nations), ed. by L. Cheikho (Beirut 1912) p. 8 f., in Philip K. Hitti's English transl.
in his *History of the Arabs*, 4th ed. (London 1949) p. 526 f.

What courage must it have taken for Jews to settle in the capitals of Khazaria or Yemen and even try to persuade the rulers of these remote lands that Judaism was superior to all other creeds! What tremendous pioneering was involved in the penetration of tenth-century Kiev by a sufficient number of Jews to give one of its thoroughfares the name "Jewish gate"! Any informed reader can readily sense the tremendous drama hidden behind the dry, matter-of-fact travelogues of Benjamin of Tudela or Petahiah of Ratisbon or the brief hints concerning the peregrinations of pilgrims to the Holy Land.

Even closer home we have yet to be told in full and illuminating detail the story of the great civilizing and pioneering function which Jewish merchant adventurers played in opening up the American frontier. The Jews appeared on this continent in more or less permanent groups a short time after the Pilgrim Fathers. Often going into unexplored territories, they were among the first to establish themselves in parts of Georgia, Pennsylvania, Kentucky or southern Illinois. Even today a whole century after the California gold rush we know extremely little about those hardy Jews who helped push the American frontier to the West amidst greatest perils. A closer examination of these remarkable exploits on all continents, or even of the more "prosaic" story of the numerous peddlers and traveling salesmen who frequently were the strongest link with the outside world for far-flung isolated settlements,[15] would offer plenty of "drama" for the retelling of Jewish history in terms attractive to the rising generation.

Lest my intention be completely misunderstood, I do not herewith advocate the rewriting of Jewish history in the traditional biographical-anecdotal vein of Graetz, even if the biographies of saints and scholars be now replaced by the life stories of pioneers and fighters. Personally I have always been more interested in underling social and ideological trends than in their personalized symbols. Much as we all realize the pedagogic difficulty of teaching any kind of history to youngsters in terms of broader movements rather than personalities most of us certainly recognize that,

[15] *Cf.* Rudolf Glanz's "Notes on Early Jewish Peddling in America," in *Jewish Social Studies*, vol. vii (1945) 119-36; and Lee M. Friedman's *Pilgrims in a New Land* (Philadelphia 1948) p. 277-96, 430-38.

at least to mature and adult minds, such basic trends and movements explain the past much better than many of the accidents of
birth and personal career which affected the destinies of individual
leaders. Yet even the simple record of a people's struggle for survival, its tenacity in the face of untold adversities, its capability for
adjustment to varying, often extremely trying, circumstances, the
quiet rhythm of its daily chores highlighted by Herculean efforts
in emergencies—all these and other facets of an extraordinary mil-
lennial experience furnish ample material for an endless succession
of vital and illuminating stories which will serve to enlighten the
Jew, as well as his neighbor, and to help uplift his morale after the
traumatic experience of the Great Catastrophe.

NEW ASSIMILATION

A word of warning is in order, however, against exaggerations
in the novel direction. Were the total replacement of saint and
scholar by pioneer and hero to become the keynote of the new historiography, it would reflect a new attitude to life and the Jewish
heritage which, paradoxically, would be the expression of a deeper
and more far-reaching assimilation of non-Jewish ideologies than
that usually ascribed to extreme "assimilationists." It would be total
surrender of the traditional Jewish values to those dominant in
western civilization today. The ancient battle cry of the generation
of Samuel, "That we also may be like all the nations," has assumed
a new realism today. Like other nations Jews have a state and an
army of their own, they have their statesmen, heroes and pioneers,
the record of whose achievements makes their hearts overflow with
legitimate pride and joy.

This trend is insofar dangerous, however, as it is but a superficial reflection of surface realities. By itself this "me too" attitude
would necessarily place the Jewish people among the many small
nations, which have seen their theoretical "sovereignity," their
freedom of *ultimate* decision, gradually whittled down by the
clashes among the great powers. The Second World War has shown
that even a great country like Holland, with the vast resources of a
colonial empire behind it, was occupied in four days. Powerful

states like Czechoslovakia and Denmark lost their independence without firing a shot. It will take Israel many a generation before it will rival in military and industrial strength either Czechoslovakia or Holland.

More significantly, such an identification with other nations is historically untrue. The very rise of Israel, as stated above, has underscored the uniqueness of Jewish experience. None of these other nations were created by a diaspora, none of them continued, after their formation, to possess a diaspora vastly exceeding in size the population of the homeland. No matter what one thinks about Israel's absorptive capacity or the speed of Jewish assimilation in other nations were created by a diaspora, none of them continued, for Israel's population to equal that of the Jewish dispersion. Certainly the world's intense interest in everything occurring in Palestine, the almost daily comprehensive reportage in the world press concerning every strategic move there and every discussion thereof at the United Nations is owing to the existence of a far-flung Jewish dispersion much more than to the intrinsic significance of these events, if measured by the usual yardstick of international relations.

Nor is this an unprecedented situation in Jewish history. Let us not forget that, according to Israel's own historic recollection, it was a diaspora of slaves released from Egyptian bondage which established the First Commonwealth and that only after it had received its training in nationhood and religion by a foremost leader during a forty-year migration outside the Promised Land. There certainly is no question that the Second Commonwealth was created by the manpower, economic strength and political influence of the great Babylonian diaspora. All through the six centuries of that Commonwealth's existence the ever more dispersed Jewish communities far outnumbered the Jewish population of Palestine. The only possible, but unlikely, exception was the period of John Hyrcanus and Alexander Jannai at the turn of the first century B.C.E., during whose reign the rapid expansion of the Jewish kingdom and the speedy assimilation of conquered populations may have raised the total number of Judea's subjects above the corresponding total in other lands. But the subsequent political reversals, migrations and missionary successes quickly restored the balance in favor of the dispersion.[16]

In the very midst of these expansive movements there arose that remarkable apologetic literature of Hellenistic Jewry, which emphasized the differences rather than the similarities between Judaism and other creeds. In Palestine itself the Maccabean regime became ever more entangled in a hopeless conflict with the Pharisaic movement which, as its name indicates, stressed above everything else the disparity between Judaism and the surrounding civilizations. Conscious of world Jewry rather than of the Palestinian center alone, Pharisaism developed that unique combination of ethnic and religious mores and ideas which subsequently secured the Jewish people's immortality under varying civilizations. Long before the fall of Jerusalem a philosopher arose in neighboring Alexandria who tried to synthesize the Jewish tradition with the ideas dominant in the Graeco-Roman world civilization, not by drawing shallow parallels and identifications between them, but by pointing up their differences and by underscoring the uniqueness of the Jewish heritage.

This seems indeed, on a novel plane, the task of our generation and of those coming after us. Like Philo of Alexandria, but with far greater historic exactitude, we may emphasize the Mosaic—we usually prefer to call them Judeo-Christian—foundations of Western civilization. At the same time reviewing the further extraordinary evolution of the last two millennia and what they transmitted to us we cannot possibly escape the recognition of that uniqueness of Jewish experience. Again dissimilarities must be given equal weight with the similarities in the Jewish contributions to human civilization in the past, the present and the future.

We may indeed abandon the lachrymose conception of Jewish history. But this can only mean that we shall endeavor to see the ancient and medieval periods, the pre-emancipation and emancipation eras from all angles and perspectives and in relation to the world at large in which they unfolded. We shall have to emphasize the story of saints, martyrs and scholars as much as that of pioneers

---

[16] Our knowledge of ancient statistics is, of course, both limited and uncertain. *Cf.* my *Social and Religious History of the Jews* (New York 1937) III, 33 f.; or preferably in its forthcoming revised and much enlarged edition.

and fighters. Most of all we shall have to tell the story of the people itself, the ordinary Jew, who was neither a hero nor a saint, but who in his patient and unostentatious achievements was at least as responsible for the totality of Jewish history as were his more famous coreligionists. We must do this not only because as historians we owe, as do students of any other discipline, an obligation to the quest for truth and to the presenting of truth as we see it, but also as a matter of public service to the community which, today more than ever, needs many new guides through the perplexities of our age.

The Beginnings of the Jewish Doctrine of Immortality

BY LOUIS FINKELSTEIN

Jewish Theological Seminary of America

*D*URING the first millennium of its existence, Judaism was the scene of concentrated effort to win insights into the nature of existence. Judaism had appeared on the stage of history as the protagonist of monotheism and of human worth. But these conceptions were believed consistent with the inherent corporeality of both Deity and man.[1] Indeed, natural science and metaphysics of the patriarchal age, as generally understood even by many of the intelligent, denied all existence except physical. Man was believed to survive death; but only as a shade, which was a tenuous, vapor-like abstraction from the body.[2] The shade was itself a phys-

[1] *Cf.* the views expressed by John Skinner, in his commentary on *Genesis* 1:26, in *International Critical Commentary;* those of Professor Louis Ginzberg in his article, "Anthropomorphism," in *Jewish Encyclopedia;* Hehn, J., *Biblische und Babylonische Gottesidee* (Leipzig 1913) p. 288 ff.; Robinson, H. Wheeler, *The Religious Ideas of the Old Testament* (New York 1913) p. 60 ff.; Duhm, Hans, *Der Verkehr Gottes mit den Menschen im Alten Testament* (Tuebingen 1926) p. 12 ff.; Albright, W. F., *From the Stone Age to Christianity* (Baltimore 1940) p. 202; Pfeiffer, Robert H., *Introduction to the Old Testament* (New York 1941) p. 150, 174; Rowley, H. H., *The Re-Discovery of the Old Testament* (London 1945) p. 133; Frankfort, H. and H. A., Wilson, J. A. Jacobsen, Thorkild, Irwin, William A., *The Intellectual Adventure of Ancient Man* (Chicago 1946) p. 232.

[2] The frequent assertion that the ancient prophets did not know of the doctrine of the resurrection or immortality, and that these, in any form, made their appearance in Israel only after the exile, appears to be baseless. *Cf.* Noetscher, Friedrich, *Altorientalischer und altestamentlicher Auferstehungsglauben* (Würzburg 1926) p. 208 ff.; and especially Patton, L. B., *Spiritism and the Cult of the Dead in Antiquity* (New York 1921) p. 268 ff. (He comments: "The same process by which the 'other gods' were degraded from mighty beings, the rivals of Yahweh, to 'feeble ones' is seen in the case of spirits of the dead. In pre-prophetic days, they were believed to possess such

ical entity with approximately the relation to the living personality of visible droplets of steam to water. The spirit was, in fact, identified with the breath which, under certain circumstances, became visible and tangible.[3]

Because the shade was less than the quick body, its appearance produced a jolt or shock like that of seeing a deformed person. The spirits, lacking the gifts and power of the living, were thought to envy them, and therefore had to be appeased with sacrifices, a form of legalized blackmail, rather than a free-will offering.

In this primitive age, to call God, as the prophets understood Him, a "spirit" would have been blasphemy, or worse. God had to be distinguished from His creatures and especially from posthu-

large powers that the temptation was strong to render them some of the worship due to Yahweh alone; in the prophetic period they were stripped of their energy so completely that they became mere shadows, unable to help or hurt, to whom it was futile either to pray or to offer sacrifice."); also Wohlgemuth, J., *Die Unsterblichkeitslehre in der Bibel* (Berlin 1899) p. 5 ff.; Oesterley, W. O. E., *Life, Death, and Immortality: Studies in the Psalms* (London 1911) p. 146 ff.; Quell, Gottfried, *Die Auffassung des Todes in Israel* (Leipzig 1925) p. 28 ff.; and Kaufmann, E., *Toledot ha-emunah ha-yisraelit,* vol. ii, part 2 (1945) p. 534 ff.

[3] This tenuous and deformed quality of the ghost was for the primitive consistent with a belief in its overwhelming power to do mischief. *Cf.*, however, Kaufmann, *op. cit.,* p. 544 ff. Superstition even in the Middle ages preserved this paradoxical belief at once in the vapor-like, vague condition of the spirit, and of its fearful energy. In later prophetic tradition, there was a tendency to negate the *power* of the dead, and on the part of the great literary prophets, a reluctance to refer in any way to the "shades." From the days of Hosea until the exilic period, they are ignored, just as are the "angels of the Lord." (I have discussed this subject at length in *The Pharisees* [Phila. 1938] p. 161 ff.). No acceptable explanation has yet been offered for the curious fact that the word *rephaim* is used both for ghosts and for primitive giants. Perhaps the word suggested supernatural beings, and was applied therefore equally to the ghost separated from the body, and to the demons or half-gods of the age of giants. It is evidence of the complete vindication of monotheism during the exile, that the prophets of that period and later felt so little hesitation in using Canaanite mythological images for the effectiveness of their teaching. Thus the author of *Isaiah,* ch. 13-14, draws a picture of the *sheol,* populated by the *rephaim,* as might be conceived by any Canaanite writer. Ezekiel, his contemporary, has no qualms about referring to *Danel,* whom we now know to have been a hero of the Canaanite epics. (For a full discussion, see Spiegel, S., in *Louis Ginzberg—Jubilee Volume* [New York 1945] p. 305 ff., and literature there cited.) The post-exilic psalms quite freely refer to *rephaim,* life in the *sheol,* and the imagery of Canaanite mythology, generally (See Albright, *Archeology and the Religion of Israel,* [Baltimore 1942] p. 128).

mous shades. The prophets could not assign the all-merciful Deity to the realm of beings which included the spirits who were resentful of their own impotence; who were worshiped from fear and not love; communion with whom might be a sad necessity, but never a welcome opportunity. God was beyond death, but He was equally beyond any ghost-like immortality. For the prophets, the conception of God as such a "spirit" was intolerable. He might be invisible to mortal eyes,[4] unless He chose to reveal Himself, but that was consistent with real corporeality. To their mind, God was man's Creator, not his inferior; He was man's benefactor, not his enemy; communion with Him was man's highest good, not a curse.

The Scriptures, recoiling from the identification of God with the spiritual beings of contemporary thought and parlance, emphasize His corporeality. The anthropomorphisms of the Pentateuch are not therefore to be regarded as simply concessions to primitive thought. They are part of the prophetic struggle against the confusion of the Deity with the popular "spirits" and the shades of animistic doctrine. In Scripture, God essentially resembles living man, having shape as well as a spirit. The teaching of *Genesis* that God created man in His image has a twofold purpose—to stress the dignity of man, and also to enhance reverence for God. But, from the beginning, the body and spirit of God were not, like man's, inseparable. God could take on many shapes, for He was Divine, not human. He was not limited by space. To behold His awesome face was to court death; but there was a Face, there was a Form; there was corporeality.[5]

The Scriptures therefore offer no apology for their constant reference to the physical appearance of God, to His descent to earth on inspection of His handiwork;[6] to His speaking to man, "mouth to mouth";[7] to His appearance before Moses, so that the Prophet

---

[4] *Cf. Exodus* 33:18 *et al.*

[5] The importance attached to the belief in the corporeality of God was such that the doctrine survived until comparatively late. See below, for the struggle between the Pharisees and the Sadducees regarding it. But even within the Pharisaic sect there were those who, until late in history, asserted the corporeality of God. See *The Pharisees*, vol. i, p. 323.

[6] *Gen.* 11:5.

[7] *Num.* 12:8.

could not see His Face, and yet could catch a glimpse of Him as His glory passed by.[8] At Sinai, the people of Israel saw their God.[9] Isaiah beheld Him in the Temple.[10] Ezekiel beheld a complicated vision, which he describes in detail, including in it a verse,[11] which the rabbinic sages forbid[12] one to ponder over, for it almost expressly states that God has human form.

Modern research realizes that this anthropomorphism of the prophets and the Scriptural writers was consistent with an insight into the transcendent and spiritual nature of the Deity. For the greatest prophets, anthropomorphism was apparently a pedagogical device, similar to that employed by the geometrician who trains his pupils in abstract thought through the use of diagrams. The truths of theology had to be inculcated to children and to adults whose consciousness was not advanced far beyond that of children. Even the prophets and teachers who were able to conceive of God as a Spirit, of a nature far different from that of the ghosts of the cemetery, spoke of Him in human terms to make His Being intelligible to their hearers, and respected by them.[13]

The ancient, like the modern teacher, thus resorted to imagery, which at once revealed and concealed the truth, giving men an insight into reality, and yet withholding from them—because of their inability to grasp it—the nature of the reality, of which they are granted a glimpse.

[8] *Exodus* 33:20.
[9] *Ibid.* 24:10.
[10] *Isa.* 6:1.
[11] *Ezek.* 1:27.
[12] *B. Hagigah* 13 b.
[13] The Pentateuch has not yet been fully studied as a pedagogic work. *Cf.*, however, Julian Morgenstern's fascinating work, *A Jewish Interpretation of Genesis* (Cincinnati 1920). It is interesting to notice that the Pentateuch grades its lessons, as it were. The first chapters are addressed primarily to young children; they therefore employ the simplest, most naive imagery. The technique is reminiscent of that used in the Tannaitic Midrashim, where the *Sifra* (the *midrash* to *Leviticus*), being the first to be studied at school, and thus addressed to young people, opens with two chapters which are frankly exercises in the rabbinic method of hermeneutics, applying the formulae and terms of that method to the easily understood issues, rather than complicated legal questions. It seems probable, too, that the mishna of *Berakot*, which deals with the familiar subject of the liturgy, and is almost wholly semi-haggadic, was placed at the beginning to provide such an easy introduction to the difficult text.

While the prophets and the psalmists repeatedly discuss the physical appearance of God, they are significantly silent regarding the spirit in man. Man's kinship to God could not, for them, inhere in the lowly human spirit, the natural and inevitable habitat of which was the *sheol*. If man had dignity, it was because his face, rather than his soul, bore the stamp of his divine origin. Men were equal not because after death they all were insignificant ghosts, but because in mundane life, they alike reflected divine reality.

Rephaim or shades are mentioned by the prophets only in passing, in poetical visions, utilizing the common vocabulary of contemporary metaphysics. The widespread animism, the worship of the dead, the superstitions associated with the rites of ancestor worship, made the very thought of "shades" abhorrent to prophecy. The patriarchs are "gathered unto their people";[14] and King David "slept with his fathers;"[15] but these expressions are designedly ambiguous. They do not define whether it is the body or the spirit which is reunited to family and kin.

The rabbinic sages struggled hard, and vainly, to find a single unmistakable reference to the immortality of the soul or the resurrection of the dead in the Pentateuch;[16] and only a few, and by no means explicit, suggestions testify to the recognition of these doctrines in prophetic literature.

This silence of the prophets does not mean that they were either ignorant of the general belief in man's immortality as a spirit; or rejected it. On the contrary, they shared their neighbors' conviction that man is inherently immortal. They could not enter into any discussion of it or use it in their message, for in the form in which it prevailed in their generation, it could not be integrated into their philosophy of religion. Its relation to contemporary paganism compelled religious teachers to ignore it.

Such was the aversion of early Judaism to any assertion of the

---

[14] *Gen.* 25:8, 17; 35:29; 50:29, 33. These passages are assigned by higher critics to the Priestly Code, and according to them are of comparatively late origin. This would only emphasize the survival of clan psychology.

[15] I *Kings* 2:10. This is so agreeable a prospect that Bath-sheba does not hesitate to refer to its imminence in her conversation with David regarding the succession (I *Kings* 1:21).

[16] B. *Sanhedrin* 90b ff.

belief in immortal spirits, that the immortality of Enoch[17] and Elijah[18] is described as a physical translation into heaven. Yet both translations are portrayed with a reticence suggestive of theological and metaphysical perplexity. Both saints were taken into heaven, and were immortal; but obviously they did not become gods or demigods. What then was their status? The sacred writers avoid the issue, which was fraught with infinite complexity, and could be clarified only with the rise of a new metaphysic.

The development of the metaphysic which was to clarify the relation of man's spirit to his body and to God, and to open the way to the integration of the belief in human immortality with monotheism and religious ethics, was the work of several centuries. Indeed, the full impact of the new metaphysic on religious thought became apparent only in the Hellenistic and the Maccabean Age. Yet faint traces of the changing concepts are discernible in earlier generations.

The later prophetic writers stress, rather than avoid, emphasis on God's transcendence. They insist that He is beyond human conception, invisible not simply because He conceals Himself in darkness,[19] to protect the possible observer from death,[20] but because His essence is beyond recognition by man's material senses. Thus in his prayer at the dedication of the Temple (which in its present form reflects apparently the views of the exilic age), King Solomon

[17] *Gen.* 5:24. The extensive Enoch literature of later times proves that the belief in his immortality as a physical being was never obliterated. The obvious aversion of the majority of the rabbinic sages to assert Enoch's immortality (he is unmentioned in either tannaitic literature or the two talmudim) simply preserves the biblical attitude toward him. *Cf.* Ginzberg, L., *Legends of the Jews*, vol. v, p. 131; Cassuto, M. D., *Me-adam ad Noah* (Jerusalem 1944) p. 165. Perhaps the rejection of Enoch was emphasized in early rabbinic times precisely because of the importance he assumed among the sectarians. It is interesting to note, in connection with the rather low opinion held of Enoch by the rabbinic authorities, that Rabbi Jose ben Halafta, who rationalistically denies that Moses or Elijah ever ascended to Heaven alive, does not even take the trouble to make this negation of Enoch (*B. Sukkah 5a*).

[18] II *Kings* 2:1 ff.; *Mal.* 3:23. The immortality of Elijah as a physical being is repeatedly emphasized in rabbinic literature, and even in the Liturgy. Thus the benedictions following the prophetic reading on the Sabbath include a prayer for the coming of Elijah.

[19] I *Kings* 8:12. See especially the reading of the Septuagint.

[20] *Exodus* 33:20.

asks: "But will God in truth dwell on the earth? Behold the heaven and the heaven of the heavens cannot contain Thee; how much less the house that I have built" (I *Kings* 8:27).[21] Deutero-Isaiah makes the transcendence of God a basic theme.[22] The difference between the ways of God and man, and between divine and human thought, rather than their similarity, is the burden of his prophecy.

A generation later, Zechariah breaks away from all precedent in his portrayal of the prophetic vision. The word of God came to him, he maintained, not directly, but through visions, which an angel interpreted for him.[23]

In the fourth century B.C.E. we discover religious writers so impressed with the transcendence of God, and His difference from all physical being, that they regard the pronunciation and even the use of a proper name for Him as irreverent. They say *elohim* (simply "God") rather than YHWH; and when they come across the word YHWH in the older literature, they read it *elohim*.[24] The ancient name of God, YHWH, has become for them ineffable. It is the *shem ha-mephorash,* the name which is "read otherwise than as it is written."[25]

In the debate about the justice of God in the book of *Job,* the word YHWH is regularly replaced by *elohim*.[26] The writer of *Chronicles* replaces the word YHWH by *elohim* even in citations from older writings.[27]

The teachers in this later generation, who so emphasized the transcendence of God, were dealing with a new theological peril. They were no longer concerned lest their description of God as spirit lead to animism or ancestor worship. The concept of God as Spirit no longer involved disparagement of His being to the level of the "shades" of the earlier metaphysics. Men had now come to recognize the "spiritual" as something more than the material; to

[21] *Cf. Isa.* 66:1.

[22] *Isa.* 55:8 *et al.* This passage is often attributed to a "Trito-Isaiah," but that issue of authorship is irrelevant to the main theological question.

[23] *Zech.* 4:1.

[24] See Jacob, B., *Im Namen Gottes* (Berlin 1903) p. 165 ff.

[25] Schaeder, Hans Heinrich, *Iranische Beiträge,* vol. i (Halle 1930) p. 205 ff.

[26] The term *eloah* is sometimes used as a variant in the discussion; the tetragrammaton occurs only in the Prologue, the Epilogue, and the chapters in which God answers Job out of the whirlwind.

[27] *Cf.* Jacob, *loc. cit.*

describe God as non-anthropomorphic was now to see in Him a Being beyond man, rather than below him.

But there was another danger—that the concept of God might become so abstract as to lose all significance for most men. The prophets of this generation wanted men to recognize the spirituality of God; but they also wanted them to continue to recognize in Him their Father, their Creator, their loving Leader and Guide.

The term *elohim,* which the sacred writers now used to suggest God's transcendence, was employed by philosophical skeptics to indicate the distance between Him and man, to create an unbridgeable gulf between His Being and that of nature. It was only a step from the premise that God was beyond all human experience to the conclusion that He was also beyond all human interest and concern.

One of the traces of the apprehension which this development evoked in the minds of the pietists of the third century B.C.E. was their reversion to the use of the name YHWH at least in writing. In their unwillingness to pronounce the name, they now substituted the pronunciation *adonai* for it, reserving the word *elohim* for those passages in which it actually occurred.[28]

---

[28] It is possible that a more specific development brought about the substitution of *adonai* for the rather abstract and philosophical *elohim*—the identification by many Hellenists of the God of Jerusalem with Zeus and the Syrian god of heaven, Baal Shamem. Antiochus tried to enforce this identification by setting up a statue of Baal Shamem in the Temple of Jerusalem (See Bickermann, E., *Der Gott d. Makkabäer* [Berlin 1937] p. 112; Ginsberg, H. L., *Studies in the Book of Daniel* [New York 1948] p. 44-45.) But it may be assumed that this identification was not initiated by him; and that his persecution, which was brought. to a climax by this desecration of the Temple, reflected support of views current in Judaea itself. The situation seems clearly analogous to that which occurred in later times, when Hadrian turned the Temple into a sanctuary of Jupiter Capitolinus. Then, too, the prevalence of Jews who saw no distinction between the God of their fathers and the Roman god of heaven, and regarded the issue as simply one of unimportant nomenclature, compelled pious Jews to revert to the original pronunciation of the tetragrammaton even in secular conversation, such as personal greeting (see Mishna *Berakot* end). Rabbi Hanina ben Teradyon was apparently among those responsible for this innovation, and it was asserted in later times that his cruel death was in punishment for his pronunciation of the Divine Name as it is written (*B. Aboda Zara 18a*). Abba Saul, apparently taking note of this practice, declares that those who pronounce the Name as it is written lose their share in the future world (Mishna *Sanhedrin* 10.1). But even those who rejected the extreme practice of pronouncing the Name as it is written, reverted to the use of the form *adonai*, which in that generation, had been replaced

These developments have left a curious imprint on the Third Book of the *Psalms*,[29] which was like Book II compiled in this age. The earlier hymns in Book III (73-83), like all in Book II, represent the word YHWH by *elohim;* the later ones in Book III (84-89) re-

widely by *elohim.* This can be seen from the difference in the form of the prayers which come from the first century, and which generally use *elohenu* in the introductory formula, whereas those of the Hadrianic times and later use *adonai elohenu.* See further my discussions of the subject in *Jewish Quarterly Review,* vol. xvi (1925) 8 ff.; *Harvard Theological Review,* vol. xxxvi (1943) 296 ff.

[29] The discussion and analysis of the various books of the Psalms have been impeded by the failure to give sufficient emphasis to the fact of their transmission as the repertoire of particular guilds, in purely oral form, and their commitment to writing only at a late period, perhaps when they were incorporated into the Psalter itself. Hence it has come about that these books retain in writing the form *elohim* in the psalms where that form was used in the daily practice and repetition. Whether it was also used in the chanting of the hymns in the Temple remains undetermined. Thus Psalm 53, which is identical with Psalm 14, replaces the tetragrammaton each time with *elohim.* Obviously Psalm 14 was committed to writing and transmitted at a time when the tetragrammaton was still pronounced in its original form; Psalm 53 retains the form in which the hymn was rehearsed by the guild, which included it in its particular repertoire, and thus transmits only the form *elohim.* The guilds may of course have used informal scripts to help them remember the words, but these would be in the form in which the hymns would be sung in rehearsal, and not at the solemn service of the Temple. Because the term *elohim* was recognized as a cypher, a careless copyist would sometimes, in his forgetfulness, write the tetragrammaton in his transcription. This occurred according to the Massoretic text in *Psalms* 47:3 and 48:1. (In *Psalms* 46:8, 12, the tetragrammaton occurs; perhaps the original pronunciation or the form *adonai* was used in the refrain.) In *Psalms* 72:18, the tetragrammaton was written to guide the responding audience in the regular service, but *elohim* follows it, because it was the form used in rehearsal. In modern times, Jews use the symbol *ha-shem,* "the Name," instead of the tetragrammaton, except in reading Scripture or in prayer. In the rehearsal of hymns, too, it is the usual form for cantors, choirs, and students to replace the pronunciation *adonai* with *ha-shem.* In the transcription of hymns there will be a wide diversity of practice, often by the same person, who will at one time write *ha-shem,* in accordance with his practice in rehearsal; at other times he will write out *adonai* so as to protect himself and other readers, when looking at the script. This corresponds to the confusion in the Psalms of Book II, which sometimes revert to the tetragrammaton, though in their rehearsals they never pronounced it. Books IV and V of the *Psalms* were compiled when the pronunciation, *adonai,* had become universal, and hence they always include the tetragrammaton where it properly belongs. For a full discussion of the dates of the Psalm collections, see Pfeiffer, *op. cit.* p. 626 ff.

tain the orthography YHWH.[30] This phenomenon, which has puzzled ancient commentators and modern critics, simply reflects the fact that toward the end of the period when the collections took form, the form YHWH returned into use in writing, but under the distinctive pronunciation, *adonai*, which has been retained in the synagogue until this day.[31]

The new metaphysic, which stressed the transcendence and spirituality of God, is further reflected in such works as the *Septuagint* and *Ben Sira*. In these works, products of the third and early second century B.C.E., anthropomorphisms of Scripture are avoided or explained. The fear of the religious teacher in this later period was not that his reader would fail to recognize the reality of an abstract God; but that he would fail to appreciate the spirituality of the real God.

Such a profound change of emphasis and form of expression could not go unchallenged. This is evident from two phenomena of the third and second centuries B.C.E. The Passover Haggadah preserves a document, which I have elsewhere[32] described as "the old-

[30] Psalm 109 was composed by a singer, through a combination of parts taken from Psalms 57 and 60 (much as modern collectors of hasidic hymns, which were sung in European ghetto communities, sometimes produce curious combinations of elements taken from different songs, into a new composition). The word which is written *adonai* in the Massoretic text of *Psalms* 57:10 is replaced by the tetragrammaton in the Massoretic text of *Psalms* 109:4, indicating that the author of this psalm presumed that *adonai* is the equivalent of the tetragrammaton, and therefore that in his days that is the way in which the tetragrammaton was pronounced. The dates of Psalms 78 and 105 can be fixed; they clearly belong, as I have indicated elsewhere, to the period of the Egyptian domination of Palestine (*Harvard Theological Review, loc. cit.,* p. 299 ff.). This is demonstrated by their omission from the list of the plagues which the Egyptians suffered at the time of the exodus, those which might seem particularly humiliating (lice and boils, in Psalm 78; boils in Psalm 105). Psalm 78 also omits the plague of darkness, because, according to Egyptian antisemitic teaching, the God of Israel was identical with Seth the god of eclipses, storms, and darkness. (*Ibid.,* p. 301.) In Psalm 105, this plague is taken out of its order and given a special verse (105:28) in order to enable the Psalmist to clarify "darkness" as an agent of God, not as His personality. The date of these psalms of course *ad quem* indicates that the collection was still open in the third century B.C.E. Psalm 78 still uses the form *elohim* instead of the tetragrammaton.

[31] Hence in the prayer of Daniel (*Dan.* 9:4 ff.) the tetragrammaton and the form *adonai* predominate.

[32] *Harvard Theological Review,* vol. xxxi (1938) 291 ff.

est midrash," and which, from both internal and external evidence, appears to be a product of the late third century B.C.E. In this document, the core of the prescribed service for Passover eve, especially stress is laid, peculiarly enough, on God's visible appearance to deliver Israel at the time of the exodus. The interpretation is so forced, and so out of harmony with the spirit of its age as we know it from other literary products, as to suggest the desire to drive home a particular lesson to the people assembled to celebrate the Passover in Jerusalem. The high priests, whose views are reflected throughout the document, apparently believed heretical the current doctrine which rejected any depiction of God in human form, and that it had to be extirpated. They attempted to inculcate their particular orthodoxy through the prescribed Passover lesson, which told how ancient Israelites redeemed from Egypt eternally saw God.

This interpretation of the ancient midrash is confirmed by the record, preserved in the Talmud, of a controversy between the Pharisaic and Sadducean sects, concerning the ritual of the Day of Atonement. As is well known, the Pharisees insisted that in the ceremonies of the holy day, the high priest had to place the incense on the fire *after* he had entered the Holy of Holies. The Sadducees maintained that the act must be performed *before* his advance into the most sacred precinct. The controversy could not, like others, have originated in a difference of custom. There was only one high priest, one Temple, and one ritual of the Day of Atonement. The Sadducean tradition presumably preserves the actual practice of the high priests; for the sect of Sadducees was built about the high priests. The Pharisees, in this instance, adhered to the literal interpretation of Scripture, and condemned the usual Temple practice as contrary to the will of God.[33]

The Sadducean high priests departed from the word of Scripture, apparently because they believed that God appeared in visible form in the Holy Shrine, above the place of the ancient Ark of the Covenant. They believed, too, that if they entered and beheld the Vision of God, they would instantly die. The incense burning

---

[33] See *The Pharisees*, vol. i, p. 188 ff.; and references there given. See also *Harvard Theological Review* (1938) p. 309. *Cf.* in addition Morgenstern, Julian, in *Hebrew Union College Annual*, vol. xii-xiii (1937-38) 9 ff.; *American Journal of Semitic Languages and Literatures*, vol. lv (1938) 19 ff.

on the fire, which they brought with them, was intended both as an offering to God, and by its smoke, as a protection against seeing the glory of God.

The Pharisees, who considered the conception of a visible God repugnant to Judaism, and held that God could only be described metaphorically as dwelling in the Holy of Holies, tried to dramatize their view, by demanding that the high priest act upon it during the solemn service of the Day of Atonement. Accordingly, they forbade the high priest to seek protection from the supposed vision of God in a smoke screen of incense; and demanded that he place the incense on the fire only after he had entered the holy chamber.

A careful study of Scripture demonstrates that the controversy, which has come down to us as one of the two great sects, had its origin in earlier times; in fact, is suggested in the words of the Bible itself. The Bible records various examples of incense offerings, outside the prescribed ritual. In each of them the Sadducean form of the ritual was followed. Thus Nadab and Abihu, presenting their forbidden offering to God, "took either of them his censer and put incense thereon, and offered strange fire before the Lord" (*Lev.* 10:1). On the other hand, the ritual of the Day of Atonement as described in *Leviticus,* chapter XVI, clearly supports the Pharisaic view. It reads: "And he shall take a censer full of burning coals of fire from off the altar before the Lord, and his hands full of sweet incense, beaten small, and bring it within the veil, and he shall put the incense upon the fire before the Lord" (*Ibid.,* 16:12 ff.). The ancient rabbinic comment on this verse sums up its meaning quite accurately; it is "place it there," *i.e.,* within the Holy of Holies.

The insistence of the high priests and the Sadducees generally on the primitive custom, in violation of the literal command of Scripture, indicates the antiquity of the controversy. Clearly, the high priests of the Hellenistic and Maccabean eras were too much impressed with the concept of a visible God, appearing in the Holy of Holies, to accept the natural meaning of the Scriptural word, which commanded them to appear within the sacred chamber unprotected by the screen of incense.

The discovery of the spirituality of God was associated with the discovery of the spirituality of man. The thinkers of the third and second centuries B.C.E. who recognized the error of visualizing God in man's image, also identified anew the divine image in man. As the debate regarding the essence of God approached its climax, there was also a second debate regarding the essence of man. Thus, describing man's ultimate fate, one writer is led to suggest: "Then shall the dust return to the earth as it was, and the spirit shall return unto God who gave it" (*Eccl.* 12:7). Before he had reached this conclusion, the author had had moments of skepticism, when he had wondered whether "the spirit of man goeth upward and the spirit of the beast goeth downward to the earth" (*Ibid.*, 3:19). The question he raised suggests the rise of the view that man's spirit finds its destiny not as a shade in *sheol* (where the spirits of the animals are still believed to be consigned) but in heaven.[34]

The author of Psalm 49 shares most emphatically the view that the spirits of the righteous, at least, ascend to heaven; those of the wicked alone are consigned to the *sheol*.

> This is the way of them that are foolish,
> And of those who after them approve their sayings.
> Like sheep they are appointed for the nether-world;
> Death shall be their shepherd;
> And the upright shall have dominion over them in the
>   morning;
> And their form shall be for the nether-world to wear away,
> That there be no habitation for it.
> But God will redeem my soul from the power of the
>   nether-world;
> When He shall receive me.   (*Ps.* 49:14 ff.)

The psalmist is engaging in no metaphors. He believes literally that man has a soul, which, if he be righteous, will be redeemed by God; and only if he be wicked, will be condemned to the *sheol*. It is true of the wicked alone, that "their grave is their home forever,

[34] Lector M. Friedmann, in his *Meir Ayyin al Ha-Haggadah* (Vienna 1901) p. 109, remarks: "Because many in Israel courted martyrdom (in the Maccabean days) because of their trust in the future life, and refused to steel themselves for war against their enemies, so that (when attacked) on the sabbath day, they met death, without having made any effort to save themselves, the psalmist was compelled to remind them that the 'heavens are the heavens of the Lord, but the earth hath He given to the sons of men; the dead praise not the Lord etc. . . .'" It is clear from this comment that Friedmann realized that the simple meaning of the passage contained a challenge to the doctrine of immortality as usually interpreted; and also that he attributed the psalm and the *Hallel* to the Maccabean period.

and their dwelling-places to all generations" (*Ibid.*, v. 12). The validity of this interpretation is demonstrated by the bitter opposition this view evokes among other psalmists.

> Shall Thy mercy be declared in the grave?
> Or Thy faithfulness in destruction?
> Shall Thy wonders be known in the dark?
> And Thy righteousness in the land of forgetfulness?

asks the writer of Psalm 88 (vv. 12-13). The author of Psalm 89 seems almost to address his words to the Hasidean believers, when he says:

> O remember how short my time is;
> For what vanity hast Thou created all the children of men!
> What man is he that liveth and shall not see death,
> That shall deliver his soul from the power of the grave?
> (vv. 48-49).

Perhaps the most emphatic challenge to the doctrine of immortality of the soul, in the Hasidean sense, is included in the ancient psalm, preserved not only in the canon, but also part of the ritual of the synagogue, which reads:

> The heavens are the heavens of the Lord,[35]
> But the earth hath He given to the sons of men.
> The dead praise not the Lord,
> Neither any that go down into the nether-world
> (*Ps.* 115:16-17).[36]

We may, out of sheer perversity, insist that this emphatic denial that the souls of the righteous can "offer praise" and that God has given man heaven as well as earth has any particular significance. But the struggles of the scholars and the commentators to reconcile these passages with Pharisaic theology indicate the difficulties

[35] The Septuagint, Peshitta, and the Targum all render the first words of this passage, "The highest heavens belong to the Lord," obviously with a view to mitigating the negation of immortality apparently implied in the Massoretic text.

[36] The fact that songs of thanksgiving virtually contain a stereotype renunciation of immortality, or at least aver the ability of the dead to participate in divine worship, cannot be accidental. Apparently, it was the custom of the priests to utilize the occasion of thanksgiving (which seems to have brought many to pilgrimages) to inculcate a rejection of the belief that the dead can intercede with God. The importance of this teaching may be indicated by the requirement that the person bringing his tithe to the Temple assert that he "has not given any of it to the dead" (*Deut.* 26:14).

involved in the literal interpretation.[37] Thus an ancient homilist paraphrases the passage as follows:

The heavens are the heavens of the Lord. Twice the Lord removed His presence into the heavens. The first occasion was in the time of Adam, as it is written, "God is gone amidst shouting, the Lord amidst the sound of the horn" (*Ps.* 47:6). The second was in the time of Manasseh, as it is written, "I will go and return to My place" (*Hosea* 5:15). *The dead shall not praise the Lord.* Is it possible for the dead to praise the Lord? (Why then does the psalmist say this?) But these are the dead of the heathen. *Nor those who descend into the pit.* These are the seven nations whom the Holy One, blessed be He, will cast into Gehenna, as it is said, "There is Elam and all her multitude . . . Asshur is there and all her company . . . There is Meshech, Tubal, and all her multitude . . . There are the princes of the north, all of them, and all them, and all the Zidonians . . . There is Edom, her kings and all her princes . . . These shall Pharoah see, and shall be comforted over all his multitude" (*Ezek.* 32:24-31). You might be led to suppose that this would be the fate of Israel as well, therefore the Scriptures say, "But we shall bless the Lord from this time forth and forever; hallelujah."[38]

This interpretation is not isolated,[39] but typical. The comments indicate the Pharisaic approach to the problems set by this ancient polemic text.

The universal acceptance of the interpretation put on these passages by Pharisaism shows how effectively the Hasidean and Pharisaic teachers molded the mind of the religious world of later generations. But, in their original setting, the main purpose of these verses could hardly have been other than to emphasize the proto-

[37] *Midrash Hallel,* ed. by A. Jellinek, in *Bet Ha-Midrash,* vol. v, p. 101; reprinted by I. D. Eisenstein, in *Ozar Ha-Midrashim,* vol. i, 133a.

[38] Cited in *Yalkut Ha-Makiri, Psalms* 14:4, ed. Buber 40a. The passage is not found in *Midrash Tehillim.* Possibly it was deleted by some form of censorship, because of its implications regarding Israel's persecutors. Even as cited in *Yalkut Ha-Makiri,* it seems incomplete. *Cf.,* however, the midrash published by J. Mann in *Hebrew Union College,* vol. xiv (1939) 311.

[39] The comment of Rabbi Hiyya b. Yose in *Midrash Tehillim,* 30.3, ed. Buber 117b, and *Pesikta Rabbati* II, ed. Friedmann 5b, to the effect that only in the power of speech do the righteous alive differ from the righteous dead, would seem to reflect a desire to reconcile the literal interpretation of Psalm 115 with the usual concept of immortality. On the other hand, the homilist who, in *Debarim Rabbah,* ed. S. Liebermann, end, asserts that the righteous dead do praise the Lord, simply interprets the word, "dead," in Psalms 115:17, as referring not to physical but spiritual death, for the wicked "even when they are alive are considered dead."

Sadducean denial that the real life is that of the afterworld; that the heavens belong to the spirits of men, as the earth belongs to their bodies; that the dead can praise the Lord.

The emphatic negations of the doctrine of immortality are valuable demonstrations of its prevalence. Once this fact is recognized, new importance attaches to the vehement opposition to the doctrine included in the *Book of Job,* composed at the very latest two centuries before the *Book of Ecclesiastes.* The *Book of Job* does not ignore the concept of human immortality. The author is more than unaware of the belief. His writing suggests a keen appreciation of the new idea, of its place in theology, and of its spread among certain groups of people. His pietist debaters, the friends of Job, neither affirm nor reject the doctrine. But Job emphatically denounces it.

> For there is hope of a tree,
> If it be cut down, that it will sprout again,
> And that the tender branch thereof will not cease.
> Though the root thereof wax old in the earth,
> And the stock thereof die in the ground;
> Yet through the scent of water it will bud,
> And put forth boughs like a plant.
> But man dieth and lieth low;
> Yea man perisheth, and where is he?
> As the waters fail from the sea,
> And the river is drained dry;
> So man lieth down and riseth not;
> Till the heavens be no more, they shall not awake,
> Nor be roused out of their sleep (*Job* 14:7-12).

With specific reference to the common doctrine that man's soul is preserved in the *sheol* to be reawakened to life, at the end of time, Job continues:

> Oh that Thou wouldest hide me in the Sheol,
> That Thou wouldest keep me secret until Thy wrath be past,
> That Thou wouldest appoint me a set time, and remember me!
> If a man die, may he live again?
> All the days of my service would I wait,
> Till my relief should come
> Thou wouldest call and I would answer Thee,
> Thou wouldest have a desire to the work of Thy hands . . .
> The waters wear the stones;
> The overflowings thereof wash away the dust of the earth;

So Thou destroyest the hope of man.
Thou prevailest for ever against him, and he passeth;
Thou changest his countenance and sendest him away.
His sons come to honor, and he knoweth it not;
And they are brought low, but he regardeth them not.
But his flesh grieveth for him,
And his soul mourneth over him (*Job* 14:13-22).

This is not simply a reversion to the old prophetic unwillingness to mention the *rephaim*. The author of *Job* eagerly discusses
them. He concludes that man has no posthumous existence, save
possibly that of the shade, without either sensation or knowledge.
The friends of Job have no answer to this challenge. They insist
that all men are sinful, and therefore justly receive mundane pun-
ishments. They also insist that the righteous find mercy and restoration at the hands of God. But they decline to respect unequivocally
Job's negation of man's future. Apparently the author is here describing the state of mind of certain pietists in the period when the
long debate about man's future condition was being carried on.
Orthodoxy was not yet prepared to assert man's immortality, as it
did two centuries later; but neither was it prepared to reject it, out
of hand. Job insists that it must do one or the other.

Job's negation of immortality and resurrection indicates that the
conflict regarding these teachings, which culminated in the break
between Pharisaism and Sadducism in the second century B.C.E.,
had attained great force at least two hundred and fifty years earlier.
It also confirms the hypothesis here presented that the issue of the
immortality of the soul was associated with the issue of the spirituality of God. Factors other than metaphysical and philosophical
disagreement entered into the discussion. The groups which di-
verged on these issues were animated by opposing psychological,
cultural, and sociological views which have been discussed elsewhere. But associated with these were ethical and philosophical
considerations regarding the nature of man, the Universe, and the
Deity, which played an important role in the emergence and shaping of the final doctrine.

The evidence further demonstrates that the belief in man's immortality as a spiritual being was by no means confined to the

Alexandrian Jewish philosophers, who were under the influence of Greek thought. The doctrine of human immortality developed side by side with that of the resurrection of the body; and so far as Judaism is concerned both had their origin in Palestine. Finally, while it cannot be doubted that the prevalence of these doctrines in other peoples helped encourage their rise and spread in Judaism, the main force leading to their emergence was inherent in the maturing of the Jewish mind and of Jewish society.

Errors of Method in the Study of Religion

෫ஓ *BY THEODORE H. GASTER*

Dropsie College

*A*NYONE who takes the trouble to review the definitions of religion which have been proposed during the past fifty years will see at once that the term has been applied to two quite different things. It has been taken, on the one hand, to denote a form of personal experience—a psychic state or a behavioristic response;[1] on the other, a communal institution—a body of public rites and ob-

---

[1] Thus, Warde Fowler defines it as "the feeling of awe, anxiety, doubt, or fear, which is aroused in the mind by something that cannot be explained by a man's experience or by the natural course of cause and effect, and which is therefore referred to as the supernatural." In the same vein, E. S. Brightman asserts (*A Philosophy of Religion* [New York 1940] p. 415) that religious experience is "any experience of any person taken in relation to his God"; and G. Galloway (*The Philosophy of Religion* [Edinburgh 1914] p. 184) that Religion is "man's faith in a power beyond himself whereby he seeks to satisfy emotional needs and gain stability of life, and which he expresses in acts of worship and service." This, of course, is simply a restatement of Tylor's famous saying that Religion is "the belief in spiritual beings." A modern Jewish preacher, the late Joel Blau, has very finely expressed the basic conception in the words (*The Wonder of Life* [New York 1926] p. 45): "Religion is a hunger for space. Its vaguest and most elementary gesture is a stretching beyond."

Some scholars have attempted to determine more precisely the nature of the stimulus which evokes the response called Religion. Thus, A. E. Crawley (*The Tree of Life* [London 1905] p. 209) defines it as "the sacred"—a view with which N. Micklem (*Religion* [London 1948] p. 9) appears to agree. This, however, "puts the cart before the horse"; for Religion is surely that which makes a thing sacred in the first place. The same objection applies also to Rudolf Otto's dictum that "Religion is the experience of the holy"; this takes as *a priori* what is clearly *a posteriori*. So, too, when Lewis Spence (*Introduction to Mythology* [New York 1921] p. 14, n. 4) gives as a minimum definition: "the result of man's attitude to the unknown," he forgets that what is altogether unknown is unlikely to evoke any attitude. What Spence evidently means is the *inexplicable*.

servances, a systematized routine or regimen.[2] To Whitehead, for instance, it is "what the individual does with his solitariness,"[3] whereas to the comparative religionist it is, by and large, what groups do with their together-ness.

This ambiguity has made havoc of any serious investigation of the subject. Under its influence, two distinct areas of study—two "referents," as the semanticists would say—have come to be confused, the phenomena of the one being subsumed to and interpreted by the categories of the other. The body of rites and ceremonies, for example, which a community customarily performs during the course of the year, and which may be in fact nothing more than a strictly economic routine, have come to be regarded as outward expressions of psychic states and experiences—responses to what Rudolf Otto has described as *numen tremendum*. It has then been taken for granted that they are addressed, by way of propitiation, to those "gods" or "spirits" whom such states and experiences alone project.[4]

The confusion is particularly well illustrated in current treatments of the religions of the ancient Near East. Almost everything

[2] The classic formulation of this view is, of course, that of E. Durkheim (*The Elementary Forms of the Religious Life*, English tr. [London 1915] p. 47): "A religion is a unified system of beliefs and practises relative to sacred things, that is to say, things set apart and forbidden—*beliefs and practises which unite into one single community called a Church all those who adhere to them*" (our italics). The use of the term in this sense actually goes back to Cicero; cf. J. Estlin Carpenter, *Comparative Religion* (London n.d.) p. 43-44. Our ancestors, in fact, thought more clearly than do we; for they distinguished neatly between the conception of *religio* or *threskeia* and that of *theosebeia*.

[3] *Religion in the Making* (New York 1930) p. 47. The statement was very largely anticipated by William James when he said (*The Varieties of Religious Experience*, 33rd ed. [New York 1922] p. 31): "Religion . . . shall mean for us the feelings, acts and experiences of individual men in their solitude in relation to what they consider the divine."

[4] Characteristic of this approach is Frazer's assertion (*The Golden Bough*, one-vol. ed., p. 50): "By religion . . . I understand a propitiation or conciliation of powers superior to man which are believed to direct and control the course of nature and of human life." It is this constant confusion between functional procedure and worship that leads, for example, to the common assumption that mortuary cults are evidence of ancestor-worship, and to the failure to distinguish between *tendance* of the gods—in the sense of clothing and feeding them and sweeping out their residences—and actual *adoration* of them.

connected with a temple or performed within its precincts is referred at once to the category of worship and explained, in one way or another, as an act of subservience to a god or goddess. The fact is, however, that the temple was the center not only of worship but also of the communal regimen. Its staff were not exclusively "clergymen," in the modern sense of the word, but also, so to speak, civil servants, and although the ceremonies performed often envisaged some personified focus, this was not necessarily a transcendental deity so that they were not necessarily acts of worship. The immolation and consumption of animals, for example, need not always imply a propitiatory act nor be described as a "sacrifice." As Robertson Smith pointed out (though he generalized somewhat too freely), the purpose of such an act may be merely to confirm kinship by means of commensality;[5] and though it is usually supposed that the personified spirit of the community also partakes of the commensal fare, that being is qualitatively distinct from the "god" projected by *numen tremendum,* and men's relationship with him need not be one of subservience or worship.

I.

If the present confusion is to be ended, if the proper distinctions are to be preserved and the phenomena viewed and appreciated in their true colors, a new and more precise terminology must be coined. As a minimum definition of religion the writer would therefore propose the following: *Religion is the synthesis of thought, emotion and behavior expressing man's attitude towards his environment and towards his existence within it.* In the first place, this definition covers the entire area of study. It embraces both personal experiences and collective regimens. Second, it subsumes to a single broad category those two forms of activity which are usually regarded as mutually exclusive and antithetical and which are designated as religion and magic. While recognizing a distinction between them, it also recognizes that they are but variant expressions of a single basic endeavor and therefore but variant species of a single genus. Moreover, by reserving the term religion to the genus as a whole, it avoids the prevalent confusion which arises from using it indiscriminately in both a generic and a specific sense.

[5] *Religion of the Semites,* ch. viii.

Third, it makes it clear that religion is not merely a product of thought (when it would issue solely in speculation or philosophy), nor of emotion (when it would issue solely in trauma or psychosis), nor of behavior (when it would issue solely in action or conduct), but necessarily a combination of all three, and that no act can be called religious unless it consists in a harmonious fusion of all within a single complex. Fourth and last, this definition is elastic. It allows for the fact that both man and his environment are dynamic, not static, and that the former may expand from the individual to the group to the race (*i.e.* from man to Man) and the latter from personal entourage to communal circumstance to the world as a whole. It likewise allows for the fact—so obvious, yet so persistently misprized—that, once a certain stage of development has been reached, these different circles of interest need not be mutually exclusive, and may even be concentric: a man may have one religion as a private individual, another as a member of a group, and a third as a constituent of the human race.

II.

This broad definition must be supplemented by other refinements of conventional usage. Above all, if the term *religion* is to be reserved to the wider genus as a whole, some new designation will be required to distinguish that narrower species to which the name is so often applied, *viz.* that body of rites and ceremonies which issue out of a sense of *numen tremendum* and in which—to quote Leuba—"ideas, feelings and volitions are supposed to be awakened in personal agents by means that are not mechanical or automatic, but which may be called anthropopathic, that is to say, invocations, offerings, prayers, and the like."[6] For this we would propose the term *Theolatry* (or *Daemonolatry*), dividing the total area of religion into *theolatric* (or *daemonolatric*) and *non-theolatric* (or *non-daemonolatric*)[7] beliefs and practices.

[6] J. L. Leuba in *Journal of Religious Psychology*, vol. vi (1913) 423.

[7] We deliberately eschew the term *magic*, because it has come by association to denote a seeming antithesis to religion, and what we desire to bring out is that it is really but another aspect of it. It should be observed also that in ancient usage, magical praxis did not imply something qualitatively different from religion but merely something unauthorized by the sanctions of the prevalent cult. It had, in fact, the same sort of connotation as the derogatory "foreign isms" of the modern bigot, and thence degenerated into the sense of "mumbo-jumbo, quackery."

Into the category of the non-theolatric fall all those public rites and ceremonies which are not actuated by any sense of *numen tremendum* but are simply economic procedures. Their motivation is not the worship of superior beings but the recruitment and co-ordination, at appropriate times and seasons, of all that human effort and energy which is considered necessary to ensure the continuance of the group for a further span of existence. They are religious because they express a synthesis of the group's thought, emotion and behavior regarding its environment and its place within it; but because their motivation is different from that of theolatry or worship, so too are their foci and symbols. The superhuman beings whom they envisage and who are believed to be involved in them are not of the same type as those projected by sensations of the numinous. Therefore the same term *god* should not be applied indiscriminately to both. We must recognize that religion has two distinct foci, one for the theolatric and the other for the non-theolatric type. To distinguish between them, we would propose to borrow from the vocabulary of Semitic or Roman religion, calling the one *el* or *deus* and the other *baal* or *genius*.

The term *el* or *deus* should be reserved for the assumed agent of a psychic state—the *numen tremendum,* the "striker" who renders a man "awe-struck." Man's relationship to this type of being is necessarily one of subservience, since he is always on the receiving end of its operations. Conversely, the being's position is one of transcendence. The religious consequence is therefore propitiation or worship.

The term *baal* or *genius* should be reserved, on the other hand, for that being who personifies and projects the life and identity of the group. He is, *mutatis mutandis,* of the same order as "Uncle Sam," Britannia, Alma Mater, or the like. Man's relationship to him is one of immergence, while he, conversely, occupies a position of immanence. He is wider but not necessarily higher than man. The religious movement is *outward,* not *upward,* issuing in communion rather than worship.

The distinction between the two types is well brought out by Semitic usage, where the term *el* (which properly means "power") is applied to anything numinous, whereas the term *baal* (which properly means "ergative force, activizer") is, when relating to a deity, usually accompanied by a qualifying localization. Thus, lofty mountains or cedars are called in Hebrew "mountains, cedars of *el*,"[8] while in Akkadian the corresponding word *ilu* is also used in the sense of "ghost, spirit."[9] Baal, on the other hand, is most often specified as *e.g.* Baal Gad, Baal Hermon, Baal Zephon, etc.—names which come later to be transferred to the places themselves as marking the spots pervaded by his presence.[10]

The two concepts are not, of course, mutually exclusive, and the distinction is more schematic than rigid. The religion of a community, it must be remembered, is by no means the same thing as the communal religion, for it embraces more than the collective interest and synthesis and includes also the congress of thoughts, passions and affective reactions which stir the totality of component individuals. In the minds and hearts of such individuals, apprehension of the pervading presence of the baal may easily assume the quality of a *numen tremendum,* so that the baal himself will take on the character of an *el.* Moreover, the line of demarcation between dominant and dominator is always a thin one, so that the baal who functions as the dominant focus of the communal entity will readily come to be confused with the controlling dominator of its fortunes and thus acquire the attributes of a transcendental *el.*[11] In point of fact, this is what usually happens; the God of Western religions—a strange fusion of transcendental *el* and immanent *baal* —best illustrates the process.

III.

We have described the baal as the god of non-theolatric religion. To understand his true nature, it is necessary to bear in mind that what he epitomizes and projects is not merely the human society of a given place but its entire "atmosphere," including alike both the animate and inanimate elements. He represents, in other words, a

[8] Psalm 36:7; 80:11.

[9] *Cf.* A. L. Oppenheim in *Archiv fuer Orientforschung,* vol. xii (1939) 352, n. 29. Note also that Greek *theos* (= **dhwesos*) is likewise connected with Latin *festus, feralis.*

[10] *Cf. Joshua* 11:17; *Judges* 3:3; *Exodus* 14:2, 9, etc.

[11] Our use of the two terms is, of course, schematic. In point of fact, almost every *baal* possesses attributes of *el.*

concept like our "Manhattan" or "Brooklyn," which embraces not only its inhabitants but also its streets and buildings and institutions—everything, in short, that gives it its distinctive character. For this more comprehensive concept we would propose the term *topocosm,* formed (on the analogy of *microcosm* and *macrocosm*) from the Greek *topos,* "place," and *cosmos,* "world, systematized entity." It is the topocosm, and not merely its human community, that constitutes the center of interest of collective religion.

The topocosm has two aspects: the one, punctual and immediate; the other, durative and (theoretically) eternal. The former is immerged in the latter as a moment is immerged in time or as, say, the present generation of Americans is part and parcel of an ideal America. Everything that the punctual community does is therefore at the same time and *ipso facto* a contribution to the continuous life and career of the durative and ideal entity.

This is the basic concept of collective religion among ancient and primitive people. On the punctual level, the cult consists in a series of practices designed to maintain and continue the life of the immediate group by means of concerted effort recruited and directed under communal sanction. It is, *au fond,* an economic regimen. On the durative level, however, it is the continuous vitalization of the ideal entity. And on both levels its basic character tends to be shot through with the influence of theolatry.

In practical articulation and expression, there is complete correspondence and parallelism between the two levels. The punctual group is epitomized and typified in the person of the *king;* the durative, in that of the *baal-type of god.* The king is therefore the incarnation and immediate avatar of the baal.

Whatever the king does in punctual ritual is done simultaneously and cosubstantially by the baal on the durative plane. If the king dies or is deposed at the end of the year to symbolize the annual decline of the corporate life which he epitomizes, the baal suffers a like fate. If the king indulges in a "sacred marriage" in order to regenerate the punctual topocosm after its periodic eclipse, the baal does the same thing in order to bring a new lease of life to its durative and ideal counterpart. And if the king is the dispenser of law and order on the punctual level, the baal discharges the same function on the ideal level. From this point of view, the "divinity of kings" is inherent, not conferred.[12]

IV.

The articulate link between the two levels or aspects is supplied by *myth*. Myth is the representation of the punctual in terms of the durative.[13] In ritual, for example, the entire punctual group may indulge in sexual license at certain critical seasons of the year in order to propagate the new life which it desires. This may then be epitomized in the "sacred marriage" of the king and a representative female, performed as part of the seasonal ceremonies. In the corresponding myth, the god (baal) will mate with a divine bride. Similarly, in ritual the forces of Life (or Summer or New Year) and those of Death (or Winter or Old Year)—each consisting in live teams of human beings—may engage in formal combat. This may then be epitomized in a battle royal (mark the term!) between the king and some monster or dragon. In the corresponding myth, it will be the god (baal) who fights the beast or similar demonic adversary.

It is easy, of course, to misunderstand this parallelism and to construe it in terms of genealogical derivation; and it is just this methodological error that pervades the standard treatments of the subject. On the one hand, we have the classic dictum of Robertson Smith that myth is a subsequent explanation of ritual;[14] on the other, the contention of Brinton that ritual reproduces antecedent myth.[15] In the light of the foregoing formulation, it will be seen at once that neither, in fact, reproduces the other and that—contrary to prevalent supposition—the participants in a ritual are not to be understood as impersonating the characters of a myth. What is involved is not representation but presentation. Ritual and myth

---

[12] See the writer's paper, "Divine Kingship in the Ancient Near East," in *The Review of Religion,* vol. ix (1945) 267-81.

[13] The correct understanding of Myth is very much beclouded by the tendency to regard it as a genre of literature or art. These are merely the media of its expression. Myth itself transcends those media in the same way that Music transcends a score.

[14] *Op. cit.,* 17-18.

[15] *Religions of Primitive Peoples* (New York 1899) p. 173.

are parallel expressions of the same thing on the punctual and durative level respectively. In the language of the cinema, they are the "close-up" and "long-shot" views of a single scene.

Nor do we account for the function of myth when we explain it away—with Cassirer,[16] Langer,[17] and others[18]—as a manifestation of the pre-logical mind. For this explanation loses sight of the fact that myth is related to ritual and that the myths which are associated with ritual performances in fact run parallel in the sequence of their "plots" to a succession of ceremonial acts ordered and determined upon a distinctly logical and functional basis.

The whole question of the pre-logical mind urgently requires re-examination. It has become the custom in recent years to exploit it as a kind of catch-all in the interpretation of ancient and primitive religions. We have been told, for example, that the early Israelites or their precursors professed a prelogical monotheism.[19] This, however, overlooks the fact that monotheism is but the theological expression of the theory of a universe, and it is difficult to see how the monistic conception of a universe can develop out of that of a multiverse (which is abundantly attested as the more primitive idea) except by a process of *logical* refinement and precision. We have been told also that when a deity is represented as alternatively male or female or as both at the same time, this is evidence of pre-logical thinking.[20] The fact is, however, that the principle which that deity represents may be conceived alternatively or simultaneously as a quality of either sex; so to represent it therefore attests a process of logical thinking, however varied be the forms

[16] Cassirer, Ernst, *Sprache und Mythos* (*Studien der Bibliothek Warburg,* VI, Leipzig-Berlin 1925); English tr. by Susanne K. Langer, *Language and Myth* (New York 1946).

[17] Langer, Susanne K., *Philosophy in a New Key* (New York, Pelican Books, 1948) p. 163-64.

[18] *E.g.* H. and H. A. Frankfort, in *The Intellectual Adventure of Ancient Man* (Chicago 1946) p. 3-27.

[19] Albright, W. F., *Archaeology and the Religion of Israel* (Baltimore 1942) p. 177-79. It is true that Albright prefers the term "empirico-logical," but his meaning is made clear by the words: "The Israelites felt, thought and acted like monotheists, even though their creed remained implicit for lack of analytic logic with which to formulate it from the raw materials which they possessed." One wonders, indeed, how such an unformulated mass of feelings and thoughts could even be described as a "creed."

[20] id., *op. cit.*, p. 27-28.

of expression. Lastly, we have been told that the "preposterous" and miraculous situations which confront us so often in folktale and myth—as when characters change shape or impossible distances are traversed in a trice—are relics of primitive perceptive thought, unfettered by conceptual or logical limitations. Here again, caution is in order; for the fact is that these elements are usually introduced for the precise purpose of pointing up the extraordinary. It is not everyone who changes shape, possesses magic boots, exhibits super-human strength or meets prodigious tests. These are the qualities of special characters, and they are endowed with them just because they have to be differentiated from the normal run of men and women. In other words, they possess these qualities precisely be-cause they are extraordinary, and what makes them so is that they are able to defy the ordinary laws of logic and the requirements of ordinary conceptual thinking. Far from being evidence of pre-logical thinking, these traits presuppose logical thought and de-liberately invert it.

V.

The main theses of this essay, then, are:

(1) Religion should be defined in generic terms as *the syn-thesis of thought, emotion and behavior expressing man's attitude towards his environment and towards his place within it.*

(2) Thus defined, religion divides into two types: personal experience exemplifying apprehension of *numen tremendum;* (b) communal regimens of basically economic character. The former are termed *theolatric* (or *daemonolatric*); the latter, *non-theolatric* (or *non-daemonolatric*).

(3) A difference must be recognized between the god presup-posed by theolatric religion and that presupposed by non-theolatric religion. The former is the transcendental agent of a psychic state; the latter is the immanent personification of a society and of its environment. The former may be called *el* or *deus;* the latter, *baal* or *genius.*

(4) The center of interest in collective religion is not merely the human society of a given place, but its total "atmosphere." This may be termed the *topocosm.*

(5) The topocosm possesses both a punctual and a durative aspect. The punctual aspect is epitomized in the person and career

of the king; the durative in that of the baal. The king is therefore the immediate avatar of the baal, and everything he does on the punctual level is done simultaneously and cosubstantially by the baal on the durative level.

(6) The parallelism is conveyed by myth which expresses in durative terms that which ritual expresses in punctual terms. It is therefore incorrect to say that myth *reproduces* ritual, or *vice versa*. They are simultaneous presentations of the same thing on two levels.

(7) The theory of "pre-logical mentality," as employed in the study of religion and myth, requires re-examination.

It may be added that the theses presented here in summary form are worked out more extensively, with supporting evidence and documentation, in the writer's *Thespis: Ritual, Myth and Drama in the Ancient Near East* (New York 1950).

Jewish Social Research

⊷§ *BY H. L. LURIE*
New York City

ATTITUDE TOWARD RESEARCH AND THE LACK OF
DEMOGRAPHIC DATA

*I*N THE early 1930's Morris Raphael Cohen began to devote a considerable part of his energies to the increasingly more critical Jewish problems. For this task he sought and secured the co-operation of other scholars who joined him in organizing the Conference on Jewish Relations.

It was obvious at that time that studies of Jewish problems lacked the systematic application of the methods and procedures of scientific research. Most of the programs and activities of Jewish agencies were of an empirical and frequently of an unplanned character. There were many generalizations, aphorisms, syllogisms and stereotypes in concepts about Jews and their social problems; few facts and still fewer studies and analyses of these facts; a smattering of recorded chronicles of events but no history; considerable theorizing but little basic theory and that little representing miscellaneous and often inappropriate borrowings from anthropology, psychiatry, and economics. There were strongly held but not necessarily well-informed opinions on antisemitism and other Jewish problems. Basic demographic data were non-existent; imagination and amateur guesswork supplied what passed for population statistics.

Cohen addressed himself to these problems trying to stimulate an interest in developing scientific attitudes and accurate data. Little progress was made during his lifetime and many gaps remain; if these are to be filled we will be further indebted to Cohen for the stimulation he gave to individual scholars and to organizations to substitute fact for fancy and intelligent analysis for make-believe and wish-fulfillment.

The belated development of an acceptable and systematic program of social studies concerning the Jewish population of the United States is probably due to several basic factors: first, the amorphous and undefined character of Jews as a group entity and, second, a reluctance to face the underlying questions of the relationships of religious and ethnic groups in the United States in an environment presumably designed to mitigate these differences and to foster the development of a homogeneous American population. It is perhaps for these reasons that we have the paradox of a self-conscious group allegedly given to excessive introspection extremely hesitant in undertaking a systematic process of self-examination. An auxiliary aspect of lag in research may have been the fact that the social sciences in general, and especially sociology, have not yet arrived at maturity and acceptability in this country.

Under the best of circumstance, social research on any population group is handicapped by the lack of adequate demographic data. Studies which are undertaken without such statistics add little to the insight and information obtained from journalists, amateur observers, political analysts and arm-chair theoreticians. While the opinions of such observers and writers may be challenging and even pertinent, there is always a large measure of valid doubt concerning their factual basis. Obviously few if any sound generalizations can be derived from questionable data.

Demographic data such as those usually obtained through census methods are almost completely lacking for the Jewish population of the United States and what passes for such data is usually found on examination to consist of more or less well-informed guesses by more or less competent observers. Thus, for example, we have no reliable data concerning the number of Jews in the United States,[1] their age and sex distribution, their places of residence or countries of origin, their occupations, or economic status. Occasional and limited Jewish population studies made of specific com-

[1] Commenting on the figure of the total number of Jews as published in the 1937 U. S. Census of Religious Bodies, Cohen stated, "The figures . . . are only guesses with an unknown margin of error. Hence, the statement that the United States has 4,770,647, even though it be embodied in an official publication of the United States, is not qualified by adequate evidence and is indeed offensive to anyone with a logical or statistical sense." (*Jewish Social Studies*, vol. iii, 1941, 231-32.)

munities at different times furnish the main source of materials for prevalent notions concerning Jewish statistics.

In this country the U. S. Bureau of the Census periodically provides demographic data which are basic to much of the understanding of trends and social conditions for the population as a whole. Such data are available on a geographic basis of residence for native-born and foreign-born elements of the population and for white as distinct from Negro, Indian and oriental populations in this country. As for the Jewish population which consists of elements derived from various periods of migration from many European countries, unavailable facts are imbedded in the census information on white persons or on foreign-born individuals, classified by their country of nativity. Occasionally, Census Bureau data on Americans born in Russia or in Poland or information about the "mother tongue" of Americans are scrutinized by an eager student and with the help of the data on immigrants classified as "Hebrews" compiled by the U. S. Bureau of Immigration previous to 1942, speculation on the facts about Jews is assumed to have been derived from such material.

Other substitutes for basic census data consist of sporadic efforts which are made locally to fill the gaps. Thus, for example, a Jewish organization engaged in fund raising or in social welfare may be interested in estimating the number of Jews in the area which it serves. Increasingly some of these organizations are undertaking total population counts through various devices which, if the results are to be dependable, are time-consuming, expensive and beset with many unsolved methodological problems. Frequently those who undertake such organized attempts are satisfied if they can make some approximately reasonable guess concerning the number of Jews and their distribution in the local area. Increasingly some of them are adding to their desire for knowledge of the number of Jews, questions on age and sex distribution, occupation, and affiliations with organized Jewish activity.

Such general population studies may be supplemented by inventories of Jews in colleges and universities and in professions and by sample studies of such characteristics as participation of Jews in the armed forces, attitudes concerning religious traditions, etc. It is perhaps significant that in the United States we have almost no data on such important aspects as degree and intensity of religious observance, rate of intermarriage, economic status or size of Jewish families.

For example, in the absence of official population data concerning Jews and with the paucity and wide differences in definition and quality of the results obtained through voluntary statistical projects it is virtually impossible to secure more than occasional or regional information on the economic adjustment of Jews in the United States or their occupational distribution. A study undertaken in 1944 by the United Jewish Appeal (for the purpose of giving that organization some basic information to determine what would be justifiable amounts of philanthropic contributions that might be expected from various cities in accordance with the economic conditions of their Jewish populations) was prepared with considerable effort. The results, however, were not considered suitable for publication. When some of the findings were scrutinized, serious questions were raised concerning the accuracy and value of the information that had been secured. Previous to the development of general public assistance, some information on the extent of dependency was available from Jewish welfare and vocational agencies. Their services today cannot throw much light upon the extent of poverty or dependency or unemployment among the Jewish population. Public welfare agencies with few exceptions keep no records of the religious beliefs of relief recipients.

While the absence of basic demographic data is a serious handicap to Jewish social studies, part of the handicap could be removed were social studies undertaken on a basis of intelligent organization and operation. Those interested in knowledge concerning the American Jewish population, conscious of the gaps in information, have been suggesting that there be some national program to consolidate the sporadic efforts of local communities and establish some uniformity and standardization of their findings, and that projects be developed for overcoming existing gaps in basic information on American Jewry.[2] It is accepted as a premise that the task will need to be completely on a voluntary basis and that it is

[2] *Cf.* Robison, Sophia M., "Toward a Bureau for Jewish Demographic Research," prepared for the Conference on Jewish Demography, Sept. 1948, and "Jewish Population Studies" in *American Jewish Year Book*, 1948-49.

neither desirable nor practical to have the U. S. Census Bureau undertake any special responsibility for securing this information in its regular censuses. While this view is generally accepted it may be of some interest to review the position which has been held by Jewish organizations for many years.

The Census Bureau obtained official information on religious institutions beginning with the 1850 Census when a special schedule was developed which included a question on the number of seats in houses of worship.[3] This special study was repeated in 1860, 1870 and 1880. In 1890 the question of membership (defined as communicants) was added and for the first time the existence of two separate bodies, the Orthodox and the Reform, was recognized. (The 1890 Census reported 92,397 seating capacity and 72,899 members in Reform and 46,837 seating capacity and 57,597 members of Orthodox congregations. The 1906 project repeated at ten-year intervals in accordance with the provisions of the Permanent Census Act approved in 1902, as amended in 1906 with a further amendment in 1919, was a special undertaking outside of the regular decennial enumeration of the previous periods.[4] In all of the special studies of religious bodies undertaken since 1850 information was secured from churches and official church bodies and followed the established policy of the United States of not including the question of religious affiliation in the enumeration of individuals.[5]

Since each religious denomination has its own definition of membership which may vary from communicants of a church to the total number of those baptized for a specific religious faith, the reports cover only a fraction of the population. For example, the 1936 report which covers 256 denominations, including independent and federated churches, lists a total church membership in the United States of 55,897,366 which is about 40 percent of the enu-

[3] *Cf.* Engelman, Uriah Z., "Jewish Statistics in the U. S. Census of Religious Bodies (1850-1936)," in *Jewish Social Studies,* vol. ix (1947) 127-79.

[4] The last U. S. Census of Religious Bodies was made in 1936. No funds have thus far been appropriated for the subsequent study planned for 1946 or 1947.

[5] "Owing to the rigid separation of Church and State in the United States, no attempt has been made in the census investigation to determine the distribution of population according to religion. However one may regret this as a statistician, one has to acquiesce as a good citizen." (Joseph Jacobs, "Jewish Population of the United States," in *American Jewish Year Book 1914-1915*).

merated population for that year. This compares with the reported
1926 total membership of 54,576,346, a somewhat larger fraction of the American population for that year. The explanation for
the relative decline given in the report is that "total membership in
1936 would have been much larger if all churches had furnished
statistics."

Information on Jewish religious congregations included in this
report is secured through a special agent appointed by the U. S.
Census Bureau. In 1906 and 1916, the special Jewish agent limited
the information to actual congregational memberships and therefore reported only 101,457 (heads of families) in 1906, and only
357,135 in 1916 (heads of families, seat holders and other contributors, figures obviously considerably below the total Jewish population in the United States for these years). For 1926 the definition of
membership in Jewish congregations was enlarged to include all
Jewish persons living in communities with an established congrega-
tion irrespective of whether such families actually considered themselves members of such congregations. The reported figures, therefore, for 1926 total 4,081,242 Jews. The 1936 published estimate is
given as 4,641,184, an increase of 13.7 percent.[6] It should also be
pointed out that the information on Jewish membership is not
classified on a denominational basis such as reform, orthodox, conservative, and information therefore differs from reports on Bap-
tists with 21 denominations, Methodists with 21, Lutheran 20, etc.

Religious or racial data in federal statistics have been limited to
the census classification of white, Negro, American, Indian, oriental
and native- and foreign-born on the basis of nationality. In 1898, a
classification by racial origin was added to the statistics by country
of nativity, compiled by the Bureau of Immigration, to provide
information on ethnic groups coming from countries which contain
various nationality components. At that time, the rubric Hebrew
was utilized (on a nationality rather than a religious basis). Serious
objections to this inclusion were raised from time to time by various
American Jewish organizations and from other sources. Because of

[6] This reported increase throws doubt on the population estimates since it is
larger than the general population increase for these years. It is improbable that
there were higher birth rates among Jews during that ten-year interval than in
the general population. Immigration during that period was limited.

these objections, the classification of Hebrew immigrants was discontinued in 1943.[7]

Although it was officially denied that one of the major purposes of the "racial" classification in the immigration statistics was in response to a growing nativist opposition to eastern and southeastern European and Jewish immigrants, it is generally assumed that one of the factors leading to the urging of such classification derived from such attitudes. In 1909, according to the annual report of that year of the American Jewish Committee an amendment to the Census Bill was introduced providing that the census enumerators should "ascertain the *race* of all inhabitants in the United States." The American Jewish Committee protested such inclusion in the Census Bill since they believed that the classification "race" adopted by the U. S. Immigration Commission which would most probably have been used in the classification was open to serious objections. The word "race" was subsequently eliminated from the Census Bill, but the 1910 and subsequent censuses have included the question of "mother tongue" applied to foreign-born Americans and their descendants where a language other than English was spoken in the household.

There has been subsequent discussion of the need for more comprehensive and accurate religious statistics in the United States which has met with objections from Jewish organizations and other religious groups. One unpublished memorandum on this subject gives the following as the reason for the objection:

(1) A religious question in a census would be an entering wedge for demolition of the separation of church and state in the United States. If the federal government introduces it, it is likely to be followed by the state and local governments with the result that the idea of classifying people by religion would become a part of the American consciousness, whereas up to the present time the effort of all men of goodwill has been to efface such lines of demarcation in official fields.

(2) That such a question would open the way for various correlations between the statistics of religious affiliation and other data in the census and that such correlations may be made by ignorant or malicious people in such a way as to produce conclusions that might be invidious to various religious groups.

[7] See *The Classification of Jewish Immigrants and Its Implications—Survey of Opinion* (New York, Yiddish Scientific Institute, 1945).

It is on the basis of avoiding discrimination that various states have recently passed laws removing such questions from employment blanks, applications to universities and colleges and in other types of relationships where discrimination on religious grounds may enter.

It may be of interest to consider the question of religious classification in the political life of the United States in relation to the fact that such information both on a religious and on an ethnic basis is regularly secured and published in Canada as well as in a number of European countries where the existence of definite minority groups in the population is recognized. Mr. Louis Rosenberg, of the Bureau of Social Economic Research of the Canadian Jewish Congress, has stated that fears expressed on the consequences of official statistics on Jews obtained in the regular censuses were groundless if judged by the Canadian experience.[8]

While the fears that official statistics may increase the prejudices and tensions of antisemitism may be invalid it can be argued that a reversal of the current official position at this time will obviously be a reflection of a changing attitude toward the importance of information concerning the religious and ethnic composition of the American population. Such a changed attitude if it were developed could not be ascribed primarily to a thirst for sociological data. In this country we are usually interested in fact-finding only for practical purposes. To seek accurate statistics about the religious and ethnic composition of the American population carries with it the implication that we are becoming increasingly concerned about these divisions among our people; that there are important problems growing out of such divisions and that more facts will be helpful in the solution of these problems. Such concerns are characteristic of many Jews and many Jewish organizations about themselves, joined with the fear that publication of data without the safeguards of interpretation to avoid misconceptions may help to intensify rather than to solve the problems which concern them. There is considerable validity, therefore, to the belief that to take the step of urging our Census Bureau to secure these additional

[8] For a fuller discussion of questions involved in a classification of Jews by religion or ethnic group, see "Summary and Conclusions" by Max Weinreich in *The Classification of Jewish Immigrants and Its Implications.*

data would have a negative effect on our underlying democratic philosophy of equality of our heterogeneous citizenship and intensify the consciousness of differences along religious and ethnic groups.

The concept of fluid conditions concerning caste and class which can be listed as among the most desirable ideals of American life may have become somewhat tarnished over the course of our history. It is nevertheless a philosophy which we should strive to uphold if we are to achieve the more perfect democratic state. Distinctions of national origin, religious preference, race are considered in theory of little importance concerning the role of the individual in the life of the community. That they are not so considered in the customs and folkways of our culture constitutes a problem and not an ideal, and much energy is now being expended to erase the prejudices and discrimination that are attached to such group differences.

For these reasons Jewish social research is confronted with a paradoxical situation. We become aware as Jews of the undesirable consequences that derive from the recognition of the distinction between Jews and other groups in the American population and the dangers to our present status and future well-being that attend an undue consciousness of such group differences. Hypothetically, such an increased awareness of group differences might conceivably be on a positive rather than negative basis but that is improbable in our present culture.[9] Perhaps the utopian classless state will be able to emphasize the value of group differences as making for the enrichment of the national life. We may indeed strive for such an ideal in American society and promote it as an objective for inter-cultural education, but it must be admitted that such efforts at present are too largely involved with combatting prejudices to hold forth any promise of achieving a more positive objective.

A philosophy of American life which would offer a generally acceptable basis for maintaining group differences along cultural

[9] "The existence of cultural groups (whether or not the Jews are present among them) is no less a historical fact than the existence of individuals, and a realistic policy should seek to inculcate this fact in people so that the Jews might appear as a natural part of the whole picture" (Weinreich, *op. cit.*, p. 122).

rather than on sectarian lines has not yet become established in the American mind. In fact, the pressures of prevailing attitudes are against such a principle. Differences in ethnic, racial and national origins are factors in the creation of what the sociologists call "social distance," making for prejudices and aversions by members of the majority groups against minorities. They are differences inherent in the heterogeneous composition of the American populations, accepted not for the positive contributions which such differences can make to a varied culture, but considered as barriers to the achievement of the goals of equality and fraternity among men. The result of these attitudes is that minority ethnic and nationality groups generally attempt to minimize rather than enlarge the cultural differences arising from their national origins. Attempts by European nations to maintain cultural ties with Americans of European origin have rarely succeeded except for a temporary period as, for example, in maintaining the interest of nationality groups in the political struggles of the homeland previous to independence against a dominating or occupying nation. Such periods of heightened interest terminate in apathy or indifference once the political objective is achieved. For these reasons there is some speculation in Jewish circles that the achievement of statehood for Jews in Israel is likely to diminish rather than increase the interest of American Jews in their cultural ties to Israel and overseas Jewry.

On the other hand, the fact that there is a more widespread acceptance of sectarian differences and of the right of the individual to follow the religion of his choice had made religion rather than ethnic group or national origin a more readily acceptable basis of group differentiation to those imbued with the desire to make Jewish community life in the United States fit most effectively into the general pattern. The weakening of religious ties and practices observed among all religious groups can probably be ascribed to causes other than popular attitudes since it is a phase of modernism operative among Jews in Israel as in the United States.

The dilemma facing Jewish research in the United States arises from this conflict of Jewish group interests with these external pressures of the prevailing attitudes. There is on the one hand a recognition of problems and the need for basic information required for programs of action by workers in Jewish organizations. On the other hand, the objective of minimizing the fact of group differences has made leaders of Jewish organizations oppose the official collection of data, which would obviously detract from that objective. This position which Jewish organizations share with other religious bodies means that the groundwork for accurate data about American Jews is not likely to be made available through statistics collected by governmental agencies.

In view of the fact that the 1950 U. S. Census did not include a question on religious affiliation or ethnic origin, it is perhaps idle to speculate on how inclusive and how useful such census data might be if they were to be secured. It is true that in a number of other countries such information is regularly obtained in official censuses. In this hemisphere, Canada is an outstanding example. In most of these countries, however, the population is more homogeneous than in the United States and this information has been secured over a long period of time antedating the present changing character of religious affiliation. It is perhaps significant that in the recent World War, it was reported that only approximately 90 percent of the enlisted personnel acknowledged some religious affiliation. (The percentage of religious identification is much larger in the official Canadian population census.) The large fraction of the non-religious presented an additional statistical difficulty to the War Records Project of the Jewish Welfare Board. With Jews assumed to be less than four percent of the total American population, were Jews a similar, larger or smaller fraction of those who did not designate a religious affiliation? The purpose of the religious classification in military statistics is to provide for appropriate religious burial. In a regular census it is possible that without such motivation there might be at this time an even larger proportion of individuals who would report themselves as unaffiliated or without religious convictions. The number would probably be considerable even if not as large as that obtained in a recent unpublished opinion poll which found a considerable higher proportion of individuals who reported no religious affiliation and many others who continued only a very tenuous relationship with the religious faith of their parents.

The composite Jewish population which is presumed to consist of all descendants of persons who were members of the Jewish faith and who have not been converted to other faiths shares few conditions with other groups in the American population upon which an appropriate statistical definition can be based without distorting the classification for most other groups. Let us assume that a person is potentially classifiable as a Jew on the basis that he or his ancestors at some not too remote historical period was a member of the Jewish faith. (That is in fact approximately the definition used as the criterion for estimates of Jewish religious membership made for the U. S. Census of Religious Bodies by the special Jewish agent for the 1926 and 1936 reports.) It would stretch the imagination to apply a similar definition to all other elements of the American population even if the ambiguous term "Protestant" were applied to every person who could not be classified as a Jew or as a Roman Catholic.

The possibilities of an ethnic classification present even greater difficulties. Aside from the racial classification based on color and the problem of the person with mixed racial origin, which is a factor detracting from the accuracy of current census data on Negroes, it would be virtually impossible to establish a valid ethnic classification for the native-born American white population. In the first place there is a large amount of intermarriage among white persons of different national origins. This is especially true under urban conditions. The great mobility of the American population is furthering the processes of intermarriage at least so far as the white section of the population is concerned. With immigration restrictions and the increase in the number and proportion of native-born Americans, a suitable ethnic classification becomes more and more difficult. What is the proper ethnic classification for Americans whose ancestry, like that of the late President Roosevelt, includes forbears from Holland, England, France and other countries, or of an individual whose grandparents were Italian, German, Jewish and English. The Hitlerian period of racism even more than the problems of a scientific category is likely to be a deterrent to inclusion of the question of ethnic origin in U. S. censuses.

Though the conclusion is unavoidable that we cannot hope to base research on American Jews on adequate and comprehensive census data and that it would be bad social policy to urge that this lack be corrected by official action, we do not need to conclude that all research is therefore impossible. Whatever major social and economic differences there may be between different geographical areas and urban localities it is obvious that a first rate study of a community sheds considerable light on the Jewish population of that area. A group of selected studies in different parts of the country undertaken under voluntary auspices, preferably Jewish, would add a substantial body of knowledge. Such an undertaking is not beyond the scope or resources of voluntary organization. Most of the methodological problems can be solved. Undertaken on a continuing basis with co-ordination of local effort and with standardization of method, valuable information would gradually be made available on such important aspects as growth or decline of the Jewish population, mobility, age, composition, birth rates, occupation, affiliations and activities.

It needs also to be pointed out that important forms of social research do not end and need not begin with population statistics. Such sources of information as case histories, diaries and biographies, historical records of Jewish agencies and communal activities, the Anglo-Jewish press and periodicals and special sociological studies of available local groups can offer much valuable material for social research. What is lacking for the effective collection and use of that material is an undeveloped interest in research and the fact that a sufficient number of properly trained and competent research workers have not been enlisted for the required tasks. The Yiddish Scientific Institute and the Conference on Jewish Relations, among other agencies, have made an effort to overcome this lack. Thus far their success has been limited since they face the lack of interest, doubts about the effectiveness or value of social research and other unresolved doubts and fears.[10]

The largest and best supported efforts that may be classified as social research have been undertaken recently by national agencies mainly concerned with programs dealing with antisemitism—the American Jewish Committee, the American Jewish Congress and the B'nai B'rith. Their programs, motivated by their desire to attack

[10] *Cf.* "Jewish Social Research in America: Status and Prospects," a symposium edited by Harry L. Lurie and Max Weinreich, in *Yivo Annual of Jewish Social Science*, vol. iv (1949) 149-312.

the problem of antisemitism, also involve studies of such questions as the dynamics of group relationships and the factors which are involved in conflict and accommodation between groups. Since these research activities are relatively new (the earliest were begun in 1944) and only a small part of the studies have been completed and published, it may be premature to assess their results, especially on the value that they may have for an understanding of Jewish development in the United States. The generally accepted slogan that "antisemitism is a Christian and not a Jewish problem" whatever its validity as to the proper focus for programs of action probably implies that these studies may not offer much information to those interested in the sociology of Jewish life.

There are, however, some current indications that the agencies mentioned are becoming concerned with more than the external problems of Jewish group life and may turn their research interest to the social and cultural aspects. The agencies concerned with the needs of their individual memberships have always displayed and are now showing an increasing interest in what is popularly known as Jewish culture. While this interest may be colored by *a priori* views and opinions as to the aims and ideologies of cultural programs, there is a possibility that the recently developed habits of approaching the problem of antisemitism as a matter requiring the application of social science research may to a degree carry over to these new projects. Ideological dogmas strongly inherent in several of these, as indeed in nearly all Jewish organizations, may operate as a damper on a truly comprehensive research program, but a beginning at least may be made to find more constructive efforts for research in place of the prevalent interest in defending, apologizing for and glamorizing American Jewish life. Among the workers in these agencies imbued with the objective temperament essential for social science there is to be found an increasing interest in and desire to understand and to evaluate the social processes in which American Jews are involved. The outlook for progress in Jewish social research may therefore be set down at this time as somewhat improved and mildly promising. Any large decrease in Jewish fears and anxieties on relationships with other American groups may, however, again diminish the currently weak interests in basic Jewish research.

German Pietism and the Jews

BY KOPPEL S. PINSON
Queens College

*W*HILE some attention has been given in Jewish historiography to the attitude of Martin Luther towards the Jews, practically nothing has been done by Jewish historians on the subsequent history of Protestantism in Germany and its relation to the problem of Jews and Judaism.[1] The background for Jewish emancipation and toleration has been studied exclusively in terms of the *philosophes* of the Enlightenment. While it is true that the movement for civil emancipation associated with the work of Dohm and Lessing is derived primarily from the Enlightenment, this is not the entire story. The intimate relations between leading figures in German romanticism, such as Schleiermacher, the Schlegels and Varnhagen von Ense, with Jews, and the subsequent wave of Jewish converts can only be understood in the light of the religious developments in 17th and 18th century Protestantism. Nor can the role of the Protestant churches with respect to the Jewish problem under the Nazi regime be adequately comprehended without a more intimate insight into the various currents within German Protestantism after Luther. Our modern disinterest in theology, and particularly Christian theology, is responsible for the huge gap in this field of study. It is the purpose of this essay to make some contribution to this important but neglected field of investigation.

I.

The most important movement within German Protestantism after the time of Luther and Melancthon was that of Pietism. The role of Pietism as a factor in the general development of modern Germany has been increasingly recognized in the past two decades.[2]

[1] Salo W. Baron makes reference to this lacuna in his *Social and Religious History of the Jews,* 3 vols. (New York 1937) vol. iii, p. 135-36.

[2] See the author's *Pietism and the Rise of German Nationalism* (New York 1934) with full bibliography of the general literature of Pietism.

It is not surprising, therefore, to find that German Pietism also made
a distinct contribution to the changing Christian attitude towards
Jews and Judaism. Before analyzing this contribution, however, it
is necessary to review the position of Martin Luther on this
question.[3]

The attitude of the founder of German Protestantism towards
the Jews affords opportunities for interesting psychological study.
Luther exhibited a development from that of avowed friendship
towards the Jews to the highest degree of open hatred and violent
antagonism towards them. In the early years of his life, before 1521,
he had very little to do with Jews. In his lectures on the Psalms in
Wittenberg, he attacked the Jewish interpretation of the Bible, described their worship as formal and ritualistic and ascribed their
suffering to their refusal to recognize Jesus. But his attitude towards
the Jews of his day at this time was on the whole neutral.[4]

In 1521 Luther visited Worms and, during his stay there, he had
an interview with two Jews. Out of this experience emerged the
feeling that he had a message for Jews as well as for Christians. His
first extended treatment on the Jewish question, *Dass Jesus Christus
ein geborener Jude sei,* appeared in 1523. The chief reason for this
pamphlet was to defend himself against the charge by his opponents that he preached the doctrine that Jesus was of the seed of
Abraham, *i.e.* a natural descendant of Abraham.[5] But at the same
time, he seizes upon the mistreatment of the Jews as another
weapon in his fight against the Roman church. "Our fools," he
writes, "the popes, bishops, sophists and monks, the thickheaded
asses, have up to now so dealt with the Jews that whoever was a

[3] Even the question of Luther and the Jews has not yet received the exhaustive study it requires. The best account is still the older study by Reinhold
Lewin, *Luther's Stellung zu den Juden* (Berlin 1911). See also Gurian, W.,
"Antisemitism in Modern Germany," in Pinson, Koppel S., ed., *Essays on Antisemitism* (2d ed., New York 1946) p. 218-65. Nazi studies of this question
are found in Grunsky, Karl, *Luthers Bekenntnisse zur Judenfrage* (Stuttgart
1933) and Walther Linden's introduction to his collection of *Luthers Kampf-
schriften gegen das Judentum* (Berlin 1936).

[4] The Nazi writer, Linden, denies that Luther was originally favorable to
the Jews and cites as evidence Luther's *Dictata super Psalterium* of 1513-1516
at the University of Wittenberg and his *Operationes in Psalmos* of 1519-1521.
See Linden, *op. cit.*

[5] See Köstlin, M., *Martin Luther,* 2 vols. (2d ed., Elberfeld 1883) vol. i,
p. 680.

good Christian might better have become a Jew. And if I were a Jew and had seen such fools and blockheads rule over the Christian faith and regulate its teaching, I would much rather have become a sow than a Christian."[6] He berates the Catholic church for having treated the Jews as if they were dogs, of cursing them and despoiling them of their possessions after it had converted them.

Luther makes a plea in this tract for a friendly attitude towards the Jews. He points to their blood relationship to Jesus, Paul and the Apostles. "We are pagans," he writes, "while the Jews are of the blood of Christ; we are only relatives by marriage and strangers; they are blood relatives, cousins and brethren of our Lord. Therefore, if one is to pride himself according to flesh and blood, the Jews belong more to Jesus than we do."[7]

The most important thing for Luther, however, is to convert the Jews to true Christianity. This can be realized only if the Jews are not abused and mistreated. The failure to convert the Jews thus far Luther attributes to the erroneous doctrines of the Roman church. "They were never shown any Christian teaching or Christian way of life."[8] He tells of having heard from pious converted Jews that "if they had not heard the Gospel in our time, they would have remained Jews under their Christian cloak for the rest of their lives. For they confess that they had never heard of Christ either from their baptizers or from their masters."[9] Now, he felt, he had the great opportunity to accomplish what a thousand years of Catholic teaching was never able to realize—the conversion of the Jews. "Now," he wrote in a letter to Bernhard, "that the invaluable light of the Gospels is rising and emitting its glowing rays, there is hope that many Jews will be converted earnestly and sincerely, and that they will be attracted to the Lord Christ with all their hearts."[10]

A great change in Luther's position towards the Jews took place in the years between 1530 and 1540. This transition is best exhib-

---

[6] *Werke*, ed. by J. G. Walch, 24 vols. (Halle 1739-51) vol. xx, p. 2231. The most authoritative edition of Luther's works is the Weimar edition, vols. i-lviii (Weimar 1883-....) but it is not yet completed. The Walch edition brings all of Luther's writings on the Jews together in vol. xx.

[7] Walch, ed., vol. xx, p. 2232.

[8] *Ibid.*

[9] *Ibid.*

[10] Walch, ed., vol. xx, p. 2268-69.

ited in his letter to the famous Court Jew, Jossel von Rossheim, in
1537,[11] and in his *Wider die Sabbather* of 1538. Luther still pro-
fesses his friendship for the Jews, but plainly shows his impatience
and aggravation at their not accepting his teaching. He denounces
the Jewish rabbis as the popes and monks of Judaism who misled
the Jews just as the Catholic church has led the Christians astray.
Unsuccessful in his hopes to convert the Jews, he became still more
incensed when he heard of instances of Christians turning Jews.
This was too much for him. His violent temper and strongly passionate nature, which had already shown how virulent he could be in
his attacks on the peasants and the Anabaptists, let loose a storm of
abuse and slander against the Jews that, for venom and coarseness
of expression, can be matched only by the pages of *Der Stürmer* in
our own day.

The later views of Luther on the Jews are set forth in detail in
two pamphlets published in 1543, *Von den Juden und ihren Lügen*
and *Vom Shem Hamphoras.*[12] He no longer has any sympathy for
the wretched plight of the Jews. He describes it with great relish
and with immense satisfaction. Jewish suffering is well deserved
and can be due only to their failure to embrace Christianity and
accept Jesus.[13] He berates the Jews for their vanity and boasting
and goes into great detail to demolish the various sources for Jewish national pride, such as ancestry, circumcision, the revelation of
Mt. Sinai and the association with Palestine, Jerusalem and the
Temple.[14]

The economic condition of the Jews arouses Luther's resentment even more than their religious ideas. All the Jews are described as being wealthy and as living by the exploitation of the
Gentiles through trade and usury (*Schacher und Wucher*). The
Jews are pictured as the parasites of the community, aliens living
on the fat of a land that is not theirs. "They live in our house," writes
Luther, "under our protection and shelter, and use our land and
roads, market place and streets. And with all this the princes and

[11] See Walch ed., vol. xx, p. 2269 and Weimar ed., vol. i, p. 309. See also
Luthers Briefwechsel, ed. by Enders, Kawerau, Fleming *et al.*, 19 vols.
(Frankfurt and Leipzig 1884-1932) vol. xi, p. 229-30 and p. 240-42.

[12] Weimar ed, vol. liii, p. 412 ff.

[13] *Ibid.*, p. 418.

[14] *Ibid.*, p. 419 ff., 491, 513.

rulers . . . allow the Jews to help themselves from their open purse and strong-box, to stand up and rob what they want, *i.e.*: they allow themselves and their subjects to be fleeced and milked by Jewish usury and to be made beggars by means of their own money. For the Jews, in their wretched state, certainly should not have anything, and what they have must certainly be ours."[15]

In place of the former hope of converting Jews by befriending them, Luther now warns Christians to beware of meeting with Jews. "Wherever you see or hear a Jew," he says, "don't think other than that you hear a poisonous basilisk which can poison and kill people also with his face."[16] There is no use hoping to convert them. "Do not dispute the articles of our faith with Jews," he warns his followers. "They are, from their youth, so brought up with poison and rancour against our Lord, that there is no hope that they will ever reach the point where, by their misery, they will finally soften and be forced to recognize that the Messiah has come and that he is our Jesus."[17] To convert the Jews, he says in another place, "is about as possible as to convert the devil. A Jewish heart is so stone-, iron-, devil-hard, and callous that there is no way at all of moving it. In fine, they are young devils damned to Hell."[18]

What then is to be done with the Jews? To allow them to live on as before is, for Luther, unthinkable. They are unbearable. Luther had his program ready and it is a program that bears striking resemblance to the program carried out by the leaders of the Third Reich four hundred years later. Luther's program called for the almost complete annihilation of both Jews and Judaism in Germany.[19] All synagogues and schools are to be set on fire and destroyed. The homes of the Jews are to be torn down. All prayer books and Talmudic literature are to be confiscated, for they are full of insults and slander to Christianity and its founder. The training and teaching of rabbis is to be forbidden. Lending of money on interest is to be prohibited. All gold and silver is to be taken away from them, for all that they possess is rightly not theirs. Finally, they are all to be set at hard manual labor.

[15] *Ibid.*, p. 481 ff.
[16] *Ibid.*, p. 446.
[17] *Ibid.*, p. 419
[18] *Ibid.*, p. 417.
[19] Weimar ed., vol. liii, p. 523.

II.

Such, in brief outline, are the two positions of the founder of German Protestantism on the Jewish question, and it is between these two positions that later German Protestantism oscillates. The later and hostile attitude of Luther's *Von der Juden und ihren Lügen* becomes the tradition of orthodox Lutheranism. It forms the basis and theological foundation for the violent antisemitism revealed in later German Protestantism. But it also slams the door to those Jews who wished to escape persecution by abandoning the faith of their fathers and find refuge in the Evangelical church. According to this view, it was pointless to try to convert a Jew since they were so utterly corrupt and incapable of genuine and sincere conversion. "Three kinds of water go to waste," wrote the orthodox Lutheran, Dannhauer; "the sweet water that flows into the ocean, the water mixed with wine and the water with which a Jew is baptized."[20] Caspar Calvor declared that "it is easier for a negro to change his skin and a leopard his spots than it is to convert a Jew."[21] Popular folk-lore expressed this sentiment in a saying which became current in the early part of the 17th century:

> *Wenn die Maus die Katze frisst*
> *Wird der Jud' ein rechter Christ.*[22]

This antisemitic tradition of orthodox Lutheranism reached its climax in the notorious work of Johann Andrea Eisenmenger, *Entdecktes Judenthum,* published in 1700 but not allowed to circulate until 1711. But it was also the persistence of this tradition in the Evangelical Lutheran church that made it possible for Lutheran pastors and theologians under the Nazis to accept the racial theories of Hitler and Rosenberg and apply them to converted Jews

[20] Quoted in Schudt, Johann Jacob, *Jüdische Merckwürdigkekeiten,* 4 vols. (Frankfurt 1714-17) vol. ii, p. 482.

[21] Cited by G. Frank, *Geschichte der protestantischen Theologie,* 4 vols. (Leipzig 1862-75) vol. ii, p. 291.

[22] *Ibid.,* p. 292; also quoted in Schudt, *op. cit.,* vol. ii, p. 482. Schudt reproduced a plaque which bore this saying on one side. Schudt as well as other writers also cite another variant of this saying. According to this version, a converted Jew of Cologne left behind him, after his death, silver figures of a cat and a mouse and added the inscription, *"Wenn die Katze das Maüsslein frisst, So wird der Jude ein rechter Christ."* This is cited to prove the insincerity of the Jewish convert. For a similar treatment, see the anonymous little tract, *Abschilderung des jüdischen Greuels im kleinen* (Jena 1733) p. 73-76.

or to the offspring of converted Jews. There is a direct and continuous line from the later writings of Luther to the German Christians and to theologians like Gerhard Kittel in the Third Reich.

The milder and more lenient view of the early Luther is taken over by the Pietist movement and its offshoot, the Unitas Fratrum, or Moravian Brethren. Pietism, in many other ways, represented a return to early Lutheran views as against the formalized orthodoxy that followed him. It harked back to the earlier individualistic spirit of the Lutheran revolt. In its attack on state absolutism, it likewise represented a return to Luther's early principles and away from the orthodox view that developed after the peace of Westphalia. So also, in its attitude towards the Jews, Pietism represented a return to the early Luther. Weary of the eternal wranglings and hair-splitting disputations of the post-Reformation theologians, Pietism turned toward a more inward form of religion and placed its chief stress on practical morality and the exercise of love and sympathy. This called for a more tolerant attitude towards all religious differences,[23] and also involved a milder treatment of Jews.

III.

Philip Jacob Spener, founder of the Pietist movement, was born in Alsace and lived a good deal of his life in Frankfurt a. M. In both places he came into contact with compact masses of Jews. He studied Talmud with a Jew and then continued Hebrew studies with Buxtorf in Basle and with Edzard in Hamburg. His collections of sermons include quite a number which deal immediately and directly with the Jewish question.

Like all Christian theologians before him, Spener explained the suffering of the Jews as a just punishment by God for their failure to accept Jesus.[24] Their greatest sin is the crucifixion, for which all the Jews as well as the priests are guilty.[25] Spener, however, drops the violent and vituperative language of the later Luther and of Eisenmenger. Instead of the "arrogant, stubborn and poisonous Jews," described by orthodox Lutheranism, Spener always refers

[23] For a full treatment of Pietism and toleration see ch. iii of the author's *Pietism and the Rise of German Nationalism.*

[24] Spener, P. J., *Die evangelische Glaubenslehre* (Frankfurt 1717) p. 1385.

[25] The basis for this is Matthew xxvii, 25: "Then answered all the people, and said, His blood be on us, and on our children." *Ibid.,* p. 1391-93.

to "*die arme Juden*" and expresses sympathy for their wretched plight. Coming from Alsace, where Jewish poverty was most apparent, he knew that not all Jews were great magnates and usurers, and that the great masses of Jews were just as poor and as unhappy as the great masses of Christians. That is why he lashed out vigorously against those Christians who, influenced by their preachers, "attack these poor people with curse words, kick them around with open insults, and even perpetrate physical injuries upon them."[26]

Christian love, says Spener, knows no distinction of race or religion and it is to be practiced with Jews as well as with Christians. It is in this connection that Spener, like later Protestant theologians, makes use of the important chapters 9-11 of Paul's *Epistle to the Romans*.[27] The physical relationship of the Jewish people to Jesus and to the apostles is given prominence and their special role in the divine plan given special attention. "In the *officis humanitatis*," says Spener, "we are connected with the Jews before all others. They were once the most important people in the entire world, from the seed of holy patriarchs. And if their present situation is due to God's judgment, nevertheless the remembrance of their extraction makes it fitting that we show our love to them more than to others."[28] He calls the Jews "the noblest people in the world, according to their ancestry, with whom God made a glorious covenant which has not yet been entirely liquidated. From them our Saviour was descended, and because of His sake, therefore, His relations according to the flesh should be loved. They are still under the wrath of God but they still have before them glorious promises of a future which will have to be fulfilled in time and which must therefore always be before our eyes."[29]

A query was addressed to Spener whether Christian midwives

[26] Spener, P. J., *Letzte Theologische Bedencken und andere briefliche Antworten*, 3 vols. (Halle 1721) vol. i, p. 288.

[27] For the most recent treatment of this see Schmidt, Karl Ludwig, *Die Judenfrage im Lichte der Kapitel 9-11 des Römerbriefes* (Zollikon-Zürich 1943, 2d ed. 1946), which is Heft xiii of the *Theologische Studien* edited by Karl Barth; also Eckardt, A. Roy, *Christianity and the Children of Israel* (New York 1948).

[28] Spener, P. J., *Theologische Bedencken*, 4 vols. (Halle 1712-15) vol. ii, p. 275.

[29] *Letzte Theologische Bedencken*, vol. i, p. 286; see also *Theologische Bedencken*, vol. i, p. 216.

should be permitted to attend Jewish women. Spener provided an extended reply in which he again emphasized the need for showing Christian love to all persons. The refusal to attend a Jewish woman, he says, would be an indication of the fact "that we pay light attention to the command of our Saviour."[30]

Spener argued against the theory that the Jews were destined to remain in their wretched state of suffering as living symbols of God's wrath and justice. They should be converted to Christianity and an all-out effort ought to be made to effect their conversion.[31] He admits that conversion in many cases is only superficial but he hopes that the children of the converts will be better Christians. Christians, therefore, are to pray for the conversion of the Jews; they are to try to get Jews to attend Christian sermons and they are to regulate Christian behavior to the Jews in a manner which would induce conversion rather than antagonize the Jews.

In these activities for the conversion of the Jews, Spener assigns a special role to the regent. "A Christian regent," declared Spener in a sermon delivered between 1681 and 1684, "is not only authorized but is conscience-bound to try to bring the Jews under his rule to the knowledge of salvation and to true Christianity."[32] He owes this duty to Jesus, to Christian love and to his sovereign power. The prince is placed in his position by God to care for the welfare of his subjects. This includes the purification of their souls. Jews, as subjects of the prince, therefore, deserve the same attention. The rulers, continues Spener, "must always remember that God did not place the Jews in their lands in order to derive temporal profit from them but rather that the Jews might draw spiritual benefits from them."[33]

Force, urges Spener, is not to be used by the rulers in the conversion of the Jews. "They must remember that conversion belongs to the spiritual realm of Christ; it is not of this world and, therefore, worldly force has no place in it."[34] Spener lists several sug-

---

[30] *Theologische Bedencken*, vol. ii, p. 274-76, *"Ob Christliche hebammen oder wehemütter sich bey gebahrenden Jüdinnen gebrauchen lassen dörffen."*

[31] *Ibid.*, vol. i, p. 214-18; also p. 170 f.

[32] *Ibid.*, vol. iv, p. 87; also the sermon in *Letzte Theologische Bedencken*, vol. i, p. 286-93.

[33] *Ibid.*, p. 88-89.

[34] *Ibid.*, p. 89.

gested ways in which the regent may help in the conversion of the Jews. First of all, he is to see to it that the Jews in his realm are not persecuted. The prince, himself, is not to perpetrate any "injustice and evil against these poor people" and he is to keep the Christians in his realm from "sinning [against the Jews] by cursing, beating or cheating them."[35] Persecution only helps to harden the Jews against Christianity and serves to disprove the Christian teaching of love. The regent is to further conditions for peaceful conversion through the spread among the Jews of Christian literature and thought. The New Testament should be made available to them, but he realizes that most Jews do not read German. Direct conversation helps; but not all Christians are skillful enough for such persuasive powers. The most effective means is by special preaching to the Jews. Spener recommends that one preacher in each community equip himself especially for such a task. Although, declares Spener, the prince does not have the power to force the Jews to accept Christianity, he does have the power to force the Jews to attend sermons arranged especially for them.[36] This is the only act of coercion in Spener's program. Beyond that, the Jews were to be assured that no force would be exercised upon them after this.[37] All efforts should be made, said Spener, to reduce the amount of compulsion to a minimum. The sermons might even better be held outside of regular churches. The manner of the sermon is to be gentle. It is to be friendly and without bitterness or vehemence so that the Jews see that "all stems from an inner love for them and from compassion for their misery."[38] They should be made to realize that "we do not despise their nation nor hate them but bear only love for them. When such confidence can be established, there is more chance of influencing their hearts."[39] In a later sermon on the same subject (September 22, 1702), Spener abandoned even this amount of coercion and admitted that it was inadvisable for the prince to force the Jews to come to such meetings. The best method to bring the

[35] *Ibid.*, p. 90.
[36] Spener had such meetings arranged for him in Berlin.
[37] *Ibid.*, p. 93.
[38] *Ibid.*, p. 94.
[39] *Ibid.*

Jews to see the light is through personal contact with them by men trained for this work in Jewish learning and teaching.[40]

One of the most interesting proposals made by Spener for the purpose of "solving" the Jewish problem is concerned with Jewish vocational retraining. Long before either the Christian writers of the *Aufklärung* or their Jewish disciples of the *Haskalah* began their propaganda to wean the Jews away from trade to agriculture and handicrafts, Spener, at the close of the 17th century, pointed to Jewish concentration in industry as one of the most aggravating factors in their plight. Exclusive preoccupation in trade, he said, "brings numerous cares to the heart, even to those who are moderately well off. . . . As for the poorer Jews, and they form the largest number, they do not have any strong desire to engage in trade. Is it not quite possible that they could earn their piece of bread without fraud in places where there are cattle? Instead, they must dream day and night and figure out what schemes and fraud they can use to maintain themselves in their poor existence. In such a condition they can hardly think of anything godly. . . . Were they all to be resettled, however, in unbuilt or semi-populated areas and restored to the mode of life of their ancestors in agriculture and dairying, not only would the government have more use from them, but they would come to the position where the body worked more but the spirit had less cares."[41] Spener advocates what amounts to the setting up of trades and agricultural schools for young Jews to effect this occupational transformation. However, he concludes that such a program could not be carried out by each local prince separately. It would require an over-all plan for the entire Reich and he ruefully admits that, under the political circumstances of the time, this could hardly be realized.[42]

Spener's general attitude towards the Jews is best summarized in the closing prayer of one of his sermons. "May the Lord have mercy upon His poor nation whom He once loved so much and

[40] *Letzte Theologische Bedencken,* vol. i, p. 292-93.

[41] *Theologische Bedencken,* vol. iv, p. 89-90; also *Letzte Theologische Bedencken,* vol. i, p. 288.

[42] Spener expressly urges Christian princes, however, to forbid Jews from using Protestants as *"Schabbas Goyim."* He suggests to the Jews that they use Catholics for this purpose. See *Theologische Bedencken,* vol. iv., p. 91.

whom He had chosen to be His above all other nations but whom
He has so long rejected. May the time soon come when the cover
of Moses be removed from their hearts and they be converted to
the true King David. May He give us in all our classes the necessary
wisdom that we know how to act without harm against them and
that we patiently bear the love which, for the sake of a Jew, Jesus,
we owe to all His brothers according to the flesh; that we work
among them with gentleness and that we dutifully apply all methods for converting them, in fear of Him and in accordance with
His Spirit."[43]

IV.

What Melanchthon was to Luther, August Hermann Francke was
to Spener and the Pietist movement. It was Francke who did most
to disseminate the ideas of Pietism and above all to create the institutional agencies to realize in practice the objectives of the movement. In Halle, Francke created a network of religious agencies
that left a deep imprint on the entire subsequent religious and cultural development of Germany. Among these institutions was also
one to deal with the Jewish question.

Francke, like Spener, had studied Hebrew and Rabbinics with
Ezra Edzard in Hamburg. From Spener as well as from Hochstetter,
he was imbued with the importance of converting the Jews. He
followed Spener completely in the lenient approach to the problem
and, like Spener, he rejected the orthodox Lutheran view that the
Jews could never really be converted. Missionary activity in general and missionary activity among the Jews in particular became
one of the important preoccupations of Halle Pietism. Francke interested one of his disciples, Johann Heinrich Callenberg, in this
work and Callenberg dedicated the rest of his life to this activity.
Spener and Francke had already called attention to the need of
Christian preachers to learn Yiddish. Callenberg studied Yiddish
as well as Hebrew and as Professor of Theology at the University
of Halle, he lectured on semitics and Yiddish and offered a special
course on "How to Aid in the Conversion of the Jews." He collected
sufficient funds to establish, in 1728, the Institutum Judaicum at
Halle, which became the center for Protestant missionary activity

---

[43] *Ibid.*, vol. iv, p. 99.

among the Jews.[44] The purposes of this institute were (1) to print Bibles and other missionary literature in Yiddish, Hebrew, Arabic and Turkish, and (2) to send missionaries to the Jews. On the advice of Wagenseil, Callenberg taught Yiddish to all his workers. In 1760, Callenberg died and was succeeded by Stephan Schultz as director of the Institutum Judaicum.[45] Schultz, in turn, was succeeded by Justus Israel Beyer. Neither of these were as forceful in their work as Callenberg. Nor was the spirit of the Enlightenment of the late 18th century conducive to their work and on January 24, 1792 a royal rescript ordered the dissolution of the institute.

Spener's attitude towards the Jews was also echoed in many of the lesser known figures in the Pietist movement such as Gottfried Arnold, Ernst Christoph Hochmann, J. W. Petersen and his wife, Johanna Eleonara, and the Württemberg theologian, J. A. Bengel.[46]

[44] The whole problem of Protestant missionary activities among Jews, from the Lutheran point of view, is treated in the exhaustive study of J. F. A. de le Roi, *Die evangelische Christenheit und die Juden,* 3 vols., vol. i (Berlin 1884), vols. ii-iii, 2d ed. (Berlin 1899). For this period see vol. i, p. 206-407. See also Goldmann, Karlheinz, "Die Bibliothek des Callenbergschen Institutum Judaicum zu Halle 1728-1791," in the Nazi publication *Weltkampf* (1942) 50-53, which contains a valuable list of the manuscripts included in this library. These manuscripts presumably are still in the main library of the Frankesche Stiftungen in Halle.

[45] See de le Roi, *Stephan Schultz,* 2d ed. (Gotha 1878); Schultz's own diaries, *Fernere Nachricht von der zum Heile der Juden errichteten Anstalt* (Halle 1762-76) and his autobiography, *Die Leitungen des Höchsten,* 5 vols. (Halle 1771-75). This early missionary literature has been almost completely neglected by Jewish historians. A detailed study of these materials should yield fruitful results for the inner life of Jews in Germany, Bohemia and Poland and should also be analyzed for relations to the Frankist and Hasidic movements. Gershom Scholem is, as far as is known to this author, the first one to make extensive use of some of this material in connection with the history of the Sabbatian movement. See his most interesting study, "Contributions to the Knowledge of Sabbatianism from 18th Century Missionary Literature," in Hebrew, in *Zion,* vol. ix (1943-44) 27-38 and 84-88. See also Plaut, W. G., "Two Notes on the History of the Jews in America," in *Hebrew Union College Annual,* vol. xiv (1939) 575 ff., which analyzes several letters about the Jews of Georgia sent to and published by Callenberg. A good deal of this missionary material is to be found in the libraries of the Hebrew Union College, in Cincinnati, and the Union Theological Library, in New York City.

[46] See Gottfried Arnold's *Das eheliche und unverehelichte Leben der ersten Christen* (2d ed., Leipzig 1732) p. 247-49 and his famous *Kirchen- und Ketzergeschichte,* 2d ed. (Schaffhausen 1740) vol. iii, p. 40 ff.; Hochmann's *Briefe an die Juden* (1699, new ed. 1709); Petersen's *Selbstbiographie,* 2d ed. (Frankfurt 1719) p. 51-53.

But it is even more apparent and likewise more significant in the thought of Count Nikolaus Ludwig von Zinzendorf (1700-60), founder of the Moravian Brethren or Herrnhuter. Zinzendorf's religion is best described as a *Herzensreligion*. More than any of the other currents in the Pietist movement, it was based on the emotional reactions of the heart and on the feeling of love. This showed itself too in his attitude toward Jews.

> I don't suffer myself to become prejudiced against any person, [he wrote]. If I find him a Mohammedan, I thank God that he, of course, will have a notion of the Old Testament, and hope his unknown Friend, but who is honored by him many times more than I find he is by thousands of my fellow Christians, will appear to him once in some of these books. In the meanwhile, I approve myself to him a true follower of that Person, the holiness of whom he reverences, but whose cross he shudders at, and I strength as much as I can, all the true notions that he has besides, and content myself with hinting to him the deficiencies of his, but with the utmost delicacy too for fear of hardening him. That is not the case absolutely with a Jew. I love that nation very much, and 'tis wonderful how they love me; the more as we have none of those matters to treat with one another, which they are so wholly taken up with. Those of my brethren who came from their tribe, remain always fond of their brethren according to the flesh, and we cannot but hope that our ever-blessed Jew, will not forsake his generation.[47]

Very early in his life, Zinzendorf became interested in the work of Callenberg and in the conversion of the Jews.[48] He 'travelled among the Jews and was especially active among the Jews in Bohemia.[49] "We cannot help having a sympathy and concern for the Jews," wrote Zinzendorf, "we being only Branches of the wild olive grafted into *their* stock, *John* X, 16, *Rom*. XI, 15, 23, 24, 25. When his Sign appears in the clouds, it will certainly have the effect described *Zech*. XII, 10, 11, but we pray that they may be converted sooner and in a gentler manner by the same object presented to

[47] Zinzendorf, N. L., *An Exposition or True State of the Matters Objected in England to the People Known by the Name of Unitas Fratrum* (London 1755) p. 47-48.

[48] See his *Der Passagier oder Sonderbare Gespräche*, ed. by A. Petersen (Jena 1880) conversations 12 and 13, and *Saat auf Hoffnung* (Ostern 1864); also de le Roi, *op. cit.*, p. 259-72.

[49] See especially his Letter to the Jews of Wetterau, reprinted in de le Roi, *op. cit.*, p. 360-62.

them spiritually."[50] Zinzendorf, for a while, even had a plan to constitute a special community of "Jewish-Christians" in his Brüder-gemeine and his followers were the first Protestant sect to introduce a prayer for the Jews in their Sunday liturgy and a special prayer for them on *Yom Kippur*.[51]

V.

Pietism thus was responsible for introducing a much friendlier attitude towards the Jews and, wherever it penetrated, it induced a softer spirit among the Christian population. It would be wrong, of course, to claim that Pietism was either solely or chiefly respon-sible for the movement for toleration and emancipation of the Jews. It was rather the interaction of Pietism and *Aufklärung* in the late 18th century that produced the climate of opinion from which emancipation eventually developed. Only in the light of the inter-action of these two major trends in German intellectual life is it possible to comprehend the relationship of the later Pietist Johann Georg Hamann to Moses Mendelssohn,[52] the Swiss Pietist Johann Caspar Lavater and his efforts to bring about the conversion of Mendelssohn,[53] the interest of Johann Gottfried Herder in the "spirit of Hebrew poetry,"[54] and the interesting and complex rela-tionship to the Jews of his day, of the "enlightened Herrnhuter," Friedrich Daniel Schleiermacher.[55] And it is no accident that, when

[50] Zinzendorf, *Maxims, Theological Ideas and Sentences* (London 1751) p. 355. See also Uttendorfer, O., *Zinzendorfs Weltanschauung* (Berlin 1929) p. 42.

[51] de le Roi, *op. cit.*, p. 364.

[52] The problem of Hamann in general is very complex; that of his relations with Mendelssohn is even more difficult. See Unger, R., *Hamann und die Aufklärung*, 2 vols. (2d ed. Halle 1925); Bamberger, Fritz, *Die geistige Gestalt Moses Mendelssohns* (Berlin 1929) and the Nazi essay by Walter Grundmann, "Mendelssohn und Hamann," in *Germanentum, Christentum und Judentum*, vol. iii (Leipzig 1943) p. 1-48.

[53] All the texts of the Lavater-Mendelssohn interchange are found in the Jubilee edition of Mendelssohn's works (Berlin 1929-38) vol. vii; see also Rawidowitz, S., "Moses Mendelssohn," in *Hatekufah*, vol. xxv (1929) 498-520 and vols. xxvi-xxvii (1930) 547-94.

[54] *Cf.* Herder, J. G. von, "Vom Geist der Hebräischen Poesie," in his *Sämtliche Werke*, ed. by Bernhard Suphan, 33 vols. (Berlin 1877-1913) vol. xi, p. 213-466 and vol. xii, p. 1-308.

[55] See Geiger, L., in *Zeitschrift für die Geschichte der Juden in Deutschland*, vol. iv (1891) 57-64.

the Nazis began their systematic study of the emancipation period, one of their leading writers placed the chief responsibility for opening the gates of German civilization to the Jews upon the Pietist movement.[56] *Aufklärung* and Pietism complemented each other. Just as Dohm later rejected the notion of a *"durchaus unverbesserlichen Menschen-Race,"* Spener and his followers rejected the notion of an "unconvertible" Jew. Both of these notions ran counter to the racialist theory of *Blut* and *Boden* and both, therefore, had to be rejected by the adherents of the Nazi regime.

[56] Grau, Wilhelm, "Die innere Auflösung des europäischen Antijudaismus in den Jahrhunderten vor der Emanzipation," in *Weltkampf* (1942) 1-16 and 131-88.

Jewish Ideologies in Austria During the Revolution of 1848

BY JACOB SHATZKY

New York City

*T*HE complexity of national, social, and religious ideologies which the revolution of 1848 brought to the fore existed well before the onset of the revolution. The upheaval of 1848 gave more color, passion and vigor to the clash of conflicting forces, which stemmed from the political and economic situation in Austria. They were well covered under a patched quilt of monarchial despotism, and the Viennese government remained blissfully ignorant of the turbulence beneath the various parts of that multi-colored national fabric.

In 1841 an Austrian of the old school made an observation that actually Austria was nothing but a fictitious name which did not express the existence of a definite people. "It is neither a country, nor a nation," he wrote. According to him, Austria was nothing but a conventional name spuriously uniting sharply separated national groups. There was no such thing as an Austria. There were Italians, Germans, Slavs, Hungarians. But one would search in vain for an Austrian national. "One who leaves Vienna," writes this Austrian, "finds no sympathy, no memoirs of the hundred years of unity and greatness, no historical ties, no national dignity of feelings. Patriotism one may find perhaps in villages and in some regions of the country. But this is local patriotism which has nothing in common with the country called Austria."[1]

The booklet from which the foregoing has been quoted was very popular and widely read. This indicates the extent of popular interest in the problem of the future of Austria as a national entity. The revolution of 1848 proved how right he was in his description

---

[1] von Adrian Wesburg, Viktor, *Oesterreich und seine Zukunft,* 3d ed. (Hamburg 1848) p. 8.

of the actual state of national consciousness in the Hapsburg monarchy.

On the eve of the revolution, when the censorship was looser and milder, political writing disclosed the stream of nationalistic trends and ideas of the peoples and ethnic groups populating Austria. Each group had its own problems derived from local social and historical conditions. These problems could not be solved by merely giving freedom of expression. The Austrian crown lands tended to be liberal, but were also intensely patriotic, and it was this patriotism for Austria that came into sharp conflict with the desires of the subject peoples, who were interested primarily not in freedom, but in national self-determination.

The problem of pan-Slavism, for instance, raged hotly in the Slav sections of Hungary and Bohemia. But in Galicia, the pan-Slav issue took second place since the two Slavic nationalities of Galicia, represented by the Ruthenians and the Poles, had a conflict which could be solved neither by pan-Slavism, nor by annexation to Poland. The Ruthenians, the weaker element in this conflict, were eager to join the pan-Slavistic camp, hoping that Russia, considered the mother of the Slavic people, would defend them against being absorbed by the Poles. However, the Poles were very hostile to Russia and looked upon Austria as the defender of their national rights. The Jewish population of Galicia had important problems of their own, and did not wish to become involved with the two contending groups, nor to help them in solving their political problems. The "slavery" of the Poles and Ruthenians, in the eyes of the Galician Jews, had more of a semblance of freedom than what they possessed. The Galician Jew looked for a revolution which would release him from the economic burden of over-taxation and from intolerable misery.[2]

The problem of cultural Polonization in Galicia was important only for the Poles, the leaders of the revolutionary movement, and for a host of superficially Polonized Jewish intellectuals. The Ruthenians, a people without intellectual leadership, did not even dare to think of winning the Jews to their camp. Their only hope and desire was that the Jews should not support the Polish claims for eastern Galicia, because this would mean that the Jews would

[2] *Yivo Bleter*, vol. xxvi (1945) 338-39.

support the Polish gentry against the Ruthenian peasantry. In Galicia, the problem of the demarcation line between the Ruthenians and Poles was relatively easier to solve. This, however, was not of much help to the Jews, who were engaged in economic activities all over Galicia, for the partition of the country would rather harm than improve their economic condition.

Quite different and unlike that in Galicia was the Jewish problem in the Italian provinces of Austria. Here there was a homogeneous Italian population with only a small number of Jews who spoke Italian and leaned more toward Italy than toward Austria politically.

A sharp conflict in which the Jewish population was involved took place in Bohemia. There the German population was not separated from the Czechs geographically as were the Poles and Ruthenians in Galicia. The Germans populated the cities, both large and small, and gave them a German character. The Bohemians lived mostly in the villages and in the poor quarters of the big cities. The problem of Bohemian freedom was primarily a national-cultural problem which could not come to its expression until the people had attained political-territorial self-government which would enable the Bohemian people to fulfill their destiny as a national entity. For the Bohemians the problem of culture was more important than the problem of political power, although they understood that the latter was imperative in order to achieve the former. They looked upon the Germans as their most dangerous enemies and therefore their drive for emancipation was concentrated upon the goal of emancipating themselves from the Germans. The liberal Jews, on the other hand, had turned toward the Germans for their culture and education and hoped to obtain emancipation through the Germans.

The philosophy of Bohemian history expressed itself in a mortal battle against everything German and this anti-German orientation became the main characteristic of Bohemian patriotism.[3] Herder's dictum that language is the very essence of national existence found enthusiastic approval and acceptance among all the Slav nations, the Bohemians included. Linguistic nationalism, therefore, became the main foundation of the Bohemian nationalist move-

[3] *Palacky, Dějiny národa čéského,* (Prague 1836) p. 12.

ment to a greater degree than among the Poles or Ruthenians in Galicia.

The outstanding Bohemian historian, Palacky, maintained that the chief criterion of Bohemian nationalism is a strong hostility to everything German. Years later when a Jewish-Bohemian movement of mutual fraternization developed in Bohemia one of its theoreticians borrowed this maxim of Palacky and developed it into a philosophy of "Jewish-Slavdom." "Czech-Jewish striving," he wrote, "tends primarily against the unnatural assimilation of Jews with Germandom."[4] Another protagonist of the same camp of Czech-Jewish assimilation expressed his philosophy in the following aphoristic sentence. "The Czech Jew is a central European Jew who has grown up in the sphere of a German culture which is not his culture." Therefore the problem of Czech assimilation was not political, as in other countries, but rather a question of ethics.[5] But when Palacky gave his formulation of the essence of Czech nationalism as applied to the Jews, it meant simply that the Jews should demonstrate the same hostility to everything German as the Czechs did. This was to be the only criterion of their Bohemian patriotism. The question whether such an anti-German orientation would make them Czechs in a cultural sense was secondary and not acute enough to be widely discussed at that time. If the Czechs considered the language problem as the central issue the most they could expect from the Jews was collaboration prompted not by emotional causes but rather as a result of political calculation. Neither Palacky nor the other eminent Bohemian writers and patriots expected great support from the Jews. The upper class of the Jewish population in Bohemia was culturally German and considered German as the only medium of cultural expression. The Jewish masses, although they spoke Yiddish, had no cultural nor language consciousness.

The Bohemian leaders looked upon the problem of "Slavisation" not as a mechanical adaptation of the language of the country, which was the final goal of assimilation. The Slavs considered

---

[4] It was *Jindřich Kohn* (1874-1935); see his *Asimilace a veky* (Prague 1936) vol. i, p. 14.

[5] Lederer, Edvard, *Předmluva k nenapsané knize. Kalendář Česko-Židovský*, XLI (1921-22) p. 31-42.

assimilation rather as a psychic readaptation in which language played a very important role. The very talented Bohemian writer Karel Havlíček Borovsky (1821-1856), for instance, had no confidence or hopes in turning the Jews in Bohemia into Czechs. "How can a Jew be a Czech," he declared, "when he is of semitic descent? It is much easier for us to consider Germans, Frenchmen, Spaniards, and Englishmen as part of our people than Jews, because these peoples have much more in common with us than do the Jews." Havlíček considered the Jews "a peculiar nation," a "semitic people," who lived among the Czechs but understood them, at best, only half the time. Havlicek came to the conclusion that in general Jews could not become Czechs, because in order to become a Czech one had to "cease to be a Jew."

Havlíček looked upon a national tongue as the strongest demonstration of national instinct. Jews, he wrote, who abandon their own language, by which he meant Hebrew, lack ethnic instinct. The best illustration, he wrote ironically, was that for many Jews, German had become a "second mother tongue." It was his contention that the Jews would do better to ally themselves with the Germans. Havlíček's attitude to the Jews, in spite of his sarcastic tongue, was not antisemitic. His almost racial approach to the Slavic problem was partly responsible for his nationalist credo that Jewish liberalism and Bohemian nationalism were incompatible. The extreme Czech movement demanded total assimilation and not an assimilation which would be a product merely of political opportunism. For Havlíček, to be a Czech was not a practical thing but rather a lofty ideal. One who did not belong by blood and history to that camp was not capable of understanding that ideal and would therefore be unwilling to sacrifice much for it. However, he did not consider Jews unworthy of equal rights. One should not dislike the Jews because they could not become Czechs, he felt, although he implied that there was no obligation to like them. The problem of emancipation of the Jews was simply not a Czech problem. What Havlíček desired was that the problem should not become a German one either, but should remain a purely Jewish one.[6]

[6] *Slovan* (Prague 1850) October, quoted from the text reprinted in *Žide a židovsti v Česke Literatuře,* by Oskar Donath (Brno 1923) vol. i, p. 141-43.

However, there were some Czechs who looked upon the Jews as dangerous enemies and for whom the mark of a good Czech was that he was a good antisemite. But this conception was not very popular. At the Congress of the Slavs held at Prague in 1848, the Slavic scholar Pavel Joseph Šafařik (1795-1861) declared that even converted Jews should not be admitted to the sessions of the Congress because they might be sent there as informers for the Germans. "These people should not intervene in international affairs." However, this assertion did not prevent him from stating at the same Congress that he envied the Poles their greatest poet, Adam Mickiewicz, who was of Jewish descent. Apparently Šafařik was not a racial antisemite if he could accept the greatness of the Polish poet despite his Jewish ancestry.[7]

There were, among the Czechs, individuals influenced by the western European conception of assimilation who were willing to work for Jewish-Bohemian fraternization, not in terms of racial nationalistic diffusion but rather in terms of cultural rapprochement. One of them was Wenzl Nebesky (1818-1882). After 1843 he resided in Vienna and mingled with a group of his Jewish countrymen who wrote in German. This group, the first "young Bohemian circle," which employed German as a medium of creative expression, had deep sympathy for the Slavs and utilized in their writings themes from Slavonic folklore and history. The Czechs were greatly pleased with this group, especially Nebesky, because the Jewish writer from Bohemia and Moravia presented to the world the beautiful and colorful life of the Slavs. Since it was written in German it helped develop great sympathy for the oppressed Slavs among German-speaking people. Nebesky believed that this literary goodwill movement would sooner or later bring about political fraternization.

There was also a group of Galician-born Jewish writers, allied with the Polish camp, who lived in Vienna and published poetry in favor of Poland. The Poles did not attribute too great importance to this group because, compared with the Czechs, they had a much larger class of intellectuals of their own. In Vienna Nebesky realized how small his own camp of writers was and therefore he con-

[7] *Slavische Centralblätter* (1848) 9; *Oesterreich*, 1918, vol. i, 521; *Korrespondence Šafařika. Vydal V. A. Francew* (Prague 1928) passim.

sidered it advisable to utilize his German-writing compatriots for
the benefit of the Bohemian cause. Somehow he believed that he
might influence them gradually to switch from German to Bohemian. Nebesky had a very high opinion of the literary abilities
of the Jews. He envied the Germans to whom the Jews had given
Heine and Boerne. He hoped that the Jews from his country might
become Bohemian writers and give to his country a galaxy of poetical names such as they had given to Germany. He therefore considered the frequent utilization of Slavic themes by his German-writing
compatriots as a great contribution to the Slavic cause and as a
unique opportunity to demonstrate the richness of the Slavic culture.

The Bohemian-Jewish writer looked more realistically upon the
problem of writing in Bohemian. It is true that the Slavic world
was rich in motifs and poetic themes, yet its potential audience was
small since there were few people who read Bohemian. In addition
to this they looked upon the language of the Czechs as immature,
undeveloped, incapable of expressing adequately the problems and
aspirations of modern times. Liberal-minded, slightly tainted by
cosmopolitan life, they could not comprehend the importance of a
language. For them, the expression of sympathy for the country
from which they came and for the national aspirations of its Slavic
inhabitants were tokens enough of attachment and solidarity. By
making such assertions they emphasized the bi-lingual character of
Bohemia, of which one language, Bohemian, was for internal consumption, and the other, German, for great cultural and literary
achievements.

"Our education shall be in German," wrote one of the main protagonists of this camp. "This, however, should not prohibit us from
participating in the literary movement of our Czech compatriots
and from supporting this movement according to our means, supporting it also in its other aspirations, as long as it is confined to
the province of literature."[8]

The Czechs had a different attitude to the problem of language.
For them this was not only a problem of literature but of life and
their very ethnic existence. The Bohemian German-writing Jews
could not understand such an attitude. When the Czech writer

[8] Among them were Morits Hartmann (1821-1872), Ludwig Frankl (1810-
1894) and others. *Cf. Orient* (1844) 38.

Vaclav Kličpera (1792-1859) approached the German-Bohemian poet Frankl and asked him also to write in Czech, Frankl replied that this was for him a matter not of principle but of readers.[9] Among the outstanding members of this circle in Vienna was a young student of medicine, Siegfried Kapper (1821-1879). He later became an eminent student of Slav folklore and a pioneer of Bohemian-Jewish assimilation and of total identification with the Bohemian political and cultural cause.

Among the first adherents of such Slavic assimilation was a young student, David Kuh (1818-1879), who had lived in Vienna since 1841. In an article published in *Allgemeine Zeitung des Judenthums* Kuh declared himself to be a great admirer of Slavic nationalism. The Slavs, he maintained, desire to win for themselves a place in the culture and history of Europe. Such a desire deserves sympathy and Kuh declared himself a Slav. But as a Jew, Kuh appealed to the Slavs to abandon their conception of racial Slavdom and thus enlist the support of non-Slavic talent. Kuh advanced the theory that with no group of people had so many Jews found shelter as among the Slavs. Therefore Slavic-Jewish friendly relations had a long historical background. He appealed to the Slavic scholars to become more liberal-minded and emancipate themselves from their primitive racial antisemitism.

The Slavs, Kuh stated, had the opportunity to convert the Jews into a middle class of their own, since there were three times as many Jews among the Slavs as among the Germans. Jews could not demand political rights from the Slavs for the very reason that the Slavs had no power to grant them. However, Kuh was very pessimistic as to the future of the Jews among the Slavs. He openly stated that if the Slavs had had the power they probably would not have given such rights to the Jews. Although he did not have confidence in the possibility of the Jews becoming citizens on terms of equality with the Slavs yet Kuh came to the conclusion that because of the precarious situation of the Jews, since they were not a nation, they had to decide which nation they should join. The Jews, Kuh maintained, could not exist as a separate people and he assured his readers that they had no desire to be such a people.

[9] Hanuš, J., *Život a spisy Nebeského* (Prague 1896) p. 72 ff.; Frankl, L. A., *Erinnerungen* (Prague 1910).

Therefore the Jew faced the dilemma as to which nation to join in Bohemia and it was his contention that they should identify themselves with the Slavs.

Simultaneously Kuh appealed to the Jews to study the Slavic literature and to abandon the "Talmudic culture" which was "alien to our times." By being educated in the language of the Slavs, Kuh maintained, the Bohemian Jew would cease to look for education among the German Jews. Gradually he would have his own publications and books. He would hear from the pulpits of the synagogues sermons delivered in the language of the country and thus gradually would become part and parcel of the country in which he dwelt. This declaration by Kuh solved only in theory the crux of the problem of the German-Bohemian conflict. By accepting the Czech stand that the country was Slavic he gave no support to those who defended the bi-lingual character of the country's culture. Moreover, in another article Kuh greeted "the peaceful victory of the Bohemian language," which was accepted on an equal basis with German. He maintained that from a cultural point of view German was still stronger than Bohemian. The best illustration of that was that the Czechs themselves, up to then, had benefited more from the German language and culture and had found it necessary to employ the German language, particularly in the realm of higher education. Kuh was not so fanatically pro-Slav as to blame the Jews who wrote in German. He considered them good patriots of the country of their birth by the fact that they employed themes taken from Bohemia. All those who perpetuated in German the history of Bohemia and the national heroes of the Bohemian people as well as those who wrote short stories and poems describing the life of the Bohemian Jews he considered good Bohemians. Among them he mentioned also Siegfried Kapper, whose *Slavic Melodies* appeared in 1844 in German. He valued the literary products of the Bohemian-Jewish writer as expressions of Bohemian patriotism manifested through the medium of the German language.[10]

[10] A. Z. J. (1844) 14, 15, 16; (1845) 41, 629 ff. Kuh's Slavophilic activities were of short duration. Two years later he switched to the German camp and became the editor of a German liberal paper. During the years 1862-1873 he served as a member of the Bohemian Diet. He died in 1879. *Cf.* Teweles, H., in *Mitt. des Vereines fuer die Geschichte der Deutschen in Böhmen,* vol. xvii (1879) 309-15.

Bohemia had, already, the first visible symptoms of a trend toward Czechization. The press gave exaggerated publicity to these evidences. The indifference to the Bohemian movement was defended as a result of anti-Jewish occurrences which took place in Prague in 1844 when Christian workers demolished the machinery in textile factories which happened to belong to Jewish manufacturers. The over-zealous adherents of Czechization among the Jews accused the Jews of cowardice and maintained that the conflict of 1844 was grossly exaggerated. The rumors of antisemitism, they asserted, served the purpose of the central government authorities. "Jewish hostility in Austria is a well-calculated issue which helps to maintain the balance of the country." Of course, Jews could not be forced to study Bohemian, but the youth had to be admonished to do it because its future was bound up with it.[11]

Nebesky was deeply moved by Kuh's pro-Bohemian declaration. He saw in it the first public utterance of importance, the first step toward drawing the Jewish intellectuals closer to Bohemian culture. "I shall continue to work in that direction," Nebesky wrote, "This can enrich us with good talent from the Jewish camp. The Jews are a wonderful, marvelous people, full of spirit and activity. They help the Germans immensely. Now they shall help us also."[12]

In an article entitled "The Relation of the Jews and Slavs," published in the same year, as a reply to Kuh's writing, Nebesky once again took up the very popular contemporary theory of "the historical hospitality of Slavdom toward the semites."[13] He complained that, despite the fact that only among the Slavic people could one find densely populated Jewish communities, yet the Jews were of very little cultural assistance to the Slavs. This, he maintained, was a great calamity for both parties.

The Slav would have gained a great deal from the assistance of this dynamic spiritual people [wrote Nebesky]. One has only to recollect how many valuable individuals the Jews have given to German art and science. The Slavs have nothing. The Jews shall aspire to one goal with

[11] Schulhof, Ignaz, "Ueber die Vernachlaessigung des Böhmischen," in *Orient* (1844) 42.

[12] Hanuš, *op. cit.*, 72.

[13] Opět něco o poměru Slovanu a Židu," in *Kvety* (1844) 314 ff. The Mickiewicz cult as a symbol of total Slavo-Jewish spiritual fusion is treated in my study on Mickiewicz and the Jews (*Zukunft*, 1923, January).

those people with whom they live together. They shall be inspired with the same thought and the same will and of the same aspiration. This will lead to the disappearance of the prejudices the Czech Christians still hold against the Jews and of which the Jews complain so strongly.

In another article, Nebesky alleges that the Jews show little patriotism towards the Slavs. In Germany, he wrote, three hundred thousand Jews had seven publications of their own, all of them in the language of the country, whereas the Jews in the Slavic countries had none, although they numbered two million souls. This separatism must cease, he said. He understood that this was not so easy to achieve, yet he felt that an effort had to be made. The Slavs were realists. They understood very well how much they could benefit from the two million Jews who were so "ingenious."

A people [Nebesky wrote] who plays such a great role in the history of humanity, in whose language the Bible is written, that book of books, a people who put up a resistance against the most furious storms of the tragic centuries and yet preserved its character, religion, this oldest people of the world, cannot be of light spirit.

He referred to Adam Mickiewicz, who said in one of his lectures on Slavic literatures, that Jews possessed great spiritual qualities and therefore it was no calamity that the Jews lived in large numbers among the Slavic people. Nebesky not only endorsed Kuh's appeal for closer Bohemian-Jewish relations, but reviewed with great enthusiasm Kapper's poems. These poems, entitled *Česke listy* (Czech Leaves) appeared in 1846 and were dedicated to the Austrian count Leo Thun, and to the Jewish banker, Leopold von Laemmel.[14] Thun represented the Bohemian nobility who demonstrated a benevolent sympathy for the cause of the Czech cultural revival. Laemmel was a Jewish patron of art and literature, one of the first few wealthy Jews in Bohemia who contributed financially to the cause of Czech cultural institutions. The dedication itself disclosed the political orientation of the young poet who was the first Jew to write in the language of the country.

It was obvious that Kapper tried simply to win the Jews for the

[14] Leopold von Laemmel (1790-1867) represented the upper group of Jewish bourgeosie, who looked upon Bohemia as a crown land of Austria of bi-national character, but historically destined to become more German than Czech. "We are living in times of dissolved historical rights," he declared to Palacky. *Cf.* Kazbunda, *Česke hnuti roku 1848* (Prague 1929) p. 115.

Bohemian cause. The political program of the radical Bohemian
patriots was not his concern. By dedicating his book to a Jew and
to a non-Jew, who definitely were not in the camp of those Czechs
who wanted to separate entirely from Austria as a territorial unit,
he gave testimony to his credo as to the desirable future of Bohemia. It was more a token of emotional pro-Czech sentiment than
a manifestation of unequivocal political orientation. Kapper wanted
to win over the Jews to the Slavic idea. Bohemia he considered
his fatherland, and therefore, he had no longing for that remote
land where "his ancestors rot." In his veins, the young poet assured
his readers, ran the same blood as in the veins of Nebesky, the
Czech. He therefore appealed to his "compatriots" to accept him
as a Czech.

Nebesky, who encouraged Jews to write in Czech, saw in Kapper's writings the first realization of his dream. He welcomed the
"proud son of Israel" who at the same time was a good Czech, and
"encourages his co-religionists to ally themselves with our national
life." Nebesky was also overjoyed by the fact that a group of Czech
liberals made possible the publication of the first Czech translation
of the Hebrew prayerbook.[15]

In general, Kapper's Czech poems were well received by the
critics, except for Havliček. The latter praised the Jewish motifs
which, according to him, comprised the best part of the book, and
he also had a friendly word to say about Kapper's idea of Czech-
Jewish fraternization. But he took strong exception to the literary
qualities of the poems. His chief argument was that, despite Kapper's poetic declarations that he was a Czech, Havliček could not
consider him a Czech because a Czech would never have written
books in German as Kapper had done. Havliček repeated the argument of the radical Czechs that it was impossible to be both a Jew
and a Czech.[16] Some writers on the history of the Jews in Bohemia

---

[15] The Czech writer Josef Jarosláv Kalina (1816-1847) suggested a Czech
translation of the Hebrew prayerbook. In February 1847 such a translation was
printed in four hundred copies and appeared in Vienna. It was reissued as late
as 1884. *Cf.* Salač, K. *Zapomenuté modlitby a Kapperóv odkaz českym Zidům,
Kalendař Česko-Židovsky*, XLV (1925-26) 160-162. On earlier efforts see,
A. Z. J. (1844) 46.

[16] *Česka včela* (1846) November 6. See also Donath's study of Kapper in
Jahrbuch der Gesellschaft für Geschichte der Juden in der Č-S. Republik, vol.
vi (1934) 341.

of that period have alleged that Havlíček's partly negative review
of Kapper's first book of Czech poems was mainly responsible for
his cooling off toward the idea of Czecho-Jewish fraternization and
also for his ceasing, for a while, to write in the Czech language.

It is a well-established fact that Bohemian pan-Slavism aroused
among the Jews certain critical reservations of a purely ideological
nature. Some liberal Jews held that the Slavic movement was reac-
tionary because it gravitated toward Russia and was concerned more
with nationalistic than with social and political problems.

One of the leaders of the Jewish liberals in Cracow, Dr. Joseph
Oettinger, a candidate for the Austrian parliament in 1848, declared
in an election speech that pan-Slavism was contradictory to democracy and therefore should be opposed by the Jews. In reality there
were two trends of thought regarding pan-Slav nationalism. At the
two congresses of Slavic peoples, held almost simultaneously in
1848, one in Prague and the second in Breslau, the differences in
attitude toward pan-Slavism were very pronounced and conclusive. While the Poles represented, in spite of their Slavic origin
and even pro-Slavic tendencies, a definite anti-Russian camp, a
great number of eminent Czechs, Croats, Ruthenians, Serbians, and
Bulgarians had strong leanings towards Russian pan-Slavism.

From a Jewish point of view, hostility toward Russia rendered
impossible even faint sympathy for those who identified themselves
with "Byzantian pan-Slavism." The very fact that the German democratic and liberal groups were strongly anti-Russian caused the
Jewish groups to base their hopes for emancipation on the progressive Germans of those days. These democratic Germans, however, had very little sympathy for any cause fought by the Slavs.
Their main goal was a centralized Germany and they considered
the Slavic aspirations to be a great hindrance to this goal and even
a danger for the very freedom of the people.[17] Even the Slavic

---

[17] A release of the "Verein zur Wahrung der deutschen Sache an den östlichen
Grenzen," dated Leipzig, May 1, 1848 (in author's collection). It is signed by
two non Jews and two Jews (Julius Fürst and Ad. Jellinek).

Among the Poles the anti-German, and consequently also pro-Russian, feel-
ing was not as strong as among the Czechs. Hence the sharp conflict between the
radical Czechs and the Poles. The Czechs supported the Ruthenians' claims in
Galicia and thus caused dissatisfaction and resentment in Polish circles. *Cf.*
Kazbunda, Karel, *Havlíček a c.k. úřady w době předbřeznove. Česky Časopis
Historicky*, vol. xxxii (1926) 44 ff.

ideology of the prominent Czechs and Poles, who embodied the
so-called pro-Austrian orientation and desired to rebuild Austria
on the principles of a federal state, was totally ignored by the more
enlightened Jewish leaders of those days. They ignored the differences in nuance between pro-Russian pan-Slavism and anti-Russian
pan-Slavism and showed a well-balanced indifference to them both.

In the circles of the liberal Jews Slavic nationalism was almost
synonymous with anti-Judaism. The more nationalistic the Slav
becomes, writes a correspondent of the *Allgemeine Zeitung des
Judenthums* (1844, 46), "the greater is the cleavage between him
and the Jew." The question of integrating the Jews with the Slavs
provoked many contradictory interpretations. Some interpreted
this concept as complete Slavization of the Jews, whereas the moderate and more realistic interpreters took it to mean simply the
acquisition of the language of the country by the Jews. The first
Reform Rabbi in Galicia, Abraham Kohn, of Lemberg, interpreted
the problem of languages for the Jews in the light of both the language of the province in which the Jew resided and the language of
state to which this province belonged. In an article written in 1847,
he declared that the Jews ought to know Polish because it was the
language of the country. But German was also necessary not only
because it was the language of the country but also because it is
the universal language of culture. Such linguistic dualism was not
acceptable to the radical patriots of the various Slavic nationalities
in Austria. Language was to them not only a token of the might of
culture but also a manifestation of the culture of might. The most
representative Jewish man of letters of those days did not want to
indulge in the complicated problems dealing with the variety of
cultural manifestations and with the fluidity of cultural boundaries,
both of which made the work of reassimilation and assimilation
difficult. He tended rather to follow the line of least resistance by
simplifying the issue of language identification, an issue to which
the various nationalities of Austria attached too great importance.

"The situation of the Jews in a country where a struggle of nationalities arises and, with that, a struggle for language hegemony,
is a very hard one," wrote the Prague correspondent of the *Orient*
(1844, 7). However, he had to admit that the Jew could not afford
to take a neutral position in that struggle. He had to align himself

with one side or the other because this was the only solution. In Bohemia, the central government of Vienna suppressed the Slavic element. The great men of Bohemia, on the other hand, strove to develop and to build their language on a scientific basis. What should the Jews do? The paper advised the Jews to be of assistance to the Czechs and thus manifest their Bohemian loyalty. The few Jews who had already expressed their active sympathy for the Czech cause, like Kapper and others, are frequently mentioned as illustrations and as examples for others to follow. The "cowards of the Jewish community" were persistently attacked, and accused of sabotaging the noble attempts to disseminate the Czech language among the Jewish population of Prague, due to their fear of the Austrian government. "Frightened," writes the *Orient*, "they believe that they will arouse the dissatisfaction of the government if the Jewish Bohemians support the Christian Bohemians in their indefatigable striving to develop the mother-tongue."

It is worth while to mention in passing that this was the first time that the expression "Jewish Bohemians" was applied to the Jews, and that the Bohemian language was identified as the language of all the inhabitants of the country, Jews included.

Suffering from a cultural inferiority complex, the Czechs realized that their language was still in the process of development from a folk language into a cultural medium capable of unlimited expression. "Every educated man," Havliček wrote, "looks like a German. Slavdom is looked upon as fitting for the common people and whoever is concerned with the promotion of his national language is considered peculiar."

Jews were confident that emancipation would open the doors of education to them and education was considered synonymous with German education. Bohemian nationalism was the ideology of the middle classes, which looked upon the Jews as their economic competitors. The foundation of national patriotism was the peasantry, hence the strong pro-peasant sentiments and the predilection for the ethnic peculiarities of the peasant's life to the extent of trying to revive them in the almost completely Germanized cities of Bohemia. Slavic mythology, folk-songs, traditions and dances were the very foundation of the Czech national upsurge. The Jews who sympathized with the Czech movement realized that this movement

was partly alien to them, since the Western European conception
of assimilation was concerned with the higher cultural aspects and
not with the primitive manifestations of folk life. They could not
understand a patriotic obligation or moral duty to study the Bohemian language and literature when such study did not offer
ample possibilities for application in everyday life. Since history
did not develop in Jews the notion of identifying national consciousness with language affiliation, the emotional attitude toward
language and culture manifested by the Czechs was alien and in-
comprehensible even to those Jews who approved of it as a matter
of principle.

The Czechs, in looking for national regeneration, expected little
short of a miracle, since the most representative leaders of the
Czech culture had very little faith in the possibility of national
survival. Hence the peculiarly sensitive attitude of the Czech leaders, not only to those who ridiculed their over-zealous efforts to
introduce their language rapidly but also to those who were too
practical and therefore realized the difficulties involved, thus hurt-
ing the feelings of the sensitive Czechs.

This whole situation had the effect of creating an opportunity
for the Jews to state that they also had a language of their own
and there was no reason why they should abandon it. "The Jews,"
the *Orient* writes, "are frequently inclined, in order to demonstrate
their patriotism, to deny any independence of their own and to
accept any other form. Our Jews ought to know and to study the
Bohemian language and literature. But they also should not neglect
Hebrew as is being done up to now." This formulation was indi-
rectly a rejoinder to the accusations of Havlíček that the Jews had
forsaken their sacred language. But it also had much deeper con-
notations. It was the first reformulation of the entire problem of
integration, so persistently underscored and disseminated by the
nationalists of the Pan-Slavic camp, who demanded total assimilation not only of the Jews, to whom they denied nationhood, but
also of the Germans, who had a higher cultural development.

Since the Slavic nationalists identified themselves primarily with
language, the Jews had to counterbalance this identification with a
similar one of their own. The "enlightened" Jews, except for a few
in Galicia, did not consider Yiddish a language, although Yiddish

was the language of the masses, not only in Galicia, but also in Bohemia, Moravia, and in the Slavic regions of Hungary. Propounding Hebrew as the language of the Jewish people, though it was no longer a spoken language, the Jews put forward a much wider program than pure linguistic identification. Hebrew was still the language of traditional Jewish education; it was thus deeply rooted from time immemorial in the communal life of the country and it had a considerable literature expounding the philosophy of the *Haskala*. Jews were different, the protagonists of the Hebrew camp argued, even when they spoke the language of the country. Historical conditions caused that difference. There was, for instance, a profound difference between the history of the Jews in Bohemia and the history of Bohemians in Bohemia. Of course there were parallels and analogies between Bohemian and Jewish histories, very frequently quoted and interpreted with gusto by many Czech philosophers of history, poets and novelists.

Leopold Kompert (1822-1886) wrote, in 1846, a short story in which we find for the first time a claim of Jewish national uniqueness: "Being a Jew, he could not understand the role of religious struggles in Bohemia . . . but their political significance he understood very well." Here he saw a battle for good will, freedom, and independence; here his own feelings were emphathic. "Jerusalem and Bohemia! The same nightmare embraced the two giant corpses with the silence of the grave. . . ."

" 'Shall I tell you,' Moritz said a few days later, 'with whose history the history of Bohemia has great similarities?' 'With none,' answered Honza proudly. 'And I tell you it has great similarities with Jewish history.' Honza did not stop laughing. 'Have you a Žižka?' he exclaimed. 'Have you Hussites?' 'Oh, yes,' replied Moritz. 'We have the Maccabeans.' "[18]

This interesting dialogue between a Czech and a Jew presents the essence of the philosophy of history then in vogue, not only among the Czechs, but also among the Poles. This was not the only argument for an historical heritage of their own which was a necessary counter-argument against the widely-held accusation that Jews

[18] The title of the story, obviously of an autobiographical nature, is "Die Kinder des Randars." It is quoted here from a study by Paul Amann, *Leopold Kompert's literarische Anfänge* (Prague 1907) p. 97-98.

lacked a sense of historicity. The young physician of Moravia, M. Teller, one of the first Jewish democratic intellectuals who was interested in the social welfare of his people, appealed to the Czechs to work for the good will of Czechs and Jews and influence their compatriots in the spirit of tolerance toward the Jews. He showed great sympathy for the cause of the Slavic peoples and he was one of the few Jews who opposed the Hungarian attempts to Magyarize the Slavic peoples of Hungary. Teller attacked the propensity to divide the population of a country into hosts and guests, the latter term usually applied to Jews. He underscored Jewish attachment to Bohemia and Moravia and he appealed to the Jews to study the history of the Jews in these countries in order to prove that Jews were settled there long before the Czechs. It is obvious that such an appeal was a psychic necessity to create a defense mechanism against the inferiority complex widely developed among the not over-confident Jewish intellectuals as to the future of the Jews in these countries.[19]

Ignatz Kuranda, a native of Bohemia, wrote extensively in the same spirit of Jewish historicity. He urged the organization of a general Jewish historical society and one for Prague in particular. The task of such a society would be to study the history of the Jews in the Slavic countries. Such a study, Kuranda stated, would prove to the Jews that they dwelt in these countries much longer than the Slavs. In his opinion it was necessary and important because it would be "of use in the struggle for emancipation."[20]

"How is it," Kuranda asks, "that among so many Jewish communities there is no historical society for the purpose of assembling material for a Jewish history?" Kuranda could not comprehend how Jews, who possess such a strong "instinct for reality," did not grasp the idea that digging in the past led to "encouragement and sup-

---

[19] Teller wrote on the earliest history of Jews in Prague in *Oest. Centralorgan* (1848) 19. See also *A. Z. J.* (1845) 44, 46. In his *Reise in Böhmen* (Dresden 1844) p. 161, the well-known traveller-author Kohl asserts that "Judaism in Bohemia is much older than paganism and Christianity, and older than Germans and Slavs." Since such a statement came from a non-Jew, the Jewish literati were deeply impressed by it. Concerning poetic interpretation of the Jewish past in Prague by Jewish and non-Jewish writers, much has been written, but no synthetic study is available. Compare Meissner, Alfred, *Geschichte meines Lebens* (Vienna 1885) p. 56, 194, etc.

[20] *Grenzboten* (1844) 165-66.

port for the present and the future." He appealed especially to the "educated Jews of Prague" and was surprised at their unforgivable indifference to their own history. He concluded that it proved that Jews lacked a sense of history.

Teller and Kuranda, who represented two different ideological camps, one with pronounced pro-Slavic sympathies, the other with definite central-German inclinations, though tainted with liberalism, both came to the same conclusion, namely that Jews should study their own history in the countries in which they are struggling for freedom. Jews were not given the opportunity of choosing their *own freedom*, derived and formulated on the basis of their own historical processes, but were forced to jump on the historical bandwagon of the "host people," and to identify themselves with a history which was not their own.

The problems of language and history were not the only ones to attract the attention of the Jewish writers of that era. The problem of how Jews as a group should be identified in the *great* family of *small* nations in Austria also began to concern some of the more sensitive young Jews. Simon Szantó (1819-1882), a Hungarian-born journalist and later editor of a Jewish yearbook, asked why the Jew should not be registered as a Jew in the struggle for emancipation rather than being content merely to follow blindly the national groups of the countries in which he was born. Everyone but the Jews, he wrote, shows his national colors by which he is recognizable. "Our colors are white and blue," he declared. "Let us, therefore, demonstrate them and the question of language will automatically drop."[21]

The Jewish intelligentsia, as previously mentioned, had no conception of language patriotism and considered it to be an artificial issue. What made the situation particularly difficult at the time was that in the struggle for language self-determination, the negative issue of anti-Germanism was much more strongly emphasized than any positive program. In their eyes language was nothing but a medium of cultural expression and they could not understand why priority should be given to a rustic language over a cosmopolitan

---

[21] "Wappen und Farben," in *Oest Centralorgan* (1848) 43. Szantó was the editor of *Neuzeit* in collaboration with Kompert. He may be considered the first precursor of Zionism in Austria.

language like German. Those who expressed sympathy for the cultural nationalism of the small nations were suspected, not by the Slavs only but also by some Jews, of being politicians rather than reasonably convinced adherents. The poets of Jewish descent were brushed aside as individuals immersed in the artistic possibilities of the colorful Slavic life rather than in mature political thinking. As previously stated, none of the Jewish intellectuals showed any sympathy or understanding for the importance of Yiddish. Yiddish became a subject of study only for the German and Slavic scholars who were interested in the rudiments of old Slavic and German words still preserved in that language. Since the conception of a Jewish national minority had not yet been broached, no one dared to advance the theory that Jews, by declaring their identification with the Yiddish language, could thus ease their precarious position of being wooed by the various camps in the intra-national strife.

The argument that nationality is based fundamentally on language was applied to the Jews in one case only, and in a negative sense. Because Yiddish was a language hence the Jews were a nationality; therefore Yiddish had to be eradicated so that the Jews should cease to be a nationality. This was the line of reasoning by Anton Reé, who wrote as follows: "The Jewish masses still speak a separate dialect which means that they still remain a separate people." It was, therefore, his opinion that the wisest thing would be for the "defeated" Jews to accept the language of the "victor."[22]

Very few Jewish intellectuals looked upon Yiddish with favor. Most Jewish intellectuals who were deeply rooted in the old traditional Jewish life propounded the Hebraic tradition as a cultural program for the Jews. In a letter to the *Orient* there appeared a strong appeal to continue to cultivate Hebrew. "Write in that language that it may become alive in us. Express your thoughts in the old but delicate and powerful phraseology." A *maskil* from Koenigsberg assured his readers that Hebrew was not dead yet. With the disappearance of Hebrew, he wrote, the Jewish people will disappear. "The Hebrew language," he wrote, "is the most important, the most sacred symbol in our religious and national history. This language was and is the most vital medium of our memories and

[22] Reé, Anton, *Sprachverhältnisse der heutigen Juden* (Hamburg, 1844) p. 41, 50.

development."[23] Similarly, another Jewish intellectual, the Galician-born scholar, Moses Ehrenreich (1818-1899), propounded his theory of Jewish nationalism. It was his contention that it was important to clarify the conflicts between Jewishness and the principle of emancipation at the inception of the struggle for equal rights. Jewishness was primarily the way and form of Jewish education, which was more important than language. It was therefore imperative, he concluded, that the Jew should not lose the very essence of the Jewish nationality in his struggle for emancipation. "If the Magyar, the Pole, or the Czech in Austria insists upon not being hindered in cultivating and developing their languages, this is 'patriotism.' If a Jew demands the same he is called 'unpatriotic'." Arguing against those who maintain that Hebrew was no longer a living language, Ehrenreich stated that regardless of that, it was the language of "our forefathers."[24]

There was also a school of thought among those Jewish intellectuals who were opposed to all manifestations of nationalism, Jewish or non-Jewish, which maintained that there was a much higher mission imposed upon the Jews, namely to cure the other nations of their nationalistic vanity and to prove that language was not as important as freedom. The difference between Jew and non-Jew, one of them asserted, consisted in the very fact that whereas the Czechs were struggling for the life of their language the Jews were struggling for their very life.[25] And in order to put up a successful struggle for "their very life," some of them expressed doubt whether "that very life" could be attained through the benevolent actions of other people, no matter how liberal they were. Teller, for instance, maintained that Jews should elect their own representatives to parliament, since no one else could be entrusted to defend the special rights of the Jews.[26]

The demand for the democratization of Jewish life was not only confined to the external political arena. The necessity to democratize Jewish communal life was also realized and demanded. The community bureaucracy became the object of attacks by the demo-

[23] *Orient* (1847); Dr. Falkenheim in *A. Z. J.* vol. xviii, 267-69.

[24] Born in Brody, he was a son-in-law of Isaac Samuel Reggio; see *Oest. Centralorgan* (1848) 149-51.

[25] *Ibid.* (1848) 30; see also *Orient* (1844) 36.

[26] *Ibid.* (1848) 178.

cratic-minded Jewish leaders. Some of them demanded that the plutocratic leadership of the communities be removed, as others demanded that the autocratic rulers of the country be abolished. If everything is for the people, then what about the communities? asked Simon Hock, the historian of Jewish Prague. "If the man on the throne recently enacted this disastrous principle, that everything is for the people but not through the people, why should the men around the 'green table' not do the same thing, and do it no less radically?"[27]

In order to clarify what should be done for the people one had to give a definite declaration of the kind of freedom the Jewish masses needed. In a very daring article which was the first pronounced manifestation of deep democratic convictions, Leopold Kompert gave expression to that idea. He maintained that a revolution from a Jewish point of view would fail unless it gave not only equal rights but also opportunities to the poor Jews. "In him [the poor Jew] lies our kernel, our power, our Judaism. The beautiful, delicate, and inspiring that we possess is found in these crippled and afflicted creatures. What we have lost in spirit and soul in our conflict with the world, he still possesses untouched." Kompert regretted the absence of social classes among the Jews. The peasant would always be a peasant, so would the burgher always remain a burgher. But the poor Jew could only become a "rich Jew." He dreamed that the revolution would pave his way to wealth. Kompert maintained that it was necessary for the Jewish intelligentsia to fuse with the people. "We can't," he writes, "and will never be able to be something different but what our people is."[28]

Kompert was very much opposed to the Jewish "money aristocracy," which pretended to be the exclusive representatives of the Jews. He, together with others of his generation, accused the wealthy Jews of doing more harm than good to the Jewish masses. "We are the disciples of freedom, and they are the servants of the *ancien regime*." Shall we be proud, he asked, of our little and big

[27] Hock, S., *Über jüdische Zustände in Prag* (Prague 1848) p. 53-54, 69-70, 201-202. Hock was very optimistic as to the future of the Jews in Europe. He predicted that the year 1948 would look upon the previous century with disgust and contempt. See also David Kaufmann's introductory essay to Hock's *Die Familien Prags* (Pressburg 1892).

[28] "Für unsere armen Juden," in *Oest Centralorgan,* vol. i (1848) 19-20, 36-37.

Rothschilds? He answered in the negative. The "money aristocrats," the Rothschilds, he maintained, with their frequent loans, helped to fortify the old absolutistic system of government. He even rejected the common belief that the rich Jews gave charity generously. Whatever they give, he maintained, was nothing but a "drop in the sea of their sins." By giving charity they benefited, thus obtaining political rights for themselves. He concluded his militant article with the slogan: "We do not want any more of a money aristocracy."[29]

The contemporary radical poet Karl Beck also accused the Rothschilds of "demoralizing the Jews." In one of his poems Beck asked why the Rothschilds did not come, like Moses, to demand freedom for the Jews. "The Jewish bankers represent the Jews just as little as the old-clothes merchants represent them."

These social notes in the Jewish journalism and poetry of that era comprise a still unexplored chapter in the history of the ideology of 1848.[30] The Jewish writer for the first time discovered the existence of Jewish proletarians in Bohemia and in Galicia. The social-minded Jewish journalists started to reinterpret the problem of Jewish emancipation from a social angle. They found discernible differences in the possibilities of enjoying that desirable freedom and emancipation and formulated for the first time the doctrine that Jewish emancipation could not be an emancipation for the rich only and not for the poor. A Belgian writer who visited Galicia concluded his observations by saying: "The Jewish prole-

[29] "Die Geldaristokratie und die Juden," *ibid* (1848) no. 3; Shatzky, J., "The Revolution of 1848 and the Beginning of Socialistic Ideas among the Jews," in *Undzer tzeit* (January 1948) 47-52. Historian Gerson Wolf (1823-1892) was in sympathy with socialism, as is discernible in his pamphlet entitled *Die Demokratie und der Socialismus, das allgemeine Wahlrecht und die Gleichberechtigung der Nationalitäten in Osterreich* (Vienna 1849).

[30] Beck, Karl, *Lieder vom armen Mann. Mit einem Vorwort an das Haus Rothschild* (Leipzig 1846); *idem.*, "Der Trödeljude," in *A. Z. J.* (1846) 13-14; *idem.*, "An Rothschild," in *Oest. Centralorgan* (1848) no. 3, 35-36; Schmidt, W. S., *Gedicht an Herrn Rothschild* (Vienna, 1848) (in author's collection). Concerning the feelings against the wealthy Jews see also Kazbunda, Karel, in *Česky Časopis Historicky*, vol. xxxiv (1928). Roubik, F., *Česky rok* 1848 (Prague 1931). Concerning anti-Jewish skirmishes and their relation to the revolution, Friedrich Schwarzenberg, an old Austrian aristocrat and cardinal, wrote: "Judenhetze is die Vorläuferin oder Begleiterin einer jeden Revolution." *Cf.* Wolfsgruber, *Friedrich Kardinal Schwarzenberg*, vol. i, p. 176.

tarian is only as Jewish as the Christian is Christian. Their real religion is the proletarian religion."[31]

In this choir of ideological voices, unorganized as yet into a *unisono* because of the variety of conditions from which they stemmed, the voice of the orthodox Jew was also heard. As a rule the orthodox kept aloof from the camps of passionate political discussion. It was not so easy for an orthodox Jew to reach public attention since the Jewish journals were more or less in sympathy with the liberal trends of Jewish life. But their importance in communal life none denied. Labelled as uncompromising fanatics, they ignored entirely the political discussions of those days and had more courage than any other group in defying resolutions passed by the radical leaders and superimposed upon the Jewish population. Some sporadic voices, however, are recorded and deserve mention.

A Talmudical student from Pressburg, Solomon Polak, was very much interested in the political events of his time, although he was sympathetic to neither the right nor the left. In a letter to his father he expressed his regret that there was no moderate trend in the revolution. He was also indifferent to the Magyar hyper-patriotism then prevailing in Hungary.[32] With very few exceptions, the Jewish voices in Hungary showed no sympathy for the people oppressed by the Hungarians. Only from the camp of the orthodox is such disapproval of totalitarian Magyarization recorded. The rabbi of a Polish prayer house in Vienna, Leizer Hurwitz, in a sermon delivered March 18, 1848 in connection with the constitution granted to the peoples of Austria, said that the hopes of the Jews did not lie in a constitution because the future of the Jews was still in the *Torah*. He agreed with the leaders of the Pressburg orthodoxy who were not in favor of emancipation, seeing in equal rights for the Jews a danger threatening the very existence of the Jewish religion. The same Hurwitz issued a leaflet on July 17, 1848 in which he discussed the question of Jewish rights and gave the following explanation: The conclusion that Jewish emancipation did not mean complete rights for the Jews could be drawn from the very

[31] von Wouwermann, Aimé, *Die Juden in Galizien* (Leipzig 1848).
[32] Wachstein, B., "Pressburger Briefe eines Rabbinatskandidaten aus dem Jahre 1848," in *Bnai Brith Magazin* (Vienna 1930) vol. xxx.

condition upon which the Jew would be considered worthy of becoming a citizen. It was expected, he wrote, that the Jew would turn to agriculture, whereas such a condition was not given to nor demanded from the non-Jews. In Galicia, orthodoxy stood aloof and did not interfere in the political events of the country. When the Polish national committee resolved that memorial services should be performed in churches and temples in memory of two executed Polish patriots, the orthodox ignored the appeal of the Polish patriots, and the Reform rabbi of Lemberg was the only one who complied with this resolution. He was severely criticized by the orthodox leaders of the country.[33]

These ideological trends prevailing in Jewish life in Austria on the eve of the revolution of 1848 and during the revolution gave impetus to the growth of the social and political credos which later developed into the ideologies of Zionism, Socialism, cultural nationalism, and, in part, Yiddishism. The seeds of these movements and ideologies, some of them to mature two decades later, are deeply rooted in the perplexities of the revolution of 1848, in the intricacies and difficulties in solving conflicting national as well as social problems and issues. The credos of all these movements, which became an integral part of the life of the Jewish people in several European countries for almost a hundred years, stemmed from the first sporadic, faintly articulated, ambiguously expressed notions, desires, and cravings which the revolution of 1848 created and brought to public attention.

[33] Horwitz, L., *Rede über die Constitution, gehalten im polnischen Bethhause in Wien, am 16 März, 1848; Oest. Centralorgan* (1848) 275-276; Gelber, N. M., *Aus zwei Jahrhunderten* (Vienna 1924) (about the loyalty of the orthodoxy to the monarchy); Shatzky, J., *Galician Jewry during the Revolution of 1848* (in press).

Biblical Criticism
in the Middle Ages

✦✦ BY ISAIAH SONNE
Hebrew Union College

*E*VER since Schechter unearthed, half a century ago, from the Cairo Genizah the fragment designated as "The Oldest Collection of Bible Difficulties,"[1] this strange medieval literary product has continued to puzzle the scholarly world. From its first appearance, the fragment revealed itself as a relic of a janus-faced monument, with two antithetical facets, the one expressing radical, negative criticism, the other loyal adherence to rabbinic authority. Indeed, the bulk of the composition, endeavoring as it does to lay bare all the alleged weak spots and defects of the Bible—both stylistically as well as in the realm of ethical teachings contained therein— seems to aim at the negation of the divine origin of the Sacred Scriptures, and thus to undermine their authority. On the other hand, there is no want of passages lavishing praises on the head of the academy, the "Gaon" of Jacob,[2] and his seven associates (*haberim*), which seems to indicate that our author not only dissociated himself from such heretical sects as dared attack the Written Law, but actually was a staunch partisan of the Rabbanites, affirming the authority of the Oral Law as well.

In view of the presence of these two diametrically opposite positions in the fragment, it was inevitable that scholars, from the very beginning, should have been startled and perplexed as to which of the directions to follow. Any attempt of harmonizing the two components of the fragment appeared futile; the only way out

---

[1] *Cf. Jewish Quarterly Review,* vol. xiii, O.S., 345 ff. A new critical edition of the text was published by Judah Rosenthal in *Hebrew Union College Annual,* vol. xxi, 29 ff., Hebrew section.

[2] Rosenthal, *l.c.* p. 51-52, sect. SH.

of the dilemma seemed to be to select one aspect as expressing the true purpose of the composition, to which the other element should be made subservient and explained away. After a short period of hesitation, the controversy among scholars crystallized around two schools of interpretation. The one, dismissing all the orthodox-conservative manifestations as hypocrisy and disguise, maintained that the author pursued a heretical, subversive purpose; the other school asserted the author's intention to defend the gaonic authority and turned the alleged subversive criticism of the Bible into an aggressive weapon against the adversaries of the Rabbanites.

The heretical interpretation of the fragment prevailed at first since, as noted above, the cynical objections against the Bible occupy a far greater part of the pamphlet than the protestations of loyalty to the heads of authoritative Judaism. Furthermore, the composition, in style as well as in content, shows a great many features in common with the notorious heretical work of Hiwi Al-Balkhi which lists two hundred objections against the Bible. All this was painstakingly pondered by the first editor, and led him to decide in favor of the heretical interpretation of the fragment. Authorship was ascribed to one of the skeptics in sympathy with Hiwi Al-Balkhi and his circle.[3] The interspersed praises for the head of the academy and his associates were interpreted as mere lip service, a screen of protection against the fury of the official Jewish authorities.

No sooner had this theory been embraced by the foremost scholars in this field, Bacher and Poznanski,[4] than it was challenged by N. Porges.[5] Conversant with medieval literature and a keen interpreter of its difficult texts, with a bent for detail, Porges subjected the fragment to penetrating scrutiny and minute analysis. He succeeded in shedding much light on its many obscure passages, restoring its mutilated text. By the very nature of his mind Porges was bound to focus his searching eye on minute details so as to bring to light many of the hidden clues which escaped the atten-

[3] For Hiwi Al-Balkhi's "Questions" *cf.* Davidson, *Saadia's Polemic Against Hiwi Al-Balkhi* (New York 1915) and Rosenthal, J., "Hiwi Al-Balkhi," in *Jewish Quarterly Review,* vol. xxxviii, n.s., 317 ff.

[4] *Jewish Quarterly Review, l.c.,* note 1, 741, 748.

[5] *Jewish Quarterly Review,* vol. xiv, o.s., 133 ff.; vol xx, 198 ff.

tion of those whose main interest centered in the general substance and meaning of the pamphlet as a whole. In displaying in bold relief the subtle allusions of the passages unmistakably of orthodox, traditional origin, Porges made these passages more articulate, more convincing, not allowing them to be easily disposed of as mere disguise. These passages, so little cared for by Schechter, became, under Porges' treatment, the central theme of the composition. In this new perspective the work turns out to be an attack on sectarians, Masoretes, and Karaites. The whole critical apparatus and the objections against the Bible serve the purpose of strengthening the standard argument of the Rabbanites against the Karaites that without oral tradition the Written Law remains a sealed book and cannot be interpreted.

With a few exceptions all scholars adopted this view, abandoning the heretical interpretation of the fragment. Schechter himself, the principal exponent of its heretical origin, now went to the other extreme and declared the pamphlet to be the work of Saadia Gaon, the arch-opponent of Hiwi Al-Balkhi as well as of the Karaites.[6]

Porges' success may be ascribed to various reasons. In the first place his valuable contribution to the clarification of many inexplicable details and to the restoration of the mutilated parts of the fragment lent weight to his hypothesis concerning the nature and import of the work in general. A more cogent reason for the wide acceptance of Porges' hypothesis was its emotional appeal, since it rescued the remains of an old Hebrew monument from the domain of heretics and sectarians and restored it to the treasury of traditional, official Judaism. No wonder that almost at once Porges' theory became the prevailing one among Jewish scholars.

The recent discovery of Saadia's polemic poem against the Masorete Ben-Asher and against the Karaites, "Essa Meshali," gave new impetus to research concerning this fragment. Almost all the scholars who contributed to the discovery of various parts of this work by Saadia (Levin, Marmorstein, Davidson, Mann, Brody)[7] could not but note parallels in language and poetical structure be-

---

[6] *Cf.* Ginzberg, L., *Ginze Schechter*, vol. i, p. 546.

[7] On the various fragments of this poem, see Levin, B. M., "Essa Mashali," in *Rav Saadya Gaon* (Jerusalem 1943) p. 481 ff.

tween the two poems. Special weight is given by some scholars to the fact that along with the Karaites the Masoretes too are made the target of Saadia's attack. They concluded that, like "Essa Meshali," our fragment, which likewise contains an assault upon the Masoretes, belongs to an anti-Karaite circle and possibly to the same author.[8]

The discovery of various compendia of "Two Contradictory Scriptural Passages" compiled by Rabbanites was also adduced by some scholars as support of Porges' hypothesis.[9] For, it was argued, a goodly number of the Bible difficulties raised in our fragment consist of such "Contradictory Scriptural Passages."

The recent discoveries mentioned above stimulated later scholars to resume the controversy about our fragment in terms of a Schechter-Porges dilemma. They provided some additional arguments in favor of Porges. But thus far these discoveries have failed to offer any new key to the enigma of the pamphlet nor have they helped provide a deeper insight into the core of the problem. As a matter of fact, the later scholars did not attempt a re-examination from within but contented themselves with widening the area of analogies from without—by linking our Genizah fragment with other similar Genizah material, such as "Essa Meshali" and compilations of "Two Contradictory Scriptural Passages." Therein lies the weakness of their approach; it remains on the periphery and all the analogies merely touch the surface and do not penetrate into the substance of the fragment.

It should be obvious that an assault upon the Masoretes is no evidence of Rabbanite authorship. The sting of scorn and ridicule for those who count the letters in the Scriptures is to be found also among the earlier Karaites. They too insisted on the use of "interpretation" and they emphasized that "reading the Torah without grasping its interpretation is also done by fools and simpletons . . . of whom the Bible says . . . 'Behold the word of the Lord has been put to shame . . . and he said, Behold Thou art to them as a song

[8] The anti-Karaite tendency is especially stressed by J. Mann, in his *Texts and Studies in Jewish History and Literature,* vol. ii (1935) p. 58-60.

[9] *Cf.* Mann, J., "Some Midrashic Genizah Fragments," in *Hebrew Union College Annual,* vol. xiv (1939) 338 ff.

of flutes . . .' "[10] Can we not hear an echo of our author's scorn for the "flutes of the cantillations?"[11]

Is there any need to stress that "Two Contradictory Scriptural Passages" may be used either to tear down the very basis of tradition and destroy it, as did Hiwi Al-Balkhi and his followers, or to build up and protect the Oral Law, as did Saadia Gaon and his supporters? Whether our fragment belongs to the first or to the second group can be determined only from an analysis of the questions themselves, the method of their formulation, and the tone accompanying them.

Poznanski's contention that "if our author's intention was merely to deride the Masoretes and demonstrate their folly, why did he use such biting language . . . to the point that the conscientious reader would see that, in addition to ridiculing the punctuation enthusiasts, he was actually making a farce of the Torah,"[12] still holds good.

Moreover, the reader who at one glance scans the more than a hundred questions in the fragment cannot but wonder at the paucity of references to texts and debatable subjects which were prominent in the controversy between the Rabbanites and the Karaites and at how few and far between are questions which constituted the central theme in their polemical writings.

Last but not least, the earnest reader will hesitate to assume that the Rabbanites were so naive as to believe that they could overwhelm their opponents—Karaites or Masoretes—merely by skill in explaining difficult words and passages and in reconciling chronological contradictions. In general, we do not find that the Rabbanites ever pretended to possess traditional, indisputable answers to most of the questions set forth in the fragment.[13] A close study of the questions themselves can only strengthen the viewpoint of Poz-

[10] *Cf.* Commentary on the Ten Commandments, attributed to Nissi ben Noah, in Pinsker's *Likute Kadmoniyot*, Appendix—*Nispahim*, vol. i, p. 9 and 10.

[11] Ed. Rosenthal, p. 37, sect. HH, lines 6 ff.

[12] Poznanski, S., "Hiwi Habalki," in *Hagoren*, vol. vii, 30-32.

[13] The Gaonic position concerning difficult passages in the Bible is clearly stated in a responsum attributed to Hai Gaon. In it the Gaon stresses that we cannot maintain that there is only one way of interpretation definitely established, but on the contrary we should admit the possibility of various interpretations. *Cf.* Berliner, *Targum Onkelos*, vol. ii, German section, p. 175.

nanski, which was also Schechter's original opinion, that the questions are couched in a negative tone, and cannot very readily be reckoned as questions meant to defend the Oral Tradition.

Since there is ample room for doubt as to the defense function of our compilation of questions, this writer takes leave to challenge the existence of any such compilation of questions by Rabbanites, designed solely for refuting heretics and Karaites. Collections of "Two Contradictory Scriptural Passages" belong primarily to the realm of exegesis or homiletics, serving either as an illustration of a hermeneutical principle or as a point of departure, an exordium, for an oration. These collections are far-removed, both in time and in content, from the polemical pamphlets of the Rabbanites against the Karaites.

A few questions published by Wertheimer[14] follow a pattern resembling that of our pamphlet, but there we learn that these questions actually derive from heretical and Karaite sources, collected in order to embarrass the Rabbanites. We do not have even one example of questions of which we could state with certainty that they were collected primarily to serve as defense material for the Rabbanite principles. Common sense too would dictate that the Rabbanites would have no interest in amassing a treasure of questions such as these, which, like a double-edged sword, could be and in fact were used to create confusion and doubts in the minds of ingenuous believers.

Once again, then, we find ourselves confronted by the dilemma of the two opposite currents of thought in our fragment. Have we no alternative but to return to Schechter's first opinion, supported by Poznanski, *i.e.* to discount the relatively less conspicuous traditional trend, consign it to the realm of hypocrisy, and declare the pamphlet to be entirely the work of a dissident sectarian, either heretic or Karaite?

In my humble opinion, a more realistic approach to our fragment may open a perspective which would do justice to both currents. Scholars have tacitly assumed that our pamphlet is but one of the many polemical writings prompted by the conflict between heretical sects and Karaites on the one side and the loyal traditionalists on the other side, such as Hiwi Al-Balkhi's "Objections,"

---

[14] Wertheimer, Solomon A., *Leket Shelomoh* (Jerusalem 1899) p. 69.

Salmon ben Yeruhim's "Book of Wars," and the "Responses" of
Saadia Gaon. The same scholars, however, could reach no agreement on the question as to which cause our author espoused.

The very fact that we are unable to determine with certainty in
which camp the fragment originated should render our assumption
of the polemical intention of the pamphlet more than doubtful.
Moreover, in our analysis above it was pointed out that the author
of the fragment refrained from including Biblical passages which
formed the battleground in the conflict between Rabbanites and
Karaites. We sensed that it was with deliberate intent that he
stayed away from material which was of a polemical nature, and
endeavored to remain in neutral territory. We may therefore safely
conclude that the author was not particularly interested in controversy, and polemics were not his purpose.

What then was his purpose in this rhymed treatise? In my estimation the whole pamphlet was not conceived as an independent,
complete composition in itself but rather as a commendatory preface to a larger exegetical work—probably to the "three extensive
and marvelous books" boasted of by the author at the end of the
fragment—similar to the rhymed introduction by Abraham Ibn
Ezra to his Pentateuch commentary. A glance at the development
of Biblical exegesis in the tenth century may help us to see how our
author endeavors to make clear his position concerning Biblical
exegesis and to avoid the obstacles which he might encounter.

It should be borne in mind that the watchword "Search in the
Scripture" enhanced, as is known, the exegetical studies among the
Karaites, and gave rise to two exegetical schools—the grammatical
(Al-Dakdukin), akin in spirit to the Masoretes, and the "interpretative" (Al-Mefasrin), a counterpart to the Midrash. The interpreters *(Baale Ha-Pitron)* disdained the grammarians, who were
unable to explain strange idioms or irregular forms, and could,
obviously, supply no "interpretation" for all those Biblical difficulties and contradictions transcending the purely grammatical
domain.

In the tenth century, the Karaites occupied a leading position
in Jerusalem which they built up as an intellectual center of great
reputation. There the renowned exegetes—Daniel Al-Kumsi, Sahal
ben Masliah, and Yefet ben Ali—displayed their prodigious activity.

Students from various countries, desirous to acquire knowledge of the Scriptures, flocked to this school where the interpretative method reigned supreme.[15]

Spurred by this spectacular success of the Karaites, the leading Rabbanite scholars in Jerusalem also founded an academy for the "Science of the Scripture" (*Hokhmat ha-Mikra*), and adopted the same exegetical method of "interpretation." As is known, the students of the Rabbanite school in Jerusalem approached in many regards the view of the Karaites. The Rabbanite school in Jerusalem attracted young, militant students zealous to attack the Karaites with their own weapons.

While these young students enthusiastically espoused the "new science," the conservative elements, especially in the East under the sway of the Babylonian academies, were far from approving the new trend in the study of the Scriptures, *i.e.* the study of the Bible for its own sake and not for homiletic purposes. The new "interpretative method" was looked upon as innovation and those who adopted it were suspected of heterodoxy. This was still the attitude of certain orthodox circles at the time of Ibn Ganah.[16] There can be no doubt that the new exegetical approach represents a more rational, more worldly, attitude towards the Bible, and can rightly be compared with that of Mendelssohn's "explanation" (*Beur*). It is well known that the *Beur* enthusiasts were stigmatized as schismatics by the orthodox authorities.

The author of our fragment was, as he informs us, one of those young students who came from the East "to the West"[17] to attend the famous school for "Scriptural science" in Jerusalem. There, for many years, he devoted himself entirely to exegetical studies and became an ardent champion of the new "Scriptural science," to which he made a considerable contribution with "three extensive, marvelous books."

It may be safe to assume that after his "years of study," as soon as he had acquired full mastery in the "new science" of exegesis, our author hastened to return to his native land, to the East, to

[15] *Cf.* Mann, *Texts and Studies,* vol. ii, p. 8 ff.

[16] *Cf.* Jonah ibn Ganah, *Sefer Hariqma,* ed. Wilensky, Introduction, p. 12, line 3.

[17] Rosenthal, p. 52, sect. SH, lines 21-22.

divulge the wisdom of the West, the new science of Torah interpretation, among his countrymen. But he could not fail to realize
that the Jewish authorities in the East looked askance at the expo-
nents of the Palestinian school and considered them as "destroyers
of the world," as schismatics. To counteract this suspicion our
author keenly felt the need for demonstrating the inestimable
apologetical value of the "new science" of the West.

For this reason he did not hesitate to use certain compendia
of "questions" and "objections" put in circulation by Hiwi Al-
Balkhi's followers, which caused confusion in the ranks of the
Rabbanites. He implies, obviously, that his new, "marvelous" commentary, prepared along the lines of the Palestinian exegetical
school, would supply his countrymen with the necessary answers
to these embarrassing questions and remove their perplexity. In
view of the diversity of the "questions," it is a fair guess that our
author's "extensive" commentary—again like that of Ibn Ezra—included explanations of linguistic character, which had engaged the
attention of the grammarians and Masoretes, as well as interpretations of difficult and contradictory passages, the main task of the
men of "interpretation."

This fully explains the contemptuous tone in the "questions,"
drawn as they are from the treasury of arguments stored by Hiwi
Al-Balkhi and his followers. The author presents them in the language of the original, with all its derision and disrespect for the
Torah, in order to point out even more sharply the indispensability
of his commentary. With it, his Rabbanite colleagues could more
readily ward off the scorn and abuse heaped upon them by their
opponents.

On the other hand, knowing how easily the adherents to the
Palestinian school were suspected of Karaite leanings, our author
from time to time unsheaths the full fury of his pen and attacks
"the lame ones . . . who heap words of abuse upon the sages of my
nation, saying . . . the Scriptures are our exclusive heritage."[18] But
he refrains from any overt literary battle and any disputations with
them, for in his commentary he follows, in the main, the exegetical
pattern common to the Rabbanites and the Karaites in Jerusalem,
in the academies for "Scriptural science."

[18] *Ibid.*, lines 23-27.

Changes in Land Tenure in the Middle East

BY BERNARD D. WEINRYB

Dropsie College

*T*HE SYSTEM of landownership in the Middle East was, and still is, a basic part of the foundations of the social and, to a certain degree, also the political structure of society in that area.

The Middle East is mainly an agricultural region. About 75 per cent of the population is engaged in agricultural occupations. The main characteristics of agriculture are derived from natural conditions such as quality of soil, amount of rainfall, etc. and from social and legal conditions prevailing in land tenure. The form of landownership is, therefore, the basis of the agrarian society which comprises a large majority of the people, with the rest of the population either originating from that group or having some connection with it.

The landownership system in the Middle East stems from Islamic legal institutions, the Ottoman regime, the Land Code of 1858, and Land Registration Law of 1859. According to the legal theories and practices, the Islamic conquerors, or the heads of the states, were regarded as the supreme owners of the conquered lands, or of those parts which were in the hands of non-Moslems. Such supreme ownership by the crown (*miri*) spells restrictions on the cultivator or owner as to the right of inheritance, transfer, etc. As a result of tribal ownership—and probably for fiscal reasons —collective landownership developed over a great part of the land. Another specific institution of the Middle East is the endowment for religious or charitable purposes (*waqf*), which withdrew lands from private ownership. At the same time, as a result of the tax-farming system and grants of fiefs by the rulers, a feudal system developed with large landownership and tenants living in much worse conditions than those of their counterparts in medieval Europe.

These systems were, for the most part, based on tradition and practice, without always being properly recorded and legally sanctioned. This naturally left plenty of opportunity for abuse. Tradition and the land regime survived the government's attempts to give landownership some legal forms. The abolition of the feudal system, the cancellation of the rights of the large landowners in 1811-14 in Egypt, in 1838 in Syria and Palestine, and in 1839 in the rest of Turkey, led to little change in practice, just as the land code of 1858 and the Land Registration Law of 1859 remained mainly on paper and never succeeded in enforcing registration of title.

The Ottoman Land Code was seldom carried out, while lands which nominally belonged to the state passed ultimately in one form or another to a new landowner class. *Musha*—community owned land—was expressly forbidden by this code but for one reason or another the Ottoman administration was unable to break down custom and tradition.[1] Other stipulations of the Land Code helped to create a new landed property class. The abolition of the feudal system did no more than to effect "an exchange for the previous overlords for the nominal rule of the State while the factual rights of possession were as a rule appropriated by new classes."[2]

The requirement of the Turkish Land Code that land in the villages be entered in the land register often resulted in village sheikhs or heads of tribes entering the land of the villages as their property. In other cases the government put up for auction such lands as the peasants failed to register under their own names—for fear of taxation or military service—and sold them to absentee owners. Generally, notables, money lenders and bankers were either buying up or seizing for debts large stretches of land in Syria and Palestine, leaving the cultivators as tenants. In Iraq, too, the tribe chief, the leading family, or the middlemen became

---

[1] In some localities only the Ottoman government succeeded, partly by means of pressure, in dividing some lands or introducing a certain order in land tenure "against the will and the wish of the people."

[2] Bonné, Alfred, *State and Economics in the Middle East* (London 1948) p. 188.

owners of a great deal of land. In Egypt, in 1813, Mohammed Ali seized large possessions and divided them into small holdings, giving each villager in usufruct 3-5 feddans.[3] In 1871 Ismail Pasha offered all tenants full ownership of their holdings in exchange for payment of six years taxes. Although this law was repealed nine years later the principle of peasant landownership was established and the state continued to sell plots to the *fellaheen*. But at the same time Mohammed Ali and his successor, in order to encourage cultivation, turned great stretches of land over tax free for ten years to wealthy notables and even to foreigners. These groups became the great landowners, while the farms of the peasants were constantly declining in size because of the increase in population and division by inheritance. These farms mostly shrank into dwarf holdings. Such was the situation at the time of the collapse of the Ottoman government at the end of World War I.

Six forms of land tenure were distinguishable although some are extensions of each other. They were: (1) *Mulk*[4]—land which belonged to private owners or freehold, with rights of sale and disposition by will. It most nearly approximated our common law fee simple. (2) *Miri*[5]—land officially owned by the ruler or the state (crown lands) either under their own administration, or, as was more often the case, leased out indefinitely to a cultivator. The latter had in fact hereditary rights of occupation and in this case the *miri* land was approaching the status of *mulk*. Although officially the land was not transmissible upon death, the claims of the deceased holder's family to such land were admitted by prevailing custom. The disadvantage of this type of land ownership as against private ownership is that the cultivator cannot bequeath it through a will or dedicate it to a religious or charitable organization. Also, if the land is left uncultivated for more than three con-

---

[3] One feddan = 1.038 acres.

[4] From *malaka*, to own freely.

[5] Belonging to the ruler (*el Arazi el Amiri*, land of the ruler). In Iraq the term *miri* usually describes land belonging to the state to which the cultivator does not have legal tenure, while state land, the usufructuary possession of which has been granted to the cultivator, is termed *tapu*, freehold. *Tapu* regions in Iraq, however, constitute only a small part of the state lands. (The word is derived from *tap-mak* = to worship, hence an acknowledgment of oneself as a vassal). *Cf.* Dowson, Ernest M., *An Inquiry into Land Tenure and Related Questions* (1931) p. 16-17.

secutive years, the owner forfeits his rights to it. (3) *Waqf*[6]—was land dedicated to a religious or charitable organization or given in trust to such an organization for the benefit of heirs, etc. The management of *waqf* lands was in the hands of the religious authorities. *Waqf* lands might be *mulk* (privately owned lands) on which the *waqf* authority has ownership rights (true *waqf*) or *miri*, in which case the *waqf* authority has usufruct rights only, not ownership. (4) *Musha*[7]—was land which was not the property of the individual or the family working it, but was regarded as the property of the village.[8] Instead of each member owning a specific parcel, he was the owner of a fractional share or shares in the village. The land was redivided every two or three years among the members of the group.

In addition to the above types of ownership there were still *matruka*[9] lands (utility lands) which were not divided among individuals but belonged to the whole community (grazing ground, local roads, threshing floors, community woods, etc.). And also *mewat*[10] lands, uncultivated areas lying beyond the boundaries of the community and not claimed by anybody.

The division of land according to the type of ownership varied from country to country. While in Lebanon most of the land was privately owned (*mulk*), the proportion of such ownership in Iraq and Transjordan was only about 20 per cent, and slightly higher in Palestine and Syria. The prevailing land ownership in Iraq was *miri* (estimated to be about 80 to 90 per cent of the available land), and in Palestine and Syria this sort of ownership prevailed together with *musha* (community ownership).

In Egypt the *waqf* was already partially reduced in the 19th century, while in the former Turkish territory it sometimes comprised one-half or more of the land.

[6] From *waq-afa*, to hold steady; Moslem religious endowment.

[7] From *sha'a*, to share; *musha*, common undivided land.

[8] The communal type of landholding or *musha* is to a certain degree similar to that of the old Russian *mir* and the south-Slavonic *Zadruga*. These, however, included a more communitarian way of living and landholding than the mere community ownership of land in the villages of the Near East, although some common features may be found.

[9] Literally, "left over." Somewhat similar to the English "commons" before the enclosure.

[10] Literally, "dead."

Official classifications of the land (*mulk* or *miri*) notwithstanding, the categories often came to mean almost the same thing in actual practice. Large ownership prevailed, with the tenants, mostly sharecroppers, being badly exploited and abused and with titles and rights unsettled and confused. Lack of land registers and records combined with the strength of tradition and custom to make every system, even when motivated by good intentions, an arbitrary one.

The situation in Iraq is well formulated by Sir Ernest M. Dowson in his report of the inquiry made in 1929-30.[11] Private ownership of the land (*mulk*) was rare in Iraq; outside of towns and certain gardens, all land, with some minor exceptions, was State Domain. The lack of Land Register records and of information about grant of tenure led to many differences and disputes. "The tenure of some four-fifths of the cultivated land in the country was not governed by law . . . and was not regulated in any methodical way at all . . . the land law was defective and uncertain in its application to the other fifth" (p. 5). "Local influences helped to promote different practices in the different regions." State land "is supposed to be leased by an annual terminal agreement. . . . In practice, although such agreements, may and do exist, they are far from being an indispensable, or even an ordinary feature of the occupation and use of *miri* land. . . . Possession is ordinarily nine-tenths of the law; but neither long possession nor any other mode of acquisition confers security. Personal influence with the most effective arbiter is commonly the decisive factor at any moment in any particular land dispute: and anyone may find the most convincing claims set aside. . . . Any dispute may be reopened at any time if circumstances promise a more favorable consideration of a disappointed party's case."[12]

About Transjordan, Sir E. Dowson, who made a survey in 1926, reports: "Throughout the length and breadth of the country there will hardly be found a handful of cases in which the government can extract from the Land Register the name of the lawful possessor of any given parcel of *miri* land or in which the occupant

[11] Dowson, *An Inquiry into Land Tenure and Related Questions. Proposals for the Initiation of Reform.* Government of El Iraq (Letchworth 1931).
[12] *Ibid.*, p. 28-29.

of such land can establish therefrom his right to lawful possession."[13]

This uncertainty of rights on land holding naturally prevented people from making investments for the purpose of amelioration. It influenced the willingness or unwillingness of the small capitalist to help to develop the land by providing funds, seed, etc., and determined the attitude of the cultivator to his parcel.

Similar confusion in the matter of land holding and tenure, although to a lesser degree, is to be found also in other Middle Eastern countries. In Turkey the main groups of land holding were *mulk* (freehold), *miri* (state land), and *waqf* (belonging to the Church authorities). In the landholding system large estates predominated[14] (with the exception of Anatolia), and they were either leased to tenants—the payment usually ranging from 25 to 50 per cent of the crop—or were managed by an administrator who either employed hired workers at the expense of the owner or gave the land, in leasehold, to small farmers and supplied them with seed, in exchange for one-third to one-half of the harvest. In the course of years relations have become so complicated that often the tenant-farmer does not know whether he belongs to the category of the leaseholder or of hired laborer.

In Syria the *miri* land prevailed and was mainly concentrated in the hands of absentee landlords. More than half of the land, sometimes in groups of many villages, was owned by city absentee owners not in the least interested in farming. The common system of tenancy was "tenancy of *metayage*" (share tenancy), usually an annual tenancy which could be terminated by the landlord at will. The tenant generally paid one-half of the produce to the landlord. This tenancy system and the *musha* (communal holding), which was widespread in the Eastern part of the country, were hampering the development of agriculture.[15] Only in Lebanon did individual small ownership exist to a considerable extent. In Palestine the

[13] *Cf.* Walpole, G. F., "Land Problems in Transjordan," in *Royal Central Asian Journal*, vol. xxv (1948) 53.

[14] There are 2,000 to 3,000 landowners each possessing 1,000 to 2,000 acres or more.

[15] Khuri, A., "Land Tenure," in *Economic Organization of Syria*, Himadeh, ed. (1936) p. 51 ff.

causes of backwardness, it is stated, are similarly rooted in the social history of the country, and a Committee appointed to investigate the conditions of agriculturists (Crossbie-Johnson Committee of 1930) stated that no improvements can take place in something like half the area of the country until the *musha* system of tenure is abolished.[16] Security of tenure is essential for the orderly progress of farming. In the case of *musha* the cultivator worked his parcel with the knowledge that after a short period he would have to move to another parcel. For this reason he usually got as much out of the soil as he could, for he had no interest in the future condition of that soil.

In Egypt alone was land tenure a little more settled. Already in 1892 a land survey was started, with the help of English engineers, which was completed in 1907. Private landownership prevailed. But land was concentrated in large holdings, while the majority of the peasants owned only very small strips (averaging about half of an acre). They were, therefore, compelled to work as tenant farmers and to pay the (often absentee) owner high tenancy fees either in money or a considerable part of the crop.

TRANSFORMATION

After World War I the Middle East, formerly mostly under Ottoman sovereignty, was divided into a number of independent or semi-independent states. After the first years of confusion Turkey was molded, by the regime of Mustapha Kemal, into a republic; in 1922 Egypt became a monarchy under King Fuad with England being systematically forced to relinquish her control.

Iraq, which came under British mandate, was granted partial independence in 1922 and the mandate was terminated ten years later. Syria and Lebanon were under French mandate (till 1944) while Palestine and Transjordan were British mandatory territories (till 1948 and 1946, respectively). All these countries, striving for political independence and attempting to build up an appropriate

[16] *Report of a Committee on the Economic Condition of Agriculturists in Palestine and the Fiscal Measures of Government in Palestine Thereto,* Jerusalem (1930) p. 55.

economic and social structure, tended to make for changes in land tenure. But in the political struggle for independence, the awakening of the national consciousness, the religious motive, the customs, the retardation and conservation of the traditional way of life, all played an important role. These countries were, therefore, inclined to retain or even to foster the Moslem heritage, the customs and existing order in land ownership.

The mandatory governments in turn were anxious to retain as far as possible the *status quo*. This tendency was also motivated by the desire to appease the local forces which were opposed to change. They were, therefore, striving rather to bring some order into the recording of landownership than for the redivision of the land. Only Turkey had a revolutionary government, and there in fact a part of the land of the *waqf*, and some other lands were divided.

The government there was interested both in the self-sufficiency of the country and raising the standards of the peasantry and sought to bring about an agrarian reform, the results of which are, however, still not entirely clear. Besides the *waqf* land, which passed to the state and was mostly distributed among the peasants, the enacted law empowered the government to distribute among the landless peasants land not being cultivated by the owners. The peasants were to pay for these new lands by credits from the Agricultural Bank and the co-operative societies. So far, however, the results of this distribution have been meager. According to figures for 1937, 20,000 acres had been distributed in this way by that year and this mostly to re-emigrants from Greece. Other sources put all land distributed in Turkey up to the war years between three-quarter to two million acres. But even so there are 129,000 landless families and another 873,000 families with scant landed property. The holdings vary from five acres in the west, eight acres in the south, and twenty acres in the regions where the industrial crops are grown. At the same time, there are still large landowners with large holdings of one thousand and more acres.[17]

[17] More recently the Turkish National Assembly passed a new agrarian law which provides for breaking up of large estates and for distribution of the land to sharecroppers and the seasonal land laborers. But this has not as yet materialized.

Landholdings in Turkey according to Size (acres)

	HOLDINGS		TOTAL AREA		AVERAGE AREA PER HOLDING (IN ACRES)
	NUMBER	%	NUMBER	%	
Less than 125 (small holding)	2,493,000	99.75	37,295,000	86.35	15
Between 125 and 1,250 (medium holding)	5,764	0.23	4,300,000	9.95	750
More than 1,250 (large estates)	418	0.02	1,600,000	3.70	3,750
Total	2,499,182	100.00	43,195,000	100.00	

As the average minimum area necessary for a farm holding is estimated at 25 acres, the vast majority of agriculturists have a deficiency of land holding (the average being only 15). Over 95 per cent of the existing farms are run by peasants, leaving only 3 per cent for medium-sized estates. The 418 large estates are usually run by administrators.

In Iraq an impetus has been given to the settlement of tribesmen, by installation of pumps and by securing law and order. Efforts have also been made to substitute paid labor for the traditional share-crop labor, but these and similar reforms were curtailed by lack of sufficient means,[18] and by the specific situation of the country.

The land of Iraq may be roughly divided into two zones, the northern rainfall zone and the southern irrigation zone, between the two rivers. In the eastern part of the northern rain-fed zone a large part of the land is held by small cultivators with holdings up to 50 acres. Even in villages where the *agha* (head of the village) registered the land of the village in his name, the share paid to them by the cultivators is small, amounting to 10-20 per cent of the produce. In the rest of the northern zone and in the south the situation is different. The breaking up of the tribal system during the last four decades, the extension of pump irrigation, and the introduction of machinery resulted in the *sheikhs,* the heads of the clans (*sirkals*) and city notables, who installed the pumps, becoming owners of the land. The cultivators, unable to establish title to ·

[18] Foster, Henry A., *The Making of Modern Iraq* (1935) p. 247.

the plots, became tenants who often had to pay away up to 70 or 80 per cent of the crop.[19] The settlement of title to the land which has been going on for the last fifteen years did not do much to change this situation.

In 1932 the government passed a law providing for broad powers to settle the title of land and an attempt was made to do this on the basis of the existing rights. In the years 1933-1943 13,220,331 acres of land were settled, comprising about one-half of the whole cultivable area.[20] In some regions the sheikhs received an allotment of land comparable to their claim in produce, the rest going to the cultivators. If for instance the sheikh had been receiving 20-30 per cent of the produce, a comparable share of the land was allotted to him and 70-80 per cent entered in the names of individual landowners. In most regions, however, where the tribal system still exists as a unit and the sheikhs are powerful, the sheikh became the owner of all the land, while in areas where the tribal system is still functioning, no settlement could be undertaken at all.

In Egypt, where the Wafd Party, which was in power for most of the inter-war period, is in its social origin connected with larger and moderate landownership, and where the Court was linked up with the landowners, little could be done in the direction of agricultural reform. The number of large landholdings and owners remained almost stationary while the agricultural population increased with no appropriate expansion of cultivated areas.

The number of landowners increased from 1,556,310 in 1913 to 2,550,579 in 1944 (an increase of about 60 per cent). The greatest growth was among those owning up to one feddan and between one and five feddans; the number of landowners of larger estates dropped only slightly. In 1913 942,530 small landowners (60.5 per cent) possessed 7.1 per cent of the land, while 12,558 landowners possessed 44.4 per cent of the land; in 1944, 1,792,530 landowners (70.2 per cent of the landowners) possessed 12.6 per cent of the land while 12,132 big landowners (0.5 per cent) had 36.4 per cent of all the land.

---

[19] The information is based on Sahih Haider's *Land Problems in Iraq* (unpublished Ph.D. dissertation, London University 1942) and Doreen Warriner's *Land and Poverty in the Middle East* (London 1948) p. 103-16.

[20] *Cf.* the classifications, Warriner, *ibid.*, p. 111.

Distribution of Agricultural Land in Egypt, 1913-1944[22]

SIZE OF HOLDING (FEDDANS)	IN 1913		IN 1944	
	NO. OF OWNERS	AREA HELD (FEDDANS)	NO. OF OWNERS	AREA HELD (FEDDANS)
0– 1	942,530	405,595	1,792,530	740,520
1– 5	468,628	1,013,364	599,985	1,216,301
5–50	132,594	1,633,413	145,932	1,765,025
over 50	12,558	2,420,558	12,132	2,141,360
Total	1,556,310	5,472,930	2,550,579	5,863,206

A great part of the area in the class of over 50 feddans belongs to the very large farms. The available statistics (for 1925) show that 58.5 per cent of the area was in average holdings of 530 feddans.[23] Most of the large estates are owned by absentee owners—partly foreigners—who let out their land either directly or through tenants general, while a majority of the small landowners must work on large estates either as laborers or as tenants.[24] The state owned large stretches of land, over one million feddans. The king is also a large landowner.

The mandatories—Great Britain for Palestine and Transjordan, and France for Syria—made no more attempts than the independent states to revolutionize the social setup.[25] First of all, the intention of any occupying administration in general, and of the British Colonial Administration in particular, is to maintain the *status quo.* Among the British Colonial civil servants there is also the inclination to preserve the landed aristocracy.[26] Furthermore, the mandatories, already opposed by the nationalists of these countries, were anxious not to arouse a great influential part of the

[22] *Statistical Handbook of Middle Eastern Countries* (Jerusalem 1945) p. 60. *Cf.* also Crouchley, *op. cit.,* p. 233; *The Middle East, 1948* (London 1948) p. 101.

[23] Warriner, *Land and Poverty in the Middle East* (London 1948) p. 35.

[24] *Cf.* also Issawi, Charles, *Egypt, An Economic and Social Analysis* (London 1947) p. 73 ff.

[25] In accordance with this attitude is the statement that "land reform cannot be imposed on a country as an exotic by an outside agency." (Dowson, *op. cit.,* p. 18). Also a recently published English report (Keen, *op. cit.*) is very pessimistic about "revising land settlements and land tenures" and advocates "minor improvements" which should be "introduced in relatively undeveloped and unoccupied areas."

[26] Kohn, Hans, *Nationalism and Imperialism in the Hither East* (London 1932) p. 34.

population against them by drastic measures, and in these predominantly agricultural countries the landowners constituted one of the most important groups.

However, some changes were made, or attempted, by the mandatories, who tried to introduce a certain degree of law and order which would be compatible with western patterns, or as a result of the special situation of the country (in the case of Palestine).

As early as 1921 the High Commissioner in Syria instituted a land service to record titles and transactions in real estate, at the same time initiating a detailed cadastral survey. The system of registration was developed in the second half of the 1920's. In this period the government made provisions to facilitate the sale of public rural land to land tenants; the price of the land was to be paid in fifteen annual installments. About one-half of all the land has been surveyed and title registered. In 1926 permanent partition of *musha* land was ordered after the delineation of the parcels by the survey—an order which began to be materialized in the mid-1930's. A new land code was promulgated in 1930 which, although based on the Old Ottoman Land Code, contained amplifications which made it resemble the Swiss Code and made provisions for land registration, agricultural credit, etc.

The endeavors of the government were to some extent successful in arranging orderly registration and encouraging division of *musha* (collective property). In the region of Jebel el-Druz, where a tendency toward division of *musha* (collective landholding) was apparent, the encouragement of the government increased this trend, so that by the middle of the 1930's most of the cultivable land was divided and only pasture and wooded lands remained under collective ownership. In other regions, however, the Bureau of Cadastre "when establishing title to land in a *musha* village followed the practice of registering each villager's share in the land as a fraction of the total area, without attaching the title to any specific piece of land."[27] In this way the *musha* system was maintained even after the registration of title. The government was also instrumental in transferring tenancy from sharecropping to orderly leases for fixed rents while the big landowners remained

[27] Warriner, *op. cit.* p. 91.

in possession of the greater part of the cultivable area.[28] It seems, however, that no changes of any importance came about. At any rate figures for Syria show that about 60 per cent of the cultivated area belonged to large landowners. In Lebanon 50 per cent of the whole land was in the hands of 171 owners, while 84,111 owners owned only 35 per cent.

In 1947 the area under cultivation in Lebanon amounted to about 270,000 hectars. According to the figures of the Ministry of Agriculture the ownership was divided as follows:

SIZE OF FARM IN HECTARS	NO. OF OWNERS	PERCENT.	HECTARS	PERCENT.	AVER. PER OWNER (ha)
0.5 to 5	84,111	98.6	94,500	35	1.12
5 to 10	991	1.2	40,500	15	41.00
Over 10	171	0.2	135,000	50	793.00
Total	85,273	100.0	270,000	100	

While 98.6 per cent of the landowners had an average of 1.12 hectars of land per person, 0.2 per cent (among them the *waqf*) owned 793 hectars per person.

In Palestine the policy of the government and its results were augmented by the special situation of the country. The impact of the influx of Jewish immigrants and capital into the country helped to destroy to some extent the pre-capitalistic forms and led to the modernization, diversification and intensification of agriculture by the Jewish immigrants as a matter of expediency; because they had only small areas, new methods had to be introduced. This had an influence on the whole agricultural development of the country and on the social relations in the villages. To a certain degree it helped in the breakdown of the semi-feudal relations in Palestine. The political situation in the country and the position of the British administration also influenced this tendency. By the provision of the mandate, the mandatory was obliged to "encourage . . . close settlement by Jews on the land" (Article 11). But the administration in Palestine and the Colonial Office, which has directed it since 1921, meeting with the non-cooperative attitude of the Arabs

[28] Particulars are to be found in Khuri, A., "Land Tenure," in *Economic Organization of Syria,* ed. S. B. Himadeh, p. 51-69.

began and later developed the tendency which Paul L. Hanna calls "transposition of the terminology of the Mandate by the transfer of secondary and subordinate clauses into primary position,"[29] and regarded it as its task to protect the Arab *fellah* against the impact of the new colonization.

The government enacted one ordinance after another designed to protect the cultivator and the tenants against eviction. The Land Transfer Ordinances of 1920 and 1921 required the consent of the government for the transfer of land, which would be given only after the Director of Lands "is satisfied that any tenant . . . will retain sufficient land . . . for the maintenance of himself and his family." The 1929 Protection of Cultivators Ordinance, which replaced the aforementioned ordinances, provided for the payment of compensation to the tenant for improvements effected by him and the amendment of 1931 included a sub-tenant in the definition of tenant. The comprehensive Cultivators (Protection) Ordinance of 1933 includes the heir of tenants, sharecroppers, agricultural workers, etc.

The government also tried to arrange for land registration and to bring some order into the ownership of land holdings. The land registries in Palestine, which were compiled in the 1860's and 1870's in accordance with the Ottoman Land Code of 1858, were incomplete and in addition were partly lost during the war. In 1920 the British government initiated a system of registration of land, combined with the previous system inherited from the Turks. This system, which was not based on a cadastral survey, whereby the parcels are accurately defined on a plan, turned out to be defective. Seven years later, therefore, in 1928, the Land (Settlement of Title) Ordinance was enacted and a new system introduced. This system was patterned after the Torrens system in use in Australia, which involves a gradual arrangement of a cadastral survey and a new system of registration.[30] Thus, up to the end of 1945, 4,808,458 dunams, or about 45 per cent of the area of the country (with the exclusion of the mountainous wilderness east of Jerusalem and the southern Beersheba region), were registered.

---

[29] Hanna, Paul L., *British Policy in Palestine* (Washington, D. C. 1942) p. 67.
[30] *Cf.* Government of Palestine, *A Survey of Palestine prepared . . . for . . . the Anglo-American Inquiry Commission,* vol. i (Jerusalem 1946) p. 233 ff.

It is true that the results of these measures were not thorough because the government did not introduce an entirely new land order nor straighten out the Land Registry situation.

The Ottoman Land Code has been retained with all the difficulties involved in its various forms of ownership and tenure of land; several new laws have been passed to amend it, but it remains in essence the same complicated system, one which is not calculated to promote close settlement and intensive cultivation. Even with the amendment which it has been found possible to introduce, it cannot be deemed to be a satisfactory system in these respects.[31]

Moreover, the registration of ownership did not mean a consolidation of the farms of the villagers. Even after the Land Settlement, the holdings consisted mostly of many fragments located in different places. An investigation made in 1944 in five Arab villages showed that "out of the 690 holdings possessed by residents of the five villages, only 40, or six percent, were made up of a single piece of land . . . for holdings of all sizes there are, on the average nine fragments per holding . . . scattered widely through the village area."[32]

The government itself admitted that the Land Transfer Ordinances were not sufficiently effective.[33] The uncertainty of land tenure, lack of sufficient information about the existing situation, and the fact that the protective measures were not aimed at protection from the absentee owners and the large landlords but were intended to protect the Arabs from Jewish colonizers only, greatly reduced the value of the government measures. The ambiguous Land Registry act and the way in which it was handled offered many possibilities for abuse. The Land Disputes (Possession) Ordinances of 1932 and 1934 and the Cultivators (Protection) Ordinance of 1933, which were intended to protect the lawful owners of land against "squatters," in practice appeared to favor the "squatter" unduly against the legal owner since they specified that whenever ownership rights are in dispute the party which must establish its rights is not the trespasser but the legal owner of the land. In

[31] *Palestine Royal Commission Report*, p. 227.

[32] *General Monthly Bulletin of Current Statistics*, XI, nos. 1-3 (January-March 1946) p. 49.

[33] Government of Palestine, *Memorandum Submitted to the Palestine Royal Commission*, 1936, p. 56.

practice in Palestine these "protective" measures for the cultivator led to many difficulties, to provocation of disturbances on a tract of land by people who had never cultivated it, for the purpose of extorting money from a new buyer, etc. The State Domain Committee in 1941 expressed the view that the Cultivators (Protection) Ordinance of 1933 had become "a serious obstacle to the reasoned development of the country" and that it placed in the hands of tenants and trespassers a weapon with which they were able to victimize the landlords. A similar view was expressed by a special committee appointed by the High Commissioner in February 1942 to consider whether the Ordinance should be amended.[34]

But despite all these shortcomings about which the Permanent Mandates Commission, the different investigators, the Palestine Royal Commission of 1936, as well as the Jews, complained, Palestine more than the other Middle Eastern countries did enact protection for the tenant and introduced changes in the system of taxation. It divided lands among the cultivators and arranged settlement of these matters.

The many investigations made by different commissions in connection with disputed points served to clarify some of the problems and to suggest recommendations which led to the partial solution of the question of ownership of *musha* (communal) lands and their partition. Toward the same end were directed the efforts of some agriculturists to intensify their husbandry, a trend which developed with the growing market for agricultural products.

Partition of land held in common ownership (*musha*) continued as a result of both government measures and agreement between all the shareholders. In 1923 a government commission of inquiry investigated 753 villages and found that 56 per cent were *musha* lands; in the southern region, *musha* lands even reached 80 per cent. The Johnson-Crosbie Commission of 1930 found that *musha* lands had shrunk to only 44 per cent in the country as a whole and 69 per cent in the southern region. The French report[35] puts the

---

[34] *A Survey of Palestine,* vol. i, p. 292-93. In the same year (1942) State Domain was excluded from the scope of the Ordinance, while the Second Defense Regulations withdrew the protection of the Ordinance from persons who occupied a holding for the first time after the date of the Regulations.

[35] French, Lewis, *Reports on Agricultural Development and Land Settlement in Palestine* (Jerusalem 1931) p. 12.

communal land at 40 per cent. "Since then (1930) efforts, partially successful, have been made to effect amicable partition . . . It is being broken up gradually by the partition of areas as the land comes under settlement operations after cadastral survey."[36] As a matter of fact, in the years 1931-38, over a million and a half dunams[37] of *musha* lands were divided. This would mean that at the end of 1938 less than a million dunams,[38] or one-sixth of the whole cultivated area, remained *musha* land.[39] Another estimate puts the *musha* land in 1940 at 20 per cent of the settled area.[40]

There was also a transformation with respect to landownership and tenancy. Fragmentary figures on this subject give us some idea about these changes. Auhagen estimated in 1907 that in northern Palestine 20 per cent of the land belonged to the peasants, while in southern Palestine they owned 50 per cent. The Johnson-Crosbie Commission of 1930, which investigated 104 villages, found that 68.2 per cent of the cultivated land belonged to the cultivators while 21.8 per cent was cultivated by tenants. Another investigation in 1935 revealed that 30 per cent of the whole land (excluding the Beersheba region) and 20 per cent of the cultivated land belonged to the group of large landownership (300 dunams per owner or more), while the rest belonged to small landowners. In northern Palestine the percentage of large landowners reached 45; in Samaria and Judea (southern Palestine) it reached 14 to 23 per cent.[41]

[36] *Palestine Royal Commission Report*, p. 219.
[37] 375,000 acres.
[38] 247,000 acres.
[39] This estimate may be confirmed through other information. According to the estimate of the government in 1935 there were, at that time, in Palestine 30,053 persons who were "shareholders in *musha*." Since the number of peasants in Palestine is estimated at 80,000 to 90,000, this would mean that at that time 30 to 33 per cent of the peasantry were shareholders in *musha* land. In other words, the *musha* lands in 1935 would have been about 1,800,000 dunams, or 30 per cent of the cultivated areas. In the years 1935-38, 760,129 dunams of *musha* lands were divided. Through this partition, the communal ownership shrank by the end of 1938 to about 17-18 per cent or about one million dunams. This figure is a confirmation of our figures. *Cf.* however, Warriner (*op. cit.*, p. 67) who maintains that about a quarter of the land is still *musha*.
[40] Waschitz, J., *Haarvim Be-eretz Yisrael* (Merchavia 1947) p. 47.
[41] The figures are from Z. Abramowitz and I. Gelfat, *Hameshek Haaravi* (Tel Aviv 1944) p. 17 ff. An investigation of 1936 which concerned 322 villages showed that 27.6 per cent of the land belonged in the category of large land-ownership (1,000 dunams or more), 35.8 per cent in middle-sized landowner-

The inquiry made in five villages in 1944-45 in the Ramleh district showed that only four holdings out of 690 (0.6 per cent) were over 300 dunams (74.1 acres) and the percentage of the land of this category in relation to the whole area comes to about 9 per cent.[42]

According to these data large landownership decreased in the years 1930-35 from 31.8 per cent to 20 per cent and in the entire post-war period from 80 per cent to 45 per cent in northern Palestine, and from 50 per cent to 23 per cent or less in the southern regions. In the whole of Palestine about one-fourth of the land belongs to the large landowners, while about two-thirds is the property of the peasants. These figures, though inaccurate, indicate the general trend toward an increase in small landownership and a decrease in large holdings, and consequently in tenancy. (The decrease in large holdings was also caused by land purchases by Jews, since these purchases were, for the most part, from owners of large estates.)[43]

Transjordan had no large-scale immigration or capital import such as Palestine's, but the development of this region was partly influenced by that of western Palestine, not only because the High Commissioner held a joint commission for both Palestine and

ship, and 36.6 per cent in small landownership Granowsky, A., in *Kamah* (Jerusalem 1949) p. 30-31.

[42] In these five villages about 60 per cent of the land was in holdings up to 25 acres, and only in one of them did absentee owners own a considerable part of the land. In all five villages 80 per cent of the land was owned by the resident villagers, 15.5 per cent by absentee landowners, leaving 4.5 per cent for communal land or state domain. (*Palestine General Monthly Bulletin of Current Statistics*, XI, p. 51, 559-73.)

[43] With partition, the Arab-Israeli war, and the exodus of the Arabs from Palestine, the whole picture changed. Most of the land in the area which passed to Israel is in the hands of the state. At a later date, if and when peace treaties with Arab states are written, the State of Israel will probably have to pay the former owners some indemnity for the lands. Some of the Arabs—probably a small number—may also be allowed to return to the country and will regain their land possessions.

As things stand now in the State of Israel, there is a total of 20,422,000 dunams (about 5,105,500 acres), including urban areas. Of this, only 1,668,000 dunams (417,000 acres) or 8.2 per cent are privately owned (by Jews and Arabs). Of the rest, 1,940,000 dunams (485,000 acres) or 9.5 per cent belong to the Jewish National Fund. The remaining 82.3 per cent belong to the state. Of these, 5,788,-000 dunams (1,447,000 acres) lie outside the Negev, 10,880,000 runams (2,-720,000 acres) in the Negev, and 146,000 dunams (36,500 acres) are leased for long terms to concessionaires. (*The Israeli Economist*, March 1950, p. 65.)

Transjordan, but also because investigations made by commissions in Palestine were also concerned with Transjordan,[44] and knowledge about the situation influenced efforts for the improvement of conditions. In the years 1928-33 a fiscal survey was completed in Transjordan which covered about 10,000 square kilometers[45] of cultivated and cultivable lands. During the survey 243,000 dunams[46] of state lands were sold to private cultivators "to encourage cultivation or facilitate building"; of these, 108,000 dunams in the Jordan Valley were registered with the Adwan tribe which claimed the land for its property against payment of the registration fees.[47] The fiscal survey included also the demarcation of village boundaries and settlement of disputes over such boundaries. After this had been completed the settlement of individual rights began.

In 1933 a land settlement law was enacted, which provided for settlement of questions connected with rights to land and aiming at the partition of *musha* lands. A travelling Land Settlement Court, with authority to decide claims, was set up to settle the disputes on the spot. An article was included (Art. 10) in the law which gave the judge of the Land Settlement Court powers to determine real ownership, to ignore documents and verbal evidence which appeared to him to be false, as well as claimants of unregistered inheritances who had made no effort to assert their rights for ten years. The judge had thus the authority to decide on the rightful owner in disputed claims.

The main objective of the Land Settlement was to break the *musha* system and to partition the communally owned land. Aided by a grant from the Colonial Development Fund, the settlement progressed although in the beginning it was hard to induce the peasants to accept fewer, mostly better-shaped, plots instead of many, for the most part, long and narrow strips. In time they began to recognize the advisability of this sort of partition and instances

[44] Transjordan received from the British treasury, for instance, a special grant of £40,000 (during the fiscal years 1937-40) for a Hydrographic Survey of the country carried out upon the recommendation of the Palestine Royal Commission.

[45] About 3,860 square miles.

[46] About 60,000 acres.

[47] *Report of His Majesty's Government on the Administration of Palestine and Transjordan* (cited later as *Annual Report*) 1931, p. 193; 1935, p. 283; 1936, p. 329.

when force was necessary to secure order became rare. In the years 1933-1943 3,846,623 dunams of land were "settled," of which 2,200,443 dunams had been communally owned before. This included the northern province Ajlun Lawa, which is the richest and most densely populated part of the country. All in all, in about three-quarters of the country's cultivated area settlement was completed.[48] According to government figures before the war among 15,960 individual holdings there were only 479 (3 per cent) with more than 50 acres while 79 per cent (12,649 holdings) had an area of up to 16½ acres; 13 per cent (2,082 holdings), 16½-33 acres; and 5 per cent (750 holdings), 33-50 acres.[49]

According to government reports the results of assuring ownership began to be noticeable shortly after partition. The feeling of security of tenure led to many improvements. Walls were built, trees planted, stones removed from the land and manure spread. Sometimes they even went to extremes "where settlement has been completed the people are so keen to take advantage of every metre of land that is now really theirs that they are actually ploughing up the anti-erosion banks which have been there for many years."[50]

RESULTS

Landholding system is probably one of the most conservative of all social institutions. In central and eastern Europe the problems of landless and dwarf peasants were realized for more than a century, but little was done toward redivision of the land until social and political revolutions swept away the existing order (after the First and Second World Wars).

In the Middle Eastern countries not only the discrepancy between the big landowners and the sharecroppers and dwarf peasants was a big one, but the land register was confused and the right of the tenants and small owners uncertain and unclear. Some progress has been made in this direction in the last quarter of a century. The land has been partially surveyed and title registered, owner-

[48] Walpole, *op. cit.*, p. 57.

[49] The figures given in the *Annual Report* to the League of Nations for 1938. *Cf.* Bonné, *State and Economics in the Middle East* (London 1948) p. 135.

[50] *Annual Report*, 1937, p. 309. *Cf.* also *Annual Report*, 1934, p. 241; 1935, p. 287; 1937, p. 315; 1938, p. 324; Konikoff, A., *Transjordan, an Economic Survey* (Jerusalem 1943) p. 38-39.

ship established and, to some extent, also ownership changed. But there are considerable differences between the different countries. On the one hand we have Turkey, which abolished *waqf* and divided considerable stretches of land and adopted a new law recently calling for the break-up of large landownership, although this law has not yet been put into practice owing, apparently, to resistance on the part of the landowners.[51] On the other hand there is Egypt, where the only change has been the redivision of already small parcels into dwarf holdings, while the big landownership remained almost untouched. The other countries could be roughly divided into two groups: Syria and Palestine, Transjordan where a considerable effort at land registration and settlement of title of land has been undertaken leading to the distribution of great stretches of communal land (*musha*) and other land and to the decline, to some extent, of great landownership. Then again there is Iraq where the registration of land led to an increase of big landownership. Only a part of the land has been settled in small holdings while a greater part was given away in large blocks.

Partition of *musha*, beneficial as it may be, also has some drawbacks which might work to the disadvantage of the peasantry if the respective governments fail to step in in time. The holdings are being broken up in small fragments so as to give every cultivator

[51] As early as 1937 a bill was presented to the National Assembly calling for comprehensive agrarian reform. In 1945 the Assembly passed a law which provided for the distribution of state lands and of lands of large landowners to landless farmers or to those with insufficient farm land. The law provided for payment of indemnity to the landowners. Opposition to these measures among the big landowners in the ruling (Peoples Republican) Party has delayed carrying out this legislation.

At the beginning of 1948 the Council of Ministers introduced changes in the Land Law which gave the owner the right to choose which parts of the land he wanted to retain and specified that at least 50 hectares could be retained. It was also stipulated that large stretches of land would not be divided unless peasants without land or with insufficient land lived on the properties. Only the land needed by the peasants would be taken from the owners for division. In actual fact nothing much has been done in this direction. According to the report of the Minister of Agriculture in April 1948, nine commissions have been established to work on the application of the law, but 100 more are needed; also that the Land Law is connected with the cadastre and settlement laws for which four government agencies are working, but it was planned to set up 25 more commissions in 1949. Inadequate funds and personnel make more rapid progress impossible (*Ulus*, April 20, 1948).

his share in different types of soil. This, however, results in frag-
mentation, making the peasants owners of small strips and hinder-
ing proper cultivation. Another drawback of partition of *musha* is
that landowners having an undisputed title to their land could
mortgage their property to money-lenders. In this way "the fellaheen are gradually building up an amount of indebtedness it is
hardly likely will ever be cleared" paying 30 and 100 per cent
interest.[52] This means, in the Middle East where city notables and
money-lenders are accustomed to accumulate land, the beginning
of fresh concentration and big landownership, and depriving small
landowners of their shares. The break-up of the *musha* system during the last decades may lead to the concentration of lands in the
hands of a new landlord group just as the abolition of the feudal
system in the nineteenth century did. Avoidance of this new development will depend on the statesmanship of the countries, even
though redistribution of land may still have to wait for some time.

[52] Walpole, *op. cit.*, p. 59.